HIJINX AND HEARSAY

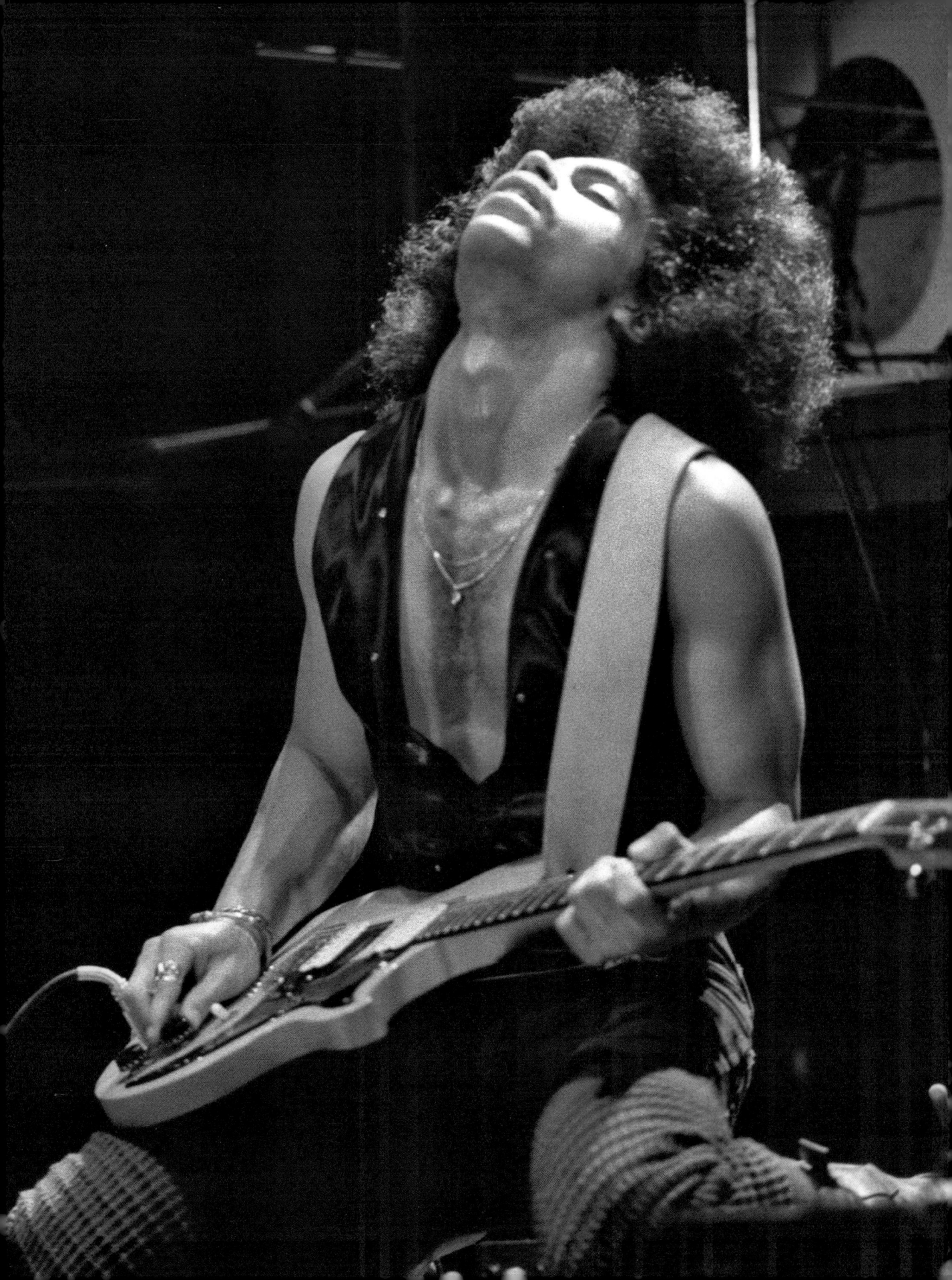

HIJINX AND HEARSAY

HEARSAY

SCENESTER STORIES
FROM MINNESOTA'S POP LIFE

TEXT BY MARTIN KELLER
PHOTOGRAPHS BY GREG HELGESON
FOREWORD BY BOB MEHR

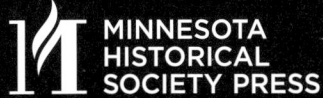
MINNESOTA
HISTORICAL
SOCIETY PRESS

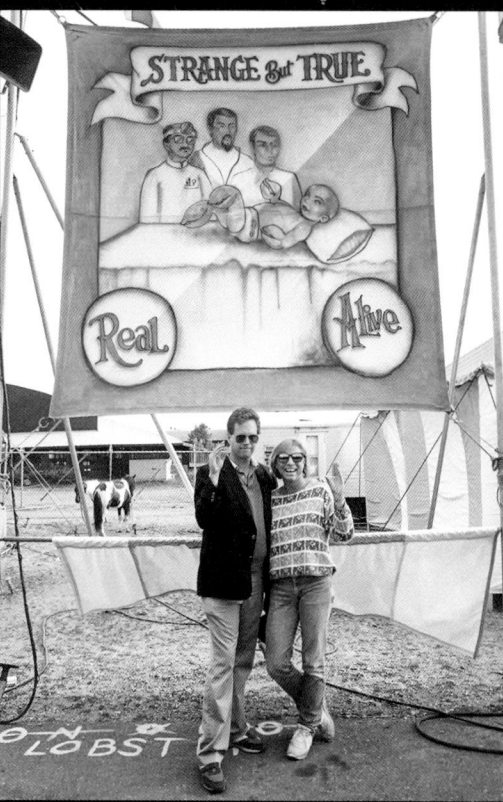

(left) *Twin Cities Reader* and, later, *New York Times* scribe David Carr with political analyst and journalist Sarah Janecek at the Minnesota State Fair in 1984

(title spread) Prince at the Capri Theater in north Minneapolis, January 1979—his first public concert

mnhspress.org

The Minnesota Historical Society Press is a member of the Association of University Presses.

Manufactured in the United States of America

10 9 8 7 6 5 4 3 2 1

∞ The paper used in this publication meets the minimum requirements of the American National Standard for Information Sciences—Permanence for Printed Library Materials, ANSI Z39.48-1984.

International Standard Book Number
ISBN: 978-1-68134-132-3 (paper)

Library of Congress Cataloging-in-Publication Data
Names: Keller, Martin, author | Helgeson, Greg, 1951–
    photographer. | Mehr, Bob, writer of foreword.
Title: Hijinx and hearsay : scenester stories from Minnesota's pop
    life / text by Martin Keller ; photographs by Greg Helgeson ;
    foreword by Bob Mehr.
Description: St. Paul, MN : Minnesota Historical Society Press,
    [2019] | Includes index.
Identifiers: LCCN 2019003394 | ISBN 9781681341323 (pbk. : alk. paper)
Subjects: LCSH: Popular music—Minnesota—History and criticism.
Classification: LCC ML3477.7.M55 K45 2019 | DDC 791.09776—dc23
LC record available at https://lccn.loc.gov/2019003394

Designed and set in type by Mayfly Design

CONTENTS

A PAIR OF STEALTHY FELLAS

Capturing the Regionally Known and the Globally Famous

Bob Mehr

Ten years ago, in the lobby of a Sheraton Hotel in Bloomington, Minnesota, I first laid eyes on Greg Helgeson—or, rather, he laid eyes on me. I was there on a mission, desperately seeking unpublished photos of the Replacements, for a biography I was writing on the band.

We'd arranged to rendezvous at my hotel. I'd never met Greg; didn't know what he looked like. I scanned the lobby for a good long while trying to pick him out, with no luck. The anticipation and worry showed on my face. Then I blinked, and Helgeson was suddenly in front of me. A diminutive, dapper figure in a long mohair coat, he smiled, stuck out his hand, and introduced himself. He'd been there the whole time, seemingly invisible, sizing me up like one of his subjects before deciding to reveal himself. I knew then that I was dealing with a true student of human nature.

As we sat and pored over his portfolio, I was struck by his earliest images of the Replacements. A famously guarded bunch, they evoked an innocence and openness that I'd never seen captured on film before. In one series of shots, the band is jumping in the air, their expressions a mix of deep suspicion and wild abandon (the two defining characteristics of the group, as it would turn out). This was an idea Helgeson had purloined from the photographer Philippe Halsman. The father of "jumpology," Halsman would ask his subjects—from Marilyn Monroe to Richard Nixon—to leap and then capture their faces in midair. He saw it as a trick of distraction: "When you ask a person to jump," Halsman said, "his attention is mostly directed toward the act of jumping, and the mask falls, so that the real person appears."

The thing I found out about Helgeson, though, is that it didn't matter if his subjects were jumping, running, playing, or sitting in repose. It was something about Greg himself—the unassuming manner, the unerring eye—that made people show their true selves.

The images in *Hijinx and Hearsay: Scenester Stories from Minnesota's Pop Life* are testament to that fact, to Helgeson's gifts as a *presence* as much as a photographer. That's why the "Crawling King Snake," John Lee Hooker, allows himself to be photographed rumpled and bedheaded in his hotel room; why the hypervigilant Bob Dylan lays comfortably, almost absentmindedly, in the grass with his family as the camera clicks away; and why we can see the true enmity in the body language between feuding soul men Sam and Dave.

In a concert setting, Helgeson brought a similar approach. His performance shots aren't about the usual glorifying angles or triumphant poses. Instead, he shoots from the margins, from behind or just to the side of the spotlight. In doing so, he captures fleeting moments of truth: whether it's a knowing, almost sensual smile shared between Prince and Sheila E., the head-cracking chaos in the heart of a Hüsker Dü mosh pit, or the penetrating amphetamine gaze of a young Elvis Costello.

That day, Helgeson told me a little about himself. He said he was a kid from a small Minnesota farm town, that he'd spent his early career in Minneapolis working for the local alt-monthly *Sweet Potato* (later to become the weekly *City Pages*), photographing drunken rock bands, living in clubs and bars. These were places he probably wouldn't have otherwise hung out in, people he wouldn't normally have socialized with. When I asked Greg what drove him to these stories and these subjects, he replied simply: "The music. And Marty Keller."

One of the Twin Cities' savviest rock writers, Keller had been his editor/partner-in-crime at *Sweet Potato*, where, collectively, they were known as the Spud Boyz. As it happened, I was set to meet Marty the next day to interview him for my own book.

The following morning, I found myself scanning another room searching for a stranger. Once again, I blinked, and Keller appeared next to me out of nowhere (these Minneapolis guys are stealthy). Right away, I liked Keller. He had the knowing manner of a racetrack tout giving you a tip on a sure bet running in the fifth. That afternoon he offered a crash course on the early history of the Replacements, and he also provided context, explaining the whole big picture of Minneapolis music in the process.

Born in Oklahoma and raised in North Dakota, Keller had been surrounded by music in his childhood: Pat Boone and show tunes from his mom, Ray Charles and Hank Williams from his dad, with Marty in the middle. It was a position Keller would come to know well when he began working at *Sweet Potato* in 1979. There, he found himself pitched between two distinct worlds: the old West Bank folk/blues culture and the emergent indie/new-wave scene.

Keller was one of the few who understood the city's rich musical heritage, yet also recognized that fresh history was being made in the nightclubs around town. A gimlet-eyed chronicler of the era through his weekly column and cover stories, Marty—like Greg—had an easy, unobtrusive presence that allowed him entrée to myriad worlds, intimate access to the key artists of the time. His writing was uniquely democratic, however. Keller afforded the same respect, the same depth of insight, whether he was profiling Prince, Bob Dylan, or the latest local band.

Together, he and Helgeson spent a decade (locally for *Sweet Potato*, *City Pages*, and the *Twin Cities Reader*, and for national rags like *Rolling Stone* and *Billboard*) documenting not just music, but the rock 'n' roll zeitgeist that defined the whole artistic spectrum of eighties Minneapolis. It was this same momentum that drove the work of comedians (Joel Hodgson, Lizz Winstead), cultural curators (Tim Carr, Steve McClellan), filmmakers (Chuck Statler), writers (David Carr, Garrison Keillor), and others.

At long last, the pictures and prose of the Spud Boyz have been brought (back) together in this fine volume. Contained here are a remarkable collection of images and words about the regionally known and the globally famous. You'll be reminded, or perhaps educated, about an incredible time in the Twin Cities. But most of all, what you'll find is the symbiotic brilliance of Greg Helgeson and Marty Keller—and the funny, wonderful way these two always seem to sneak up on you.

Bob Mehr is an award-winning reporter covering music for Memphis's daily newspaper, the Commercial Appeal. *Mehr is also the author of the widely acclaimed best seller* Trouble Boys: The True Story of the Replacements.

INTRODUCTION

Meet the Spud Boyz

Fate throws people together for better or worse. Or is it Destiny—the friendlier life force—that does?

In the summer of 1979, Greg Helgeson (aka the Helg) and I were two twenty-something guys from small towns who had been freelancing (also known as fasting) for a year or two in the big cities of Minneapolis–St. Paul. We were randomly tossed together to begin a ten-plus-year excursion in the culture zone—a zone that was undergoing a real transformation as the tumultuous decade was coming to a close. Comedy scenes were quietly sprouting in urban watering holes and unusual places, perhaps as cathartic relief valves to the excesses of the unfunny seventies. Disco and a lot of overproduced rock and empty-calorie pop were losing their fizz, while new wave, punk, and funk were loudly rising from underground. It was a welcomed culture shift. And it was happening not just in Minnesota, but around the country and the world.

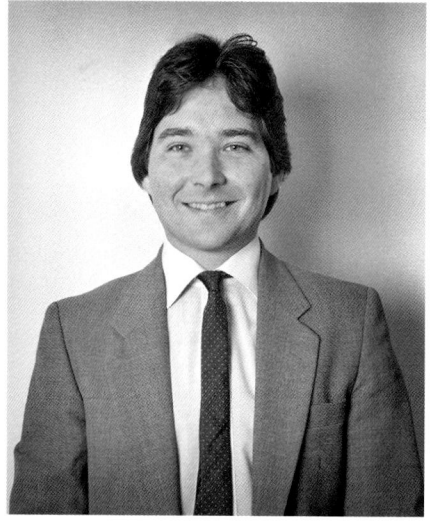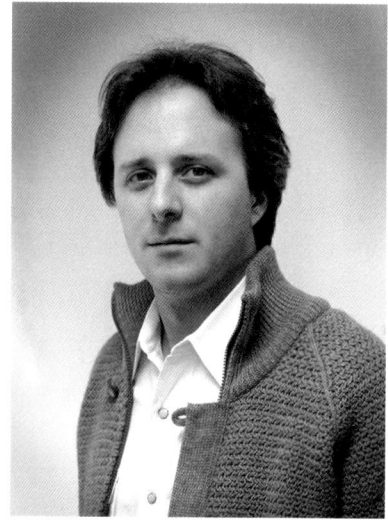

A couple of young Spud Boyz: Greg Helgeson and Martin Keller

12

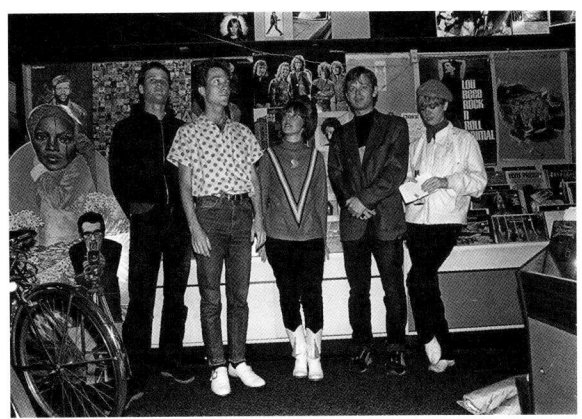 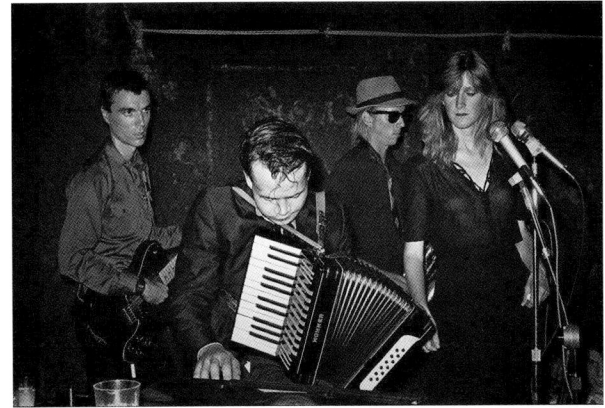

In July of that year, we went to work on a new monthly music newspaper ignobly called *Sweet Potato* (which later became *City Pages*, an alternative weekly–format newspaper with its roots in the underground press of the bygone sixties). We fondly and derisively called it the *Spud* and began referring to each other as Spud Boyz. We not only helped report for, edit, and produce the paper, but we also delivered it to drop spots near and far in our not-always-reliable cars. Because there was a stone soup freelance budget in the early days, I wrote under several assumed aliases so that it didn't look like my byline or ego were running amok.

One of my aliases was Martian Colour, which I used for the gossip column, "Highlights, Hijinx, and Hearsay: Martian's Chronicles," in which the third-person voice was often deployed to give a sense that English was not the alien's first language, even though he walked among us! (Actually, the column was thrown at me as another must-do task; I hated it at first. Today, it's the only thing I miss writing.) The name serendipitously emerged one night when Marcey Bolter, a former KQRS deejay, spotted me outside the Longhorn Bar and yelled, "Hey, Martian." I added Colour—a play on my last name (as was the Martian a play on my first), using the British spelling of *color* just because—to reflect that the Martian would be providing weekly color commentary. Surprisingly, the Martian handle is still seen and heard occasionally, more than four decades later. Might be time to slap a hashtag on it! When I crossed over to work at the *Twin Cities Reader*, after losing an employment dispute at *City Pages*, a similar column was requested, so "Diary of a Free-Lunch Writer" was born, penned by Frank "Big Ears" Schwartz, who heard all—or what he wanted to hear—from the scene and its many scenesters.

In the beginning, Spud Boy 1 (Helgeson) had Canon and sometimes Leica cameras. Spud Boy 2 (me) owned an ancient, thirty-six-pound Royal typewriter that could double as a murder weapon. Until early desktop-computer word processing and floppy discs arrived, this heavy

(above left) The B-52s pose in front of the racks at the trendsetting Oar Folkjokeopus "wrecka sto" on a day off during a three-night stand at Jay's Longhorn. Audience turnout was light, but the new-wave band out of Athens, Georgia, put on quite a show.

(above right) At the 7th Street Entry in 1979, David Byrne of Talking Heads sat in with the Wallets for an inspired version of the Dean Martin hit "Houston"—a song originally written about the big Texas city but reimagined for the famous street in New York City (pronounced *Howston*). Wallets maestro Steve Kramer is in the foreground on accordion and keyboards, and sunglasses-clad saxophonist Max Ray lurks in the background. At right is Kristine McKenna, a writer from LA who was chumming around with Byrne.

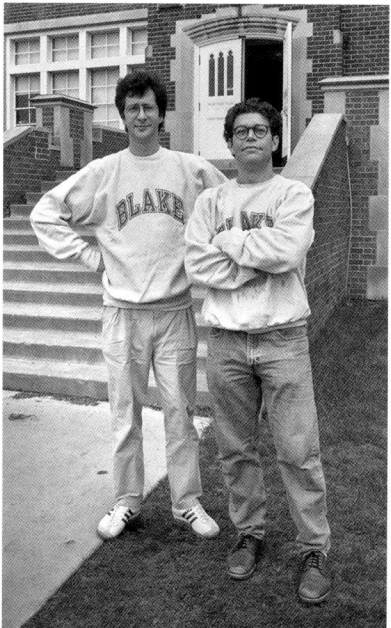
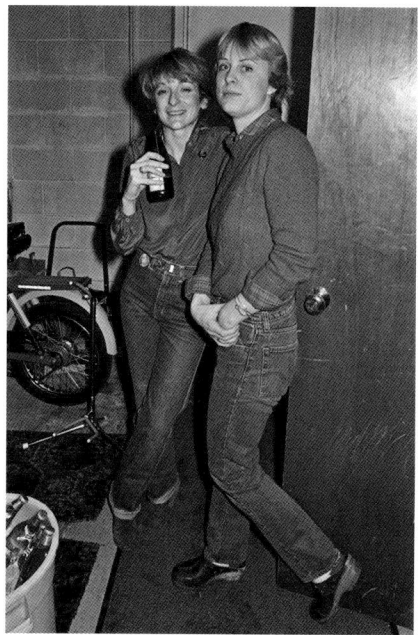

(right) Former Dudley Riggs sketch-comedy standouts Tom Davis and Al Franken went on to write for and occasionally appear on *Saturday Night Live*. Here they're pictured at their high school alma mater, Blake in Minneapolis, representing in their baggy school sweatshirts after a meeting with students.

(far right) Known as the "queen of concerts and clubs," Sue McLean was a true pathfinder for women working as booking agents in the United States. A single mom who adopted a daughter, she once quipped to a colleague, "I can't book Bob Dylan right now; I've got to change Lilly's diaper." In 1998, she founded Sue McLean & Associates, which remains an active and influential promotions firm today, following the motto, "Live music is good for your soul." McLean died of cancer in 2013. Decades earlier, she was photographed by Helgeson backstage at an XTC show at Duffy's bar in south Minneapolis, handling a cold one (with an unknown assistant).

writing tool allowed me to earn a little income and to realize my dreams. I haphazardly learned to hunt, peck, and shriek on it to cover the highlights, hijinx, and hearsay that ensued in the arts and entertainment realms for the next ten or so years. Together we worked without a map or a net, and we were never sure if our small paychecks would still be coming a few months down the road: We had already witnessed the slow demise of another monthly music paper called *Connie's Insider* (aka *The Insider* and, later, *Musician's Insider)* that started in the late 1960s and a short-lived alternative weekly, *Metropolis.* Had we made what our mothers called "bad choices"?

We didn't care.

And we got lucky! Was it Fate or Destiny? We could never tell.

For the next decade, we chronicled the so-called Minneapolis Sound and scene, plus the broader cultural landscape that featured some of the most influential artists, one or two actors, and select impresarios and entertainers, from Dylan and Prince to such disparate writers as Garrison Keillor and William Burroughs. Movers and shakers, some well-known and some known only to showbiz insiders, were our bread and jam. Thankfully, our tastes were as eclectic and expansive as those of our willing readers. Sometimes we didn't even know (as good midwesterners are apt to say) "what the heck the deal was" with our subjects until we encountered them in their natural and unnatural habitats, as was the case with Devo, First Avenue's Steve McClellan, and Hollywood's Gary Busey. We tracked outbreaks of funny from comedians Al Franken and Tom Davis (then writing

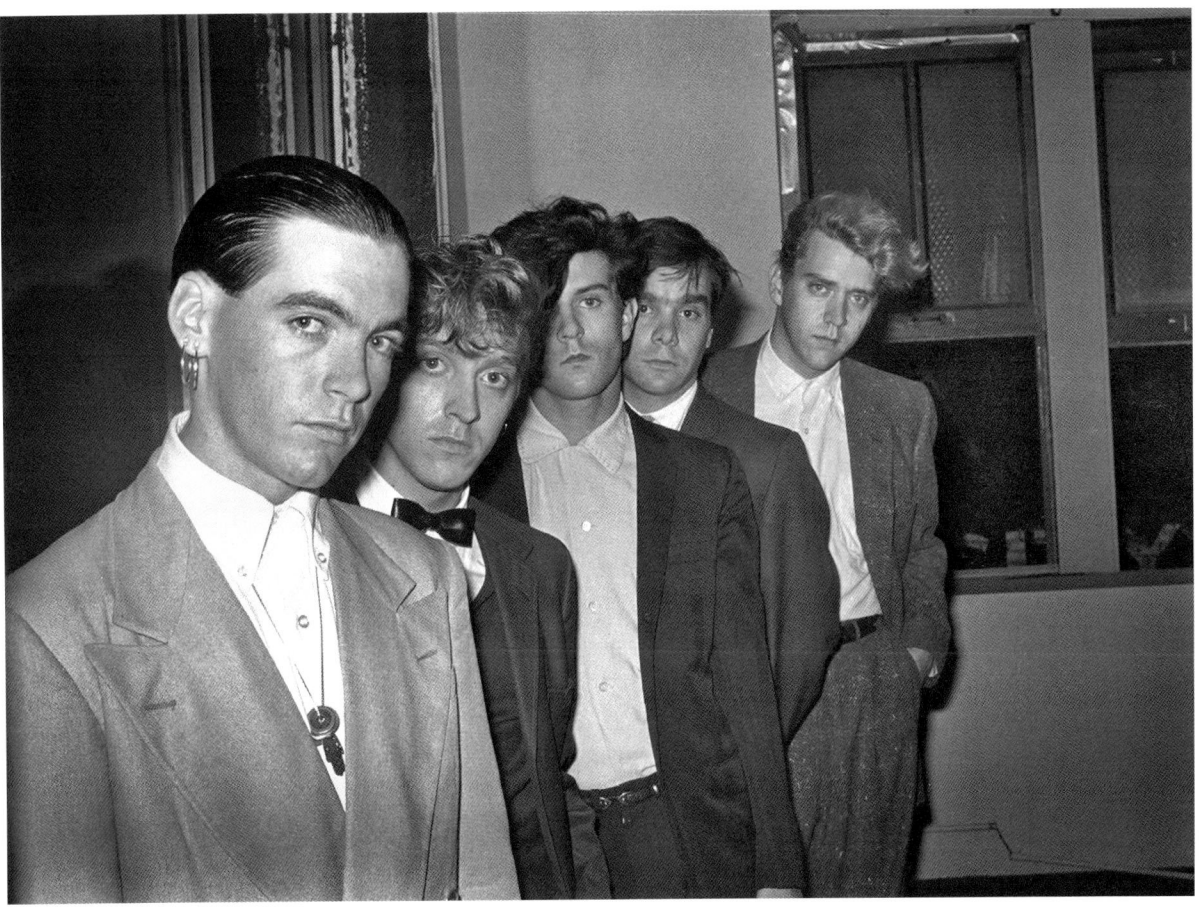

for *Saturday Night Live*), Jerry Seinfeld, Joel Hodgson, Louie Anderson, Scott Hansen, and Lizz Winstead, among many others.

Maybe because of our youthful age, the eighties seemed like a time that would never end, but in reality, it was the end of many things, especially in culture, commerce, and work. Big shifts loomed on the horizon, upheavals we really didn't see coming until we looked back at them once we started this book. The World Wide Web would change the world from comfortably round to infinitely flat with the click of a mouse; the 45 single, vinyl album, and cassette gave way to compact discs; VHS tape morphed into DVDs; and then, further downstream, the rest of the digital multimedia universe arrived like a handheld apocalypse with all of its flat-screen implications, from social media to streaming—friending, hacking, and screaming—online.

Taking that trip together, going from the analog eighties into the digital nineties, the Helg and I probably extended our adolescence by another decade or more—the Spud Boyz as Peter Pan's Lost Boys, perhaps? We were out often five or six nights a week, "working," getting paid to hang

Dressed like Rat Pack punks from the Twin Cities western 'burbs, the Suburbs band featured a hopeful romantic in keyboard player and songwriter Chan Poling (far right) counterbalanced by exceptional guitarist, singer, songwriter, and wild-card showman Beej Chaney (far left). Left to right behind Beej are guitarist Bruce Allen, bassist Michael Halliday, and drummer Hugo Klaers. The consistently reliable local band has released seven studio albums to date, most recently 2017's *Hey Muse!*

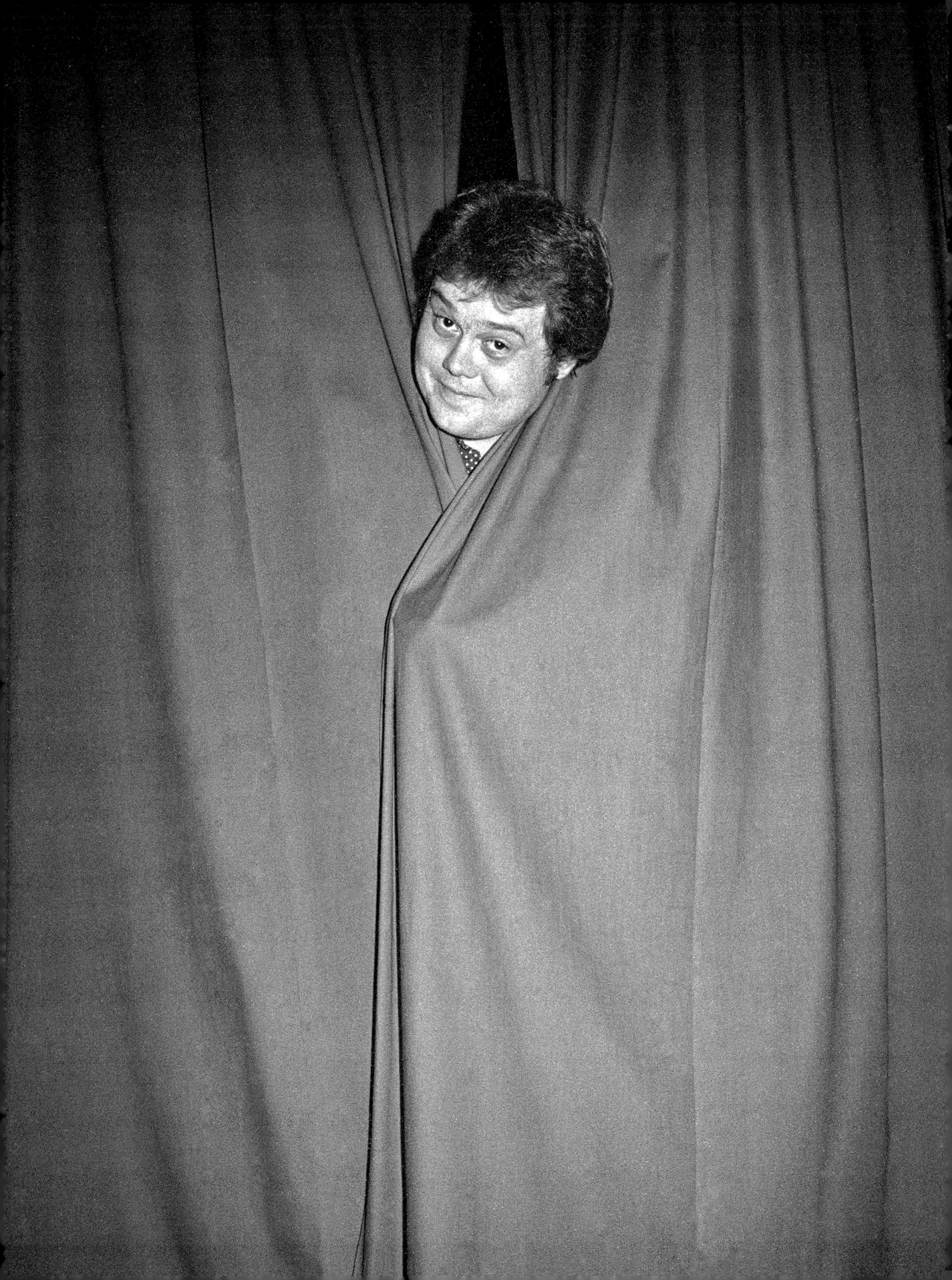

out and report back, while those around us had "real jobs" and responsibilities.

We sailed on, into the exotic ports of many legendary and influential musicians from across the high seas of pop music, from Bob Marley to U2 and Elvis Costello, Paul and Linda McCartney to Bonnie Raitt. We met a host of sunsetting rhythm and blues icons: James Brown, Sam and Dave, John Lee Hooker, Gatemouth Brown, Koerner, Ray, and Glover, and more. Seemingly out of nowhere, a new genre of music, known as hip-hop, dropped on the Mill City. Like the emerging new-wave scene at the Longhorn Bar, where we saw groups like the Police, the B-52s, Talking Heads, and others that didn't sell out, we checked it out, never guessing that rap, deejaying, and break-dance culture would become a global phenomenon. We watched and charted deep-impact Twin Cities musicians like Jimmy Jam and Terry Lewis, the Replacements, Lamont Cranston, Hüsker Dü, Curtiss A, the Suburbs, Flamin' Oh's, and of course Prince Rogers Nelson and his Paisley Park court.

We were perpetually walking the thin-grooved line between fandom and journalism. Sometimes, out of love for both, we crossed the streams.

And then, decades later, Greg and I had a series of discussions over tea about how we could share that love. Neither of us wanted to produce an oral history (it sounded too much like a dental exam). Nor did we want to simply reheat our historical reporting like stale leftovers—although we do offer occasional sample-sized portions within these pages because some stories traveled so well to where we sit today. And where we sit today is atop a bunch of mostly fresh vignettes and photos worth the proverbial thousand words.

Hijinx and Hearsay is a genuine hybrid, part fragmented memoir, part photo book, amplified by many diverse scenesters from a wickedly good, and pivotally important, time in popular culture. We survived it. Sadly, others did not. In this age where the algorithm rules, we hope that our "olde-world" exploration of an era in image and text will provide the vital themes that compelled us each to create this work. Maybe they will even somehow become viral memes.

We also hope to prove to our children and our children's children that we did not completely waste our twenties and thirties.

(opposite) Years before leaving for Los Angeles and becoming one of America's top comics, a best-selling author, and a three-time Emmy Award winner, Louie Anderson goofs at Dudley Riggs's Brave New Workshop, where he often performed with the Comedy All-Stars as the comedy boom hit in the late seventies and early eighties.

BOB DYLAN

Twin Cities Skyline

The blue-eyed kid from the North Country. The oracle from the Iron Range. The song-and-dance man with a Nobel Prize in hand. Where to begin? Maybe at the Cabooze bar on Minneapolis's West Bank. That's where Bob Dylan jump-started my writing career (even though I had Dylan dreams for years prior to first running into him in 1978). Was it fate or destiny? I could never tell.

Chicago bluesman Luther Allison was playing the Cabooze that night. I didn't really care; I was down in the dumps. Funding for my teaching assistant job at the Urban League Street Academy had ended. Pennies were being pinched. Spirits were low. Although I was reluctant to go clubbing, a friend convinced me otherwise. About halfway through Allison's set, Dylan came in with Louie Kemp, his childhood friend from northern Minnesota, and Scott Stein, a personal assistant. Without too much trouble, I bought Minnesota's most famous son a whiskey, then backed off to leave him alone. I hung around late enough after closing to ask him about a couple lines in "You're Gonna Make Me Lonesome When You Go" that I could never understand. He kindly explained that "Ashtabula" was a place in Ohio (and not the Beulah of poet William Blake's cosmic, cryptic mythology).

The next day, I interviewed Allison about the evening. He told Dylan he was looking for a record deal, and though Allison downplayed the encounter, his big smile couldn't disguise his elation with meeting him. I pitched the story of Dylan at the Cabooze to *Twin Cities Reader* editor Greg Linder, who published it the following week, even though an Associated Press photo of Bob at the Cabooze was already in circulation. *Rolling Stone* also ran a "Random Note" I submitted on the Zimmie sighting, pounded out on my old Royal typewriter. More freelance jobs followed, and Linder jokingly assigned me to the freelance "Dylan beat"—which meant nothing since no compensation was involved. And then *Sweet Potato* hired me as editor, writer, columnist, critic, and paperboy.

Bob Dylan has produced far more and greater memories than all the copy created about him, although I have written about him plenty, including a rare interview in 1983 (nearly four hours long, although much of it was small talk) with the arrival of *Infidels*, his first album after his so-called gospel albums and conversion to Christianity. The interview originally ran in *City Pages* and was syndicated around the world. I've had the extreme good fortune not only to interview the Minnesota music legend but also to spend time with him socially, along with his small circle of friends and acquaintances across the Twin Cities skyline, including Gene LaFond, Dick and Val Cohn, Paul White, and Larry Kegan. I also got to travel with the rock bard, his band, and Kegan's entourage for a weeklong Midwest swing on the Never Ending Tour in 1990.

In between there were other highlights and hijinx worth sharing in this book of select memories. They ranged from bumping into Bob backstage at a Clash concert with his Clash fankids in tow while waiting to interview Joe Strummer and Mick Jones, to driving down with his former aide-de-camp, Scott Stein, and another friend to cover an Omaha performance after his *Slow Train Coming* and *Saved* discs at the height of his "born again" period. During that time, he had disavowed his older material and many of his fans and critics savaged him. He remained undeterred and pressed on. Dylan and his band and backup gospel singers huddled in prayer before taking the stage. Despite the earthly fire and brimstone he endured in the early eighties, Dylan's artistic triumphs—and that includes many of the songs from that period—were far from over.

Looking back now, maybe there was something to being assigned to Linder's imaginary "Dylan beat." What can you get hanging around him? A few insights and some occasional laughs courtesy of his ready sense of humor, but not nearly as much as you can listening to him, poring over lyrics, or watching him in concert. After all, the artist's journey is mostly a solitary, interior one, not a spectator sport. You can't divine or define the enigmatic Robert Allen Zimmerman much. Larry Kegan, who had met Bob at Herzl Camp in Webster, Wisconsin, when they were thirteen or fourteen years old, was fond of reminding people that his friend Bobby "is never going to do what anyone thinks he should do or will do." The two remained friends until Kegan's death in 2001. (Bob gave Larry a good shout-out on *Street Legal* as "champion of all causes.") And Larry was responsible for setting up the '83 interview, although Bob initiated it by asking, "How can we do something nice for Marty?" when he learned of the cover story I'd written about disabled Americans, including Kegan, who were facing cuts to their monthly benefits under Reagan.

Kegan spent most of his life in a wheelchair. He was paralyzed from the waist down following a diving accident when he was a teenager not long after meeting Bob, and some years later, in Mexico, he rolled his hand-controlled Caddy and became quadriplegic. But nothing slowed him down; he was a rock 'n' roll scenester since the fifties, listening to the same roots rock and blues radio station in Louisiana that Bob did, even before they connected at camp.

One night in 1983, I ran into both of them at the 7th Street Entry, the small club attached to First Avenue. A search for the inevitable after-party led us to a light gathering at Willie Murphy's place, over on the West Bank. Dylan wanted to know if we should bring something, like coffee; I assured him that Willie would be holding java. Bob borrowed a bunch of Murphy's records that night, heavy on the blues. That get-together led to Dylan recording a demo with Willie and the Bees in a bad basement studio someplace in town, a cool tune about "Money." Not likely to show up on an official or unofficial bootleg any time soon, however.

Another memorable encounter was the night Chuck Statler's video crew threw a party for Elvis Costello and the Attractions at one of the first loft spaces in downtown Minneapolis that was inhabited by Chuck's talented and gregarious British editor, Dale Cooper. Statler and crew had done early music videos for Elvis and stayed in touch with the band.

Dylan, who has a home in the western exurbs, was hanging out around town a lot that summer of 1980, often with Stephanie, a Minnesota woman who'd been living in LA and seemed to be unofficially in charge of his Twin Cities social calendar that season. So, I told her about the party for Elvis. Surprisingly, Dylan showed up with a couple of his kids, including a young Jakob, who showed me how deftly he could wield nunchucks.

Before Elvis and his band arrived, I popped in a mix tape of New Orleans music that I'd put together for the event. Bob frequently interrupted to ask who was singing or playing on the fresh mix. I had been smitten with the genre since my first experience at the New Orleans Jazz & Heritage Festival a couple months earlier, and I plucked a bunch of stuff from records I'd bought there or gotten free to review from different labels, like Rounder Records.

"Roosevelt Sykes, he plays piano like I do," Dylan offered at one point after asking about one of the instrumental cuts on the tape. Finally, after a few more questions about the musicians and song titles, and as the party grew too noisy for audible music, I just gave him the mix.

A decade later, I joined Kegan and his crew in Larry's van, following Dylan's buses, for a weeklong road trip through the Midwest during the Never Ending Tour. The first night backstage in the La Crosse Civic Center, I noticed he traveled with a dresser who helped pick out his stage clothes. As he stood looking at a large, portable wardrobe in the faint light and shadows of the stage, it seemed to have an old world aspect, like a great Elizabethan actor transforming into the character he would soon play onstage. The next day, Bob got off his private bus with his dog, whose name I think was Horace, after the Roman poet. I think it was a boxer, a large, short-haired, camel-colored dog with black jowls and skinny legs and a cartoonish line for a tail. Dylan and I didn't exchange many words that whole week, as he kept to himself in the bus and hotel rooms. I was along for the ride as Kegan's guest, not his, and helping Larry write his autobiography.

In Fargo, Dylan gave a shout-out to Bobby Vee from the stage early in the show, noting with a rare broad smile that his former employer was "in the house"—referencing the time when a young Dylan, using the stage name Elston Gunnn, played piano in Vee's band. Once we got to Bismarck, I brought my parents backstage to see some of the show, including the part where the band started one tune and Bob suddenly called out "In the Garden." Somehow his guitar player at the time, G. E. Smith, grimacing like a madman, managed to lead the band out of the mess. No one in the audience was the wiser. I also noticed in the Dakota capital that most of the Dylanites who had been following the tour since I got on in La Crosse had disappeared, except for one: a young, delusional woman who was well known to the Dylan camp. She appeared at many of his shows around the country and believed she was married to him. It brought to mind something he said to me at one point, a couple years after John Lennon had been murdered by a "fan"; in his classic Dylan-esque way, he noted, "I got a lotta people on my trail."

That was surprising to hear, but it was not as unexpected as the time Kegan called in the spring of '83 with a request from out of left field. He wanted to know if I could help set up a meeting between the Duluth-Hibbing native and another homegrown-Minnesota heavyweight: Prince. During this period, His Royal Badness was represented by the LA-based management company of Cavallo, Ruffalo, and Fargnoli. At the annual Black Music Awards, held on June 29 at the Prom Center Ballroom in St. Paul, I approached one of the gents from the management agency. I offered a brief description of the Larry Kegan–Bob Dylan connection. Larry sat in his wheelchair a few rows back and nodded and smiled when I pointed him out. The agent looked briefly back at him as if he were looking for a waitress.

"That's a hell of a way to try and get a Prince interview," the manager said, brushing me off and turning around.

"No, this is on the level," I assured him. "Besides, I've already interviewed Prince." That last part caught him off guard. But it was true. I had already logged a lot of miles and spun a ton of copy about Prince. However, as promising as that improbable summit might have been, it never happened. Prince backed out, allegedly because, he admitted, "I could never deal with that mind."

The fortuitous times I got to spend inside Dylan's and Prince's home

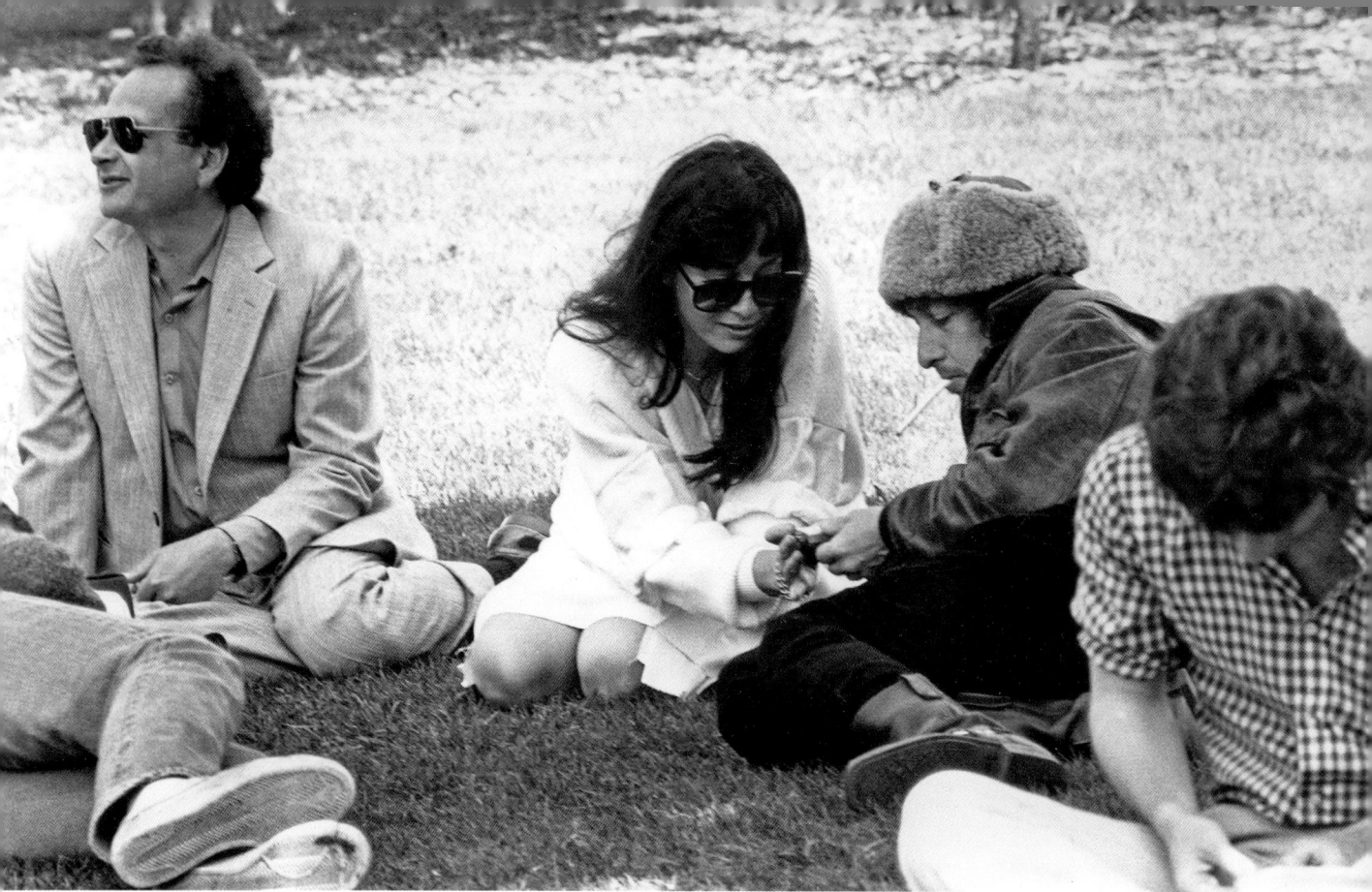

In perhaps his only true paparazzi photo, Helgeson captured Bob Dylan and family while the Helg was on assignment photographing Macalester College's graduation ceremonies in 1983.

terrain had a kind of boomeranging effect. In the late eighties, another Dylan, Bob's oldest daughter, Maria, and her former Macalester classmate Peter Berg reached out to me about a documentary they were developing on the Minnesota music scene, with Prince at the center. It was called *Erotic City*. The treatment I wrote for them explored the perfect contradictions and sublime ironies that existed between Prince, the Time, and others in the royal camp and the state of mostly stoic Scandinavian and German descendants who kept their clothes on while performing or otherwise. It also profiled then-rising rockers like the Replacements and Soul Asylum, among others. Word of the project somehow reached Paisley Park, and for a time there was even talk of Prince financing it.

Disappointment being but one of the many door prizes of showbiz, the doc never came to fruition. Berg, however, went on to have a lasting run in Hollywood as an actor, writer, producer, and director in such film and television properties as *Friday Night Lights*, *Hancock*, *Chicago Hope*, and many, many others. His IMDb profile is longer than the credits for a Ken Burns PBS series. Maria pursued her law degree in Chicago and later married Peter Himmelman, from the popular Twin Cities rock band Sussman Lawrence.

The story behind the candid photo of Bob Dylan and family lounging on the grass connects back to Maria, courtesy of Macalester College, which had hired Greg Helgeson to shoot the graduation ceremony in 1983. In what is likely the Helg's only true paparazzi-type photograph, he was able to capture a candid shot of Bob; his wife at the time, Sara; his brother, David; and two of Bob's kids sprawled on the college lawn for Maria's big day. As Greg describes it, he saw the family among the many other families there to see their children matriculate into the world. Since he was hired by the college to document the event and its participants, Greg proceeded to do just that, pointing his telephoto in the direction of one of the University of Minnesota's most renowned dropouts. That photo, too, would be bootlegged widely, somehow escaping both the Helg's and the college's control.

"The only reason I realized it was him was that he was dressed in a leather coat and winter-like hat on a really hot day in May and looked totally out of place," Helgeson recalled. "If he was trying to be incognito, he couldn't have worn more distinctive garb! Sara saw my lens pointed in their direction, and the family members slowly closed in a circle around Bob, to block out any more photos."

"I got lucky," he said.

JOHN LEE HOOKER

Between the Sheets and *The Streets of San Francisco* with the Hook

One of the earliest stories the Helg and I did together was interviewing John Lee Hooker for *Sweet Potato*. The Hook was the godfather of the boogie and, at the time, one of the last of the great, living bedrock bluesmen.

Hooker had played a trademark fiery set at the Cabooze the night before and was scheduled to play another set that night. He was holed up in the funky Fairmont Hotel, kitty-corner from the Minneapolis Institute of Art. Greg and I arrived at his hotel room at three in the afternoon on the day of the second show.

"Come in," Hooker yelled through the door in his deep, unmistakable voice. As we entered, we saw John Lee still in bed, still wearing the lime green suit pants and print shirt he had worn for the show the previous night. He was watching *The Streets of San Francisco* on TV.

Afternoon TV seemed to be a bane or a blessing for other touring musicians we met during our escapades. Jamaican drummer Sly Dunbar—who was part of the hot eighties rhythmic duo and production team known as Sly and Robbie (Shakespeare, the bassist) that played on albums by everyone from Grace Jones, Dylan, Joe Cocker, and Marianne Faithfull to reggae artists like Black Uhuru—was also in bed with the tube on while we interviewed him, a few years after our encounter with Hooker. Dunbar never moved and rarely made eye contact other than with the TV. He eventually confessed that he was hooked on the daytime soaps because they offered "moral lessons" for living.

Inside the urban motel in Minneapolis, Hooker wasn't looking quite that deep for life's meaning or guidance. Frequently distracted by what was happening on the screen, he admitted that the show wasn't necessarily a favorite of his, but he liked to watch it to see if any scenes featured the parking lots that he owned in the bay city.

As the Helg and I got comfortable in a couple of bedside chairs, we

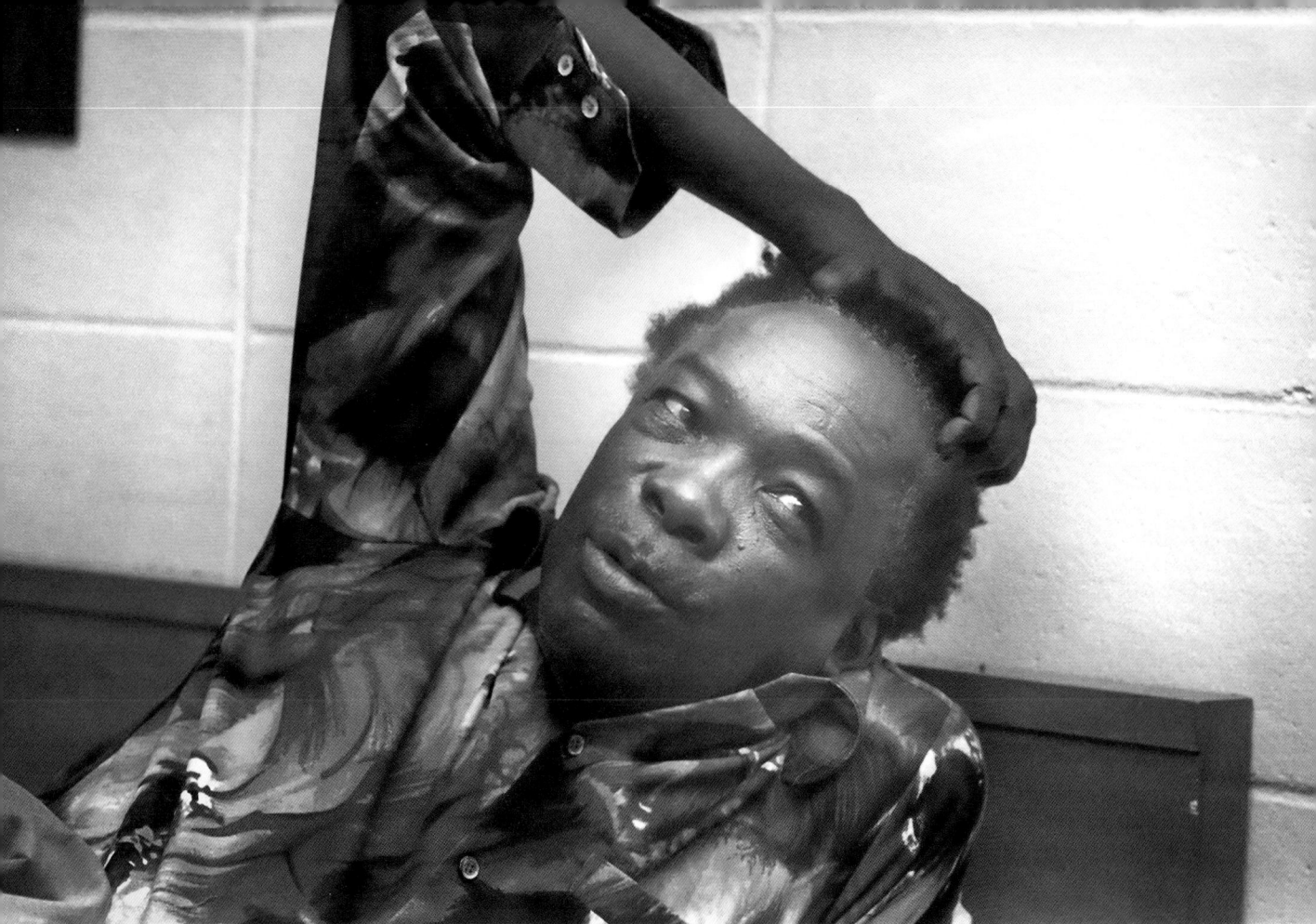

talked with Hooker about his lifetime in blues, his influences, and where the blues was headed, given the dearth of African Americans taking up the blues tradition at the time—this being prior to the arrival of the Robert Crays, Keb' Mo's, and Gary Clarks of the world.

The genre had been culturally—and lovingly—appropriated by lots of white bands and individual artists. In the Twin Cities, the legendary folk-blues trio Koerner, Ray, and Glover made impacts around the country and in Europe with their understated mixture of blues, rags, and hollers.

A handful of other Twin Cities acts were keeping the blues alive, including the Lamont Cranston Band, Lynwood Slim, and Aces, Straights, and Shuffles, featuring Kim Wilson (who would soon join the Fabulous Thunderbirds with guitarist Jimmie Vaughan, Steve Ray Vaughan's older brother). Elsewhere around the United States, Roy Buchanan (Washington, DC, area), the J. Geils Band (Boston), the Allman Brothers Band (Macon, Georgia), the Paul Butterfield Blues Band (Chicago), and others were keeping the tradition vibrant while legendary players like Muddy Waters, Willie Dixon, and Hooker entered their later years. Of course, across

The "Father of Boogie," John Lee Hooker, watching afternoon TV in search of his San Francisco parking lots the Atlantic, an entire generation of Brits and Irishmen, including Eric Clapton, Van Morrison, Rory Gallagher, the Rolling Stones, John Mayall, and the Animals, had blues at their core. And, in a twisted feedback loop that underscored the segregated, racist nature of the music business and American culture, they fed it to US audiences—many of whom were hearing the blues for the first time, but in this diluted, secondhand way.

Hooker was pleasantly conversational, despite traces of a lifelong stutter. It framed his talking and made it parse even more memorably. It was damn near as rhythmic as his electric boogie that went boom, boom, boom and how, how, how.

Despite the bounty of local, national, and international artists that we had to choose from for stories for *Sweet Potato* and, later, *City Pages*, I made a point of covering these "living legends" as they moved into their twilight years. I wanted to honor them and their deep influence on rock music and American culture, knowing the generation they belonged to had a long, varied, and important historical tradition that many Americans either were ignorant of or didn't care about, or both. Willie Dixon, Muddy Waters, Albert King, Koko Taylor, Sonny Terry and Brownie McGhee, Gatemouth Brown, and others received coverage in the early days of the *Spud* and *City Pages*.

As the Helg and I wound down our time with Hooker while he lounged in bed and the TV burbled in the background, I asked him what made his blues so powerful, so authentic. He rubbed his head back and forth with his big hand and paused for a moment. Stuttering a bit, he said matter-of-factly and with real sincerity, "Imma, Imma, vvvvery cool, very calm, very co-co-collected, natural person." It sounded like the eloquent, electric blues poetry that poured out of his guitar every night.

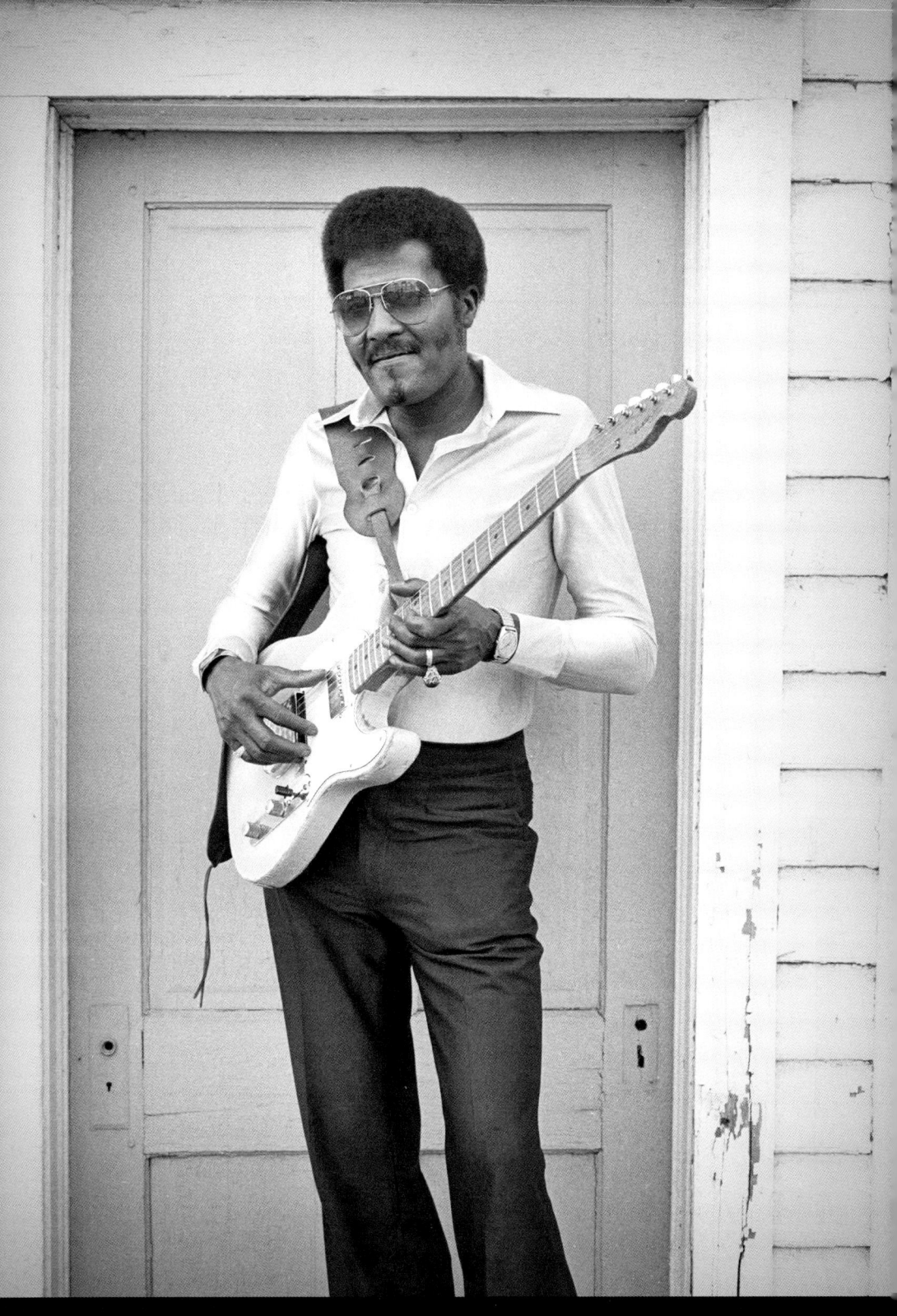

"The Master of the Telecaster," Albert Collins recorded steamy blues that often traded on cold and cool themes and titles, while his style belonged to the hot lineage of Texas blues guitar slingers before and after him.

Part bluesman, part performance artist, Screamin' Jay Hawkins is best known for his hit song "I Put a Spell on You," a diabolical marriage of voodoo and R&B that has become a standard for anyone willing to test their vocal prowess—and theatrical antics. Hawkins displayed his own antics at Northrop Auditorium on the University of Minnesota campus in 1979.

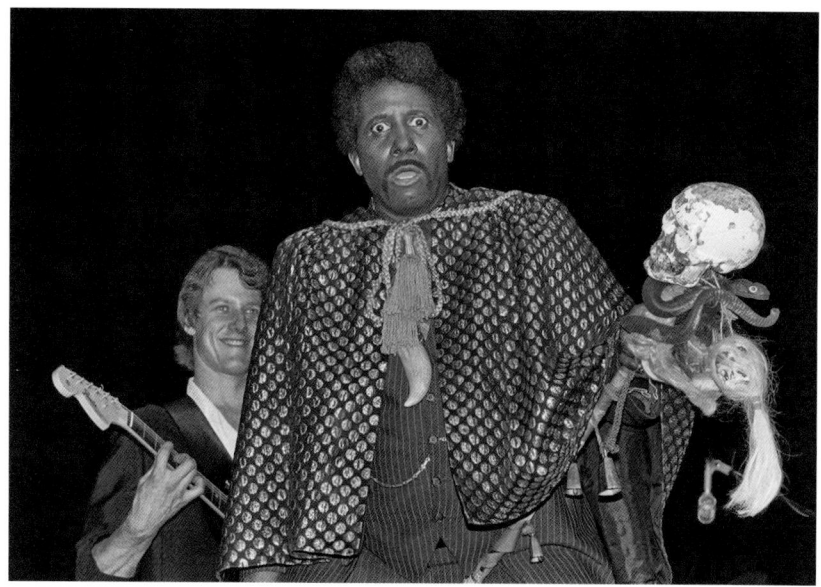

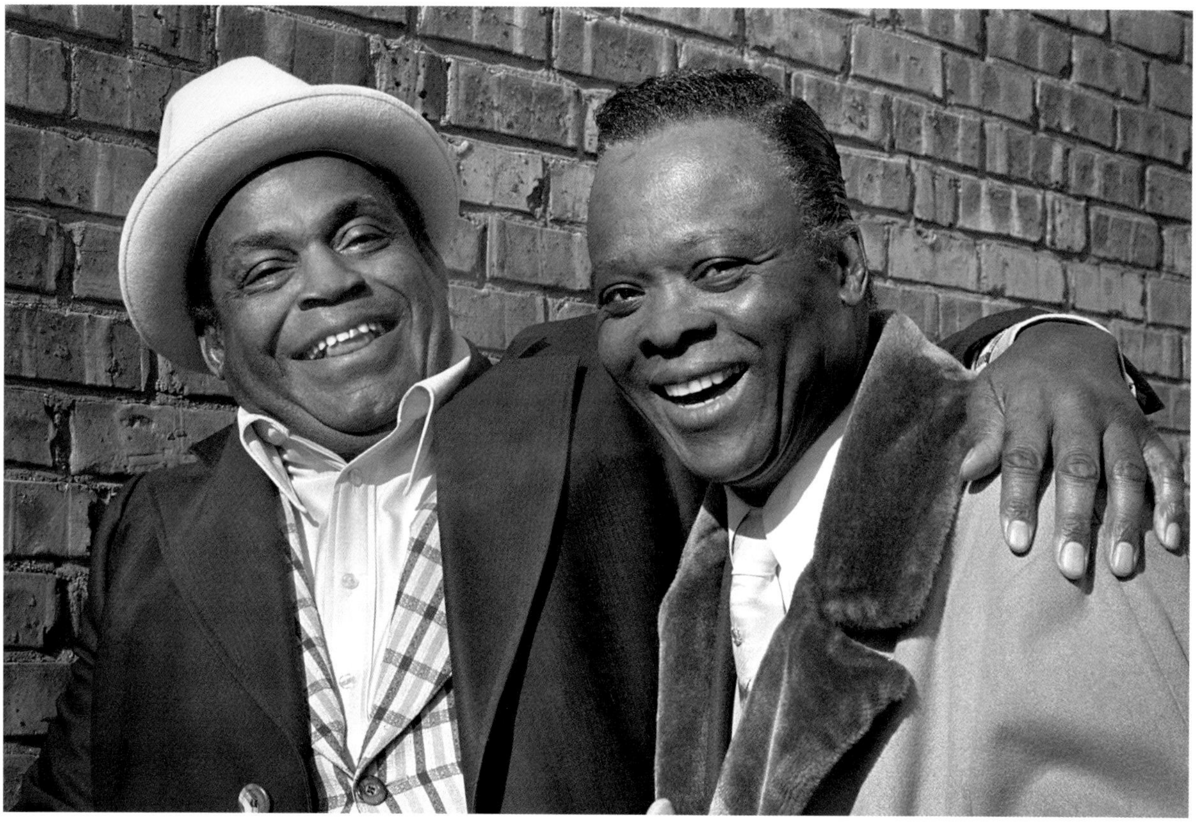

Reunited in Minneapolis with an old piano-playing friend, bassist and blues legend Willie Dixon (left) embraces Leonard "Baby Doo" Caston, with whom he played in the Big Three Trio, along with guitarist Ollie Crawford (who replaced Bernardo Dennis). Caston lived in Minneapolis until his death in 1987 and had a semi-regular gig as a solo piano man. He had a funny way of interjecting the phrase "knock a hole in it!" into many of the songs he performed live. His final album, *Baby Doo's House Party*, was recorded in Minneapolis and featured trumpeter Melvin Carter Sr., grandfather of St. Paul mayor Melvin Carter III.

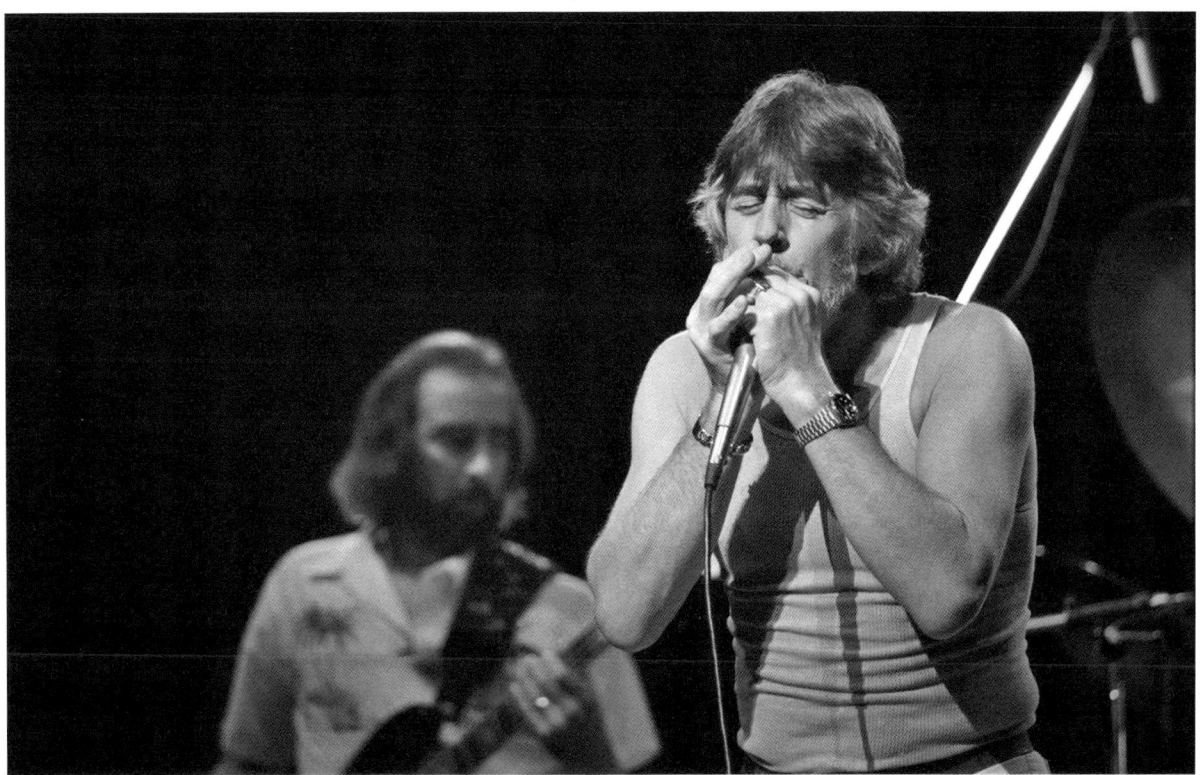

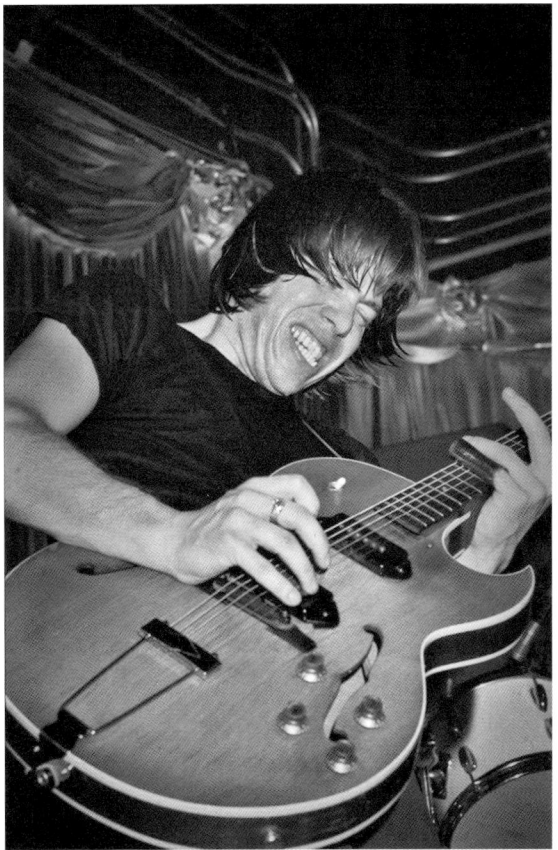

(above) John Mayall was one of the early British rockers to embrace American blues music and put his own spin on it. Over the years, his John Mayall and the Bluesbreakers included such prominent musicians as Eric Clapton, Mick Taylor, and Mick Fleetwood, among many others.

(left) George Thorogood was another white blues-rock practitioner who got mainstream airplay that his black blues and boogie forebears could only dream of. Nonetheless, he elevated and preserved the goods, playing with punk-rock fury and making the songs his own—when's the last time you heard Hank Williams's "Move It on Over" as a cement-mixer rocker? Thorogood also penned his own original tunes, like the raw, slide-guitar smash "Bad to the Bone."

ALBERT KING

The Monster Iguana Low-Down Development Blues

The publicist said it would be okay. Call Albert at eight o'clock Saturday morning. But keep it short. That was the only time he could do an interview for a story in advance of his gigs in New York at the Lone Star Cafe. The Lone Star was a relatively small, hipster combo café/bar with a Texas twang that attracted many Texans living in the Big Apple, including Dan Rather. It was located on Thirteenth Street and Fifth Avenue and featured on its roof a humongous, forty-foot iguana sculpture named Iggy. Hard to miss, it looked like another mis-bred, mammoth reptile from Japan was about to threaten lower Manhattan.

Albert King was one of blues music's true wonders, musically and physically. He was tall and heavyset, and the way he played his trademark Gibson Flying V guitar, he looked like a giant cradling a sacred lyre, one that produced some of the toughest and tenderest blues lines ever played on the instrument. Distinctive and influential, he schooled some of rock's and blues' brightest, from Eric Clapton and Duane Allman to Robert Cray and Albert Collins.

You didn't miss an Albert King show if you could help it. Personally, I would have been at every show if I could have seen him play "As the Years Go Passing By." I always saved space for him in whatever paper I was writing for. For the Lone Star show, King enlisted as an opening act Minneapolis's own Lamont Cranston Band, who were riding a pretty big wave in 1980. I pitched editors around town a bunch of stories set in New York that had local angles, and a couple that didn't.

Pretty soon Buzz Morison, a longtime running buddy and fellow scribe at the *Spud*, and I were headed east. We had one overnight stop to get our mojos workin': seeing Muddy Waters in a sold-out show at Harry Hope's, an intimate club just outside Chicago. An old college classmate of mine, Bill Kubeczko, who would go on to book the Cedar Cultural Center in Minneapolis, was running the joint. Comps and a couple of couches to

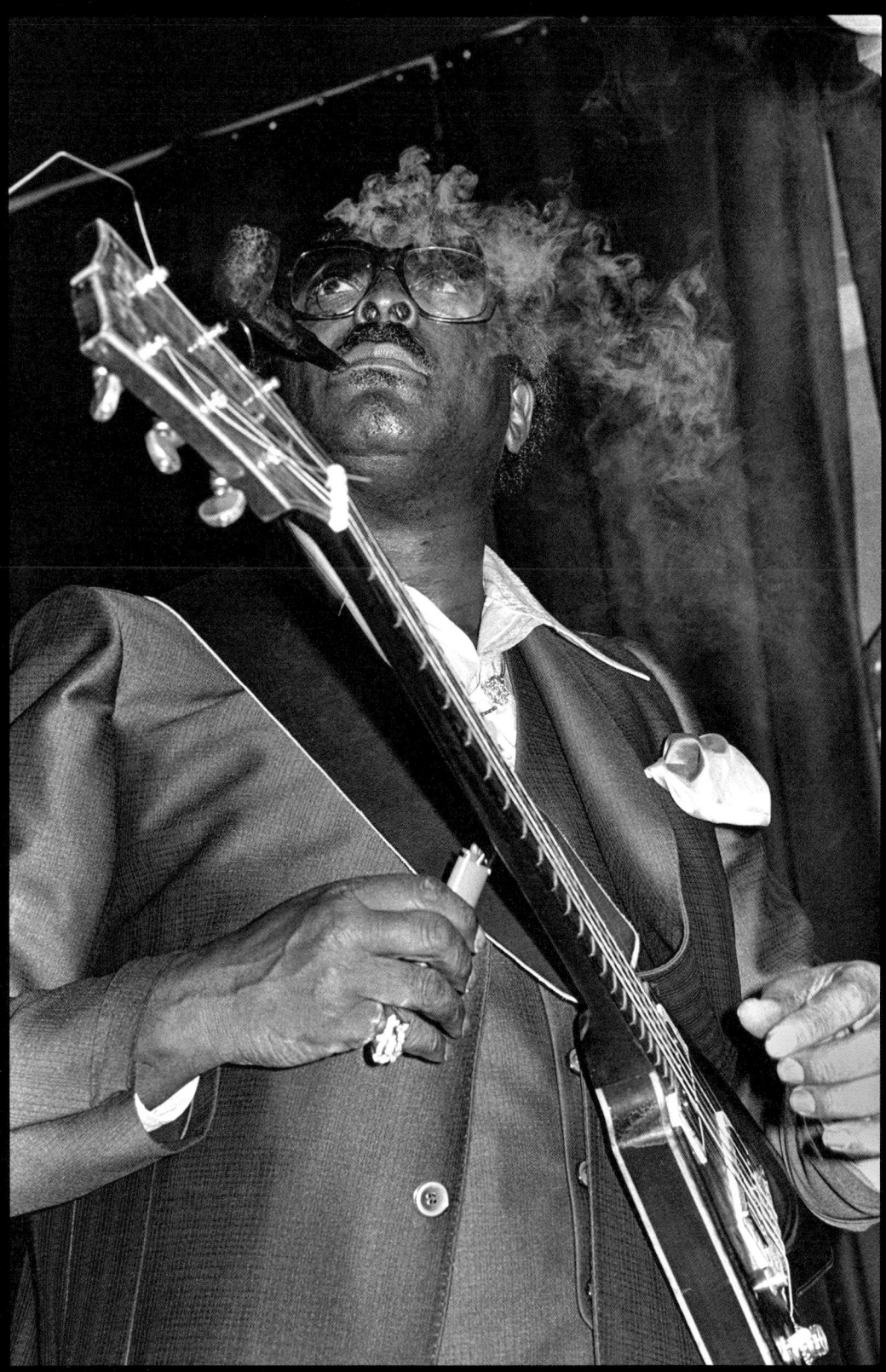

With the wafting pipe smoke, this shot of blues legend Albert King—taken at the Cabooze bar on Minneapolis's West Bank in 1981—evokes the cover photo on King's 1973 album, *I Wanna Get Funky*.

crash on made it a must-do pit stop. Waters and King were both among the top early pioneers of electric blues who shaped rock music into the next century.

There's probably a rule somewhere against calling a member of music royalty, blues or otherwise, before noon, but I trusted the publicist knew what she was doing. I set an alarm to get myself up for the 8:00 AM call, since the night before I was out someplace chasing a story or a tune.

Albert was in a hotel bed somewhere when I rang. I apologized for the early hour. He said he didn't mind. We made small talk about the Cranston band, whom he'd worked with before. I asked him about where he was in his career, which included stints as a bulldozer operator when the music wasn't paying the bills for whatever reason. That earned him the nickname the "Velvet Bulldozer," mostly for his soulful vocal attacks, and demonstrated that Albert could operate heavy machinery under the influence of "being born under a bad sign."

At about the fifteen- or twenty-minute mark of the interview, I shot him another question. Silence. I asked again. When I still didn't hear him, I tapped the line gently on the old rotary phone, thinking maybe we'd been disconnected. I asked him once more. All quiet on the set.

"Albert? You there?"

After about ten seconds, he responded with some depth-charged snores, deep, buzzing bass notes fogging up Ma Bell's long-distance lines. Just as I was about to hang up and go back to bed myself, he roared back to life.

"What's that you said?" he inquired.

"Nothing really," I said. "I think I got enough. Thanks for taking such an early call." King gathered himself as best he could.

"Okay then. You tell them Cranston boys to have a good jug of wine with 'em at the Lone Star, cuz we're gonna tear that place up." They did.

What finally, in fact, tore up the Lone Star were skyrocketing rents and neighborhood displeasure with the sci-fi beast on the roof, and by 1989, the place was closed. Another palace fit for an Albert King lost in the smoke of gentrification and time. And that was a low-down blues you could play in almost any city, including our own Twin Cities. The Prom Center, the Uptown Bar, Flyte Tyme Studios, and Nye's are just a handful of the pop culture landmarks snuffed out like Iggy, bulldozed into dust and memory rubble.

GATEMOUTH BROWN

The Texas Multi-Instrumentalist and His Special Case

S ometimes you don't get "the quote" or "the shot," no matter how long you spend with someone in an interview. So it went with Gatemouth Brown, who generously gave of his time inside the old Gopher Inn on University Avenue, once located on the western edge of the University of Minnesota's Greek row.

Gatemouth was a bandleader and multi-instrumentalist from Louisiana and Texas who played and blended many different genres, including Cajun, country, jazz, R&B, rock, and gritty Texas blues. Some regard his "blues fiddle" as one of his chief characteristics. But he disdained being lumped into a single category, especially that of a "bluesman"—and for good reason. His musical sensibilities were more akin to the big bands he led in the fifties—including a twenty-three-piece group called Gatemouth Brown and His Orchestra, which he fronted when he was just twenty-two years old. He played jazz standards by Duke Ellington and Count Basie (one of his self-admitted biggest influences, along with his own father), as well as more rockin' stuff, à la Louis Jordan. Brown confessed to not liking actual rock 'n' roll ("It's nothing you can sit up and enjoy becuz there's nothin' you can learn from it, man. That's what I'm sayin'. I mean I'm steppin' on a lot of toes when I say this, but it's true").

Ellington once told him, "You're the front-runner in what you're doin'," adding that he should be able to do anything as long as he played cleanly and precisely, continued to shape his own style, had a good stage presentation, and controlled his audience—"That's all of the most important things about music and entertainment." Of course, the Duke overlooked another key thing: what your record company would or wouldn't do for you, or *to* you.

Brown was on one of the first black-owned record labels in the world, Peacock Records. Owned and run by Don Robey, the label had its own pressing plant and distribution and was instrumental in launching the

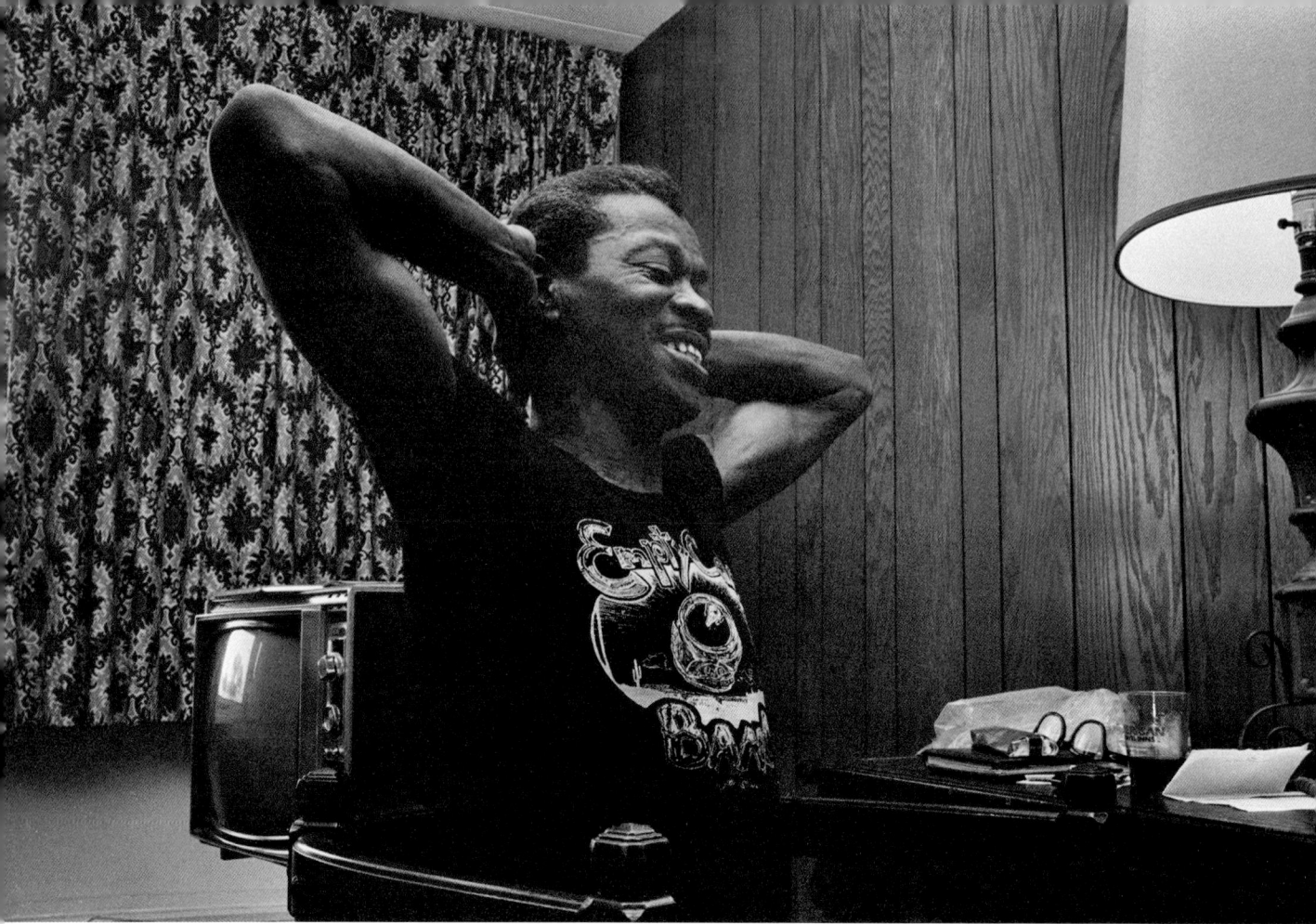

Multi-instrumentalist Gatemouth Brown shared his story and displayed his road wares during an interview in a shabby motel room at the Gopher Inn near the University of Minnesota.

careers of Bobby Bland, B. B. King, Lloyd Price, and Little Richard. Still, Brown ran into the same obstacles that were faced by black artists who recorded for labels owned by the white man: not getting paid the royalties due him and not having the freedom to record the material he wanted to record.

Gatemouth estimated that Peacock made approximately $2.5 million from his work on numerous albums and singles, which sold well in the States and worldwide, especially his big hit, "The Okie Dokie Stomp." Brown also pushed Peacock to let him record country, bluegrass, and Cajun tunes, "but my company wouldn't let me do it," he recalled.

It's not because he didn't have the goods. Gatemouth Brown was highly capable of delivering a country tune one minute and Texas blues in the style of T-Bone Walker, his biggest guitar influence, the next, then knocking down a zydeco number. I was surprised to learn that he even played on an album by New Orleans blues master Professor Longhair. It was just further proof of how accomplished his musicianship was. Brown liked to boast that he had a trademark way of staging the instruments, no matter how many musicians were in his band. He said he could make a five-piece band sound like ten: "It's the way you voice your instruments, and that's all."

Like many American jazz and blues artists, for a long time Brown enjoyed more success in Europe than at home. On these shores, he forged ties to country star Roy Clark, who helped him land several *Hee Haw* appearances. He certainly had the look down: in most of his photos, Brown is wearing killer cowboy shirts and a cowboy hat and boots. That's how he looked when he walked us through his story.

Diminutive and energetic, Brown had a quiet intensity about him when he wasn't onstage. As Greg put away his camera and I turned off my tape recorder, he took us aside to show us the "special case" he always carried with him.

Gatemouth popped open a rectangular case about twice the size of a cigar box and produced its shiny contents. In each hand he held out a Colt .45 pistol, with pearl handles, the chambers loaded—the whole shootin' match. Greg's eyes got big as bottle caps. For a moment, I had to wonder if Gatemouth was gonna go all western on us.

"Whattya carry those around for?" the Helg asked.

Brown looked us both in the eye and said: "Son, I'm a black man from Texas out on the road, that's why."

DOUG SAHM

A Lone-Star Rocker in the North Star State

People unfamiliar with Doug Sahm's story might believe he might have come from any one of three places:

1) England, because the record label that released his 1965 hit, "She's About a Mover"—which reached the top twenty in both the United States and the United Kingdom—insisted his group be called "the Sir Douglas Quintet" so people would think they were part of the British Invasion. They weren't.

2) Mendocino, California, because his Vox Continental keyboard–driven, hippie-inspired song about the town of that name put the Quintet back on the charts in '68.

3) Someplace down South, because of his classic southern drawl.

Truth is, Sahm was a Texan, through and through. This hipster's hipster from San Antonio embraced all the music of Texas—R&B, country, Tex-Mex, honky-tonk, psychedelic rock, Cajun, and whatever else struck his fancy—and it always sounded soulfully authentic and exceptionally cool. Later, he teamed up with country star Freddy Fender, Augie Meyers (his renowned Vox keyboard player), and accordion ace Flaco Jiménez to form the Texas Tornados—the four heavies you'd want carved on the Tex-Mex version of Mount Rushmore in Texas Hill Country.

Toward the end of his life (he died suddenly in his sleep in 1999 in Taos, New Mexico, only fifty-eight years old), Sahm spent a fair amount of time in Minneapolis–St. Paul visiting a "lady friend" and enjoying the pleasures of the North Star State. The Helg photographed Sahm at Duffy's bar, where his band went up against fellow Texans Joe King Carrasco and the Crowns in a kind of tequila-worm-in-cheek Tex-Mex battle of the bands. An hour or so earlier, Doug and his boys blew up the public television airwaves, playing live on the *NightTimes Variety* show on Channel 2, produced

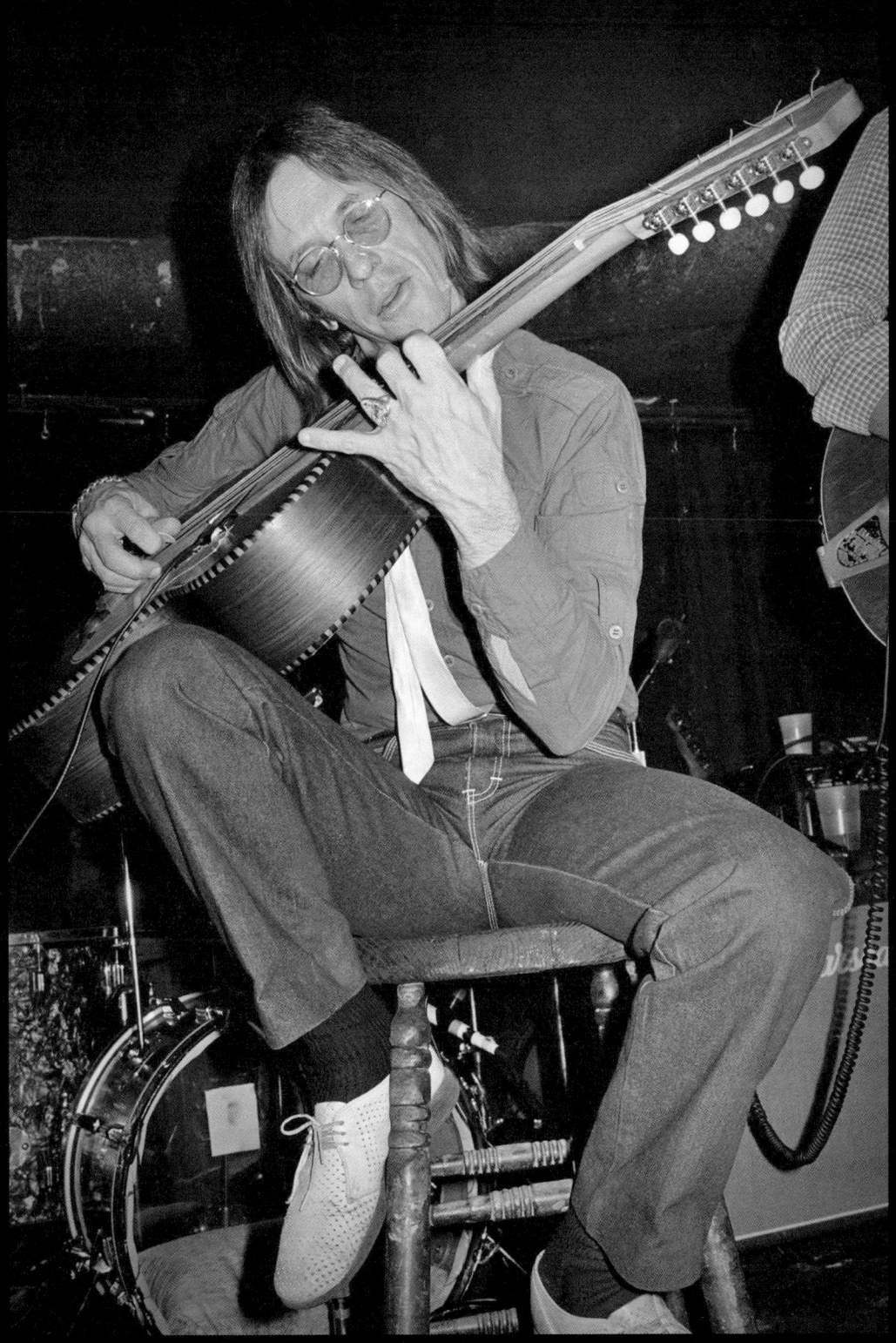

Texas-born rocker Doug Sahm spent considerable time in Minneapolis, calling it one of America's last unspoiled cities.

by Marian Moore and Kathi Riley (whom I was dating at the time, so I got to be a TV whisperer for much of their run).

Sahm caught Twins ballgames at the Hubert H. Humphrey Metro-dome—or, as it was more unaffectionately known, the Hump Dome—attended club dates and concerts, and hung out at dive bars like the Viking on Minneapolis's West Bank. The Lone-Star rocker called Minneapolis "one of the last great American cities that hasn't been spoiled," according to Tom Surowicz, a fellow Twin Cities music scribe and an old friend of mine from college. Tom often accompanied Sir Doug to events around town, such as the NRBQ concert at First Avenue, where Sahm joined them onstage for a spirited workout of "She's About a Mover."

Did I mention baseball? There was lotsa baseball. Sahm wasn't just a fan; he was on a first-name basis with many MLB players, including future Hall of Famer Goose Gossage. I lucked out one day and received an invitation to attend a Twins game with Tom and Doug. I also brought along the artistic director of the Winnipeg Folk Festival, Rosalie Goldstein, making our tight little trio an unwieldly quartet.

The Canadian impresario was in town visiting and scouting acts to book at Birds Hill Park for the internationally known music fest that drew many Minnesotans across the border each July. It was a stray "foreign" event the *Spud* regularly covered, if only to discover up-and-coming artists like k.d. lang and others. The *NightTimes* crew also had shot a long documentary about the Winnipeg event, called *A Festival of Friends*, so Goldstein had good history with many scenesters in the twin towns.

Once we got to the ballpark, it became sadly apparent that she knew as much about baseball as the three of us knew about particle physics. I wish I had known that before extending the invitation. The other mistake I made was letting Rosalie sit next to Doug during the game. She peppered him relentlessly about everything *not* related to America's national pastime. When it was over, and she went on to her next engagement, Doug growled, "Man, don't ever invite *that* woman to another game if I'm along."

If it was any consolation, the Goldstein Incident didn't dampen his appetite for the old Hump Dome. Tom remembers at another game, right before the sixth inning, the title track to Doug's latest album—"Day-dreaming at Midnight," which had just been released that week—roared through the big Teflon blimp's sound system.

Looking at the wide smile and bright gleam in the eyes of the Texas giant, you would have thought Kirby Puckett blasted one into the center field bleachers just for him. No one knows how the song got into the ball-park, let alone played, or if the person spinning the cut knew Sir Douglas was in the house. But it was a fitting salute to one of the most enduring roots music makers, a true American original that we will not see the likes of again.

GARY BUSEY

Spoiler Alert: Busey Talks Dirty

n 1979, there was no official Minnesota Film Board yet to attract film-makers with lucrative incentives like Snowbate, or even fish bait. But that didn't stop the producers of *Foolin' Around* from shooting in the Twin Cities area. The so-so romantic comedy starred Annette O'Toole, Eddie Albert, Cloris Leachman, and Gary Busey. Busey was still smolder-ing from his defining 1978 role in *The Buddy Holly Story*. Why the Oscars overlooked him for best actor that year probably had more to do with the academy's rock-history myopia back then than it did with Busey's per-formance—a stunning transfiguration into one of popular music's most enduring songwriters and innovative producers, the bespectacled Charles Hardin Holley from Lubbock, Texas.

While shooting *Foolin' Around*, Busey was active on the set during the days. But at night, he often initiated what he liked to call "rock 'n' roll time" and turned up on Twin Cities stages with groups like the Lamont Cranston Band and country rockers the Daisy Dillman Band. Pat Fred-erick, singer and fiddler from the Dillmans, remembers the movie star kicking him squarely in the cojones while Busey was "jumping around do-ing his Buddy Holly thing." National artists also got guested by Gary. The Helg got a choice shot of Busey playing alongside Tom Petty at the State Theatre (pre-restoration, when plaster occasionally fell from the ceiling during shows and your feet would stick to unknown gobs on the floor). Busey had won the respect of these artists for his work in the Holly flick, I guess. And he knew all the moves. He loved to hug-share the mic on a cho-rus or a hot guitar lick; and no one was going to push back on the beefy, six-foot Texas native who played on early Leon Russell albums in Tulsa.

In what was the first full-length feature story I ever wrote (for the *Minnesota Daily*), Busey acknowledged that Russell taught him how to play to the camera on local Okie television. "I Was Buddy Holly" was the title of the *Daily* piece, a direct quote from Busey, who felt like he really did become Buddy while in character. And he never backed off the claim.

Since I was hungry and looking for as many outlets as I could find to run my work, I would send tidbits from my pieces to Fred Schruers at *Rolling Stone* for the "Random Notes" section, which he ran at the time. I sent poor Fred so many "Notes" while Busey was in town that he began one with "Gary Busey, still foolin' around in Minneapolis," as Gary fatigue started setting in at the magazine and among the local music populace.

Busey meant well, I think. He loved the Cranstons so much he wanted them to be the musical guests on *Saturday Night Live* when he was slated to host the following spring. The closest the Cranstons ever got to 30 Rock in midtown Manhattan, though, was way downtown at the Lone Star Cafe on Thirteenth Street (see the Albert King story). But thanks to tickets from Busey—or was it Twin Cities natives Al Franken and Tom Davis, who were writing for *SNL* at the time?—I ended up on national TV, as did the left arm and shoulder of my friend and fellow writer Buzz Morison. We'd come to New York to write a bunch of stories, including on the Cranstons show and the Flamin' Oh's at the Peppermint Lounge.

Although it looks big on TV, Studio 8H, where *SNL* is shot, is relatively small. During a sketch about a fake TV show called *Women's Problems*, in which no women appear, John Belushi stood right next to me in the audience to ask a question of the fake host. Bam, there I was, dead center on the NBC camera, up close with the Peacock. For the next ten years, I knew whenever the show was rerun because I would get calls or cards from friends around the country asking, "Hey, were you on *Saturday Night Live*?"

Busey promised he would meet us after the broadcast and we'd all haul ass downtown in his limo to see the Cranstons. But when we got into the limo, it started going uptown to the Essex House hotel, where *SNL* guest hosts stayed in the big suite. Ol' Gar wanted to change before commencing "rock 'n' roll time." All the way to the hotel, he made dirty small talk with the driver, who had a nice tat on his forearm. An older man, he looked Thai and spoke limited English, but he seemed to understand perfectly well what a dragon tattoo might look like on Mr. Busey's mid-frontal appendage because he tittered like an embarrassed schoolboy for several New York City blocks.

Busey never did make it to the club. Buzz and I left after waiting more than an hour for him to get off a call with a female friend of his, an aspiring country singer and actress who was having problems with a boyfriend. We bid Busey farewell and got into a cab heading south to Thirteenth Street, figuring it was probably the last we would ever see of the man who was Buddy Holly.

Fast forward past 150-plus movie and TV roles—and one near-fatal motorcycle accident in 1988—that Busey went through since our limo ride with him. In 2012, he returned to Minneapolis for a special screening of *The Buddy Holly Story* at the Parkway Theater.

I had long since moved from pop culture journalism to doing publicity, and among my clients was the Parkway, as well as McNally Smith College of Music, and so I was on hand for the screening. I wondered if Busey would remember our New York encounter, or even filming in Minneapolis in 1979. Rumors that he had suffered brain trauma from the motorcycle accident were widespread. Was the guy all "still there"? If you ever watched him on YouTube talking about Hobbits while sitting on a lush, green hillside that might have been in the shire or a nice LA vista somewhere, you might think, naw, he definitely was not "still there." Or you might believe he was just acting in character as a disheveled, wide-eyed storyteller, drunk on his own wacky tales.

Busey didn't remember me, which was kind of a relief, to be honest. But when Greg—who coincidentally was shooting the event for the Parkway—mentioned the photo with Petty, the actor seemed to recall it. "I've got to have that!" Busey blurted, looking a little vexed. Before the event was over, he also proved he could still talk dirty, and conjure Holly.

Writing a follow-up news release for McNally Smith, I penned the following account of his visit:

> Actor-musician Gary Busey revisited his celluloid history and rock 'n' roll roots by paying homage to Buddy Holly on the fifty-third anniversary of Holly's death, February 3, 2012, in Minneapolis, working with three McNally Smith College of Music alumni. Standing in as Holly's first band, the Crickets, Josh Bourdon (upright bass), Brandon Petron (guitar), and Zach Spicer (drums) formed the perfect backing trio for the musician-turned-actor whose defining role as Holly in the 1978 music biopic, *The Buddy Holly Story*, earned Busey an Academy Award nomination and the National Society of Film Critics' Best Actor award.
>
> During a filmed sound check, Busey regaled the eager young players with stories from the movie, insights into Buddy's music, and occasional off-color jokes, before expanding the night's playlist to seven Holly songs. The band, recruited by McNally Smith's composition teacher and recording artist Gary Rue, had played in the 2011 popular musical about Holly at the History Theatre, simply called *Buddy*. Their chops still finely honed, the talented threesome connected immediately with the aging actor who says he feels Buddy's spirit every February 3 and would channel that spirit in performance. It didn't take long to happen.
>
> Busey and the trio nailed select Holly tunes like "Rave On," "Everyday," "Peggy Sue," and others. The emotion and music were so strong that Busey's Los Angeles publicist cried during their first take of "True Love

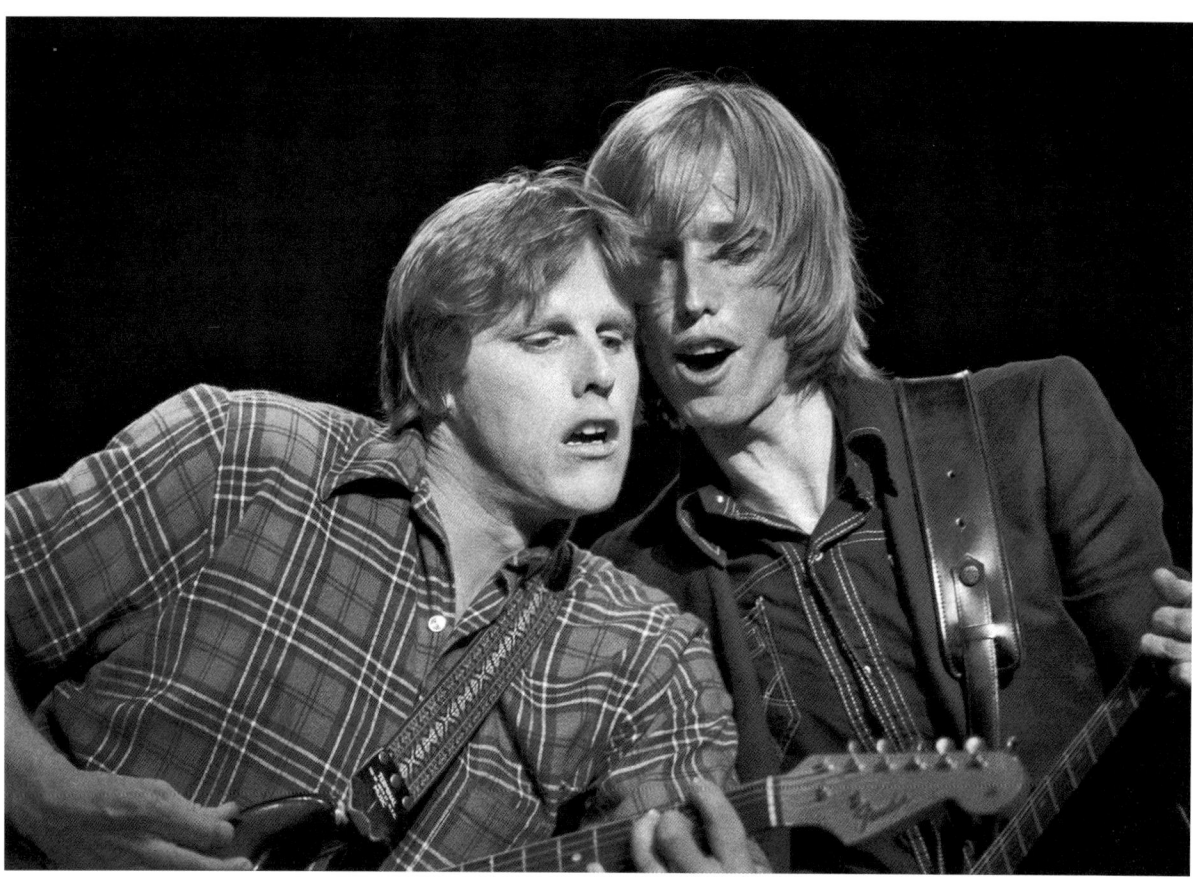

In addition to Tom Petty—shown here during a concert at the State Theatre in Minneapolis in September 1978—Hollywood actor Gary Busey shared microphones with quite a few local Twin Cities bands, including the Daisy Dillman Band and the Lamont Cranston Band.

Ways," with the sixty-seven-year-old Hollywood actor delivering a powerfully soulful version that was both plaintive and jubilant.

What I didn't write was that "True Love Ways," perhaps Holly's finest ballad, made my own tear ducts leak, if only a trickle. I turned to my fellow flak afterward and said, "There's nothing really wrong with this side of Gary Busey."

"No, there's not!" he blubbered.

Despite having looked into the hollow eye sockets of the Reaper, Busey hadn't changed his tune all that much in thirty years. As the news release—and later events—continued:

"In fact, Bourdon, Petron, Spicer, and Busey worked so well together that he promised them he would have them play with him next year at the Surf Ballroom in Clear Lake, Iowa, on February 3, 2013, which will be the thirty-fifth anniversary of the film. He also discussed having them work on a Holly tribute record he was putting together, with renowned producer Rob Fraboni (the Band, the Rolling Stones, Bonnie Raitt, et al.) and special guests."

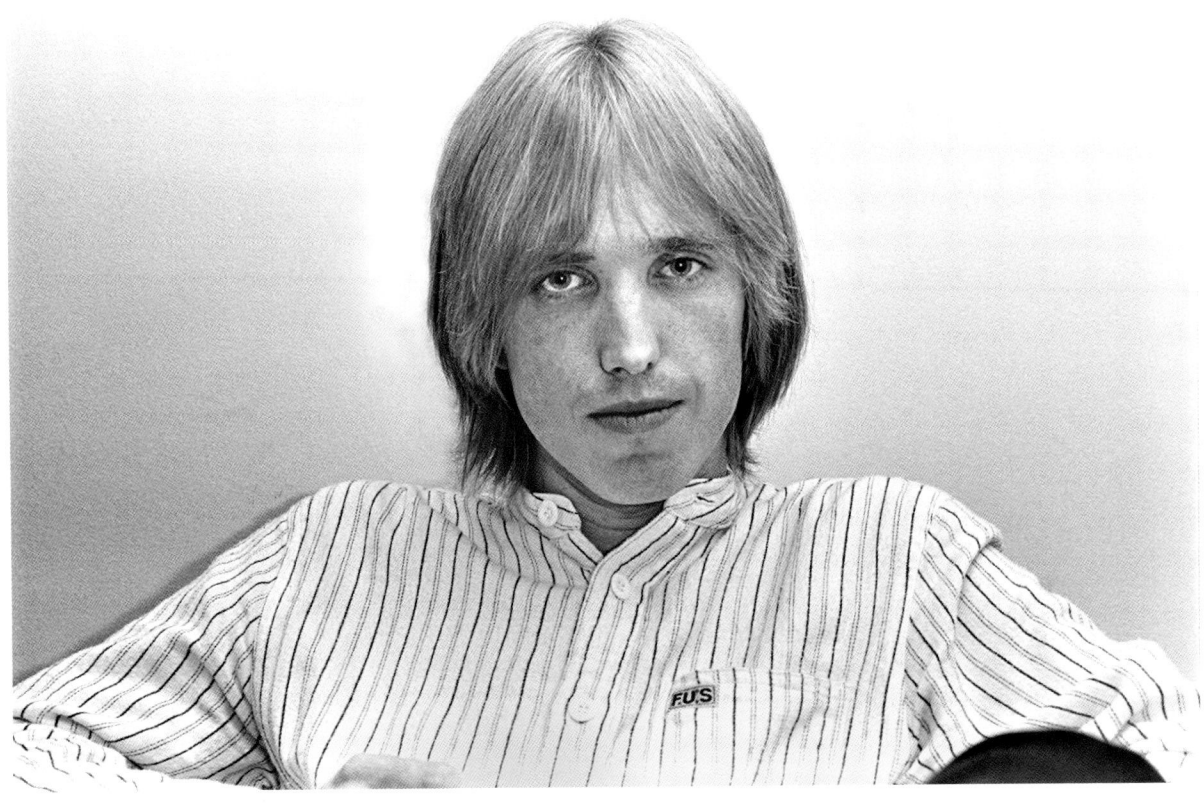

Busey did cut two Holly singles in 2018 to commemorate the fortieth anniversary of *The Buddy Holly Story*, though not with the local Minnesota guys. (To his credit, he did have them back him at an annual Starkey Hearing Foundation Gala and for a gig at the Surf.) Teddy Jack, son of Busey's old mentor Leon Russell—and Busey's godson—produced the cuts.

Among his other escapades, Busey became a poster man for celebrity rehab on reality TV. And as further proof that his "rock 'n' roll time" was winding down, as it will for all of us, he hoofed it on *Dancing with the Stars*, a show where former A-listers go for one last whack at the showbiz piñata. He also came out in support of Trump in the 2016 election, one of the few Hollywood "stars" to hazard a declaration for the Donald.

Looking at the photo of Petty and Busey now, the two of them rockin' out to one of Tom's fine tunes, you really wish, or at least I do, that Petty woulda, sorta, coulda shouldered him out of the way. Even just a little bit.

This solo portrait of Tom Petty from September 1978 was taken in his room at the hotel that once stood behind the State Theatre in Minneapolis. "He was a very smart and sharp person with a dry sense of humor," recalled Helgeson.

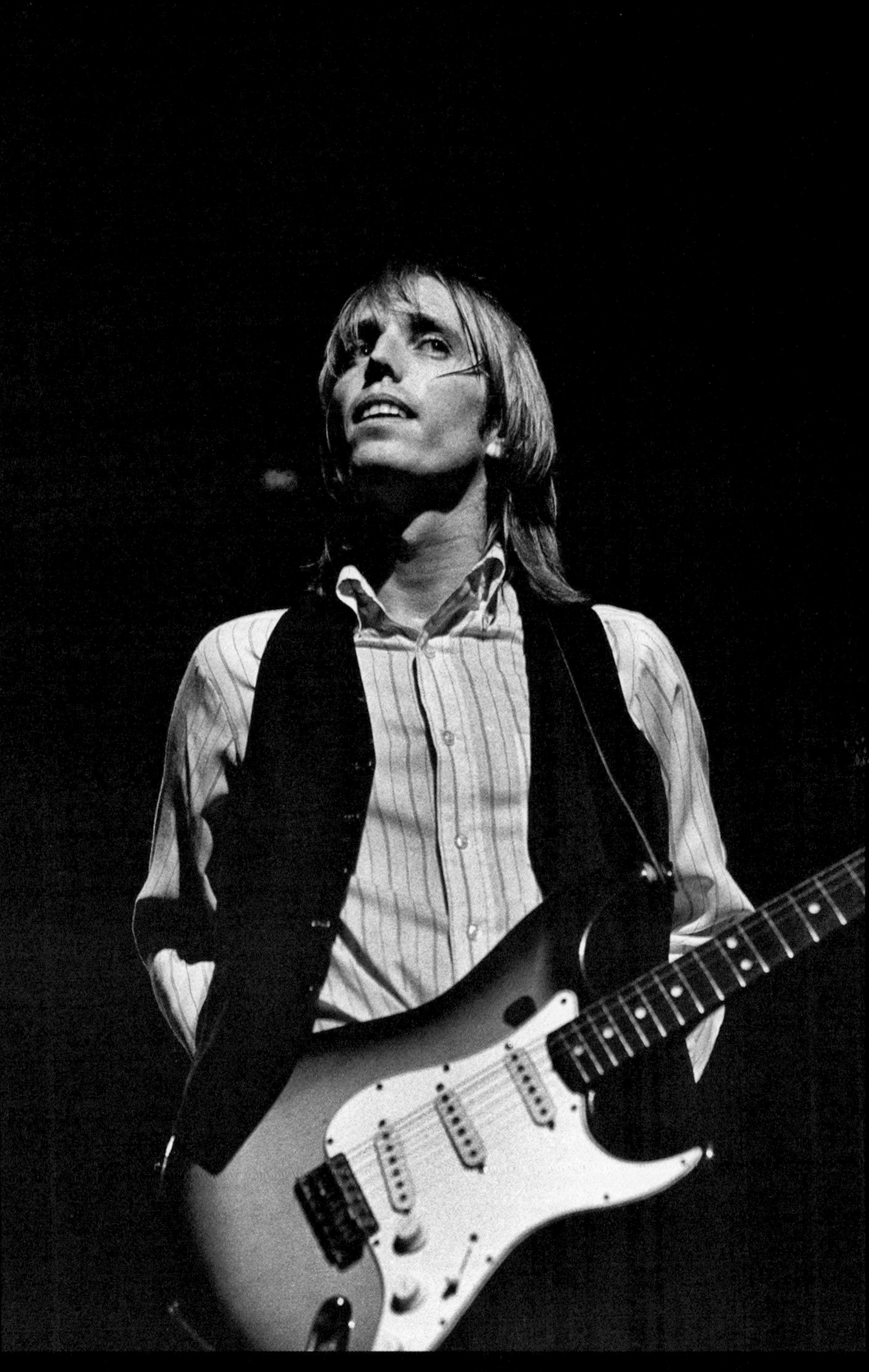

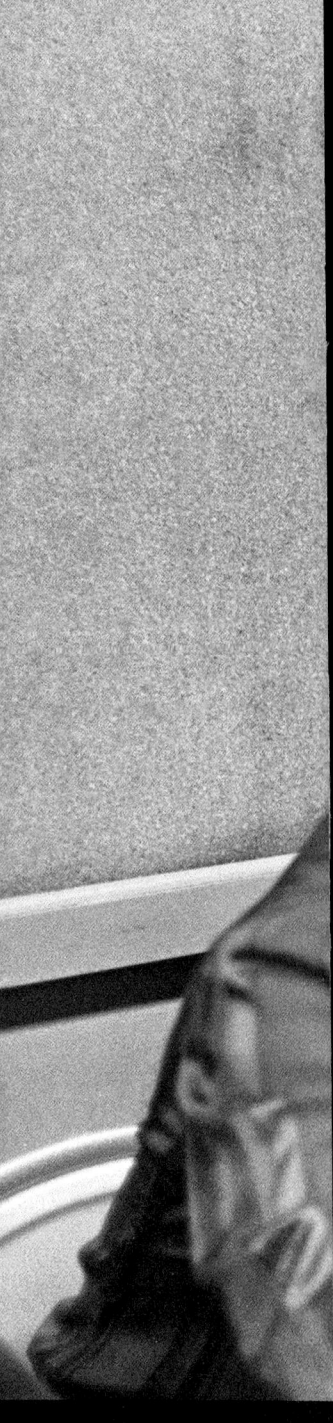

Tom Petty during one of his earliest Twin Cities performances, at the State Theatre in 1978,

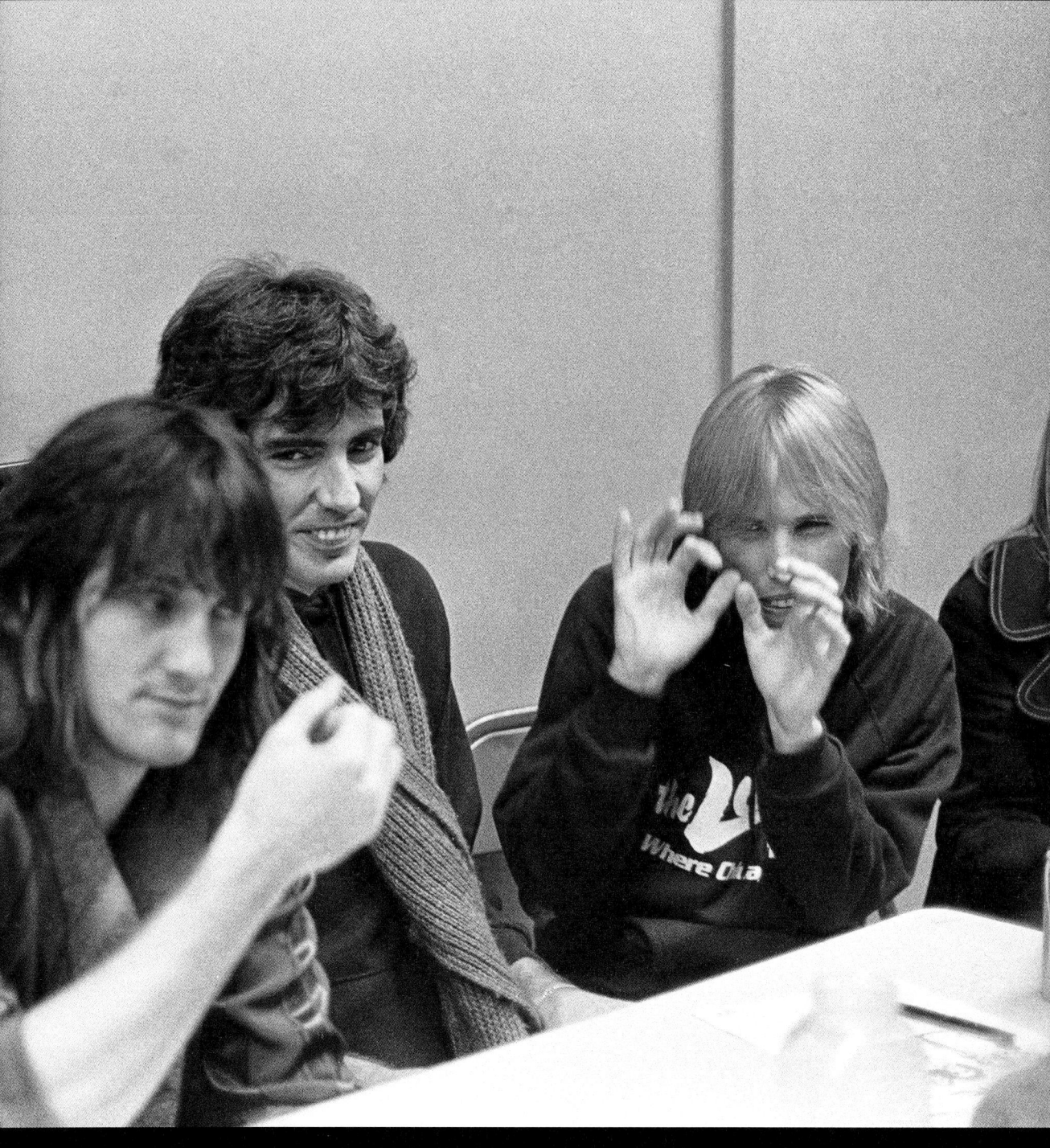
Tom Petty backstage at the St. Paul Civic Center in 1979 with Stan Lynch and Ron Blair of the Heartbreakers. "Because we had met previously, Petty started imitating me with an imaginary camera," the Helg noted.

MORRIS WILSON

The Fighter

Twin Cities jazz bands and players were rare breeds, constantly at risk of fading into obscurity during the late seventies and eighties. Supportive, but seemingly always struggling, jazz joints in that era included prime places like the AQ (Artists Quarter, then in Minneapolis), the Dakota (hidden in Bandana Square in St. Paul), the Emporium of Jazz in Mendota, the upstairs room at the Longhorn Bar, and the Rainbow Gallery Jazz Club on the West Bank. The most popular groups of the era—read, the ones working on a semi-regular basis—included the seventeen-piece Wolverines Big Band (which played at Jimmy Carter and Walter Mondale's 1976 inauguration) and the fabulous trio of Prudence Johnson, Tom Lieberman, and Tim Spark of Rio Nido. But if you had Morris Wilson in your corner—even if you weren't a jazz cat—you had a fighting chance.

Saxophone and flute player, organizer, mentor—Morris was all those things, as well as a boxer who had important friends in high places. Like that of many musicians, especially black musicians, Wilson's own career was only truly on for the public when there were gigs to play and some money to record with. In-between times were lean and mean times.

Glowing feature stories about him from time to time would put him and his colorful history, self-discipline, and strong work ethic back in a good light. Rick Mason's February 1981 cover story in the *Spud* and a much, much later profile in the first issue of *Secret Stash* in 2012 probably shared a narrow readership, despite the wide chasm in time. The legendary saxman mostly was known only to other musicians and the small retinue of jazz, R&B, and funk fans who appreciated that he was a deep, outspoken, and highly educated Twin Cities player who knew theory as well as improvisation, both largely self-taught.

Wilson picked up traveling gigs at an early age with R&B stars the Temptations and Ike and Tina Turner; jazz players such as Freddie Hubbard, Sonny Stitt, and Herbie Hancock; and bluesmen Mojo Buford and Muddy Waters. But prior to earning a place on those notable band rosters, his story took an interesting turn when the young Arkansas native transplanted to Minneapolis. There Wilson met John Coltrane, who was in town for two weeks playing with the Miles Davis sextet in 1957. Wilson reconnected with 'Trane in Chicago in the early sixties, when the Windy City was something of a bustling Jazz Central Station. Wilson practiced regularly with Coltrane, who constantly challenged him, but as Mason wrote, Wilson said, "I had no idea what he was talking about."

Side hustles for survival are second nature to musicians—other bands outside your main gig, a solid day job to make bank—and Morris had them, too. At the time of Rick's profile of Wilson, he was playing in at least three different groups. Later, he gained a reputation for helping groom young singers and musicians, like Mint Condition's Stokley Williams, jazz drummer Phil Hey, and multi-instrumentalist and producer Shaun La-Belle. He also took Sue Ann Carwell (who landed a Warner Bros. deal in the eighties with a little help from Prince) and Paisley Park Records' Taja Sevelle (née Richardson) under his wing. But before anyone—even the ladies—could do anything with him, they had to put on the boxing gloves and spar with Wilson in his basement.

"If you were part of a project with Morris, you had to put on the gloves," his son, Kevin Kirkendahl, remembered over a friendly chat in 2018 about the man he called Morris the Taurus but seldom Dad. "He said it helped them focus," Kirkendahl noted. Then he added: "Morris's boxing style was a lot like Mohammed Ali's—he was always dancing." And Wilson shared a first-name-basis friendship with the Greatest of All Time. "Prince always bugged him to introduce him to Ali," Kirkendahl said with a laugh. "But Morris always told him, 'You're not ready yet, you're not ready yet.'"

What did that mean?

"I don't know," said Wilson's son, who has his own noteworthy irons in the fire in Los Angeles, including acting, script work, and a fabulous ongoing project called "A Tribute to Johnny Mathis Featuring Kevin Kirkendahl."

Other reminiscences included some genuine surprises and some tender father-son moments, from classic learning-to-drive stories to the revelation that even though he played it, "Morris couldn't stand fusion." As to that coming-of-age ritual, imagine Wilson and son in Morris's old Fleetwood Brougham heading down the ramp to I-35W, with Pops tied in knots and his son at the wheel. Aside from the safety and the strength that the big ride provided, the Caddy served another purpose for Kirkendahl's hip parent: "He needed a cool car to drive to clubs."

"Jazz doesn't wait" was a favorite expression of Wilson's that Kirkendahl fondly remembers, underscoring Morris's dedication to his horn. He

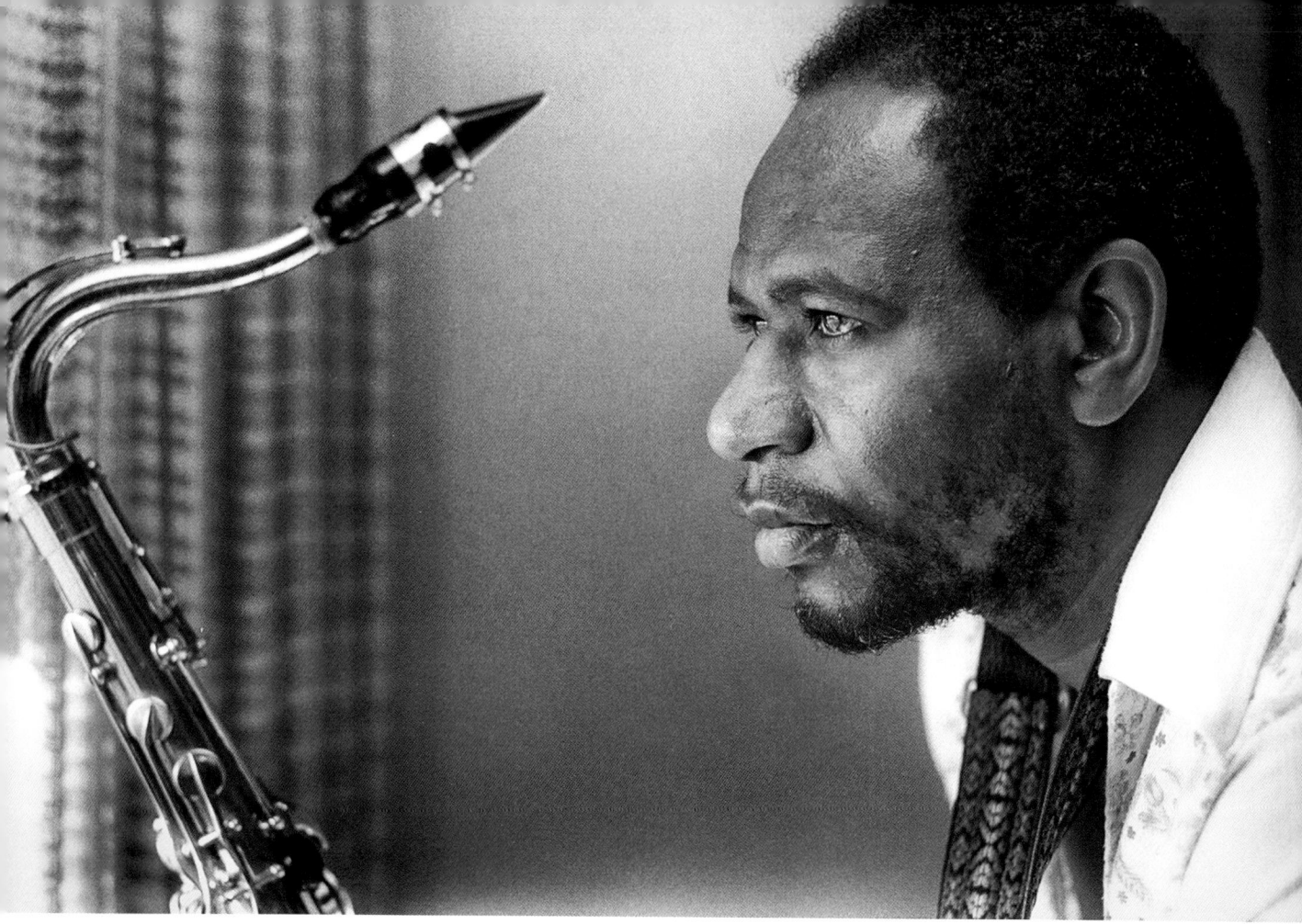

Photographed in his south Minneapolis home, jazzman Morris Wilson was a mentor and musicians' activist with friends in high places—and someone you scatted with at your own peril.

would sometimes stay up all night playing études. "A lot of people didn't know it, but he was a great scat singer, too. You scatted at your own peril with Morris." But the "Jazz doesn't wait" mantra also illustrated the urgency he felt in the late seventies and through the next decade, as he saw disco pushing out the opportunities for live gigs for African American players in nightclubs, whether jazz or not. At one point, he led demonstrations downtown to raise awareness about how electronic disco systems were putting local musicians out of work. Only a handful of people joined him to rally for the cause.

Never one to back down, Wilson saw the bigger picture even more clearly: the Twin Cities' history of locking black artists out of the mainstream art and music scene. In part, he formed the Minnesota Minority Musicians Association as a response.

"He's complained long and loudly about what he considers to be systematic discrimination by local club owners and radio station programmers to keep black musicians and jazz out of the clubs and off the airwaves," Mason wrote in 1981, less than a year after local pop stations refused to play "Funkytown"—even though it was becoming a worldwide hit—because, as one program director noted, it "sounded too black." This same theme would echo through Joe Minjares's 2015 play about the Latino rocker, and Minnesota's godfather of rock 'n' roll, Augie Garcia, *River Road Boogie: The Augie Garcia Story*, and in Alan Berks's *Complicated Fun* play about the eighties music scene a year later, both staged at the History Theatre.

Wilson died at age seventy-six early in January 2016, and his memorial service attracted a host of luminaries from across the musical spectrum, including older jazz players like Irv Williams, R&B and pop artists, and several members of Minnesota's first family of music, the Petersons. You expect to hear good things at such occasions, but the outpouring for Wilson was inspiring. (Wilson himself would have never stood for trite and tired platitudes.)

As the brief service wound down, an old friend of Wilson's, Dean Brewington, stood up and confirmed that this beloved, hardworking, and dedicated jazz musician had earned widespread respect and admiration. After reading a letter from Wilson's longtime friend and fellow musician Bobby Lyle, Dean shared a personal note from another old acquaintance and one of the last true jazz giants. You would never hear about him, or their friendship, from Morris, because Morris was not a name-dropper. It wasn't his style. But the note, brief and poignant, underscored that deeper place Wilson had in the wider jazz world. It read:

We thank you, Brother Morris. Job well done. We'll be seeing you later, you dig?"

—Sonny Rollins

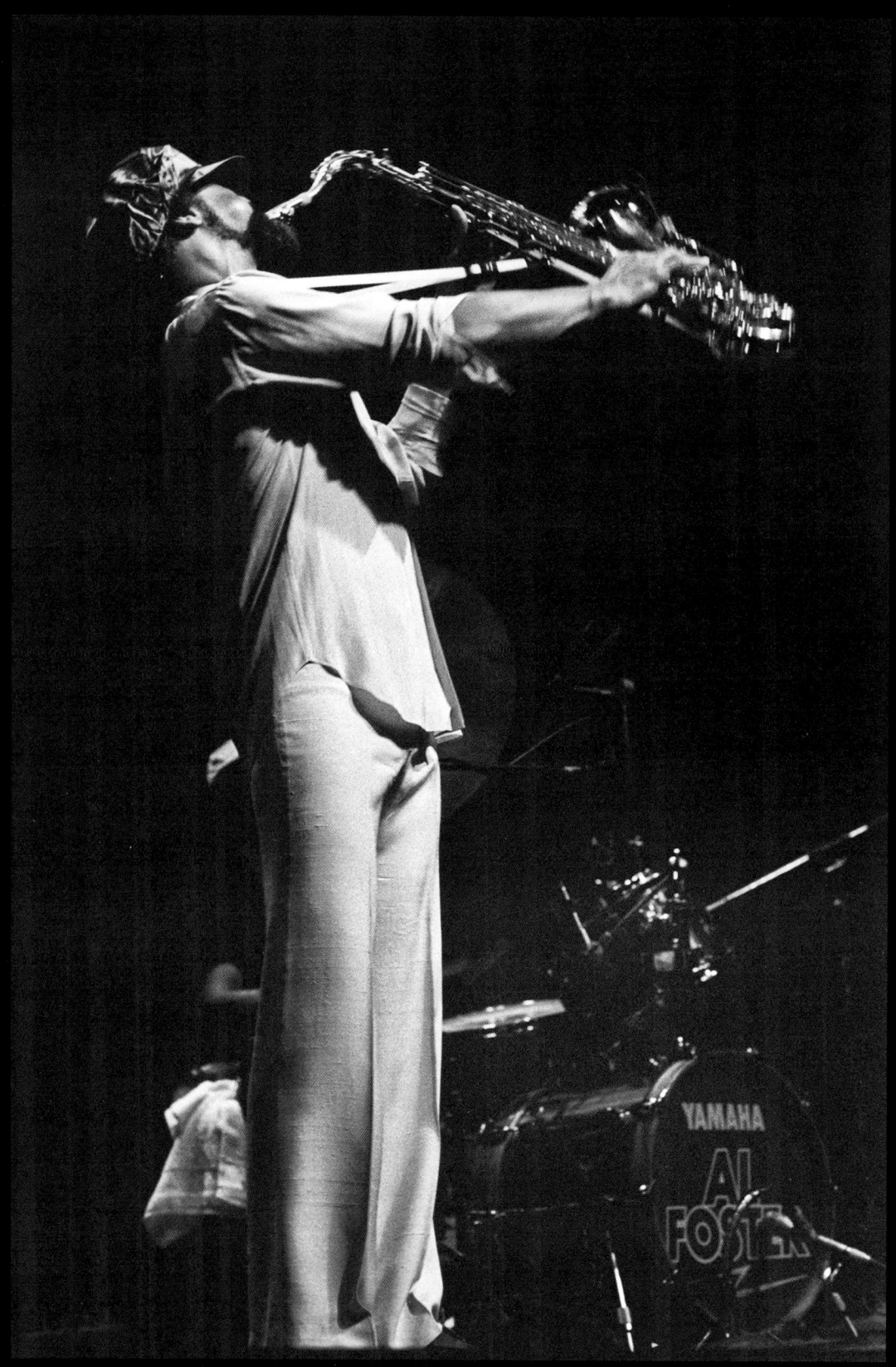

One of the last of the legendary jazz masters, Sonny Rollins performs in Minneapolis in 1980.

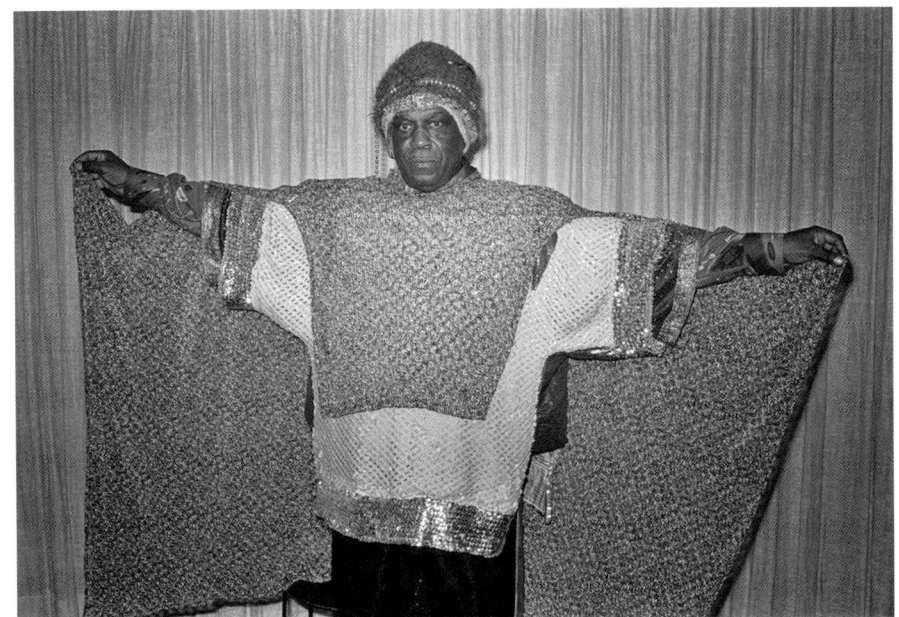

Space is the place—but in this case, the place was the Minneapolis Institute of Art theater, where Sun Ra, the intrepid and innovative leader of his cosmic jazz Arkestra band, performed in 1980.

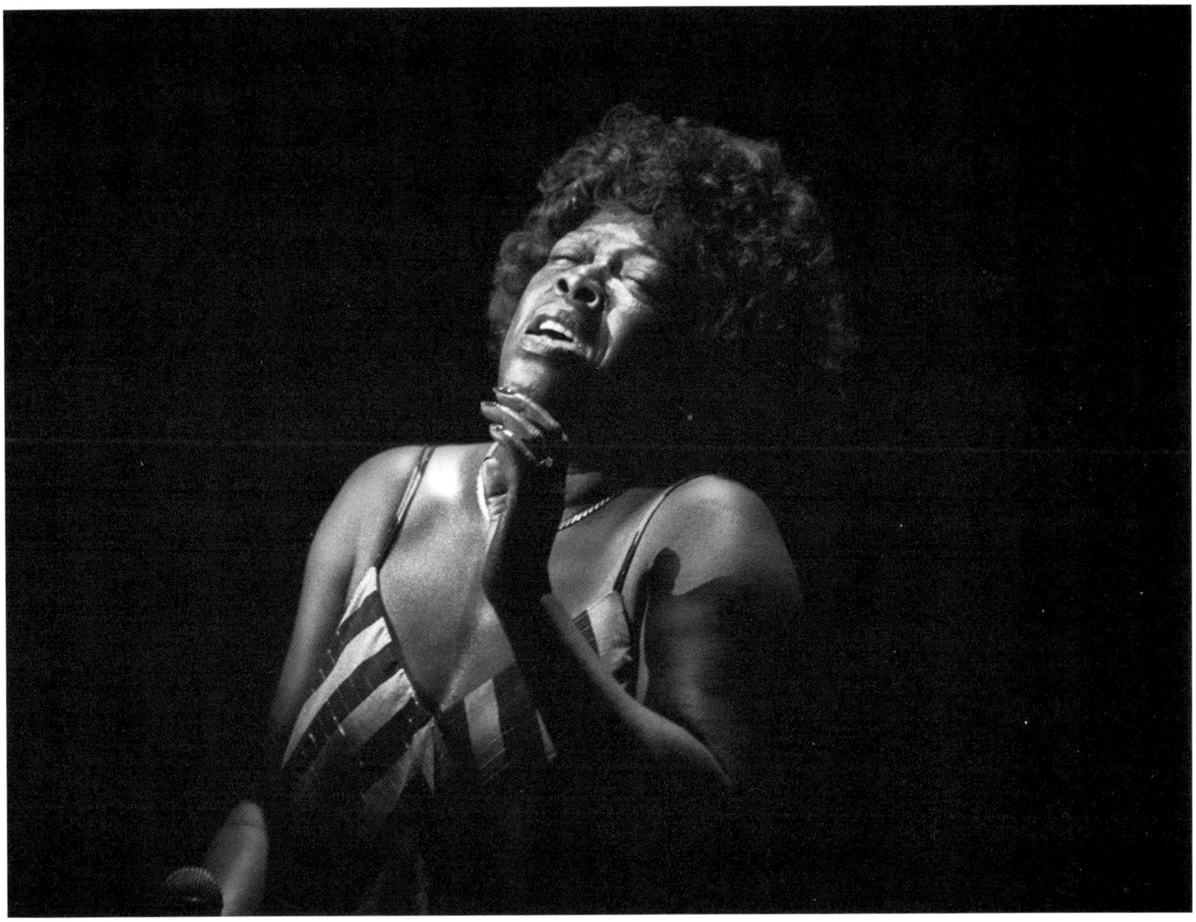

The divine Sarah Vaughan performing at O'Shaughnessy Auditorium at the College of St. Catherine in St. Paul. About the concert, Greg remarked, "There's not much to say that I remember, except that she was amazing!"

THE STEELES

Minnesota's First Family of Soul and the Arts

The famous Jacksons—Tito, Janet, Michael, and the rest—grew up in the same industrial town of Gary, Indiana, as the Steele family. But whereas the Jacksons moved to the West Coast, J. D., Jevetta, Jearlyn, Fred, and Billy Steele came northwest to the Twin Cities. And the cities have been richer for it ever since. Minnesota's first family of soul has contributed more to our artistic culture than just about any family in the history of the state.

The Steeles are known for their rousing soul and gospel performances, live and on record; their active involvement in theater locally, nationally, and internationally; and their ever-present presence in other media, from radio to film to television. Their work over the decades—including collaborations with artists such as Prince, Donald Fagen, Morgan Freeman, and others—should qualify them for a "Minnesota Lifetime Achievement Award," if the state had such an honor to bestow.

The reasons Steele fans know and love them are as numerous as the productions the family has touched. Their annual Christmas concerts, or their halftime performance with the Minnesota Orchestra at the opening game of the NFL megachurch/Vikings stadium in 2016, at which they honored the recently departed Prince—these might be a couple of your favorite Steele things.

Singing together onstage, the Steeles have so much heat and heart that they create their own weather. But their individual strengths and gifts make each one a force to be reckoned with. Although they've been in Minnesota since the late seventies, their story really takes off in 1983 when they were collectively cast as Ismene (Oedipus's daughter) in *The Gospel at Colonus*, a theatrical musical retelling of Sophocles's *Oedipus at Colonus*, set in a Pentecostal church in modern America. The captivating production was first staged as a workshop piece in 1983 at the O'Shaughnessy Auditorium in St. Paul before moving on to the Brooklyn Academy

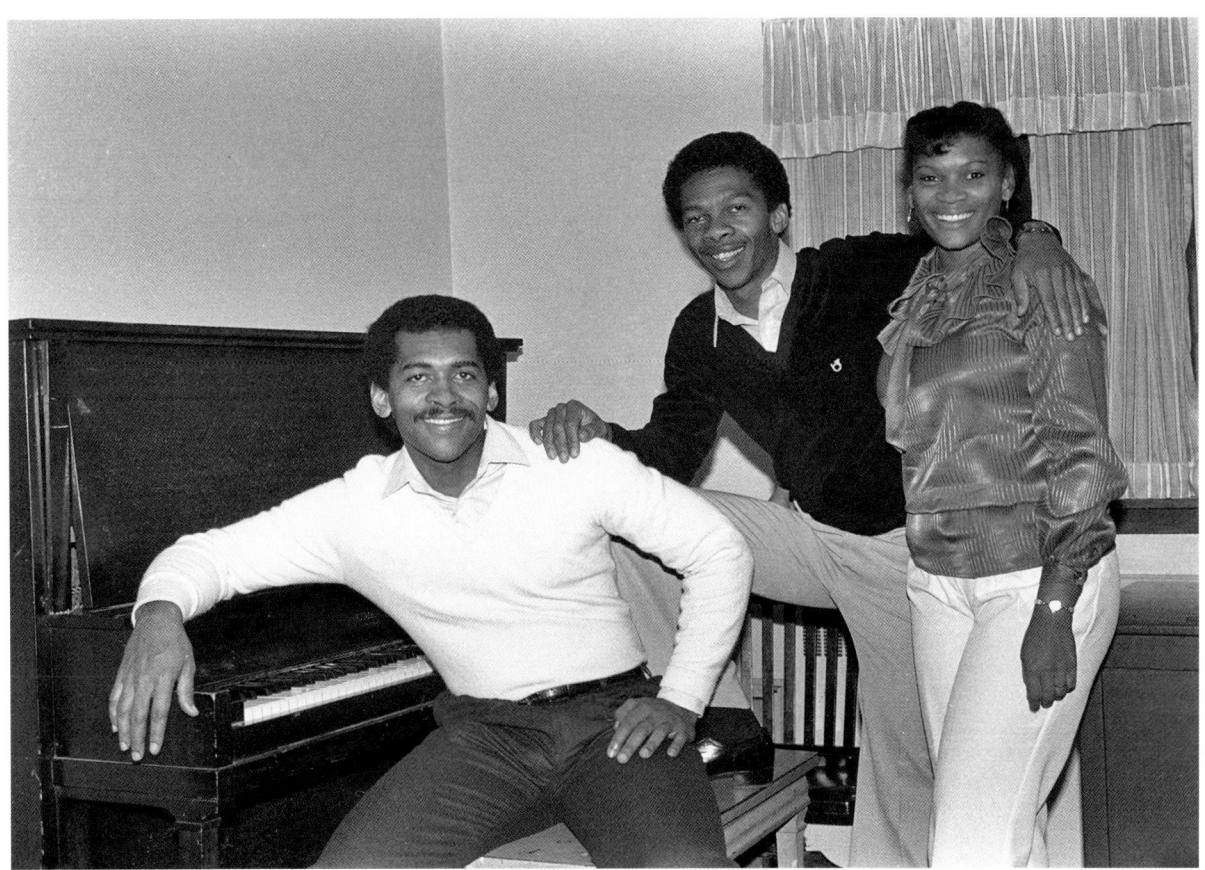

of Music's Next Wave Festival and the wider world. It featured Clarence Fountain and the Blind Boys of Alabama, including singer/guitarist Sam Butler, the Original Soul Stirrers, and the Rance Majestic Choir from Minneapolis.

Written by innovative, award-winning New York theater director Lee Breuer, with music composed by Bob Telson, the musical captured a righteous pile of critical and audience praise and the highest awards from around the world. It was *the* hot theater ticket, no matter where it was performed, from Hollywood to Paris to Broadway and beyond.

Like the phenomenon *Hamilton*, *The Gospel at Colonus* leveraged black culture to reframe historical and literary events—both musicals are a triumph of inspired multiculturism that the world needs more of. A preview of *Colonus* was the last feature I wrote for *City Pages* under my own name, but I left some of the coverage to my other voice, Martian Colour in the "Martian's Chronicles" column, in which I would discuss Butler's role and artistry. When I first called the number to talk with him, whoever answered couldn't find him. The guy at the other end of the phone kept asking, "What drawer is he in? What drawer is he in?" Finally, I had to ask

Members of "Minnesota's first family of the arts" (left to right): Fred, J. D., and Jevetta Steele. Missing from the photo are sister Jearlyn and brother Billy. The award-winning musical *The Gospel at Colonus* helped to broaden the name recognition and careers of the Steele family worldwide.

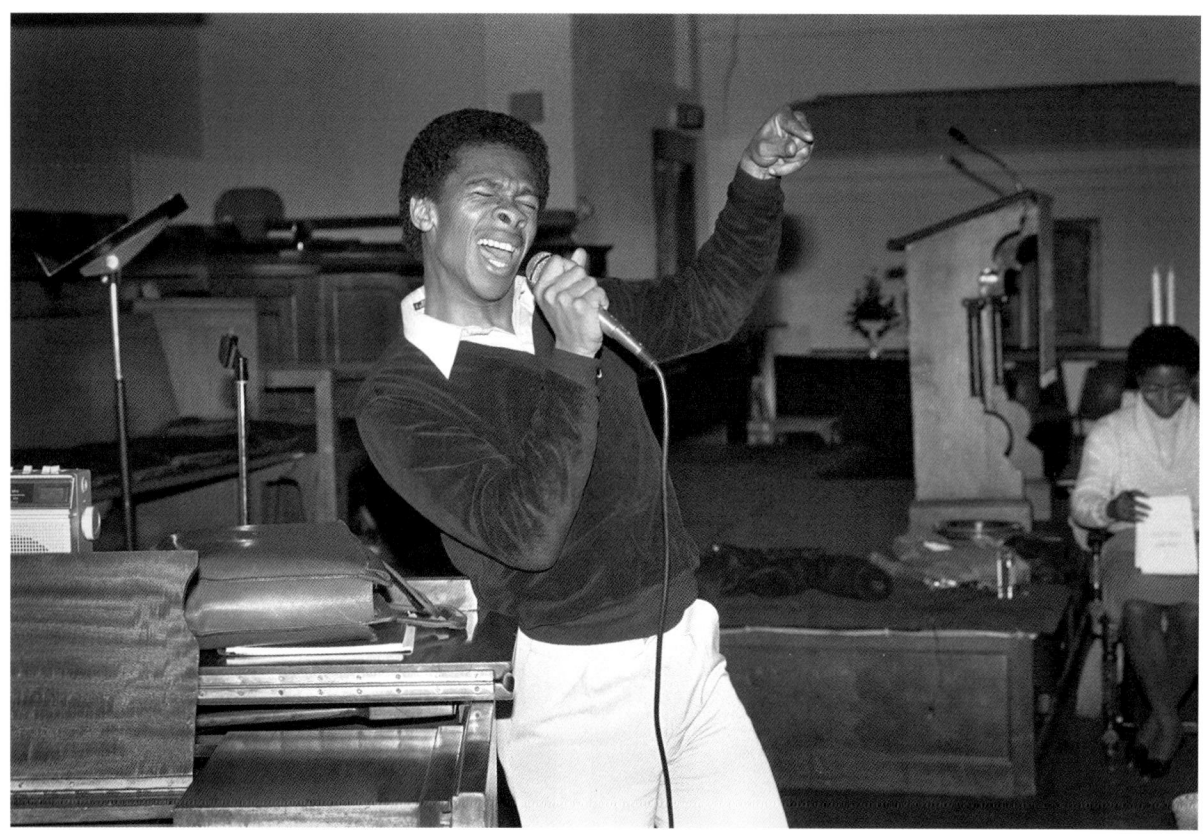

J. D. Steele has been one of the more prolific of the Steele siblings, producing numerous albums and theater productions and leading several youth choirs, from Minnesota to Africa.

what number I had reached. He replied, "the city morgue." When I did finally connect with Butler, he turned out to be a top-drawer guy, though not the kind you put in the cooler.

While *Colonus* raised Butler's musical profile significantly, it really propelled the fortunes and visibility of the Steele family members. Both Breuer and Telson were fond of the singers as a group and individually, and the five siblings all went on to develop their own successful careers.

J. D. Steele was back in a production of *The Gospel at Colonus* as recently as the fall of 2018, at New York City's Public Theater. His other stage work includes ten commissioned theatrical musicals, collaborations with entities such as Zorongo Flamenco Dance Company and Mixed Blood Theatre, and artistic alliances from Portland to New York City. His passion for music likewise extends to creating and leading youth choirs. He has served as founder and director of youth choirs in Minneapolis, including the MacPhail Community Youth Choir and the Shangilia Youth Choir, which was assembled from one of Africa's toughest slums in Nairobi, Kenya, and has since toured in the United States. Musically unstoppable is one phrase that comes to mind when talking about the guy I like to call the "Man of Steele."

For the Steeles' one album for a national label, 1993's *Heaven Help Us All*, J. D. produced and wrote twelve of the disc's fourteen songs. He repeated such tasks for subsequent Steele albums, in addition to writing, producing, and recording albums with George Clinton, Prince, Mavis Staples, the Blenders, Kim Carnes, and others. He's a heavyweight!

Breuer liked to call J. D.'s brother, Fred Steele, "the black Gable," for his resemblance to Hollywood actor Clark Gable. Later, in the mid-nineties, when Jeff Arundel's highly successful Twin Cities–based Lifescapes label went looking for a singer for their line of gospel and spiritual albums, they tapped Fred (whom Jeff said reminded him of Cary Grant, "a Cary Grant who can sing!"). He and his sister Jevetta were also both cast in the traveling stage production of *Bagdad Café*, an adaptation of the award-winning 1987 movie of the same name. Telson wrote the music for the film, which included the song "Calling You," a sparse but haunting track featuring chilling vocals by Jevetta. I still believe there hasn't been a better vocal performance by any Minnesota artist since that soulful, solitary plea. When asked about it in 2018, Jevetta recalled that she recorded it at a deeply troubling time in her life, and she seemed glad it was in the rearview mirror.

Jevetta has had her own success in the theater, as well. In addition to acting and singing in musicals like *Ma Rainey's Black Bottom*, she wrote *Two Queens, One Castle* in collaboration with J. D. The much-lauded play has been performed at Mixed Blood Theatre in Minneapolis, as well as at prominent theaters in Arizona and Washington, DC. She also has had an active schedule of album releases and live concerts around the country, performing with various orchestras and symphonies. At the time of his death, Prince was planning to record her wonderful voice for a new album project.

Sister Jearlyn (unfortunately not pictured in the photo taken by Greg in a north Minneapolis church) might be the best known among her equally talented siblings, thanks to her consistent roles over the years on radio. She was a frequent performer on *A Prairie Home Companion*, whether singing with host Garrison Keillor, nailing it solo, or teaming with sister Jevetta and other guests. Her *Steele Talkin'* program on WCCO-AM radio has been on the air since 1998. The weekly Sunday night talk show gives her a platform to discuss upcoming arts and entertainment events with artists and performers from across the spectrum.

The fifth and youngest sibling, Billy Steele (also not pictured), is a well-known piano accompanist and singer who works, writes, and produces regularly with the Grammy Award–winning Sounds of Blackness. His credits also include stints with Rod Stewart, Luther Vandross, Quincy Jones, and others.

If the Steeles aren't in your heart, they are bound to be someplace in your eyes and ears, lifting up the spirit.

THE PETERSON FAMILY

Def Jam Fam

Muscle Shoals had the soulful Swampers, LA the beastly Wrecking Crew. And where would the Motor City Motown Sound be without the ferocious Funk Brothers, or Stax Records' Memphis grooves without Booker T. and the M.G.'s? These studio session legends collectively shaped more great albums and top-ten singles than you could imagine in America's storied pop life. The Twin Cities version of those immortal, hit-making session players is called, simply, the Petersons.

Although the Petersons are more likely to be tapped to play individually rather than as a group, like the aforementioned amalgamations, this renowned family of musicians and singers would be at home in any one of those legendary backing ensembles. And they have the résumé to prove it.

Among the brothers Peterson, they share individual alliances with Bob Dylan, Prince, Fleetwood Mac, George Benson, Bonnie Raitt, the Family, Donny Osmond, Steve Miller Band, Oleta Adams, Leo Kottke, the Time, David Sanborn, Annie Lennox—your baker's dozen of outstanding musicians from varied genres. And that's just the short list! Tally up all the talent Billy, Ricky, and Paul have played with, either in the studio or live, and the count goes much higher. And let's not forget their own solo work as featured artists and producers. Throw in sisters Patty and Linda, who have solid solo careers in pop and jazz, and their unforgettable late mother, Jeanne Arland Peterson, and you have a def jam fam of the first magnitude. If you spent any time over the past four decades making or enjoying music, you've probably seen, heard, or shared a stage or recording studio with one of them.

The Petersons also have been generous with benefits and community-oriented appearances. In spring of 2011, a twister blew through the north side of Minneapolis, causing considerable damage and killing one person. Larry Long, the fearless folkie and community organizer (bassist Billy Peterson has played on his albums), helped stage a benefit concert for

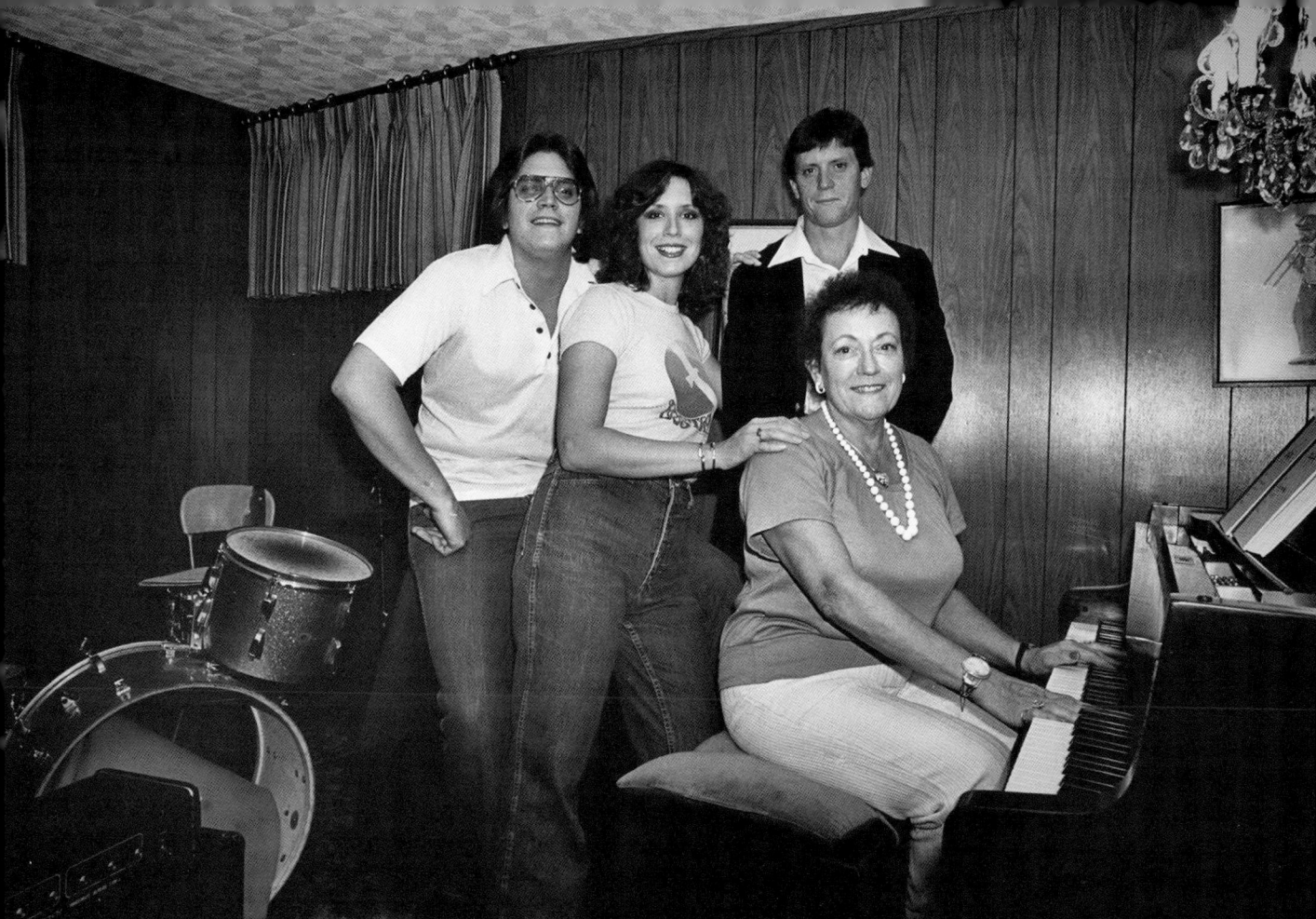

northsiders. The lineup was as eclectic as the diverse artists the Petersons have on speed dial.

Brother Ali flew in early from a hip-hop show down south to play the event. Soul Asylum, Prudence Johnson, GB Leighton, the New Standards, Sounds of Blackness, Billy McLaughlin Group, DJ Freddy Fresh, and many more joined the benefit pro bono. And yes, quite a few Petersons were on the bill that night at the State Theatre (which generously donated the space).

Family members and local musicians, such as bandleader and drummer Bobby Vandell, were out in force as part of the ad-hoc TC Jammers. That night the Jammers featured a sizable Peterson crew, including Patty, Paul, a next-generation Peterson, Jason, and the grande dame of the evening, Jeanne.

Guess who stole the show?

At eighty-nine years of age, Mama Peterson sat down at the piano and smoked it with a vibrant jazz arrangement of "Summertime," playing with the vitality and chops of someone half her age.

The musical strengths of the Peterson family were seemingly bred in the bone. Seen here are siblings Ricky, Patty, and Billy with their mother, Jeanne Arland Peterson; missing are Linda, the oldest, and Paul, the youngest.

Besides their good works in the community, the Petersons have also been seen making merry at their semi-regular Christmas show, "'Twas the Jam Before Christmas." Digging them together for the holidays is as warm a memory as concertgoers will ever get, as the multitalented family band makes everyone in the house feel like a Peterson, if only for that one night.

Together, the Petersons are something special; individually, no one Peterson can be said to out-Peterson the rest. Billy's bass playing is renowned worldwide and has accompanied disparate musicians in the jazz, rock, country, and pop genres. His session work for Dylan's 1975 classic, *Blood on the Tracks*—one of rock's most trenchant and tender breakup albums—at Minneapolis's Sound 80 bestows a particular immortality to a résumé that features artists from Les Paul to Prince to Steve Miller and Pete Seeger.

Brother Ricky, friend of the funk, fusion, and R&B realms, is a chillin' keyboard player. But that's like calling Mozart a good piano player. Ricky also arranges, produces, and writes music, and his magic on a Hammond B-3 elevates the notes to the funky high heavens and takes them to the groovy down-low place. Of the many musicians I've seen working or hanging out over time at Creation Audio on Nicollet Avenue in south Minneapolis, Ricky remains the most ubiquitous, despite a demanding tour schedule with any number of A-list artists from any camp. He's also one of the friendliest guys you will ever meet: his smile will get you right before his musical powers sink their soulful imprint on your senses.

If you haven't seen singer Patty Peterson perform or listened to her three solo albums, you've probably heard her on a slate of TV and radio jingles, or caught her on her KBEM-FM show, *The Playroom*. You might even have read her "Listen" column in the local *Edina Magazine* or heard her speaking on health, wellness, and mind-body-spirit topics. She's something of a renaissance woman who's also a first-class crooner, capable of paying homage to top female artists from Barbra Streisand to a host of jazz divas.

Winner of multiple Minnesota Music Awards for Best Vocalist, Patty has a well-earned reputation for nailing works from the American Songbook, and for capturing the soul and funk intensity of a Chaka Khan cut. This quick quip from *DownBeat* sums her up in a different light, one that shines just as true as all the other laudatory things written about her through the years: "I like her forthright sexiness and spunk." She also produced "Minnesota Jazz Legends: The Elders" for KBEM, featuring interviews with the many jazz players in town—mostly sidemen lost to the headliners of their day—who shared remarkable stories and personal histories.

As for the eldest Peterson, Linda is probably least well known in her old hometown. Nonetheless, she's enjoyed her own successful career in

California, crooning jazz standards and other material well suited to her style and the same musical sensibilities that seem to be genetically shared among the brood. Linda has recorded five albums and played jazz festivals abroad and around Los Angeles. She's a singer, songwriter, and pianist, and there's no mistaking her lineage; it's bred in the bone.

It's hard to think of the youngest Peterson as "the baby," cuz, baby, he's a star! "St. Paul" (as Prince dubbed him) is on the same high-caliber playing field as his older siblings, although he was thrust into a brighter spotlight, largely through his affiliation with the Prince camp. He appeared in *Purple Rain*, played in the Time, and was front and center with the Family, which recorded the Prince-penned "Nothing Compares 2 U" in 1985 (a few years before Sinéad O'Connor's version hit the charts). A revamped Family, called fDeluxe, formed in 2011 with Peterson and original Family members Susannah Melvoin, Eric Leeds, and Jellybean Johnson.

Along the way, St. Paul has also served as music director for Donny Osmond and played bass with Peter Frampton, who described him as "one of the finest bass players ever," according to the *Star Tribune*. He's worked with Kenny Loggins, the vastly overlooked singer Oleta Adams, Paula Abdul, and others across a range of genres. He also took over his father's special events–booking business, known formerly as Willie Peterson Productions, and rebranded it as Peterson Music and Events.

It's true that St. Paul left the Family against Prince's wishes (just as brother Ricky had turned down His Royal Badness for an early keyboard seat in the Revolution). But the purple spotlight lingers: his group, St. Paul and the Minneapolis Funk All Stars, was the house band for the September 2018 ceremony at which Prince was presented with a posthumous honorary doctorate degree from the University of Minnesota. It was an emotional and celebratory event, and one of the highlights was, naturally, St. Paul delivering the goods again on "Nothing Compares 2 U."

The Petersons can be credited as being the consulting architects behind the "Minneapolis Sound," and they are often called Minnesota's First Family of Music. There's no threat to them losing the title any time soon, even in the land of ten thousand Petersons and musicians.

WEST BANK FOLK SCENE

Meet the Folkers

Willie Murphy jokingly called them "The Folk Mafia." It had something to do with throwing their purist weight around, or perhaps the weight of their instruments—dangerous fiddles, gouging guitars, murderous mandolins, lethal Dobros, harmonicas that could make your ears bleed, and Jew's harps like trip wires. In fact, it was more about the acoustic world that a handful of mostly West Bank musicians made for the rest of us.

To the more electric-oriented music makers like Murphy, the folkie scene might have seemed impenetrable. Truth is, it was a friendly, loosely based "club" whose members carried no cards, cash, or vendettas—at least none that you could print. They formed a rich foundation on which the storied Twin Cities music scene rested, the depository in which all the historical songs resided, and the stone from which inspired original work was carved.

For a time, the unofficial clubhouse was a shabby upstairs listening room called the Coffeehouse Extemporé on Cedar Avenue (where Midwest Mountaineering is today), next to the one-time "geomagnetic center of the universe," as was written on the wall of the Riverside Café. It was a good room. Not much to look at—chairs ranged from folding units to donated rockers or recliners with the stuffing leaking out—it nevertheless provided ample comfort, song, and spoken-word tales.

The Extemp's music ranged from diehard folk fare to sophisticated ragtime piano from Butch Thompson to Peter Ostroushko's slüz düz music imported from Ukraine and seasoned with American bluegrass and swing. Iowa's great poetic singer-songwriter Greg Brown made his Twin Cities debut there. And a renowned special guest, a Maine storyteller named Marshall Dodge, told side-splitting "Bert and I" stories in an impossible accent that only made the witty, homespun New England tall tales even more exotic. I would have paid double or triple to see him again (even though music writers usually were allowed in *gratis*), before somebody rear-ended his bicycle in Hawaii and killed him.

The roster of hometown regulars also included the western swing of Sean Blackburn and Dakota Dave Hull, the latter described by folk giant Dave Van Ronk as "one of the best guitarists in the world." There was fiddlin' Mary Duchene; Bill Hinkley and Judy Larson, who knew world folk music and played multiple instruments with tremendous savvy and spirit; Pop Wagner, who mixed lariat tricks with his own tunes and folk and blues covers; and Scott Alarik, a superlative singer-songwriter and music writer whose brother, Steve, ran the place. Cal Hand showed many how a Dobro should be played, while Adam Granger, Papa John Kolstad, Charlie McGuire, and more were just a few among the rest of the Twin Cities best who played there—and at other, more upscale venues, once word got out on how good they were.

Enticed by the folk vibe of that Twin Cities culture zone in the heart of the granola-crunchy West Bank, the folkers attracted select outliers and occasional carpetbaggers. Two who rambled into the fold over the years—and became mainstays—included Paul Metsa and Larry Long, the former from the northern Minnesota mining town of Virginia, the latter by way of St. Cloud. Metsa was fond of saying that "musicians are like first responders. After the fire trucks, ambulance, and/or cop cars leave, the musicians come in to raise funds and spirits." He and Long had firsthand experience, and both became practiced at the imperfect art of holding benefit performances.

An avowed Finn and raconteur of the first order from "up north," Metsa held gigs for earthquake victims in Japan, residents of Flint with shitty water, Parkland students in Florida, dogs in need of homes—you name it. He even threw a benefit for himself after his equipment was stolen out of his garage. He played at a 1996 tribute to Woody Guthrie, presented by the Rock and Roll Hall of Fame, along with a host of marquee names, including Bruce Springsteen. Metsa had to teach the Boss the chords to Guthrie's "I Ain't Got No Home" backstage before the performance.

Perhaps Metsa's most noble endeavor, and failure, was his attempt to save the original Guthrie Theater from the wrecking ball; the Ralph Rapson–designed space had made for a wonderful rock 'n' roll stage for decades, when it wasn't being used by the Guthrie company of actors. The legendary thrust stage saw Twin Cities debuts by rock artists like the Who, Led Zeppelin, Bruce Springsteen and E Street Band, the Band, Elton John, Patti Smith Group, and Frank Zappa and the Mothers of Invention, as well as numerous jazz, folk, and world music legends like Ravi Shankar, Miles Davis, John Coltrane, Doc Watson, Steve Goodman—the list is long and impressive. Metsa tells the story of trying to rescue the venerable building and other tales in his must-read book, *Blue Guitar Highway*.

In addition to building communities through song, Larry Long worked hard to clean up the Mississippi River and the reputation of Woody Guthrie in Guthrie's hometown of Okemah, Oklahoma.

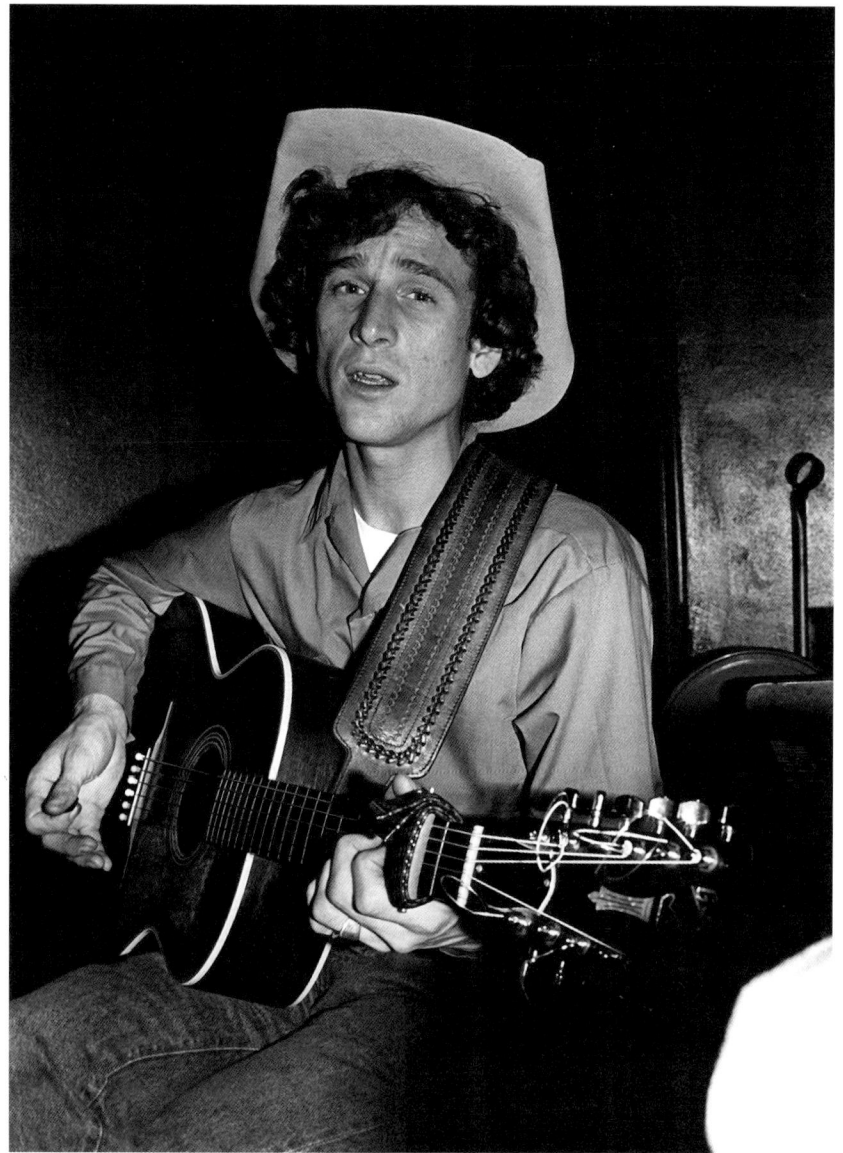

Aside from his civic orientation, Metsa's songwriting and engaging prose have been lauded across the country. The *Huffington Post* called him "Minnesota's other great Iron Range songwriter." Working within folk music's long protest tradition, whether solo or with his old loose blues-rock-and-swing band, Cats Under the Stars, Metsa writes songs that take on the social injustices and grave inequalities of American life. In response to the neo-Nazi violence in Charlottesville, Virginia, in 2017, he penned and later recorded "Ain't Gonna Whistle Dixie Anymore," a stinging protest anthem aimed at the hate and violence of our divisive times. The Sounds of Blackness joined in on the chorus, while the

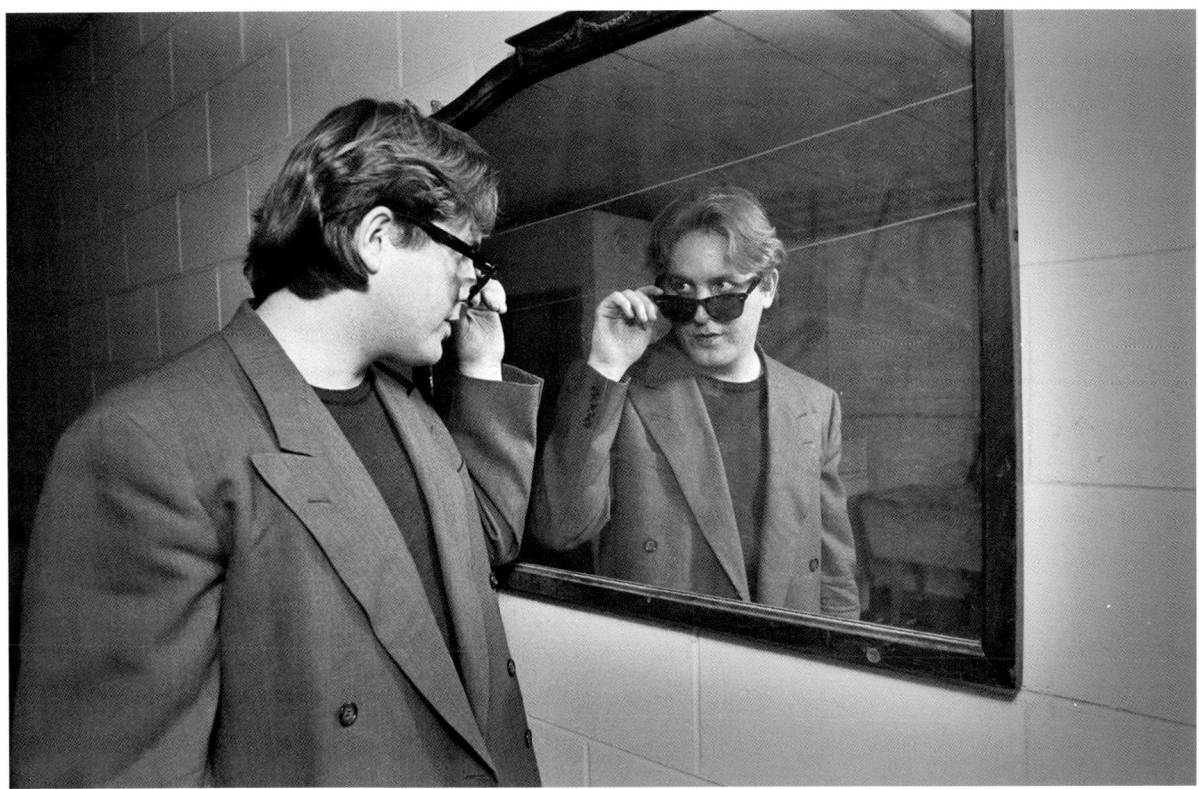

internationally known and award-winning Twin Cities blues singer Willie Walker delivered the caustic verses.

The work of both Metsa and Long was shaped heavily by the grassroots sensibilities of Woody Guthrie and Pete Seeger. But Long's connection to both folk giants has practically consumed his entire career and is evident in his prolific songwriting. His socio-political outreach has ranged from First Nations communities to environmental organizations. The Smithsonian Folkways Recordings artist is a chip off the old block of the American folk tradition: poet, singer-songwriter, community builder, rabble-rouser, storyteller, and conservationist. (He was one of the earliest to help organize the cleanup of the Mississippi River with his Mississippi River Revival, traveling lengths of the river in troubadour style with fellow music makers and river keepers.)

Where Metsa tried to rescue the theater named after Sir Tyrone Guthrie, Long resurrected the reputation of Woody Guthrie in his hometown of Okemah, Oklahoma, which had largely disowned the legendary native son because of his far-left political views and alleged "un-American" attitudes. By presenting annual tributes to Guthrie, featuring both special guests and local schoolkids, Long re-established Woody's good name, spreading goodwill in the process throughout Okemah.

The "other" great folksinger from Minnesota's Iron Range, Paul Metsa tried to save the original Guthrie Theater, taught Bruce Springsteen a Woody Guthrie song, and has been a fixture on the Minnesota folk and rock scene since the eighties.

He also has given musical voice to struggling Midwest farmers, embattled workers, striking women on the Iron Range, and forgotten veterans. He has been widely recognized for his work in schools, writing songs with kids about local community figures, from the immigrant school janitor to other unsung heroes and special elders who live among us. He's traveled extensively, going to Russia as part of the Soviet-American peace cruise, touring with Kris Kristofferson through Moscow in the days of perestroika. And he sang for Rosa Parks at the forty-fifth anniversary of the Montgomery Bus Boycott. Let's face it, the guy is a folk mensch.

Long was the only Minnesota artist—besides the one from Hibbing, who didn't show—invited to sing at Seeger's ninetieth birthday celebration at Madison Square Garden in 2009, featuring Springsteen, Joan Baez, Dave Matthews, Roger McGuinn, Ani DiFranco, John Mellencamp, and many others. Seeger and Long had been friends for many years. Once, when interviewing Seeger about his old pal, I mentioned that Larry is often referred to as the Pete Seeger of Minnesota, to which Pete replied, "I would be honored to be called the Larry Long of New York."

With decades of singing and organizing behind him, Long has turned more of his attention in his later life to producing the semi-regular American Roots Revue concerts in the Twin Cities and around the region. The show features a core group, consisting of gospel powerhouse Robert Robinson, soul singers Tonia Hughes and J. D. Steele, and a backing band that usually includes musician-producer Cory Wong and his band. Rotating special guests are also featured during each revue, ranging from bluesman Guy Davis, Soul Asylum's Dave Pirner, the Honeydogs' Adam Levy, singer-songwriter Haley, chanteuse Prudence Johnson (a fellow St. Cloud native), and Long himself.

Sadly, the old folk guard in Minnesota is passing into history and memory, as my wife, Susan Hamre (the first female editor of a national music publication called *Request*, published by Sam Goody and Musicland from the early nineties to 2003 and a competitor of *Rolling Stone* and *Spin*), reminded me when Bill Hinkley died. And with them goes not just a baseline of exemplary Appalachian tunes, British Isles hornpipe music, and old southern country blues, but a significant cultural and intellectual capital that might become even more scarce in the twenty-first century. When Hinkley made his final passage in 2010, perhaps he set the scene for the good death. Bill, along with his busking wife, Judy, held a special place in my own life. They were always great copy—and good company. During a *Reader* interview for an upcoming Bill and Judy concert in the late eighties, the three of us consumed more sushi in one sitting than seemed humanly possible. Bill could really put it away.

Fast forward a decade, they and two other musicians played at the Hamre-Keller wedding (and reception) in a little country church in south-

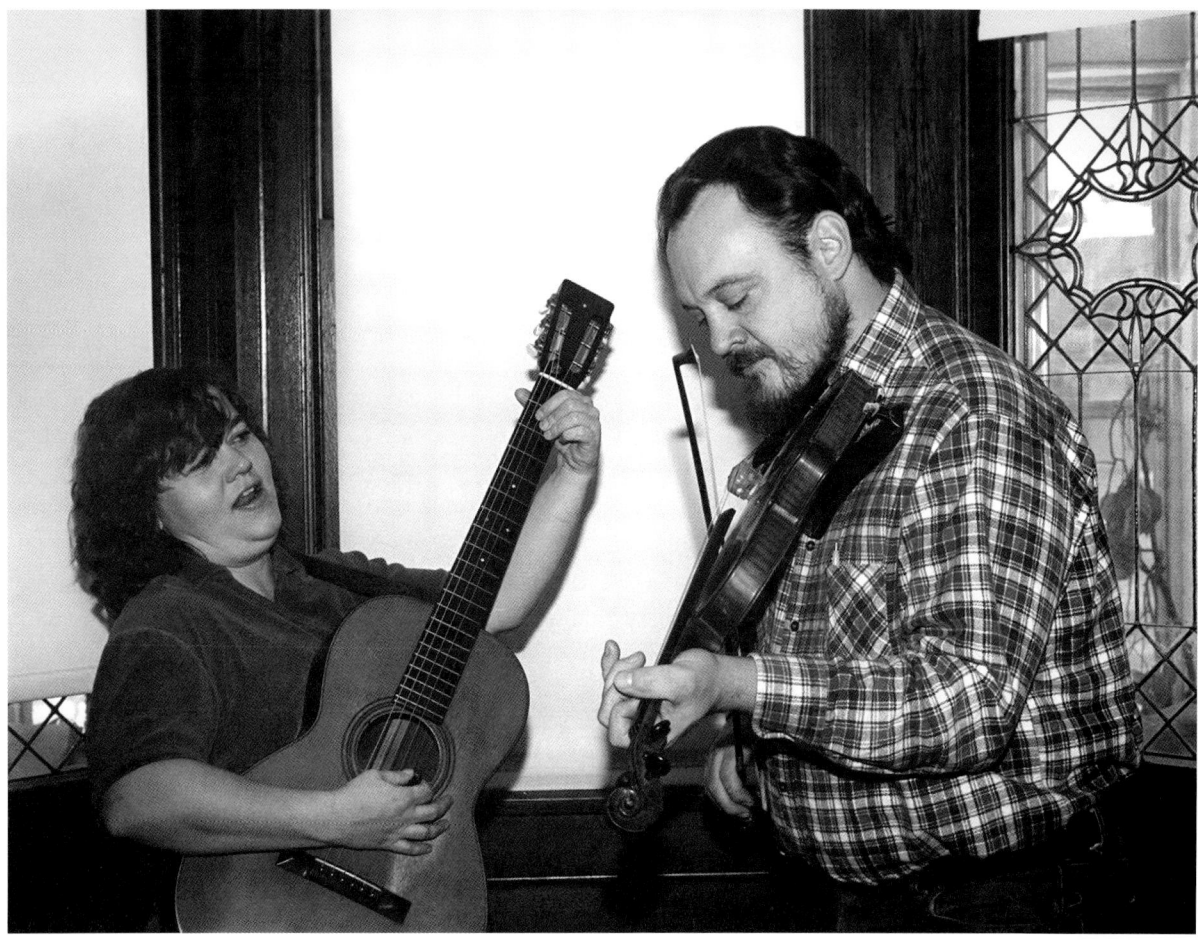

west Minnesota where my wife's family was from. They probably also played the longest processional ever—the instrumental Irish tunes "The Women of Ireland/The Morning Dew" (more widely known as the Love Theme from Stanley Kubrick's film *Barry Lyndon*)—as we stalled and stalled again, waiting for late-arriving friends from the Cities who were delayed by a daunting thunderstorm out on the prairie.

Seventeen years later, folk music marked another rite. Bill's hospice room at the VA was regularly filled with players to serenade him while he slept and to gently rile him when he was awake. Five days before he died, the musician and teacher who Metsa christened the "patriarch of the folk music world in the Twin Cities" was feted with a movable feast in the VA hospitality room. Folkers, jazz and blues players, and bluegrass musicians held an impromptu concert of old and familiar songs and instrumentals. Never one to miss a note, Bill managed to join in on his mandolin from his wheelchair for the slow, wistful Irish waltz "Midnight on the Water." There would be no encore.

The husband-and-wife team of Bill Hinkley and Judy Larson were funny, smart, and well read in folk traditions. (They could also play a mean wedding reception!)

KOERNER, RAY, AND GLOVER

Spider, Snake, and Little Sun

Over the years, at least two rock writers—and probably a bunch of fans—have noticed that, in the documentary film about the legendary folk-blues trio of Koerner, Ray, and Glover (KR&G), at one point in the movie, each musician is keeping time by tapping a foot—but none were in sync with the others. It's about as good a visual metaphor as you could hope to get for the pronounced individuality and loose group dynamics of "Spider" John Koerner, Tony "Little Sun" Glover, and Dave "Snaker" Ray.

There's no need to dwell on the group's well-known history and the resounding impact it had on generations of singers and musicians. Suffice to say, their Elektra albums could be found in the collections of John Lennon, Keith Richards, Jim Morrison, Bonnie Raitt, Eric Clapton, and later, Beck, Lucinda Williams, Charlie Parr, and others. Along with the Chicago-based Paul Butterfield Blues Band, an electric group with acoustic roots similar to those of KR&G, Spider, Little Sun, and Snaker were the north-star fountainhead of the so-called blues and folk revival of the sixties.

How deep did their influence go? Well, there's probably no Parr, for one, without them. Even the blue-eyed boy from the north country, who occasionally shared the coffeehouse stage with Koerner at the Scholar in Dinkytown, might not have become half the picker or half-assed harp player he was if he'd never shared their musical chops or lifetime friendship, especially with John and Tony. Although they are often viewed as contractual-obligation albums, Bob Dylan's two solo albums of folk and blues songs, *Good as I Been to You* and *World Gone Wrong* from 1992 and 1993, respectively, can be seen as tribute albums to John Koerner's work, style, and influence. Both embraced America's bedrock musical genres with a preservationist's spirit, putting their own mark on material to revitalize, personalize, improvise, and honor the traditions and artists before them. Plus, they're just great tunes.

As a trio onstage, Koerner, Ray, and Glover had distinct personalities and divergent personal interests, which provided as much entertainment value as their traditional repertoire and original songs. Each owned a well-defined sense of humor all his own, with Tony often taking on the role of the straight man, however sardonic.

"This is how it was: I was Sonny Terry, Dave was Lead Belly, and John was Woody Guthrie," Glover told me for a *Sweet Potato* cover story about them on the eve of a twenty-year commemorative performance at Walker Art Center in the spring of 1981. Those historical coordinates provide ample understanding of their musical strengths on stage and record.

Following them through the years and even working with them (I assigned Glover numerous stories and album reviews at the *Spud* and *City Pages* and helped Ray with publicity for his solo work in the last part of his life), I encountered more than a few of their personal antics.

Koerner singing the old nineteenth-century folk tune "The Dodger" over his twelve-string or his own "Everybody's Going for the Money" while stomping his foot is one of life's simple joys. Another is his pithy and humorous storytelling style. Spider also has a strong interest in space and astronomy. The self-described "Star Geezer" (the name of his 1996 album, which collects some of his previously out-of-print songs) isn't likely to give Neil deGrasse Tyson a run. But he knows enough about Callisto, pulsars, and quasars to keep it "interesting."

Koerner has made a handful of solo albums in his time, and you'll play any one of them again if you hear any one of them once.

Although he retired when he hit his late seventies, he never really disappeared. You could usually find him at Palmer's Bar on the West Bank at an appointed hour. On New Year's Eve in 2017, he came out to play for the closing of Treehouse Records in south Minneapolis, the site of the old Oar Folkjokeopus store, a seminal scene-making hub. Owner Mark Trehus, who had reissued Koerner records on his own label from different periods, couldn't contain his enthusiasm about having Spider John in the house, even as he shuttered the scenester landmark.

Just before his eightieth birthday in 2018, Koerner "took a fall off a six-inch cliff" on an uneven floor at a friend's house. But it didn't stop him from celebrating his octogenarian year with a walker and some musician guest friends at his favorite whiskey well. Still, old age ain't no country for old folk-blues men.

Long before I met him or heard him play a note, I first encountered Tony Glover as a byline in western North Dakota, while reading *Eye Magazine* and sucking on a cherry coke at a shopping center cafeteria with my best friend, Jim, as he read *UFO Magazine* (and then we'd trade copies). Glover had written an engaging short story about an elderly couple and sex in the short-lived *Eye*, published by the Hearst Corporation between

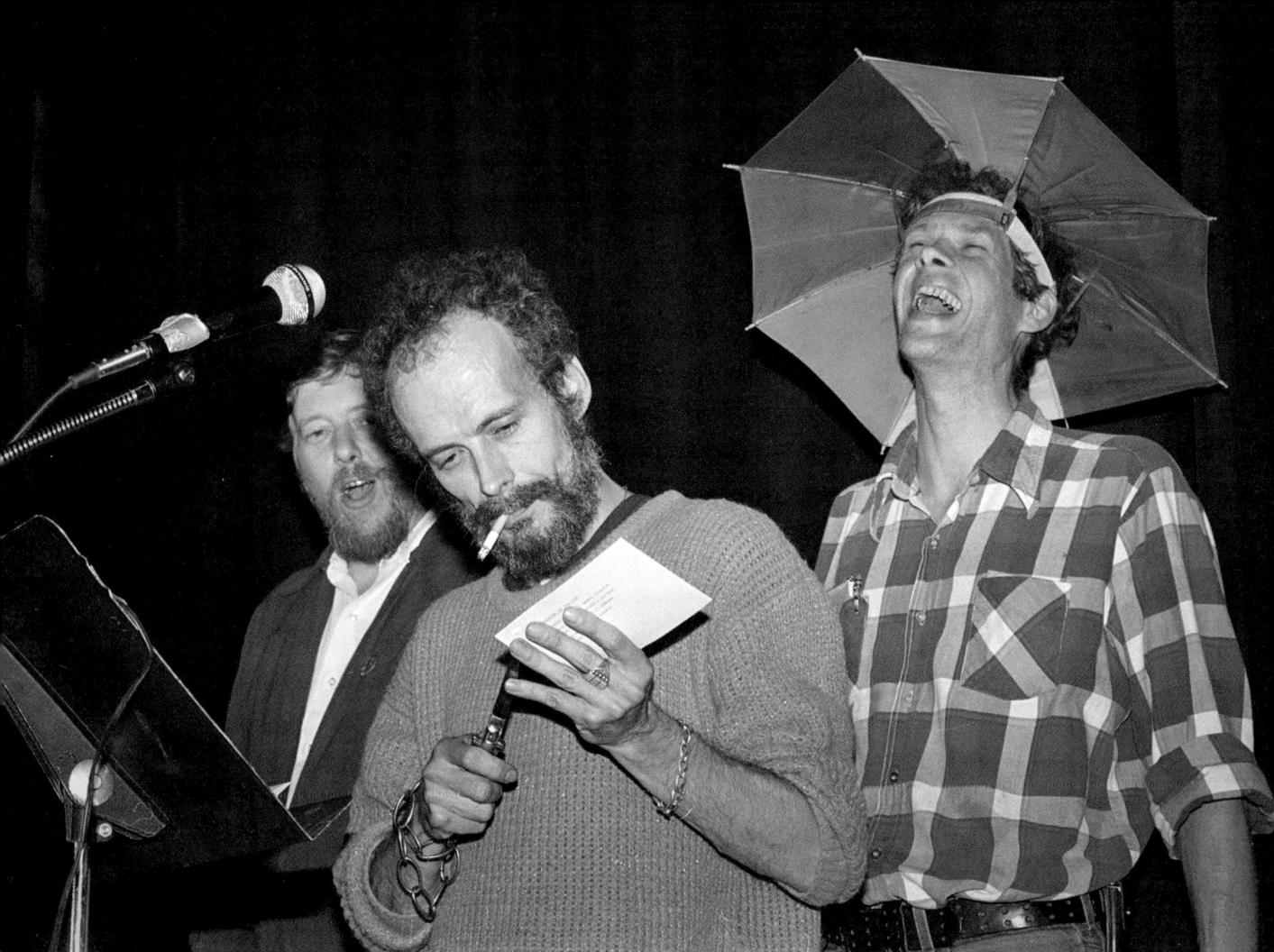

Tony Glover of Koerner, Ray, and Glover uses a switchblade to slice open the envelope containing the winner of the Musician of the Year award at the Minnesota Music Awards in March 1982, as John Koerner (right) and Dave Ray (left) look on with shock and amusement. (The award was given to Prince.)

1968 and 1969, a mainstream mag that tried to capture the good vibrations of the counterculture and some slick advertising dollars. Compared to the underground press like the *Berkeley Barb*—forget it, there was no comparison.

Tony went on to write more about sex later on, spending a year freelancing short-story porn for *Penthouse* magazine. We valued more his contributions at *Sweet Potato* and *City Pages*, whether he was profiling country singer Don Williams, writing a cover story about Willie and the Bees, waxing poetic about singer Doug Maynard's trichord vocal technique (producing three notes in one at the same time), or interviewing Beat novelist William Burroughs. He had widespread tastes, from early Replacements records to Prince, cinema, literature, the sitar (which he tried to learn to play), radio (he was a deejay on KDWB-FM after midnight), and more.

Based on his musical reputation, "the quiet one" in KR&G cultivated friendships with a host of artists, including Patti Smith and Lucinda

Williams, with whom he would often play harp when they appeared in the Twin Cities. According to Dylan, Tony was always the guy on the lookout during their early days together in Dinkytown and elsewhere. He would stand in front of clubs and watch what was happening up and down the street. Would it be accurate to call him a part-time folk bouncer, too? He did occasionally carry a stiletto.

In the late 1970s, bluegrass singer, banjo player, fiddler, songwriter, and Mississippi River tugboat captain John Hartford was on a music festival bill someplace that also featured Dave "Snaker" Ray's group Snake, one of his many post–KR&G band incarnations. Hartford was a fan, and after doing an interview with me and discovering I was from Minneapolis, he asked if I could make an intro.

I opened the door to Dave's bus, which had "Snaker" emblazed on the side in psychedelic colors, and peered in. Although it was midafternoon, it looked like 2:00 AM inside the Snake. "Hey, Dave, John Hartford is here and would like to meet you," I yelled. Not a creature was stirring, not even a roadie. I was pretty sure he was in there because I'd seen him and his girlfriend, MJ, and a few others head to the bus after their set. "Hey, you in here?"

Hartford grew uncomfortable, and just as he started to leave, Ray's boisterous voice boomed out in the dark, "John Hartford, get in here, man!" I left the two to their private conversation, but I know I would have gotten a much better opening for my Hartford story had I ventured to the black recesses of the bus, where their two muddy rivers would meet.

Over the years, Ray moved through a litany of bands and albums, including the Blackburn-Beach Blues Band and the Three Bedroom Ramblers. The succinct landing-page résumé on his website summed up a long career in a long, trademark sentence that referenced his "terrifyingly obscure bands and recordings."

Ray was from a large family, many of whom became musicians, including his brother, Max, who played sax with the Wallets, Suburbs, Angel Headed Hipsters, and others. His dad, though, had an insurance business, and the aging bluesman started working there later in life, perhaps realizing the sad truth of Koerner's comment at the twenty-year mark of the trio: "If somebody calls you legendary, it probably means you're broke." Naturally, Ray insured a bunch of musicians and became my guy, as well. My friend Buzz called him "the insurance man for the funk."

The nine-to-five didn't beat him down. When he started playing solo again, or with Tony in semi-regular gigs around town, his guitar chops were never better, his singing never more robust and expressive. There was another side of him that also fiercely improved with age: his ranting. There was no rant like a Dave Ray Rant (a few are posted on his website). While doing publicity for him, I'd get a good earful now and then by phone. The

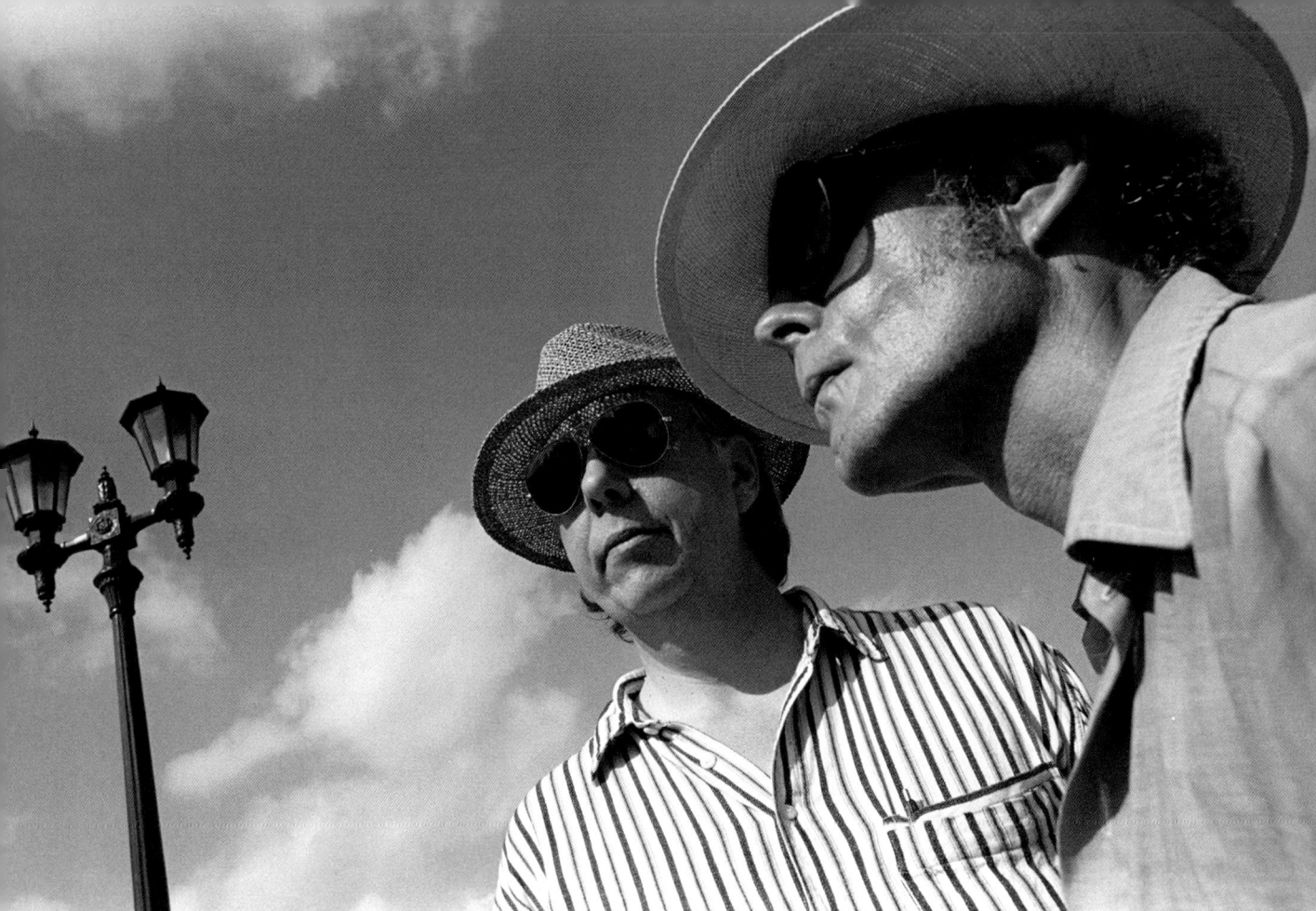

Shades-wearing Dave "Snaker" Ray and Tony "Little Sun" Glover

best ones he seemed to save for in-person meetings at his studio, tucked away in the trucking ghetto around Transfer Road off University Avenue, which was really more of a man cave—no, strike that, a Ray Cave—before man caves were a thing. It had an old barbershop chair that you could pump up and down; he sat on it like a funky throne.

Dave was fond of saying that his generation "took its retirement in its youth." It was certainly true for Snaker, who packed in more hard living than most of us ever could. But the clock ran out eventually. He died of lung cancer on Thanksgiving Day in 2002. The *Star Tribune* featured his obituary in a front-page story by Tim Campbell. I never got to say goodbye to Dave, since I stupidly delayed my farewell visit by a week.

In 2014, Glover curated a three-CD compilation entitled *Dave Ray: Legacy*, covering forty years of music and featuring epic liner notes by Tony. That same year, at the urging of his last label, Red House Records, the City of St. Paul named a small stretch of street off Franklin Avenue and Berry Street in Prospect Park, near his old office, Dave Ray Avenue. There's a good blues tune or jaunty rag about the spot waiting to be written.

WILLIE AND THE BEES

Honey from the Bee

On the best nights at the Triangle Bar—when oxygen and elbow room were scarce and a tall black man dressed in a Harlem Globetrotter's uniform played his big sax while walking atop the length of the bar where patrons drank and bopped in place—you could feel like there was no better place to be. As the rest of the band wailed, shoved into an impossible angle inside a tight corner, their funky originals, R&B covers, and rock 'n' roll blasts made you believe you had achieved something like a West Bank nirvana. Only the occasional soulful ballad would slow the spinning rotation of the Triangle so that it would not fly off into space.

No matter where Willie and the Bees played, there were no strangers, only a fan hive. The band's West Bank shows in the late seventies, while the hippie enclave was still entrenched there at Cedar-Riverside, could make you believe that flower power might yet pollinate the planet, and these Bees would provide the soundtrack. It didn't quite work out that way, but wasn't it pretty to think so?

The King Bee in the equation, Willie Murphy, phased the band out— or they phased themselves out—in 1984, a peak year for Minnesota's new-wave/punk scene and the rise of Prince. But Murphy's reputation never lost its sting. More importantly, he'll never lose his standing as a historical linchpin that bridged the racial divide in the Twin Cities, creating the kind of integrated, black-and-white group and sound in two cities that had invisible, but clearly segregated, boundaries, especially in live music venues.

As a teen, Murphy had played with the legendary Valdons, the only white guy in the African American R&B band. It was a sign of things to come.

I often wondered what a Murphy-Prince collaboration (or friendship) might have sounded and looked like. They both consciously put

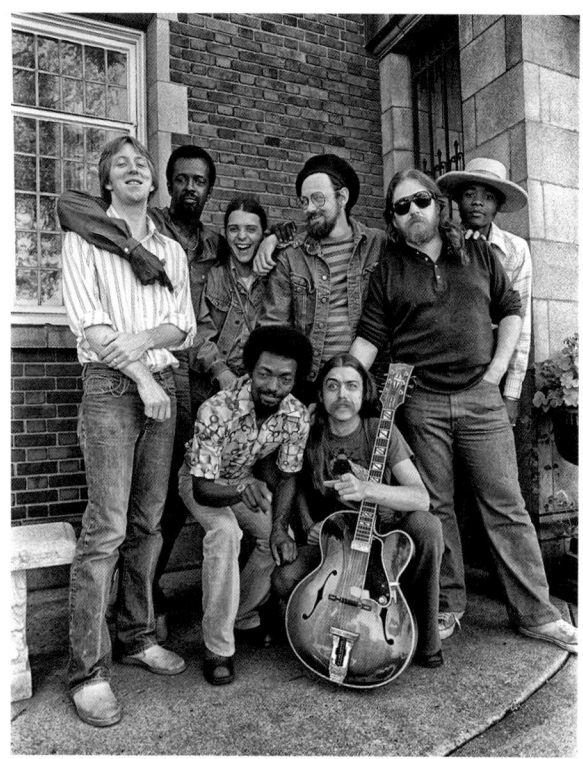

Willie and the Bees, nearing the height of their rock 'n' roll bumblebee flight in September 1979, pose in front of the old Walker Church in south Minneapolis. The church was the original site of the community radio station KFAI-FM, on the left of the dial, where Willie Murphy's show, *Jammin' with Willie*, was must-listen radio every Friday afternoon.

together racial- and gender-mixed bands, and both could play in multiple genres. As multi-instrumentalists go, Murphy was on par with Prince, and his proficiency on the soundboard as a producer was also equal to Prince's. It's fitting that he was inducted into the Minnesota Music Hall of Fame the same year as both Prince Rogers Nelson and Bob Dylan, in 1990.

Elektra Records offered Murphy producing jobs in LA and New York, but he turned them down—not wanting to appear to be selling out to "the Man." Perhaps those label executives got the same buzz anyone did listening to early albums Murphy produced, such as Bonnie Raitt's eponymous 1971 debut, which featured the Bees and special guests from Chicago A.C. Reed and Junior Wells backing her, and a stand-alone collaboration in 1969 with Spider John Koerner called *Running, Jumping, Standing Still*. *Crawdaddy*, another one of the better rock rags from the sixties, called the five-star album "perhaps the only psychedelic ragtime blues album ever made." It came out at the end of an era in which such creative innovation was the norm rather than the exception. Willie Murphy, who started playing piano at three or four, left his imaginative signature on it.

Looking back, one wonders how large or how small those Elektra offers are written on Murphy's list of regrets. We'll never know the records or artists he might have shaped, or how his own solo work might have evolved. Or if his proclivities for booze and drugs would have increased and preempted the Elektra assignment. But it doesn't take much brain sap to know that the Minnesota music scene would have been absent one of its most formidable artists ever to sit at a piano, to record at a soundboard, or to lead a band. This place simply would have been unimaginable without him.

Offstage, Murphy could be friendly, charming, and irascible, sometimes all at once. Spend any time with him and you'd discover he was a devoted cinephile (sometimes seeing nearly the entire run of local film festivals) and well read, heavy on the modern Irish novelists. After delivering part of Lawrence Ferlinghetti's poem "I Am Waiting" as part of my best man duties at writer Tom Surowicz's wedding, I was approached by Willie, who told me how much he loved the Beat poets, adding, "I just heard that same poem read at a funeral." He was a glass is half full *and* glass is half empty dude.

When the Bees disbanded, Murphy went to work on a solo gig, producing the album *Willie Murphy Hits Piano/Piano Hits Willie Murphy* as his calling card. He put out the keeper album on his own label, Atomic Theory Records. He took a tip from the DIY principle that defined much of the eighties, as bands and recording artists realized they might not need big labels anymore, despite the daunting challenges that distribution, marketing, and promotion presented.

Atomic Theory went on to release albums by other artists, among them folkie Larry Long, acclaimed country singer Becky Thompson, reggae band Ipso Facto, the punky Irish folk band Boiled in Lead, Phil Heywood's remarkable acoustic delight, *Some Summer Day*, and a blues record by legendary bluesmen Hubert Sumlin and Jimmy Rogers, with harp player Bill Hickey. There's even a quirky world music entry from the New International Trio, which blended Cambodian folk music with bagpipes, harpsichord, and other instruments! Murphy's tastes were universal to the core.

In 2009, the clean and sober artist issued a personalized paean to peace and better times with the double CD *A Shot of Love in a Time of Need / Autobiographical Notes*. This one was released by the St. Paul indie label founded by Bob Feldman, Red House Records, and it finally pushed the now-former West Banker into the Top 15 on *Billboard*'s blues chart. Murphy's most recent group, the Angel Headed Hipsters, took its name from the first lines in Allen Ginsberg's epic poem, "Howl," and their funky direction from the long-running, long-jumping, still-standing lead musician. Murph and the Angel Heads delivered another stunning, eclectic disc late in 2018, *Dirtball*, in which he decried the environmental state of the planet and the divisions among people; the aging hipster had not lost sight of the hippie manifestos from his youth.

After several threats, the Bees finally reunited in 2014, for the fortieth anniversary of the Cabooze. Surviving members, longtime fans, and younger, curious music buffs all grooved to soul-stirring covers and original band classics like "Honey from the Bee"; Murphy's put-down of excessive consumer culture, "Supermarket"; and the caustic slow burner, "You're No Good, You're Funky (You're Mean and Nasty Too)."

The horn section, including Maurice Jacox—the tall black man in the Globetrotter's uniform playing the big horn from the old days—still had their stuff, and the rhythm section kept the buzz blazing for two sets. It was a fitting victory lap for two West Bank institutions. One is still intact. The other was embodied in the man who sat down for solo gigs at places like the Richfield American Legion and proceeded to demonstrate why Willie Murphy was still the undisputed champ of rock 'n' roll here.

But in mid-January of 2019, at age seventy-five, the King Bee succumbed to the many medical problems that plagued him in the last year of his life. Fortunately, in November 2018, he was well enough to greet fans, old friends and lovers, and those who had helped him crowdfund

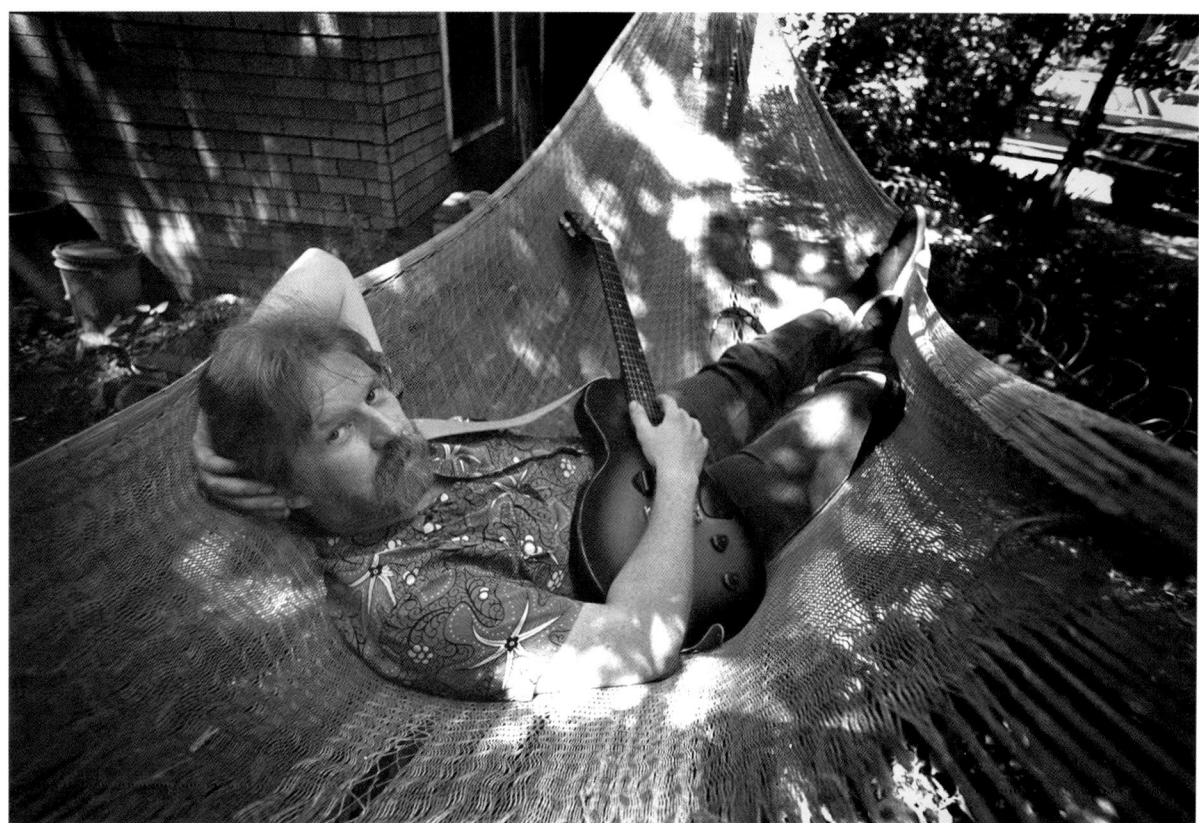

Minnesota's versatile multi-instrumentalist, songwriter, producer, and band leader Willie Murphy relaxes in a hammock at his West Bank home.

Dirtball at the Eagles Club in south Minneapolis, which has become a second home to the West Bank scene. He couldn't sing because of his health complications but still managed to fill the dance floor as the sound of his new album filled the hall. Others lined up to greet him some ten to twenty deep. "It was like kids waiting to see Santa," quipped Max Ray, one of the Angel Headed Hipsters and a longtime friend and caregiver who was with him when he passed on. Another old friend, Tony Glover (of Koerner, Ray, and Glover), lamented his final exit off the bandstand. "Willie knew where the music was—he played with the authority to get right into the core of it. There was fun in his funkiness, and his lyrical visions were as high as his blues were low down. There's a hole where he used to be," the fellow bluesman said. "The Man will be missed."

Funky angel-headed hipster ghost, come back, if only to sow your vision of harmony among the weary dancers, one more time . . .

BONNIE AND STEVE RAITT

Heart-and-Soul Siblings

The striking redhead in the room eyeballed the plush TV images of some luxury estate while Robin Leach practically wet himself over the property's exorbitant value. Sitting in her brother Steve's apartment in Uptown Minneapolis with his wife, singer Melanie Rosales, as we all watched and mocked *Lifestyles of the Rich and Famous*, Bonnie Raitt's brow furled in disbelief.

The multiple Grammy Award winner, blues-rock singer, tasty slide guitarist, activist, and songwriter and her oldest brother—an innovative soundman, inspired road manager, and seasoned soulful singer in his own right—both plunged deep into the lifestyles of Minnesota's rich music scene and its famous lakes for many years. A favorite Minnesota attraction for both Raitts was water-skiing in the land of sky-blue waters, out on White Bear Lake.

Bonnie became something of a patron to Twin Cities R&B acts like Willie and the Bees, the Doug Maynard Band, the Lamont Cranston Band, and later, the TC Jammers, which Steve joined as both singer and sound guy. Given how much respect she had for the seminal blues-folk acoustic trio Koerner, Ray, and Glover, she might have been their biggest champion ever.

Born in California and college educated back east, Raitt's deep Twin Cities connections qualify as roots. Her first record—still among her best, if only for her heartful reading of Willie Murphy's and John Koerner's "I Ain't Blue," complete with Maurice Jacox's plaintive flute solo—was produced in 1971 by Murphy and engineered by Dave Ray at his makeshift garage studio on an island in Lake Minnetonka. Her Minnesota-made musical adventures played out in the western suburbs again in 1987, when, at his suggestion, she recorded three tracks with Prince at Paisley Park in Chanhassen. But nothing ultimately came of the sessions.

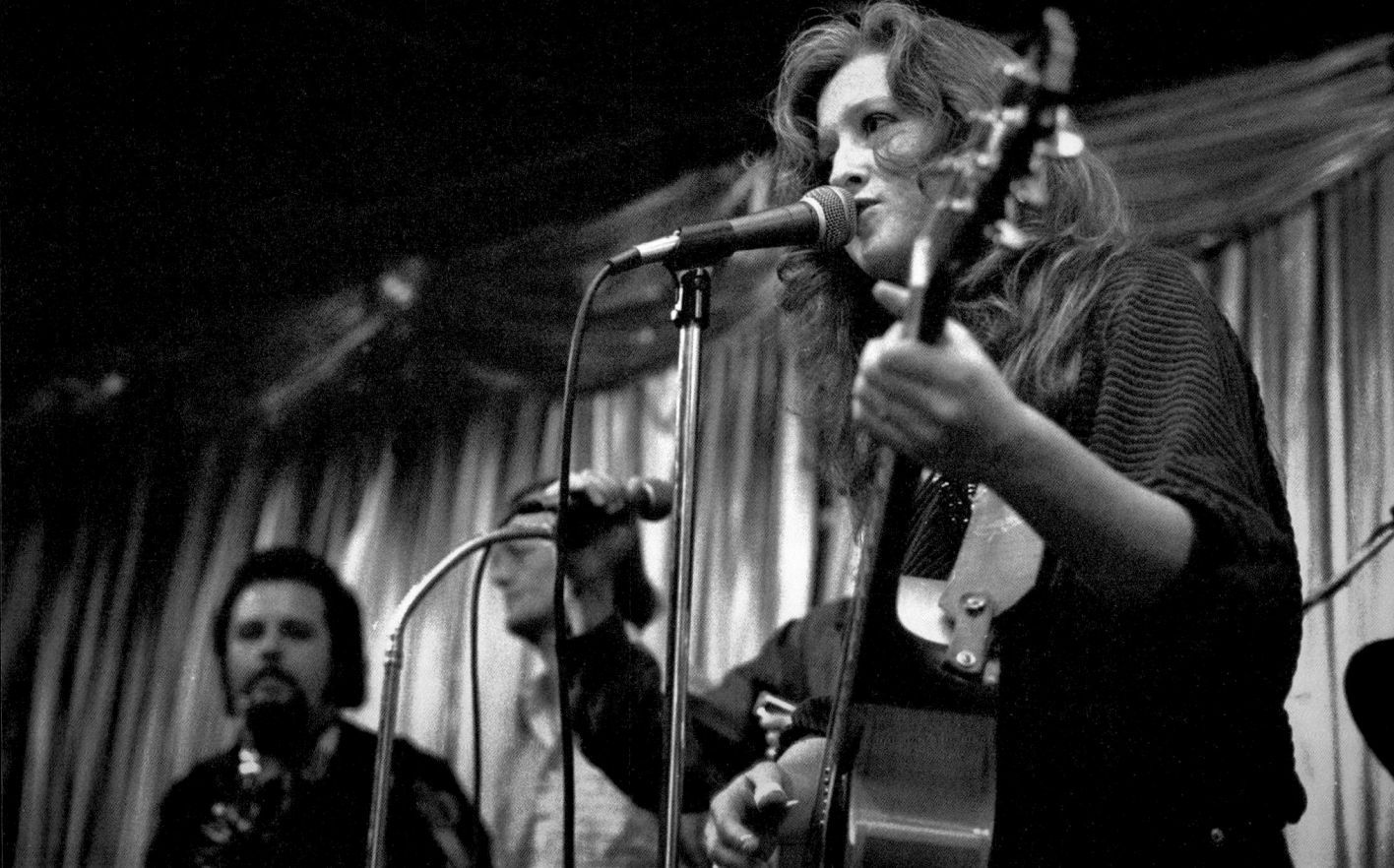

Bonnie Raitt at the Cabooze bar in 1978, performing with a couple of players from the Lamont Cranston Band. She spent a lot of time in the Twin Cities with her brother Steve and the myriad R&B bands they both hung out with.

From my eighties perch, somewhere between the computer keyboard and the concert stage, the record turntable and a barroom's backstage, I saw Raitt generated as much excitement with a pending appearance, a public concert, or a reported "Bonnie sighting" as Dylan did. There was something about both artists that transcended their caretaking of America's roots music and popular music traditions. In part, Bob's persona and charisma seemed tightly wrapped in enigmatic layers, whereas Bonnie's emitted a true transparent glow.

Her enthusiasm for blues, R&B, funk, New Orleans music, and folk extended to sharing discoveries of fresh new songwriters and resurrecting the talents of older, forgotten ladies of blues and jazz, like Sippie Wallace and Alberta Hunter. In short, Raitt has a great ear and a big heart. She often covered early material by John Prine and Randy Newman, helping those two songsmiths achieve well-deserved wider audiences. And she was early to the activism-in-music party, especially focused on environmental stewardship and anti–nuclear power. In fact, she was often the party-maker, including as a founding member of Musicians United for

Safe Energy (MUSE), as an organizer of the 1979 No Nukes concerts and film, and her ongoing benefit work for myriad social, political, and environmental causes. In Minnesota, Bonnie tirelessly played fundraising concerts for Winona LaDuke's Honor the Earth, a nonprofit organization run by Ojibwe women on the White Earth reservation that works to raise awareness of indigenous environmental issues.

Perhaps Raitt's social and environmental justice sensibilities grew out of being raised in a Quaker household, or from experiencing the radical events of the late sixties and early seventies while attending Harvard and Radcliffe. Whatever her motivation, as rock stars go, you won't find a more down-to-earth human whose warmth and empathy are as genuine as the blistering notes she conjures on a bottleneck guitar, or the emotion she conveys in a delicate ballad.

Traveling with her through the Rockies with the Lamont Cranston Band in 1980, I found her to be very gracious with her time and funnier than the boys. During the interview session on her bus, she was outspoken about the need to get off fossil fuels and turn to renewable energy sources and steadfast in her belief that no one should build any more nuclear power plants until we figured out what to do with the nuclear waste piling up around the world. She also served as a stabilizing influence as the only woman on a trek of nearly twenty men on two busses.

Not without blemishes, Raitt battled her own demons and eventually went into recovery. But when she emerged, her career stepped to the next level. She started writing her own songs, picked up multiple Grammy Awards (ten as of 2018), and was inducted into the Rock and Roll Hall of Fame, all of which underscores the significance of the second act in her long run. Better album sales also amped her career, like a second-booster-stage rocket that allowed her to soar beyond her bluesier past while never losing sight of it.

In 1989, she wrote the astonishing title track of her album *Nick of Time*, which captured the anxious feelings of friends and parents—and much of her fan base—staring down the aging process, but with the prospect of love still at the door. In one of my last record reviews for the *Reader*, I gave it a rave and asked, half seriously, half in jest, if it were too late to propose marriage. It's probably a good thing she didn't reply.

Riding shotgun with her brother in Colorado during the Bonnie/Lamont tour, I got to see Steve in a whole different light than the dimly lit barrooms where he was usually at work. He drove the Cranston bus, ran sound, and served as road manager. Sensational sound was his mantra, especially if the low, bottom end was bright and funky. The bass had to be in your face, or it wasn't happening. You've heard of the third eye; Steve Raitt had a third ear, and he used it like some high-tech intuition, whether a band was playing a low-life bar, out in an alpine field, or inside a cushy concert hall. That expert audio ability served him well later when he started his own company, designing and implementing home theater systems when that industry was just taking off.

"Rabbit" (his screwy nickname) was also an exceptional "people person," as they say in the HR world. Many times I watched him calmly deal with short-fused promoters jacked up about this or that. Maybe because he grew up in a showbiz family—his father, John Raitt, was a longtime Broadway and musical theater star, and appeared in film and television—Steve always knew how to slide out of the way of his sister's and Pat Hayes's fans—and when to step in to keep the show on the road, making sure all parties were "satisfied and tickled, too," as the old Taj Mahal song goes.

Traveling to make music is a wearisome task, no matter how many good times are being made. It takes a certain amount of discipline and indifference: You need to have enough gas in your own personal tank to charge ahead at the right time, and you are also required to carry an "indifference license" to apply to the unpredictable moods and situations that are out of your control. It allows you to advance despite how you or a bandmate might feel, or whatever lousy detour might lie ahead. Steve didn't really need that license, though. He herded musicians onto stages, or roused them out of buses and hotel rooms, just on the strength of his good nature and big smile.

There was one particular early morning in Durango when we had a long haul back to Denver ahead of us. With the sun barely up in the early dawn hours, there was Rabbit, standing at the open door of the bus, upbeat, energized, and grinning widely, greeting everybody by their first names and cajoling into the bus dreary-looking musicians, some of whom may not have been to bed that night. Perhaps even he hadn't, but it didn't show. I thought, man, this guy is something else: part dad, a tour guide, a hard-ass, maternal, part pastor, and genuinely himself at all times.

Onstage, Steve Raitt surprised many. I occasionally heard him sing along to house tapes or during sound checks back by the soundboard. By the time he became an official member of the TC Jammers, he was certifiably blow-away quality. The Jammers (still playing in late 2018 in a reconstituted formation) featured Melanie Rosales, Mark Lickteig, Eddie Brown, Pat Mackin, Bobby Vandell, Don Miner, Steve, and in some incarnations, singer Patty Peterson and others. Heavy on the R&B and funk, they developed a loyal following. It didn't really matter what they played, however; you went to see them for their musical chops and vocal prowess.

In 2009, Steve died of brain cancer, which he had been living with since he was diagnosed in 2001. He was only sixty-one when he passed. He left Minnesota shortly after the diagnosis and lived for a time in a water-skiing community in California where he could ski year-round. The last time I saw him was during a brief visit to Minneapolis a couple years

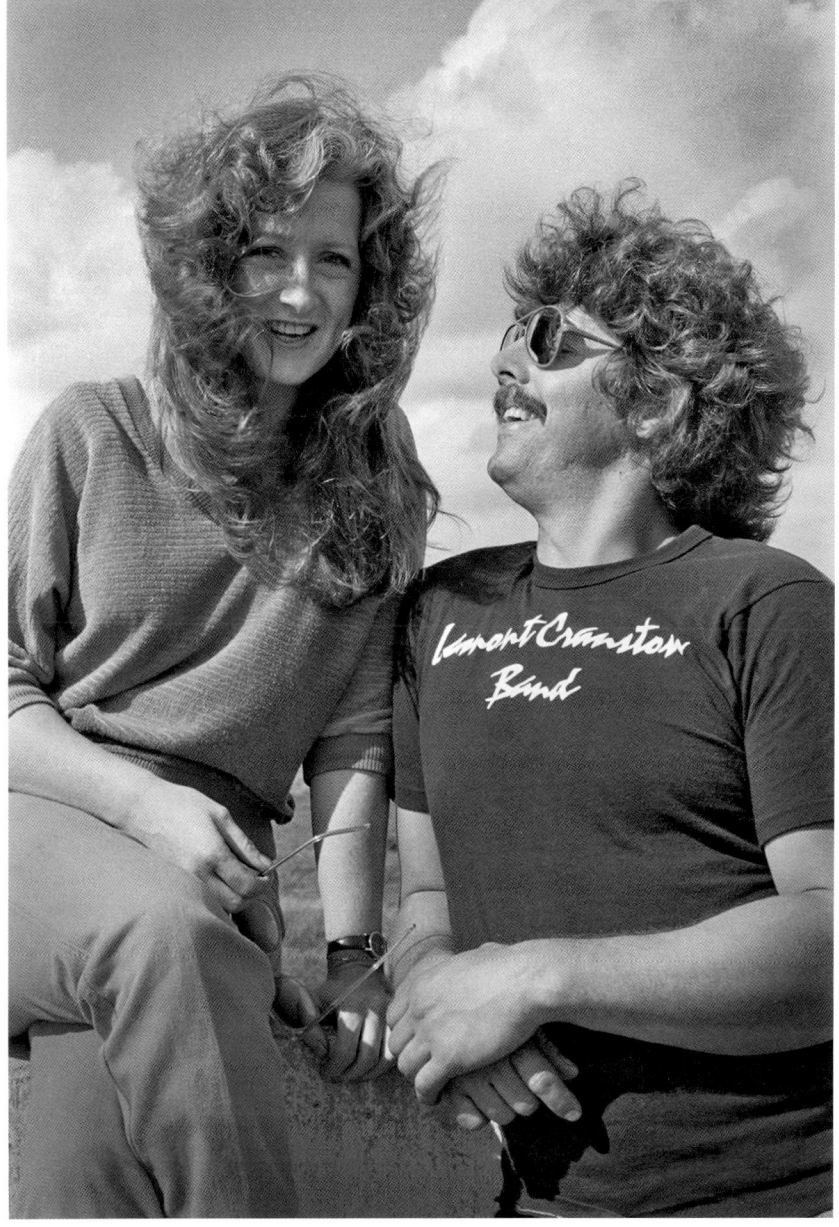

While Bonnie Raitt found global fame and fortune as one of the world's most successful blues/rock/folk/country artists, Steve Raitt made his own name as a widely respected sound engineer and as a Twin Cities scenester.

before he died. He stopped in for a show at Bunkers. His suffering did not alter that friendly, lovable grin or diminish his magnanimous spirit.

A couple years after he'd been gone, I emailed his sister a thank-you note for something she had done for the brother of a member of Têtes Noires, who was also battling the Big C. I told her I thought about Steve often and hoped he had landed in a better place, but a better place where the blues were still playing. Bonnie wrote back, "Wherever he is, he's probably yelling, 'More bass! More bass!'"

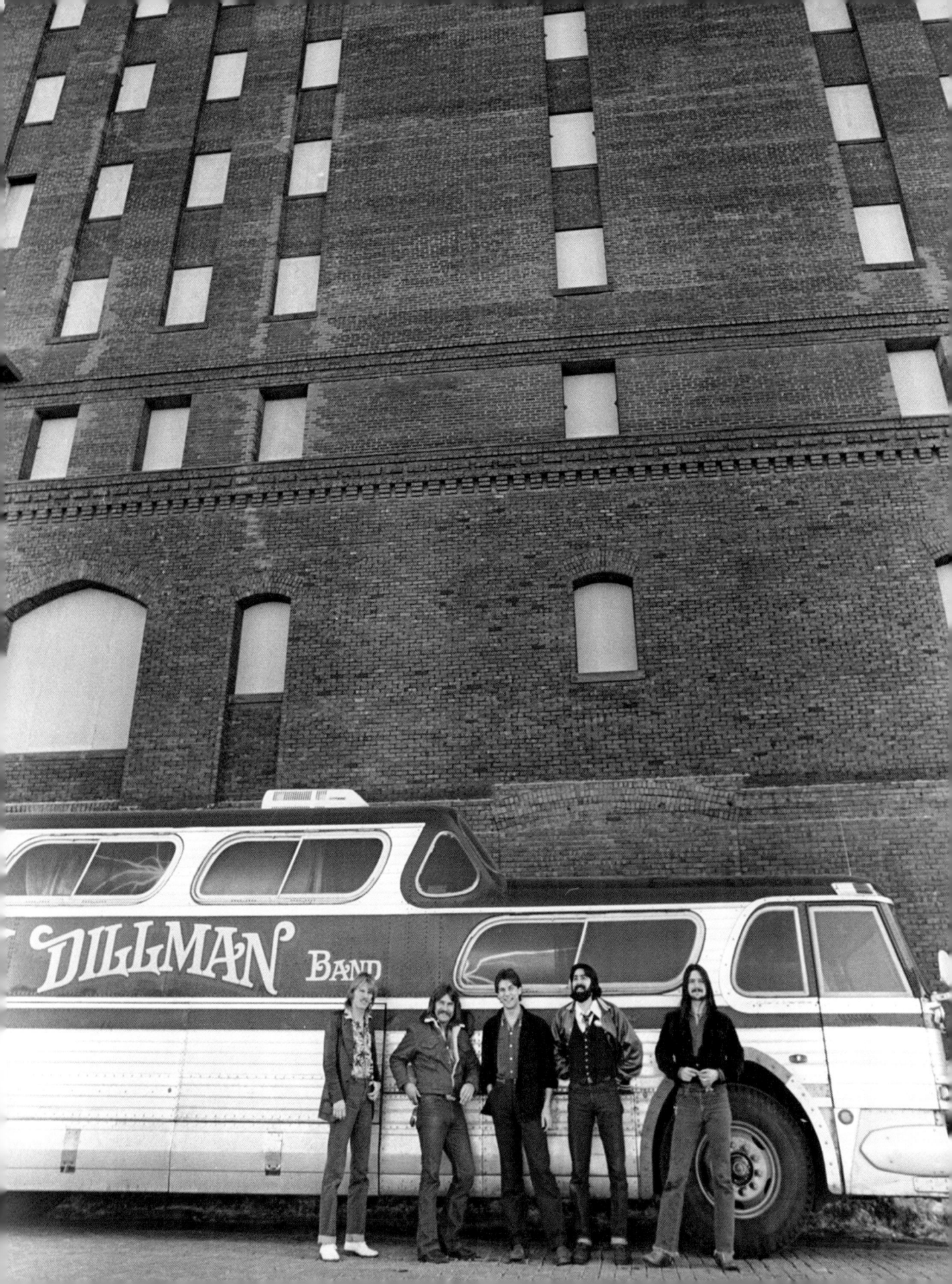

ROCK 'N' ROLL ROAD TRIPS AND RORSCHACH TESTS

You never know what you're getting into when you go on tour with a band. Any band. Life on the road can feel and look like a rock 'n' roll Rorschach test—the things you see and the things you think you see differ from person to person. One thing is certain: "normal reality" collapses into itself and reassembles under daily fragments composed mostly of putting miles on the odometer, sterile hotel rooms, wild and forgettable small talk, banal backstage settings, the roar of the audience, and the occasional musician asking to pull the bus over to throw up.

In my ten to twelve years covering "the scene," I went on a few daytrips with groups like the Daisy Dillman Band and Shangoya, the pioneering soca and reggae band led by Peter Nelson from Trinidad, and made some longer excursions to festivals to get inside music and music makers—and sometimes just to get out of the office and off the streets of Minneapolis–St. Paul. After getting canned at *City Pages* in the fall of '83, I headed to Cuba for a three-day Latin American music festival in Varadero, hoping to freelance a story nationally. After the festival, I was off for a few days in Havana, where the staggering amount of government propaganda was as laughable as the overwhelming amount of consumerist rhetoric in the United States. Although American gringos were in short supply at that time, there were tourists from all over the world, including a few Russians taking time off.

At the festival, known and unknown performers, from Celia Cruz to jazz trumpeter Arturo Sandoval (who later defected) to a personal favorite, Los Van Van, filled the evenings with unforgettable Afro-Cuban music. Then the clubs took over until dawn. The full story of my adventure is too long and too complicated to tell here. Suffice to say, the only way for an American to get into Cuba then was through cultural exchanges like

---

(opposite) The Daisy Dillman Band poses in front of their tour bus in downtown Minneapolis, prior to hitting the road in the early eighties, one of several road trips Keller took to get the inside story of the music and the music makers.

the one the Cuban Center for Cultural Studies arranged for the festival. It attracted a few elderly locals living in the city, some salsa band members from a Seattle group, and others like myself interested in the music and what the place was like.

In Cuba, Americans were always suspect, and journalists especially were suspected of being foreign agents or spies. It didn't help that I extended my visa, whereas almost everyone else went home after a few days at the festival and in Havana. The night before I left the island, three people from Cuba's immigration office knocked on my hotel door and interrogated me for an hour because "we have reason to believe you have been involved in unauthorized sociopolitical action." I feared I might be spending the holidays—maybe many holidays—in jail. Instead, they took my notebook from the festival, said I could keep my film, and went on their way.

Things fared much better in Venezuela a few years later, when I was traveling with the neo-metal pop-rock band Dare Force. I got on that trip mostly because Victor Valens, the Twin Cities' leading Latino booking agent and a Cuban native (who later opened Victor's Café), told me they had an extra seat on the plane. A local Caracas band of twelve or thirteen people joined the tour, which took place on a standard-issue school bus with no air conditioning, bad shocks, and a lead singer with a bad stomach.

The fellas in the Force and I had a come-to-Jesus moment in Caracas the first day, before two of us got altitude sickness. They challenged my presence, knowing that they had never been covered in *City Pages* while I was there, or in the *Reader*, where I was at the time of this South American trip. It was true that an anti–metal/hard-rock bias ran through the paper and its many freelancers (although we occasionally ran stories by Nany Heitzeg, who liked the genre). I affirmed their accusations and said this trip would change that, and hopefully it did.

The Dare Force sound turned out to be more like "Van Halen crossed with Thin Lizzy," as guitarist Brian Bart liked to describe it, and less like other, more formulaic hard rockers. They wrote solid songs and had a four-star drummer, and they were good company. That was a good thing, seeing as they could have dumped me at the leper colony we passed on the way to Maracaibo in western Venezuela. Or they could have left me with the two sisters that guitarist Johnny O'Neill and I met, whose parents ran a traveling circus. The sisters told harrowing stories of their large entourage crossing the Amazon River over a rope bridge, sending the elephants first as a "safety test." North America seemed so far away the longer we journeyed. Throughout the entire trip, any time we stopped at hotels or gas stations, there was always an odd, colorful extravaganza on television, like a Jerry Lewis telethon or something. It felt like we were missing the real Venezuela.

Earlier in the decade, in November 1982, I attended the three-day

"World Music Festival" at the Bob Marley Performance Centre in Montego Bay, Jamaica. It had the strangest lineup of any of my rock journeys during that time, featuring the Clash, Aretha Franklin, Squeeze, country star Skeeter Davis, Gladys Knight & the Pips, the Wailers, Peter Tosh, the Grateful Dead, the Beach Boys, the B-52s, and Rick James, to name a few. The shows ran all night in tropical, oceanside Mo' Bay. At one point, Squeeze's Chris Difford and I shared a brief, sad conversation in front of a food shack that had two young goats tethered to it as we perused a chalkboard menu of curries—including goat curry.

Rita Marley performed with the Melody Makers (featuring four of Bob and Rita's children) and served as the official hostess, welcoming the international press on the first day. I don't remember a lot of the performances—Beach Boys? Yellowman? ("You were pretty stoned," my traveling companion, Mark Rikess, reminded me recently)—but I vividly remember Rita Marley referencing her late husband and hopes of reincarnation: "We are waiting for him to come back."

Earlier in the summer of '82, I rode my thumb and a train along Route 66 to the US Festival in San Bernardino, California, put on by Steve "Woz" Wozniak before he split from the other Steve (Jobs) at Apple. Music for the three-day event was booked by the legendary promoter Bill Graham, who brought in big names like the Grateful Dead, Santana, Talking Heads, Tom Petty, Fleetwood Mac, Jackson Browne, the Kinks, and others. US was billed as a technology and music fest, although I don't recall seeing any technology—aside from the first use of giant video screens at the sides of the stage, which reminded me of going to a drive-in movie. My clearest memory of the festival is how the press conference on day one deteriorated into a shouting match between an overheated bunch of big-mouthed reporters and a besieged Graham, who had tried but failed to get it broadcast to Russia via satellite, three years before Mikhail Gorbachev introduced glasnost to the Soviet Union.

The chapter on Dylan earlier in this book touches on a weeklong swing through the Midwest on his Never Ending Tour. But of all my rock 'n' roll sojourns, the ride through the big rock candy mountains of Colorado with the Lamont Cranston Band and Bonnie Raitt and her band was the best on the pure-fun scale. It felt like going to summer camp with the cool kids you knew only from a distance. Of course, it helped that the scenery was stunning; it reminded me of the Ute Mountains around little Vernal City, Utah, where I lived as a youngster before my family moved to western North Dakota, where there were only great plains, distant buttes, excruciatingly long winters, and the redemptive badlands.

There were two rules on the Cranston bus. One, nobody (other than Pat Hayes) is allowed in the "Catfish Lounge" in the back of the bus. And two, no music other than blues music shall be played if any Lamont

Cranston Band members are on board (whether in wakeful, slumbering, or wasted states of consciousness). Although not posted, the rules would quickly become known to visiting outsiders and any guest passengers riding the old converted double-decker Greyhound.

The Lamont Cranston Band was one of the preeminent groups on the Minnesota music scene in the seventies and early eighties. The Cranstons were drawing fans even through the rise of new-wave/punk and Prince groups. And the band's reputation was well known beyond the borders of the lake state.

Featuring a mighty horn- and guitar-driven sound readily augmented by Pat Hayes's dynamic harp (and occasional guitar playing), the Cranstons mixed famous and obscure blues standards with deftly crafted original songs. The latter were penned in the blues tradition by keyboardist Bruce McCabe, Pat, and Pat's brother Larry, as well as other contributors. In many ways, Pat and Larry Hayes were the real Blues Brothers, until those two guys from Chicago came along.

Among the band's biggest fans were Bonnie Raitt, Dan Aykroyd (aka Elwood Blues), and John Belushi (aka Jake Blues). The young Jonny Lang and other well-known performers, such as the comedy duo of Al Franken and Tom Davis, also scored them high. Elderly blues giants like Albert King and Charlie Musselwhite respected them and shared bills. An English band called the Rolling Stones seemed to fancy them, too, and the Cranstons opened for the Brits through three midwestern cities in 1981.

As of 2018, the Lamont Cranston Band has recorded eleven studio albums. The 1981 *Shakedown*, one of several Cranston records released on the legendary Twin Cities indie label Waterhouse Records, included a Cranston original by McCabe and Pat Hayes called "Upper Mississippi Shakedown," which gained enough sales and airplay to chart on *Billboard*. Among the even tastier gems in their wheelhouse are the sassy "Excusez Moi, Mon Cheri," written by Larry Hayes and featured on 1977's *Specials-Lit*, and Pat's beautiful, elegiac instrumental "E Jam" from *El Cee Notes* of 1978. The "Mon Cheri" tune was later cut as the flipside for the Blues Brothers' single "Soul Man" (a remake of the old Sam and Dave hit and featured in the *Blues Brothers* film). But it was "E Jam" that could put a deep blues chill on your spine and a happy ache in your heart.

Leading up to the Colorado tour, the LC boys had just released one of their finest albums in *Up from the Alley*, which Bonnie's brother Steve produced and on which McCabe delivered some of the best tunes of his long career. The album was recorded at the infamous Del's Tire Mart space. Located in the West Bank's Seven Corners area, Del's was a refurbished garage turned rehearsal space, rather than a real recording studio, but it suited the Cranstons just fine. (Prince also used Del's as a rehearsal space early in his career, until the band's equipment was stolen.)

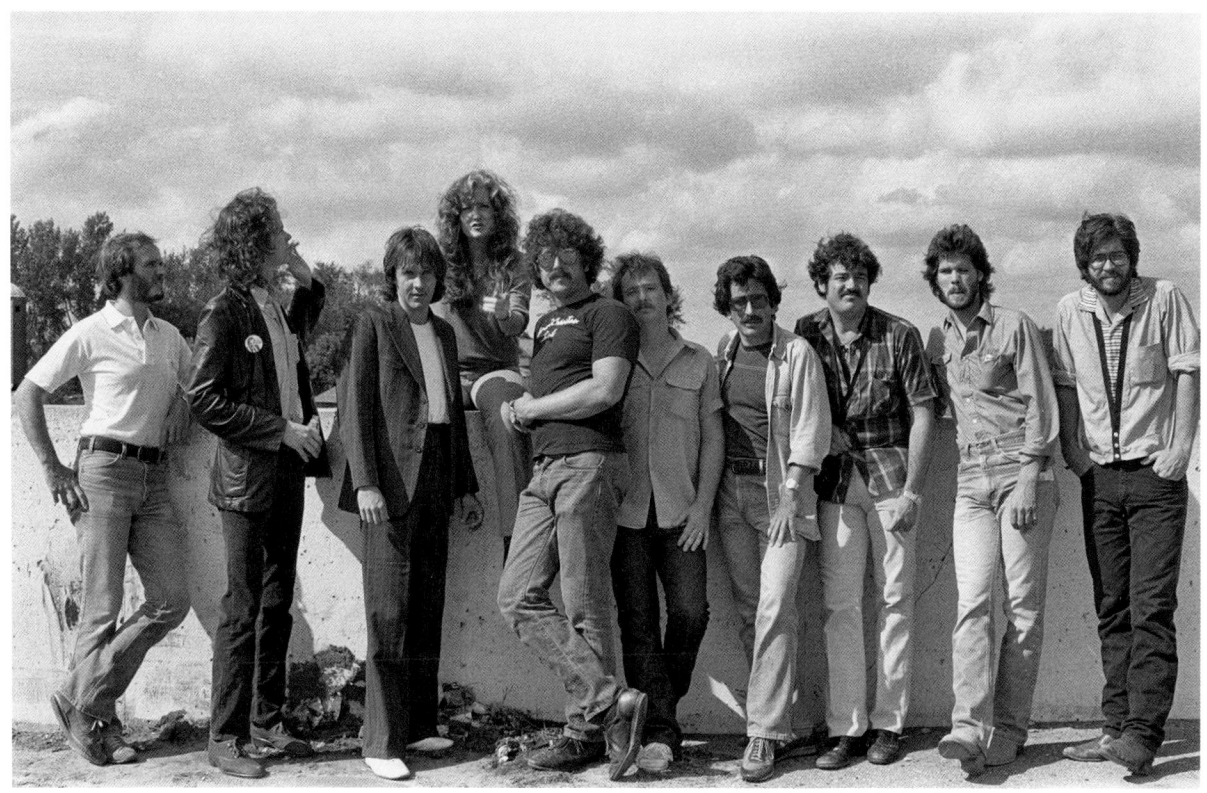

As the buses were preparing to depart Minnesota, Pat Hayes climbed aboard carrying only a big, black garbage bag of clothes and a sketch pad. An avid angler and accomplished artist, he looked like he was going fishing for a couple days. His section of the bus in the rear was cordoned off with some funky curtains and an equally funky hand-drawn sign hanging nearby: The Catfish Lounge.

Larry Hayes had departed the band before the *Up from the Alley* record and the Colorado trip. On board were Waterhouse label president and Cranston manager Gary Marx, along with the horn section of Dick Perna, Rick O'Dell, and Billy Shiell; bassist Mick Massoff; drummer Jim Novak; McCabe; guitarist Charlie Bingham; and Pat. Marx always called me "Scoop," and as we sauntered through the Rockies, it's all anyone on the bus called me. It felt like being on a baseball team where everyone has a nickname. Bonnie's bus—cleaner, leaner, and newer, with well-defined sleeping compartments—provided a comfy setting for an interview with her on one leg of the tour.

On the second day of the trip, I popped an advance cassette of the new Bob Marley and the Wailers album, *Uprising*, into the dashboard cassette player on the Cranston bus. *Uprising* was one of Marley's most accessible albums—with the irresistible "Could You Be Loved" and the timeless

Helgeson struggled to get the Lamont Cranston Band and Bonnie Raitt all together for this photo, taken at Elko Speedway, south of the Twin Cities, prior to their embarking on a tour through the Rocky Mountains of Colorado.

acoustic masterpiece "Redemption Song"—but the jeers from the back started with the first sound of the reggae rhythms on track one, "Coming in from the Cold." I quickly punched the tape out of the machine. Steve Raitt, at the wheel, winked and knowingly pushed in an old blues album.

The tour's shows were going well. The red-headed rock-blueser often joined the Cranstons onstage for a number or two before setting the stage afire with her own boys. Then it was pack it all up, rinse, and repeat. One afternoon, during a pit stop at a rest area somewhere alongside a scenic alpine stream, Marx got left behind in the men's room. About twenty miles farther up the road, somebody finally noticed. The general consensus was that we should probably go back and pick him up. Maybe it was time to institute a "Blues Buddy" system and add another bus rule: Never abandon your record label guy and manager.

That tour ended; summer camp was over. Other tours began and stopped. The band underwent many changes in the years and decades ahead. Some members died, like O'Dell; others simply moved on. McCabe left, along with Bingham, Novak, and Massoff, to form the much-loved Hoopsnakes. But the Lamont Cranston Band somehow kept going, well into the new century. Pat kept playing, adding younger guys, calling back Cranston vets like saxophonist Tom Burnevick, and always seemed to find hot new guitarists. He turned into one badass blues-rock player in his own right, and he blossomed as a songwriter.

After an odds-beating battle with brain cancer, McCabe returned to the band for the 2012 album *Lamont Cranston with Bruce McCabe*. By this time, it was Pat Hayes who had lost all his hair, a fact that he celebrated with the wry, up-tempo cut "My Hair Is Gone." It sounded like an unapologetic anthem for longtime older fans everywhere and a cautionary tale for a new generation of Lamont aficionados.

The bus in American history can be viewed as significant and symbolic for transformation, as a means for political redress and radical cultural action. Think Rosa Parks refusing to sit at the back of the bus and helping to ignite the Civil Rights movement. Think Ken Kesey and the Merry Pranksters in their psychedelic bus, "Further," that represented the beginning of 1960s counterculture and the long, strange trip. Recall all the bus cavalcades to Washington to rally for peace, women's rights, gay rights, black lives.

But from that microdot corner of my own back pages, "the bus" will always mean the old, tired Greyhound dieseling through the Rocky Mountain forests—Bobby "Blue" Bland's "Farther Up the Road" rockin' the quiet streams, Otis Rush's "All Your Love (I Miss Loving)" cryin' out the windows—as Lamont and the fellas roll to the next gig.

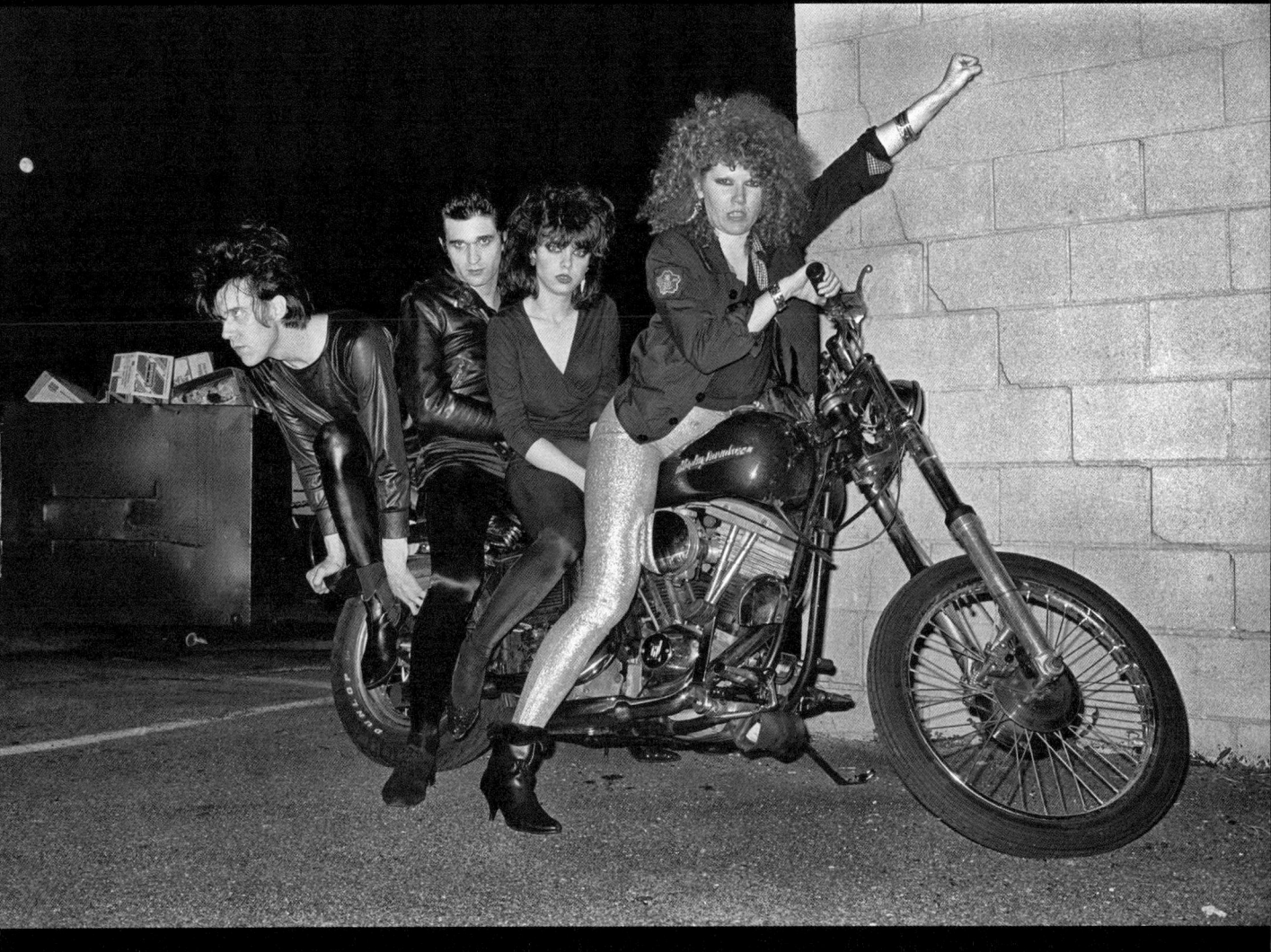

"Wanna go out and play?" asked the photog to the Cramps, in town to play at Duffy's bar in Minneapolis, circa 1980. So they did, on a motorcycle parked nearby under a full moon. Coming out of Sacramento, California, the "punkabilly" band were regulars at CBGB in New York City during the late seventies. They eventually signed to the I.R.S. Records label and recorded with the legendary Alex Chilton as producer. The Cramps are credited by some with helping to foster the revival of rockabilly music during the punk/new-wave era.

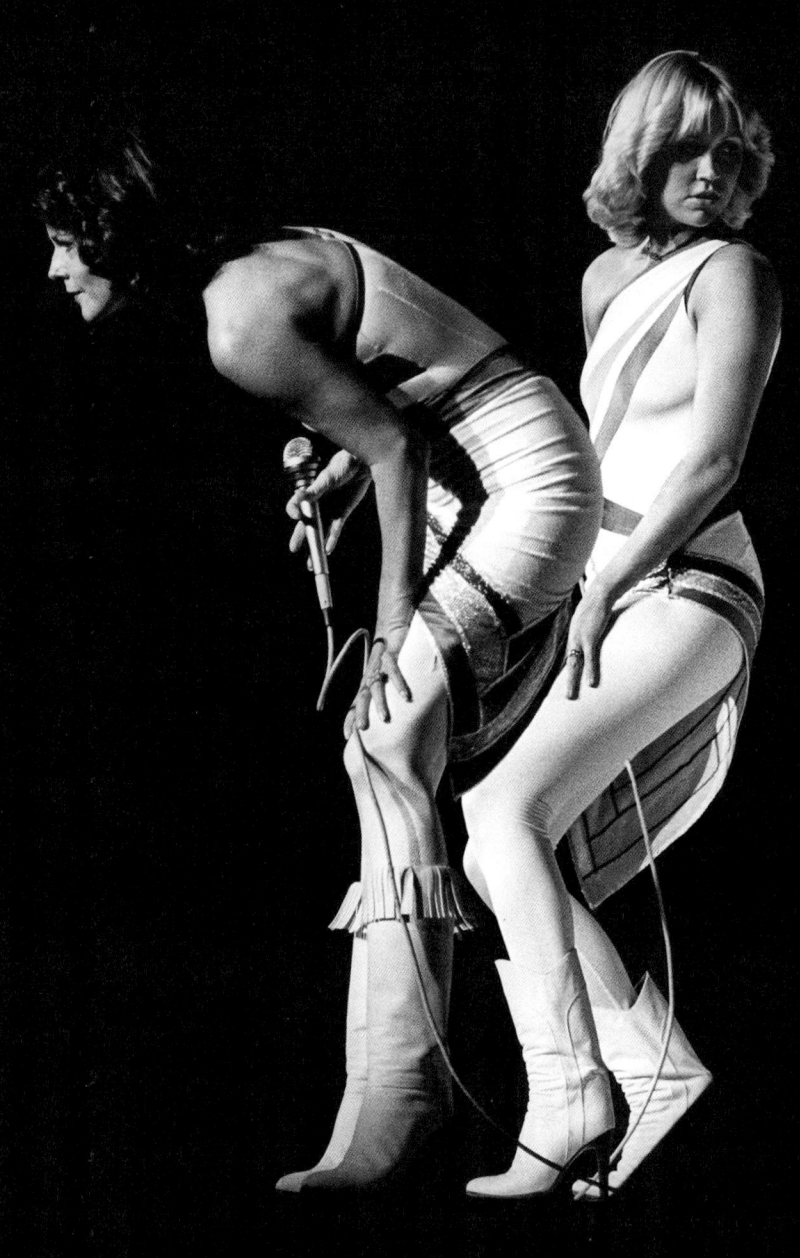

Agnetha Fältskog and Anni-Frid Lyngstad of the Swedish pop group ABBA are shot from the side while performing at the St. Paul Civic Center in 1979. The Helg assigned himself to work the show, "just to have them in my portfolio." The forty-city, six-month tour would be the band's final one.

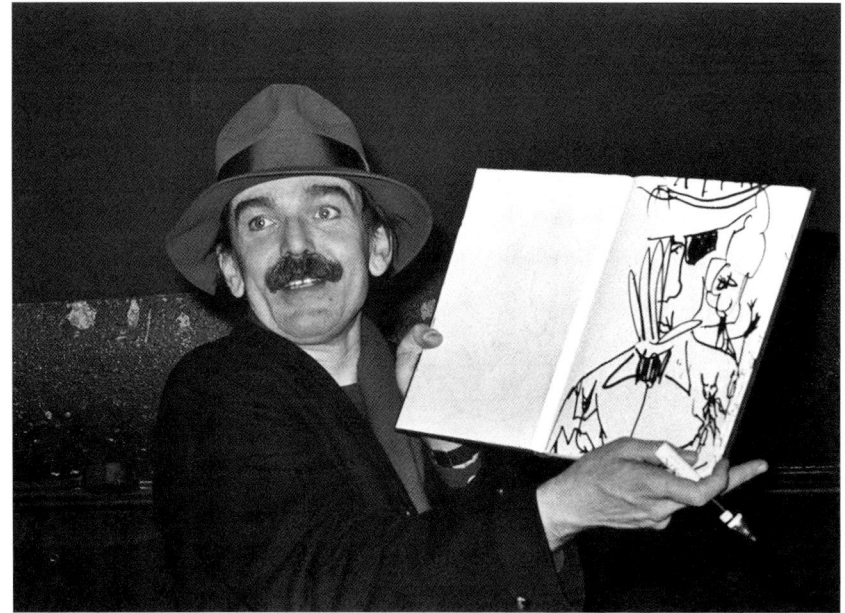

With a rare smile on his face, the enigmatic Captain Beefheart, a musical expressionist and abstractionist, shows off the sketch he was doing while performing at Duffy's in 1980.

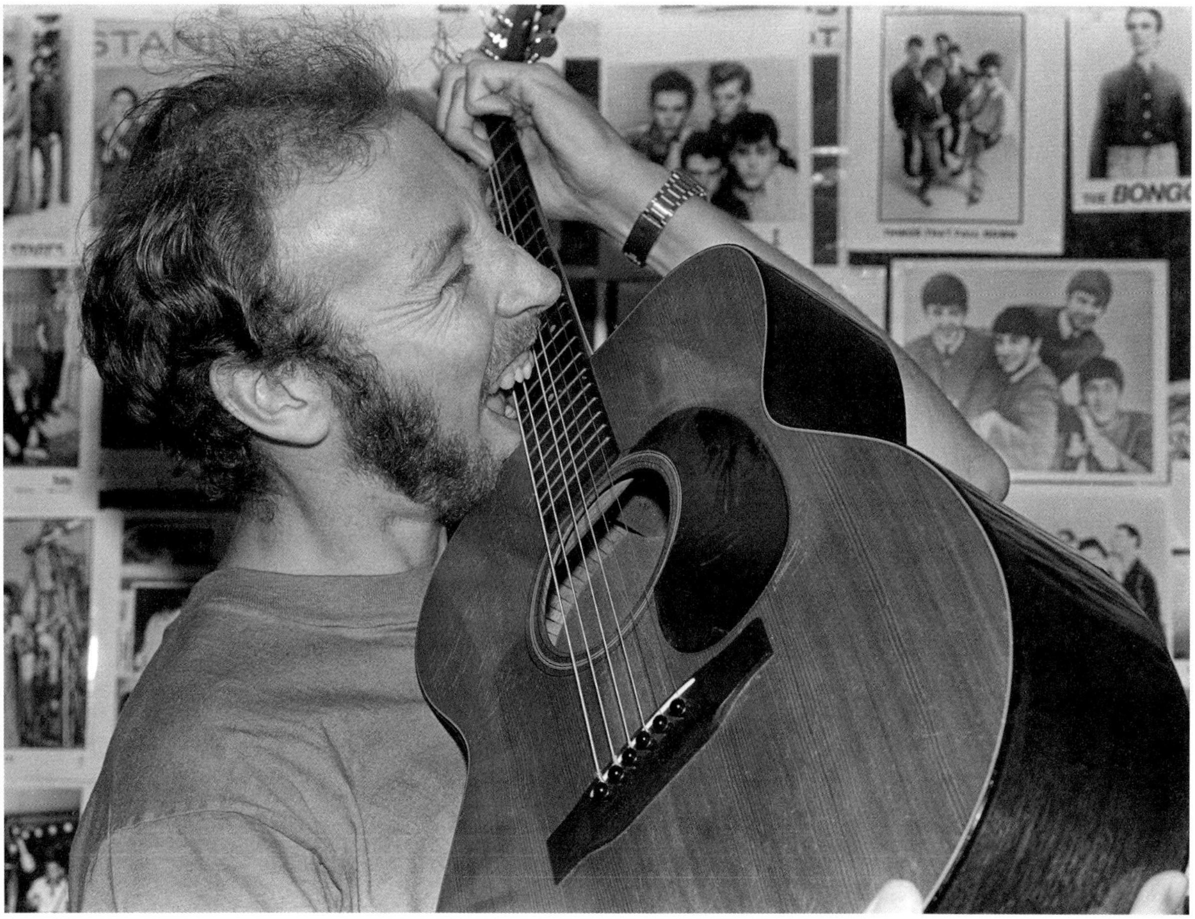

Alone with the Helg inside club manager Steve McClellan's office at First Avenue, folk-rock artist Richard Thompson puts some teeth into his acoustic. Thompson has played the legendary club numerous times over the decades.

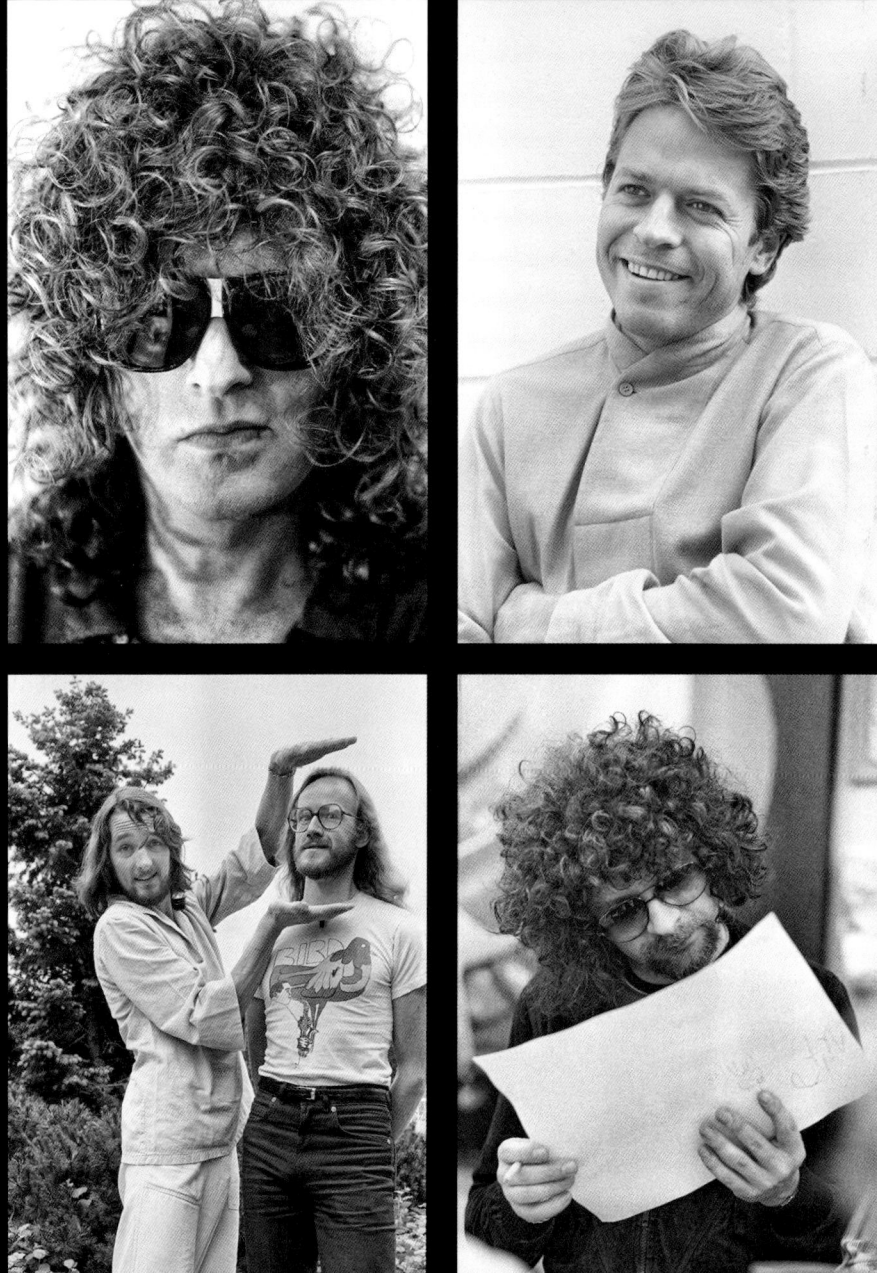

(top left) During the 1970s, Ian Hunter was the front man of Mott the Hoople, which had its biggest hit in 1972 with the glam-rock anthem "All the Young Dudes," written by David Bowie especially for the band. Hunter left the group in the mid-seventies and went on to have a solid solo career. The Helg captured Hunter in this dazzling portrait backstage in the dressing room at Northrop Auditorium on the University of Minnesota campus. **(top right)** Stylish Brit rocker Robert Palmer, who had a huge hit and equally successful MTV video with 1985's "Addicted to Love," strikes a pose for Spud Boy 1 at the offices of KQRS radio in 1986. **(bottom left)** Supertramp's Roger Hodgson frames bandmate John Helliwell for Helgeson at the St. Paul Radisson Hotel after their concert the night before behind their mega-selling 1979 album, *Breakfast in America*. The rest of the group had already flown out for their next date. **(bottom right)** ELO's Jeff Lynne (aka Otis or Clayton Wilbury, of the Traveling Wilburys) examines what might be a fan's drawing or some piece of rock memorabilia at the Great American Music record store in the Twin Cities suburb of Bloomington in the late 1970s.

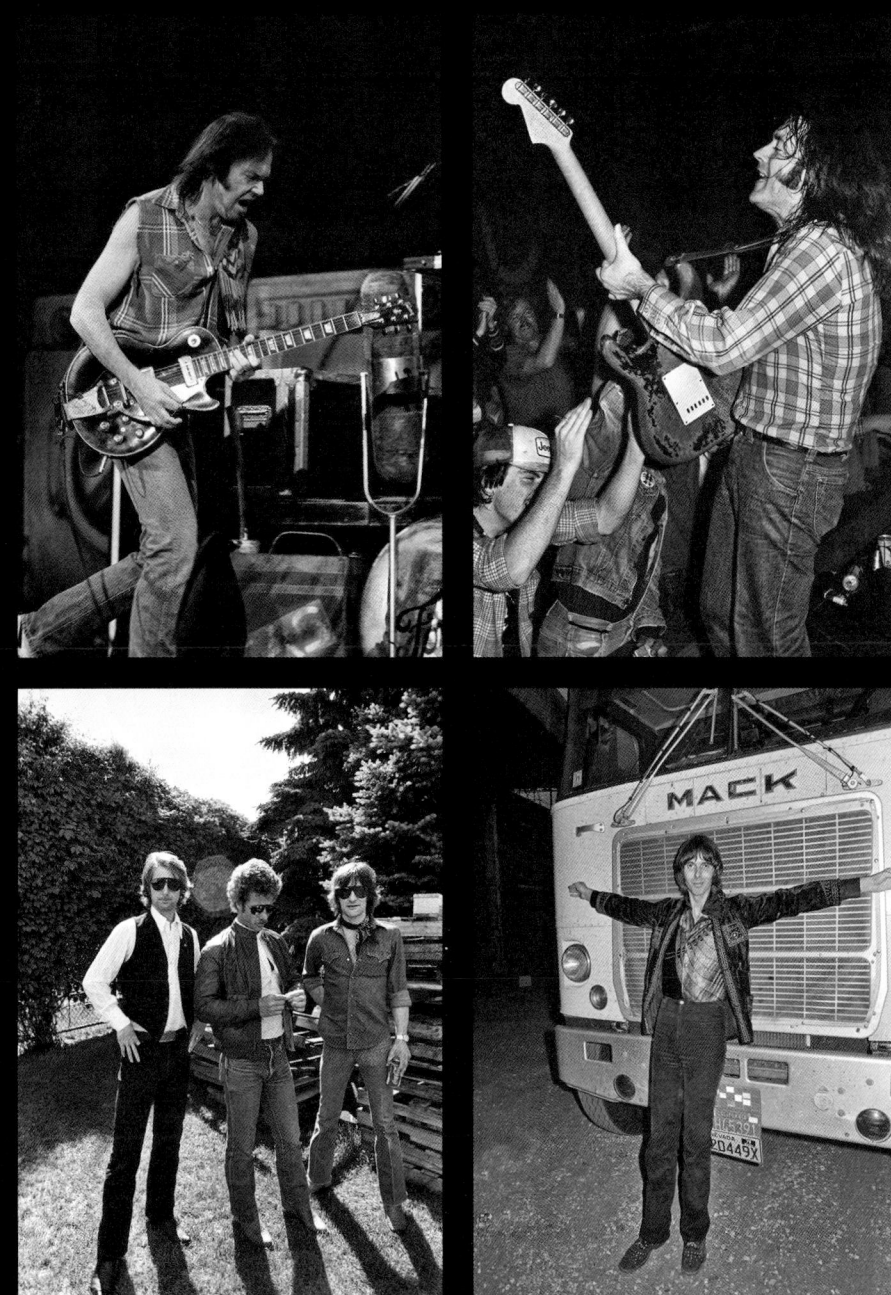

(top left) Neil Young, with Crazy Horse, rocks the Met Center in Bloomington on October 17, 1986, during the Live in a Rusted Out Garage tour. **(top right)** Rory Gallagher, from County Donegal in Ireland, was smitten with American blues and inspired many other musicians on both sides of the Atlantic with his own interpretation of the genre. Here, he rouses fans during a Twin Cities performance. **(bottom left)** Three Byrds captured at Parade Stadium in Minneapolis in 1979. According to the Helg, Roger McGuinn (left) was very friendly, Chris Hillman (middle) was shy and retiring, and Gene Clark (right) was dark and brooding but still cooperated with taking a photo. **(bottom right)** Photographer to rock star: "Pretend you got hit by a Mack truck." Piano player Nicky Hopkins—whose résumé includes sessions with the Stones, the Who, the Kinks, Harry Nilsson, and all four individual Beatles after their breakup, as well as with the whole band on "Revolution"—sprawls out against the vehicle outside Midway Stadium in St. Paul. Hopkins also played in the Jeff Beck Group, Quicksilver Messenger Service, and others in the San Francisco scene and released three solo albums.

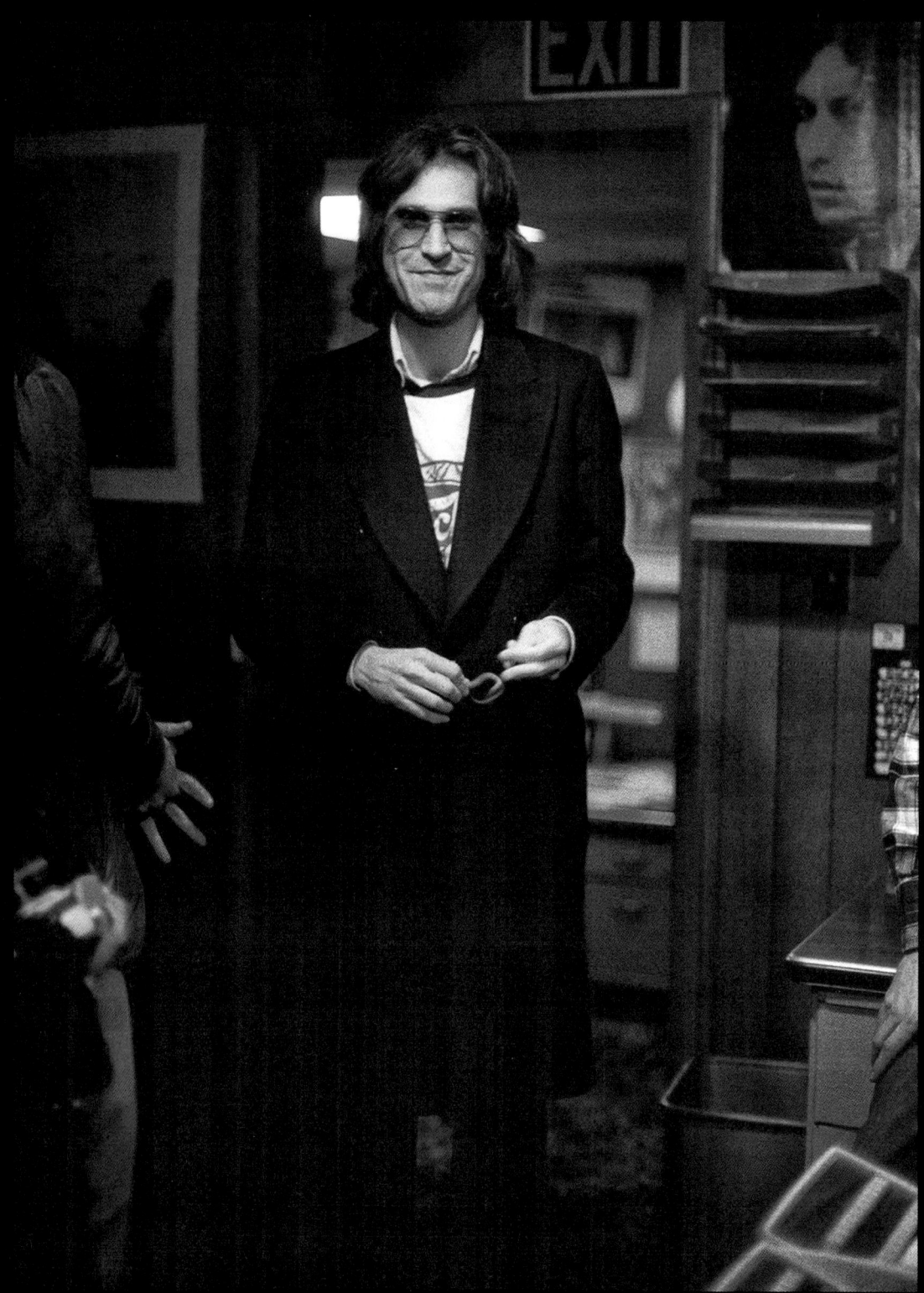

Shot during a 1976 promotional tour for *Schoolboys in Disgrace*, the literate-looking Ray Davies poses for a true Kinks fanboy, Greg Helgeson, at the KQRS radio station. Davies's brother Dave was in Kansas City the same day peddling the band's new album, which was heralded by many—including by Twin Cities native Paul Nelson writing for *Rolling Stone*—as a welcomed return to form.

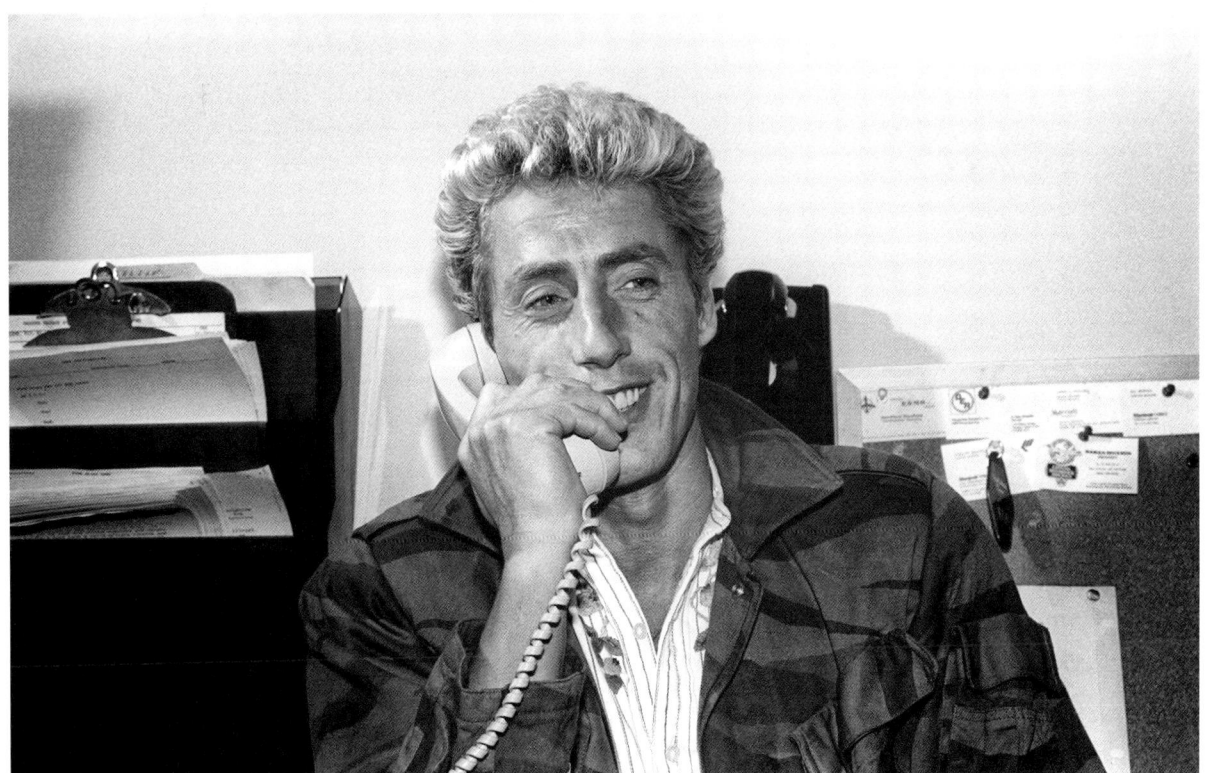

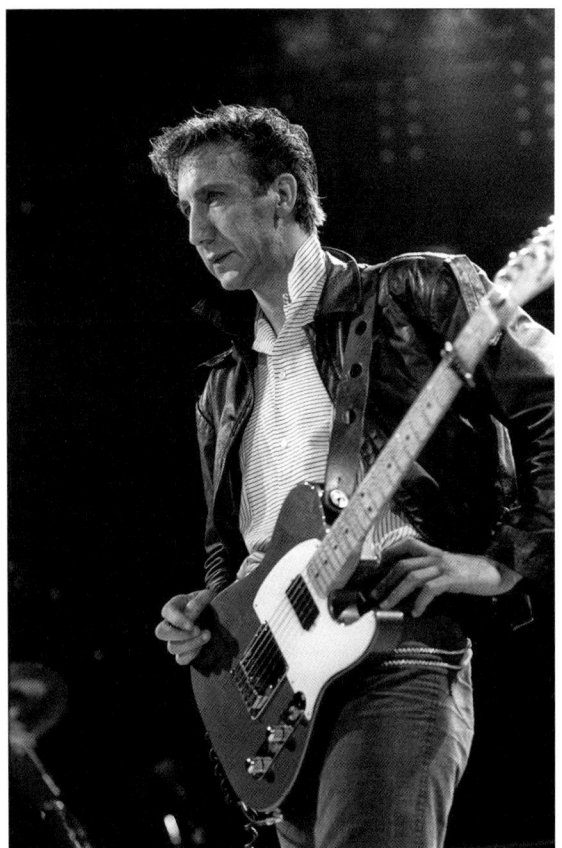

(above) The Who's Roger Daltrey makes a business call at the Minneapolis–St. Paul airport after deplaning from a private jet with his bandmates for a St. Paul Civic Center gig in 1982.

(left) Pete Townshend surveys the crowd between songs during the St. Paul Civic Center concert in '82, with the Helg at his feet. Backstage before the show, Spud Boy 2 (Keller) got Townshend's autograph on a Polaroid photo he took at a Who concert in Hartford, Connecticut, a few years earlier.

THE ROLLING STONES

Sizing Up the Stones from the Mid-Market

Chicago has been the home of the blues ever since the Great Migration from the South before and after the two world wars. Some of the world's greatest blues musicians, from Willie Dixon and Muddy Waters to Howlin' Wolf and Magic Sam, all relocated to Chi-town. The city also became home to legendary record labels like Chess Records, Vee-Jay, Cobra, Delmark, Alligator, and others. So, naturally, sweet home Chicago became the Rolling Stones' US base camp for the 1981 tour behind their *Tattoo You* album. The tour featured three Midwest stops—the Checkerdome in St. Louis, the UNI-Dome at the University of Northern Iowa in Cedar Falls, and the St. Paul Civic Center—and the Lamont Cranston Band was brought on as the opening act at those venues.

The wheel-and-spoke strategy allowed the Stones to fly into smaller cities, do the gig, then fly out again and be back in the Windy City to hit the late-night clubs or just hang at their hotel. The informal documentary film *Live at the Checkerboard Lounge, Chicago 1981* captures some of the core members jamming with Muddy Waters and his band, while the Brits' entourage parties in the background at a table full of booze. If you've never seen Mick Jagger performing in sweats, here's your chance.

The Cranstons got on the tour largely because of the relationship Randy Levy at Schon Productions had with the band's manager, Bill Graham, who liked the sound of the Cranstons' new album at the time, *Upper Mississippi Shakedown*. Levy was often the one to book the Stones when they came to the Twin Cities, except for their first tour in 1964, when one of the earliest rock promoters, Dick Shapiro, booked them to play at Big Reggie's Danceland in Excelsior, Minnesota. The band reportedly was booed off the stage by the meager crowd of fewer than three hundred. Danceland owner Ray "Big Reggie" Colihan lost money on the show—as he did at the Beatles' concert at Met Stadium in 1965.

With backstage passes from the Cranstons for both the Cedar Falls

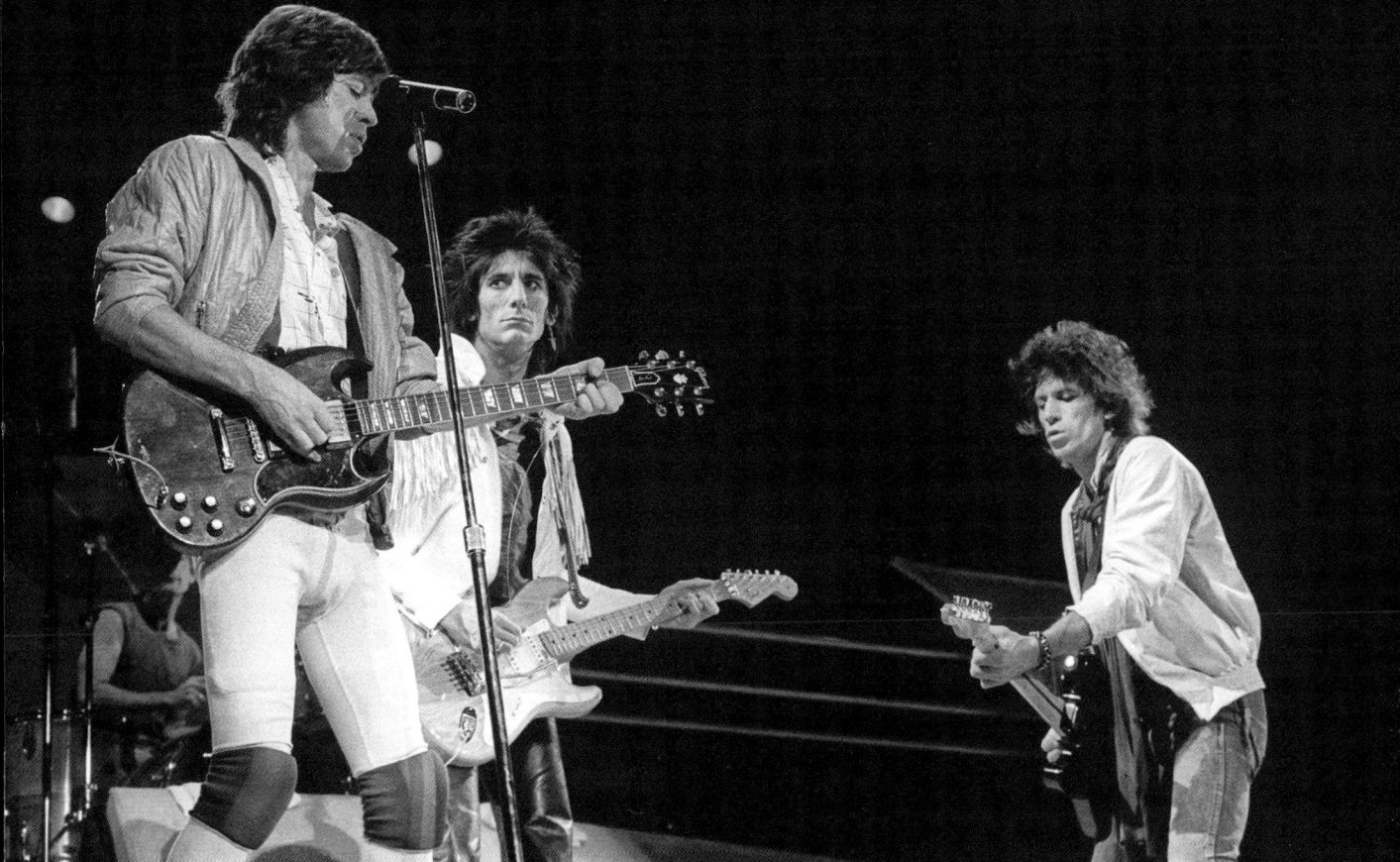

and St. Paul shows, I decided it would be a good idea to do a cover story in *City Pages*, even though I had no access to the reigning kings of rock 'n' roll. What was I thinking? One of the top media stories around the *Tattoo You* tour was that it was the first major rock tour to feature a corporate sponsor—Jovan, a musk fragrance owned by Coty. At the time, corporate sponsorships of rock tours and events was hotly debated among artists and in the press. Had the Stones succumbed to selling out to corporate interests that would co-opt their music? The question doesn't even get asked these days, as such sponsorships are generally viewed as a passive and practical way to offset the high costs of touring and/or to provide another source of revenue to bands and artists.

Instead of writing a big cover story, I should have pulled a Truman Capote. In 1972, *Rolling Stone* magazine hired the masterful writer to cover the tour supporting the Stones' masterpiece *Exile on Main Street* double LP. Capote threw in the towel—he never wrote word one. In interviews about it later, he simply shrugged, saying there was no story to write, save for a few salacious anecdotes about teenaged boys and girls coming

The Rolling Stones at the St. Paul Civic Center, November 21, 1981, touring behind their *Tattoo You* album—with a little help from a perfumery called Jovan.

onto the plane for interviews who ended up having sex with unidentified members of the entourage.

I managed to eke out a long story that was really a glorified review of both nights, with some UNI-Dome backstage color splashed here and there like a bad kid's painting. Still, some readers liked going behind the scenes.

Before taking the stage, the Stones were to come through a campus building connected to the dome. A couple of classrooms were designated as their dressing rooms, which were on lockdown. As soon as the band arrived, everyone else in the building was supposed to immediately leave the hallway and stay shuttered inside their rooms until the band was on-stage. Various local and out-of-town security types, each wearing multiple laminates around their necks, were on hand to enforce these strict hall-monitor rules.

The Cranston band had its own dressing rooms in another area of the building, and I was sequestered there with a few of the band members' girlfriends who had made the trip. The homeboys played well but were on and off the stage in about thirty-five minutes. A fleet of cars finally pulled up to the dome, delivering the headliners from the local airport after they flew in from Chicago in a private jet. It was unclear if the musicians even used their dressing rooms or consumed the giant lobsters that had been prepared prior to arrival. It was too hard to see through the tiny slats of glass that looked out into the hall.

Suddenly, a swirling mass of bodies and instruments flashed in front of us through the glass. It was too much for the women. They pushed open the door, and we all spilled into the hall and scurried to catch the band as they were about to enter the arena. We kept a slight distance so the security would not escort us away, although they were preoccupied getting "Ladies and Gentleman, the Rolling Stones" onstage.

Mick and Keith were in the rear, and seconds before the house lights dimmed, Jagger started jumping up and down in an intense aerobic warm-up that looked like Royal Air Force jumping jacks. When the place went dark, a roar went up from the arena that sent an electrical charge through musicians, interlopers, and Cranston girlfriends. Some flashlights appeared and Jagger disappeared. Just before Richards did, Kathy Winther, Larry Hayes's wife, yelled, "Keith, you are the baddest ever!"

Richards turned around with a creaky, heartfelt smile and a cigarette dripping from his face before a flashlight led him into the blackness. The roar reached its peak, and "Start Me Up" inflated the UNI-Dome to another level.

Fun? Sure! A cover story, nah. It wasn't as exciting as the night in 1978 during the *Some Girls* tour when Peter Tosh, former guitarist for the Wailers, opened for the Stones at the St. Paul Civic Center. He had recorded a duet with Jagger covering the old Temptations hit "Don't Look Back"

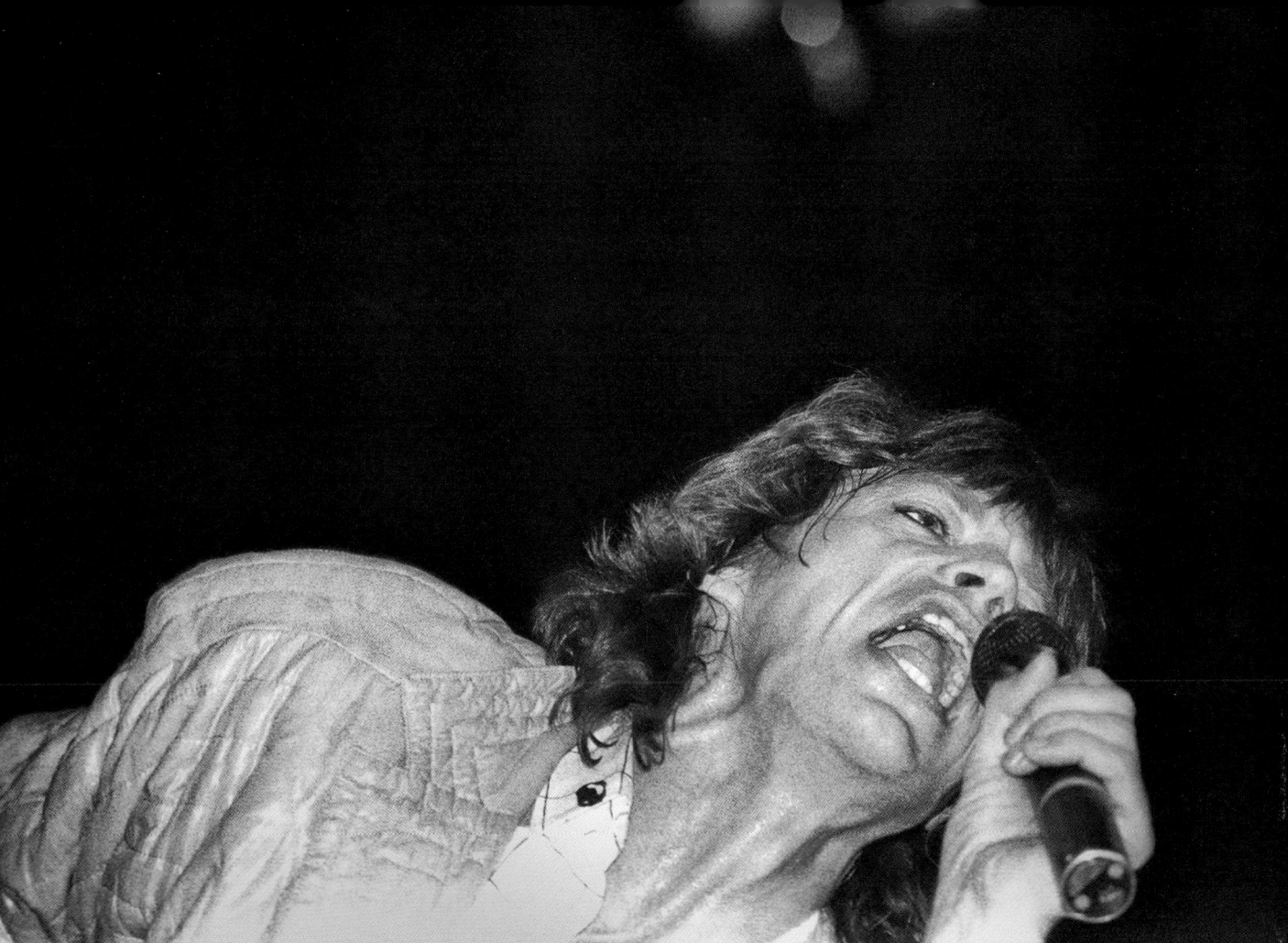

for his new album, *Bush Doctor*. Tosh was doing solo gigs in small joints during the tour, and the headlining act sometimes joined him onstage or played by themselves under assumed names. Rumors were widespread that the band would play with Tosh during his Cabooze show on July 9, the night before the Stones' date at the Civic Center. It made sense. They'd played Chicago the day before.

I was pretty much broke and just barely freelancing in '78, but I had yet to see the Stones live because I had not lived near any place they played until I moved to Minneapolis in '76. So, I gave plasma for two hours at some local Dracula-mobile and earned enough money to buy a ticket. Then I talked my way into the Cabooze for the Tosh gig, since I sort of knew the woman selling tickets, Merritt Campbell, who had connections to the Cranstons, Willie and the Bees, and other bands that her then-husband, Charlie (aka Woodchuck), booked occasionally.

There were maybe a couple hundred people inside, many who had heard the Stones rumor, and many who had not. Tosh had barely started

Mick Jagger plays to the camera during the Stones' performance at the St. Paul Civic Center. "Only two times in my entire life have my knees ever wobbled while shooting," Helgeson notes. "This shot of Jagger in my face, and that Paul McCartney photo backstage in Iowa."

performing when Mick and Keith discreetly came out from behind a curtain at the back of the stage and sat somewhat inconspicuously behind the drum kit as Tosh and company worked through some early numbers.

Somebody walked by me and reported that Charlie Watts and his wife were in the rear of the place. It was on! Then the media provided the buzzkill. A reporter from Channel 5, KSTP-TV, went on the air and reported live from in front of the Cabooze that, ladies and gentlemen, the Rolling Stones were going to play. Within minutes, the club was filled to capacity, and they had to stop letting people in. But it didn't stop the barbarians at the gates; pretty soon you could hear footsteps clomping on the *roof* of the building, sounding like a herd of wild horses (sorry, dear Stones fans).

Mick and Keith vanished as quickly as they had appeared, and ditto for Mr. and Mrs. Watts. There were reported parking-lot sightings of Ron Wood, Bill Wyman, and the two Ians, Stewart and McLagan, the group's reliable guns for hire on keyboards. Had the Rolling Stones played, there would have been a bloody good riot, real news, good copy.

You don't need a Capote, or even a middle-market rock critic, to know that *Some Girls* is miles beyond *Tattoo You*—and the concert off that tour was a much better live show, too. The Tattoo gigs were also rumored to be the band's last tour. Obviously, it wasn't. The band played in Minnesota six times between 1981 and 2015, including their outdoor concert at TCF Bank Stadium (also rumored to be the end of the road), and they're coming ashore for yet another US romp in 2019. They don't need the money; they just love to play, it seems. Is rock 'n' roll their fountain of youth?

Whatever their reasons for still getting onstage, the Stones' longevity might also have something to do with their deep blues roots, the music they grew up loving, the hallowed R&B nuggets they covered throughout their long run, stuff most of us in America had to discover secondhand via the Brits. But thank God they did it. Many fans would never have been exposed to the original R&B culture that inspired their rock heroes. Still, the racist system that made the Stones rich and famous shackled their predecessors. It's a nagging contradiction that the history of popular music will never rectify with any satisfaction, no matter how many R&B covers the Stones end up recording or playing live before their gig is really up.

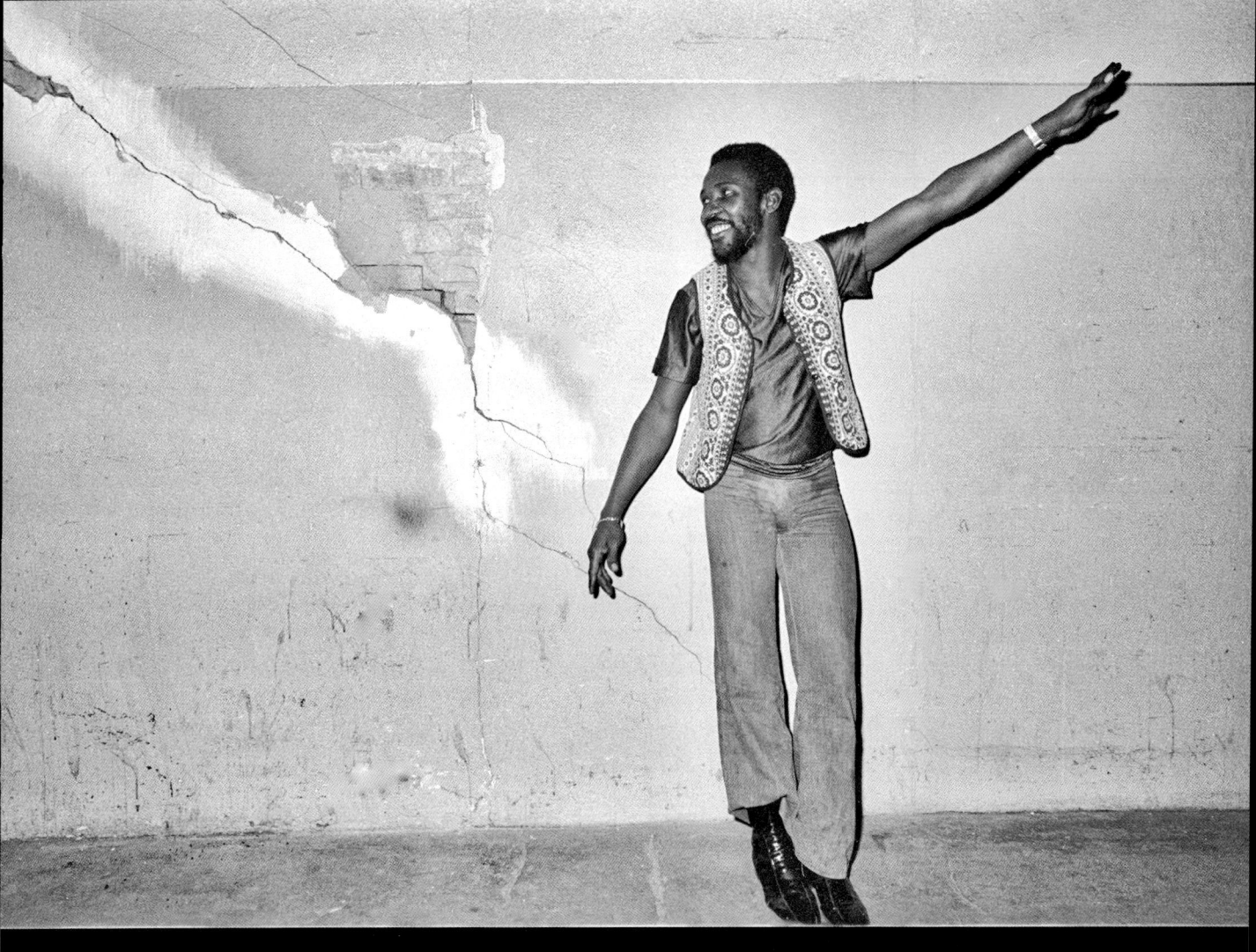

Toots Hibbert of Toots and the Maytals, one of the first wave of reggae bands to play the states after Bob Marley and the Wailers

BOB MARLEY AND THE WAILERS

Of Black Bibles, Vexed Earth, and Shredded Time

Bob Dylan admitted in my 1983 interview with him that Bob Marley was one of the artists in his lifetime that he regretted never meeting. Then, in 2017, David Letterman, who has interviewed nearly every marquee name, including Dylan, made the same confession. So how did a couple of punko journalist newbies like Helgeson and me, working in the alt-newspaper tradition of the seventies and eighties, score a Bob Marley interview for a relatively new monthly music rag called *Sweet Potato*? It wasn't that easy, given that we were not A-list media and were working in the hinterlands and for what could have been a farm journal about sweet spuds.

While Marley and the Wailers were on their 1979 Survival tour, Helgeson and I got a rare chance to spend a considerable amount of time with the artist whose picture hangs in many Jamaican homes, a local legend and hero. We earned our access after reassuring an Island Records' publicist in New York, at least twice, that *Sweet Potato* really was a bona fide music publication (one that had put Black Uhuru on a recent cover, featuring the hot Jamaican "riddim" section of Sly Dunbar and Robbie Shakespeare).

We attended the band's gig at the University of Minnesota's Northrop Auditorium and the sound check earlier that day, and we followed with an interview session the next afternoon in Marley's hotel room, a penthouse suite on the top floor of the Radisson Hotel in downtown St. Paul, overlooking the mighty Mississippi River. Then Greg accompanied him and a Warner Bros. rep to a record store for a meet and greet on day three.

We had unsupervised access to Marley and the band during sound check, and the Wailers all seemed in a good mood. Greg saw band members walking into Northrop with grocery bags filled with ganja, big stashes of the sacred Rasta herb ushered into the university building like takeout food. He joked that they were rolling joints the size of a rolled-up Sunday newspaper.

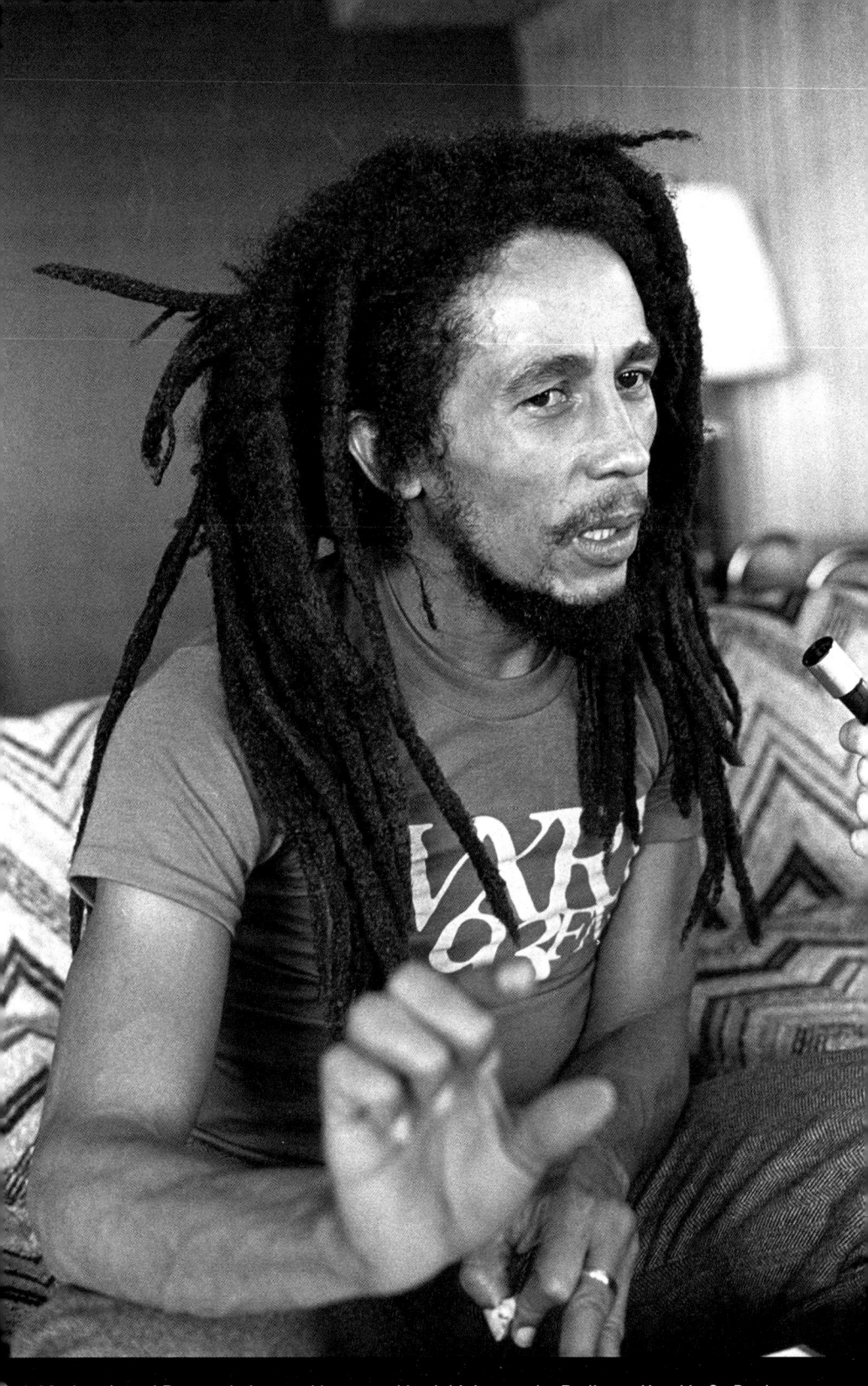

Bob Marley shared Rasta wisdom and its sacred herb high atop the Radisson Hotel in St. Paul.

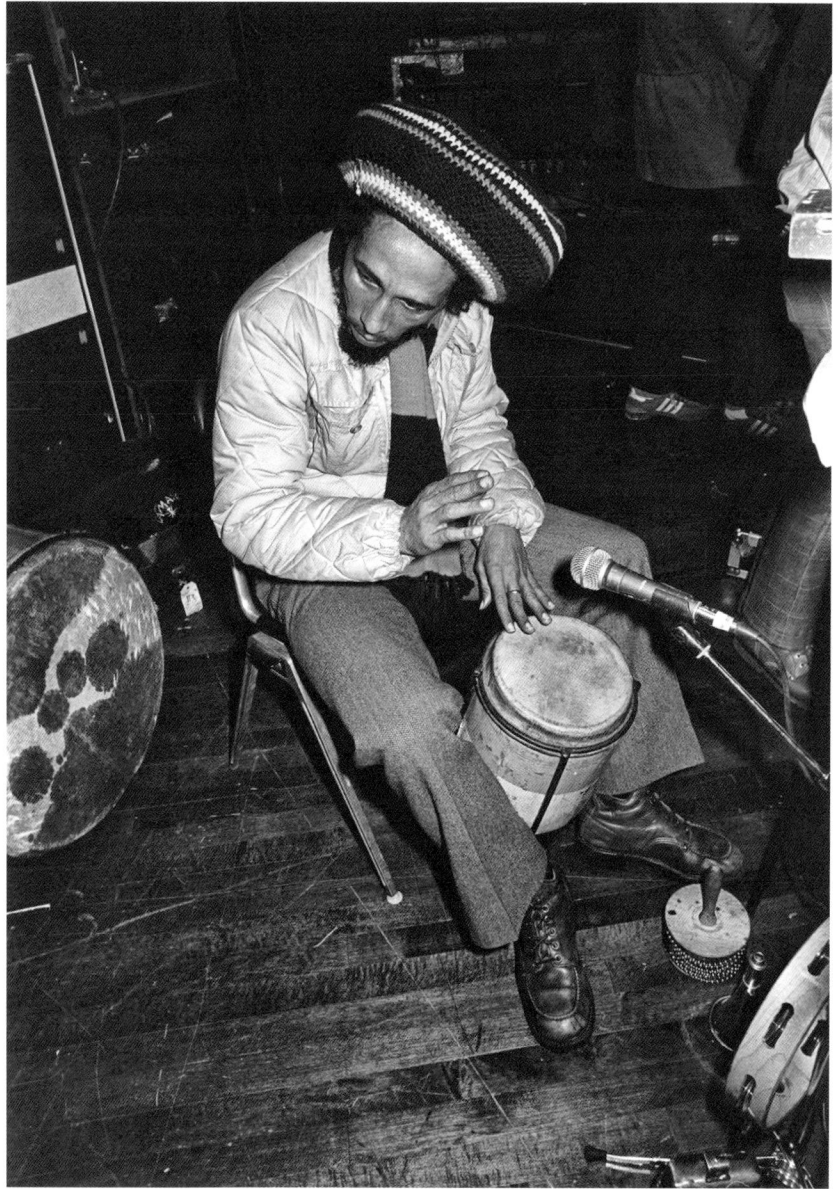

Bongo Bob doing sound check backstage at Northrop Auditorium before his concert with the Wailers in 1979.

In a poorly lit backstage area, Bob begrudgingly posed for Greg, who tried to get the best light setting on his camera, amidst a bunch of percussion instruments. He also flirted with Pauline from Schon Productions, who was minding the area and was in charge of catering (although the group ate their own prepared food, mostly curries). Marley sang a verse of the Hank Williams classic "Hey, Good Lookin'" to her with a wide smile, his dreads tucked up under his cap. "Whatcha got cookin'?"

As sound check got underway, the young British roadies, who used the n-word to describe the "n-food" they were subject to smelling at every stop, scattered to plugs and amplifiers just before the bottom of reality dropped out of Northrop Auditorium.

In Timothy White's definitive 2006 Marley biography, *Catch a Fire: The Life of Bob Marley*, there is frequent talk of "magic" around Bob and the Rastafarians that White encountered, inexplicable realities that to materialistic, science-worshipping westerners do not fit accepted paradigms. The photo guy and I never anticipated experiencing it ourselves.

After about twenty minutes of jamming during sound check—after a Rasta prayer huddle—the Wailers' heavy sound shifted so dramatically that it stopped me as I strolled through the auditorium. Even the little racist roadie bastards scurrying about onstage halted in their tracks. A groove so pronounced yet indescribable materialized from nowhere, emanating from the players onstage but coming from someplace else entirely.

It was an undulating rhythm that lasted twenty seconds, maybe—although time ceased to exist in those moments. The sound seemed to shred time-space. I have thought about it many times over the years and can never imagine hearing it again. To paraphrase Shakespeare's *Hamlet*, "Time was out of joint." Was this a real *Rastaman Vibration* that the group sang about? It's convenient to say it was, but how would we ever know? It enveloped the whole of Northrup like a mystic groove.

The concert later that night delivered everything one could expect from this powerful artist and grippingly flawless band. The balcony literally bounced to the rhythms as the second-floor audience danced in place.

The next day, I casually mentioned that ethereal sound check moment to Marley as we started the interview. I got a small grin and a "Yeah, mon," but nothing more.

The Jamaican superstar was gregarious and generous, giving us two and a half hours of his time. The interview quickly became a hazy dialogue clouded with the vapors of the herb being shared, a slow-burning joint the size of a nice banana. Smoke as thick as Marley's patois filled the room. The experience gave a whole new meaning to the phrase "high atop the Radisson Hotel."

The friendly, informal chatter ranged from discussions about music and the tour to topics more esoteric and apocalyptic. Bob talked about "the black Bible," a reading of the Good Book as sort of a living, historical cosmic horoscope. Asked to explain, he said if I was born in December, I would read the Bible from the perspective of Joseph, sold into slavery by his brothers in the Old Testament, that his story line was my story line into the rest of the New Testament.

At one point, he chided rock stars for "always singin' about pussy," with a look of both scorn and bemusement on his face. Eventually, the subject of the "end times" came up. Marley grew more serious, and it was clear that this was a topic he had spent much time considering. Oh, mon,

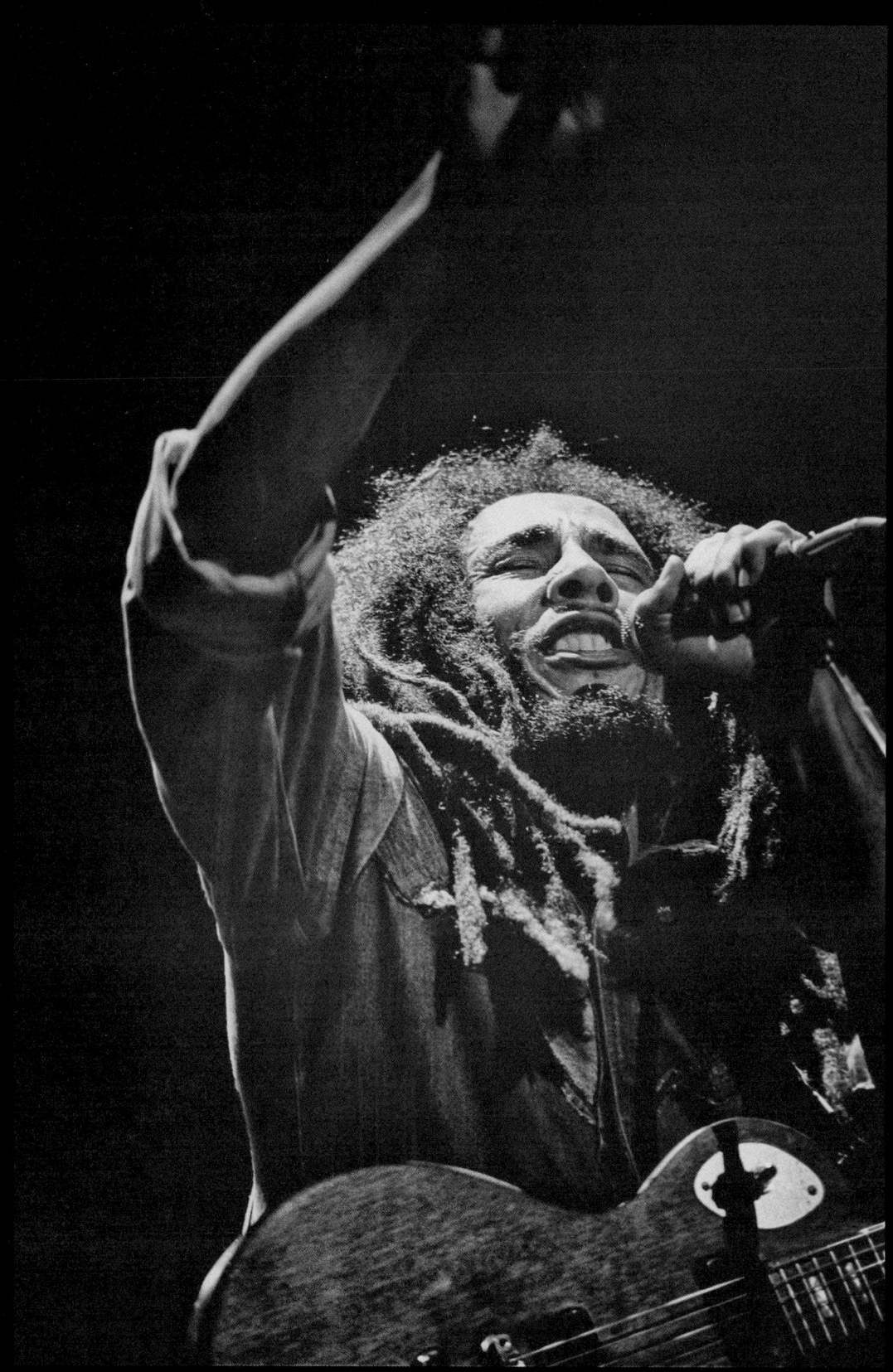

Lively up yourselves, Marley commands!

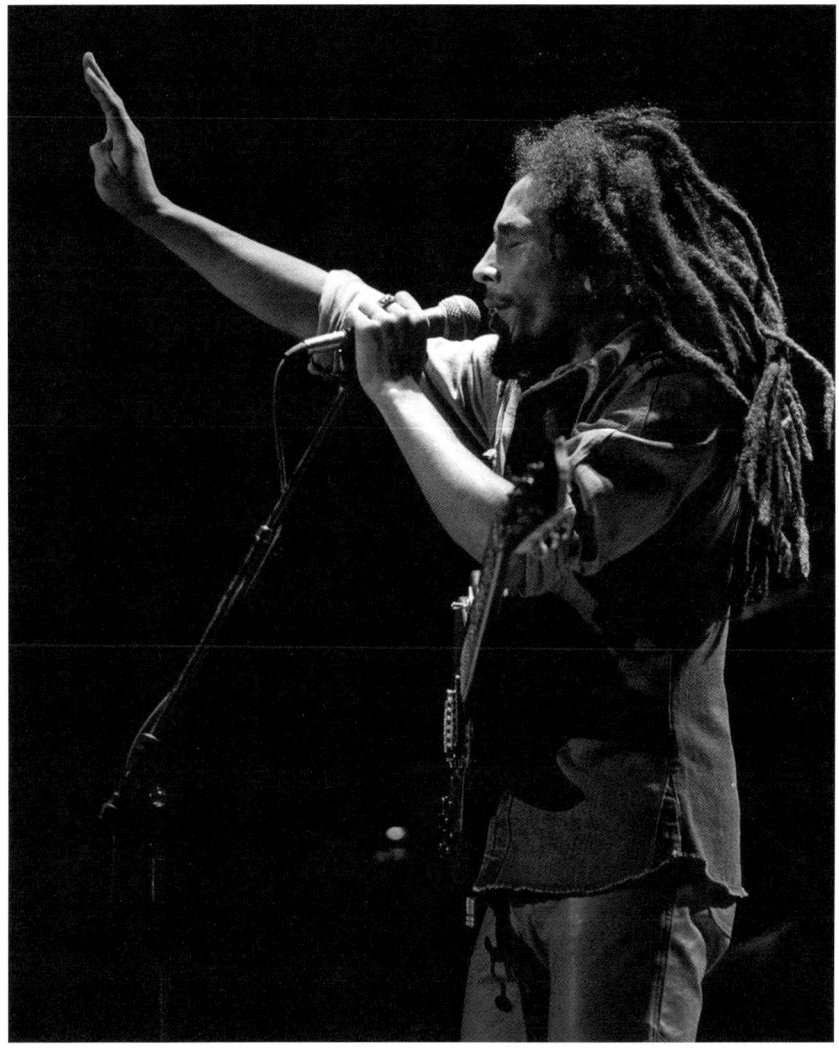

Marley stirs it up in concert during a three-day stay in the Twin Cities in '79.

Earth be vexing itself, earthquakes and upheavals. He stopped abruptly and nodded silently, like he had already shared too much.

As we wound down our time with him and thanked him again, he strolled to the penthouse window and looked out on the river below. When told it was the Mississippi River, he seemed surprised and elated. "That's it?! That's the Mississippi?" He stood in awe of it as we packed up quietly and left his orbit.

When Bob Marley died in May 1981 from cancer and we were trying to figure out how to handle his death in the paper (by this time *City Pages*), we thought of running the 1979 interview again. But the editor, Randy Anderson, nixed that idea, saying the interview was incoherent and all over the place.

Yeah, mon, it could be seen that way.

PAUL AND LINDA MCCARTNEY

A Beatle. A Press Conference. And a Scolding.

They had not been a band on the run for thirteen years. So, when Helgeson and I were offered the opportunity to cover the Paul and Linda McCartney concert in Ames, Iowa, on July 18, 1990, for the *Twin Cities Reader*, we turned into our sixth-grade Beatles-fan selves. With his new post-Wings group, Macca was playing Beatles songs for the first time since the Fabs broke up.

Of course, we would have to share him and Linda and their posh band with a horde of roughly forty fellow journalists (including one from the *Iowa Farmer*) and photogs at the preconcert press conference. We would also have to decide how much space to give to the controversy that was set in motion by the outspoken vegetarian couple among livestock producers, who were outraged that PETA was an official component of the show and that a rabble-rousing vegetarian was in their midst. The day of the show, a few farmers from nearby Keota, Iowa, leafleted the crowd with messaging right out of Nowheresville: "Adolf Hitler was a notorious vegetarian. . . . Paul McCartney has led young people down the path of drug usage. . . . Animal worship and drugs go hand in hand with most forms of Satanism. Now it's beginning to destroy food producers." Junior's Farm would never be the same, it seemed.

The foray into pork and beef country was all part of the vast Paul Mc-Cartney World Tour that began in September 1989. The spur into Ames at Cyclone Stadium the following summer also featured an official announcement from Iowa State University: it would begin offering the Paul and Linda McCartney Endowed Scholarship for an incoming student who wanted to study environmental issues.

I was freelancing again at the time, balancing the occasional feature story with newly found publicity projects, which included a few for Steven "Funkytown" Greenberg.

Greenberg got wind of our impending trip and offered to drive—and

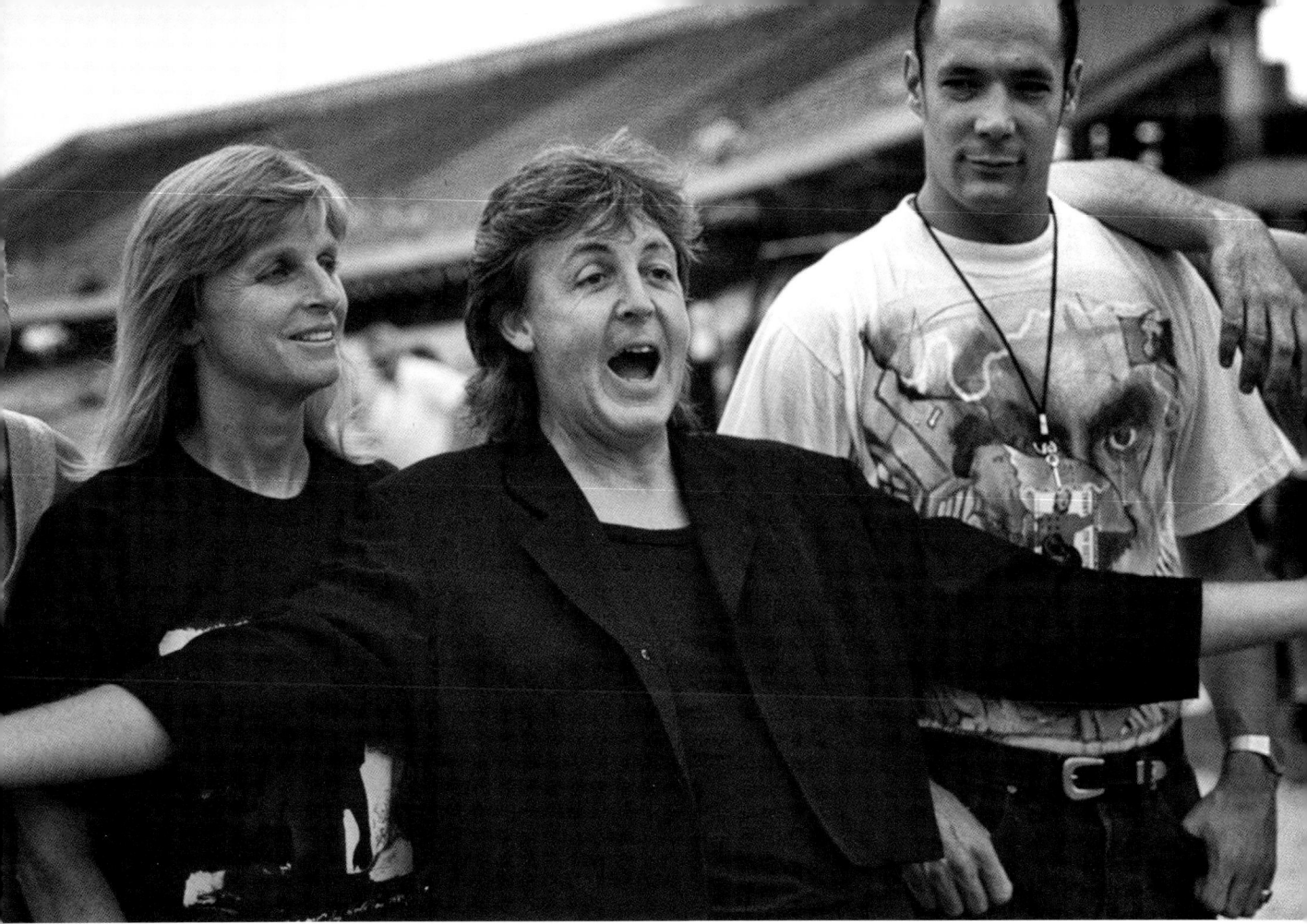

how could we refuse? He had a super nice Mercedes-Benz, equipped with newfangled roaming car-phone technology that looked like something Maxwell Smart would use. And he brought along a snazzy, state-of-the art video camera to capture the trip.

Soon, three eager fanboys were cruising 35W South into the heart of farm country, guessing at the set list and seriously pondering, "How much solo stuff vs. Wings material vs. Beatles tunes?" (Sixteen out of twenty-eight, it turned out.) Other Minnesotans were also en route in pursuit of nah-nah-nah-nah, Hey Jude bliss, surely debating these very same questions. Passengers in a few passing cars held homemade signs indicating they were still crazy about the cute Beatle.

Once in Ames, we got our media laminates and hung out in the rear of the stadium outside the facility where we could hear Paul rockin' some old classics for sound check. Greg later went off and managed to capture a photo of the McCartneys with keyboardist Paul "Wix" Wickens as the trio walked to the press conference in a nearby building. It was the only candid shot he would get, save for some performance stuff that everyone

An incurable ham, Paul McCartney mugs offstage at Cyclone Stadium in Ames, Iowa, flanked by keyboardists Linda McCartney and Paul "Wix" Wickens, in July 1990.

else was also shooting. No photos were allowed during the presser. And, as we would discover the hard way, no rogue video, either.

Somehow, I got to the first row and was asked to launch the first question to Paul. All kinds of people were walking to the dais with him: university officials, security dudes, handlers some ten deep. An entourage worthy of an ex-Beatle, I guess. The handlers parted, and Paul sat by himself near a lovely flower bouquet.

I hadn't really prepared any tough questions, or any questions really, thinking I'd probably never get to ask one. And I had barely gotten my notebook out of my bag when the press conference started. But when you're fifteen feet away from Paul McCartney and he points his finger at you and says, "this guy right here," you gotta deliver something.

"So, you've been to America quite a bit over the decades," I began. "How do you see it this time around?" It was a mushy, open-ended idea of a question, half baked. He kind of shrugged and said something like, "It's good, I like it. I like America, I like Americans. I mean, I married one, you know." Chuckles rippled among the press corps and at the big table. He still had that boyish, aw-shucks charm, and he turned it up and down as needed throughout the half-hour period. When fending off the inevitable question about meat vs. veggies, he presented the press with a big hammy money quote for the afternoon: "Look, we haven't come out on this tour to preach against meat. I mean, I'm pro-corn. How's that? I'm very pro-corn."

As soon as I finished my question, I turned around to see Greenberg, who was standing about fifteen rows back and off against a wall, with the video camera on his shoulder. I put my index finger in the air and twirled it clockwise a few times to indicate that he should roll tape. I also saw a worried look come over Mac's face as he eyeballed one of the security hands up front. He flashed another look in the direction of Greenberg, who was soon being asked to put the camera down by a very large man who could have been a Blue Meanie from Pepperland.

Great, I thought, *here's where we get tossed, our lifetime fandom privileges are revoked, and we miss the concert entirely.* Plus, the old man would probably take away the car keys, too.

Greenberg's offense was that he wasn't with the pool of other video shooters in the back of the room with their tripods set up. But they let us stay. After more questions rang out from fellow scribes assembled in the room, McCartney glanced over at me again. I thought he was looking for another question, so I floated one: "How much rap do you listen to? Do you like it?"

"Ah, let's have others have a turn," he scolded, cocking an eyebrow at me before looking out among the many hands in the air. When somebody started asking about the lost notes in "Day Tripper," one of Paul's aides leaned into a mic and said, "We should probably wrap this up." McCartney recollected that all the notes on the record were still there, or something smart like that, as he got up and thanked everyone. It was then that I reached into my bag and pulled out a copy of Prince's *Black Album*, which had just gone out to media in the Twin Cities. I walked toward the front where Paul was about to exit, hoisted the album into the air, and yelled, "Prince's *Black Album*," offering it to him as he looked over his shoulder. He couldn't hear me, however, and was soon engulfed in entourage.

A younger bloke from the entourage—with long, curly hair and facial stubble who seemed to step out of an era from twenty years earlier—had heard me and came over. I asked him to give the album to Paul, one of the geniuses behind the mighty *White Album*, explaining it was the (soon-to-be-forbidden) underground *Black Album* by Prince. He clasped my shoulder, smiled, and said politely, "Sure, mate. Thank you."

Mildly anticipating that I might get a simple thank-you note back— even from his secretary if not Paul himself—I had written my name and address on a note and stuffed it inside the cover, signing it, "A Fellow Vegahoovian" (which I was, but not nearly as strict as the McCartneys).

Did he ever get the album? Not sure. Doubtful, really. Who knows? Mail's been pretty slow and spotty from England since the nineties, with the explosion of the internet and all. The thank-you note is probably caught up somewhere with those missing notes from "Day Tripper."

THE CHIEFTAINS, PLUS ONE

Homage to a Legendary Music Publicist, Charles Comer

There is an art to getting people to do things. And proof of that lies in part in Helgeson's screwball photo of a few members of the world-renowned Irish folk group the Chieftains, horsing around at the Helg's request while in Minneapolis for a concert. Anyone who knows Helgeson knows he's not a pushy guy; he's a polite lad from Redwood Falls with a reticence he blames on his Norwegian ancestry. But he's managed to get any number of rockers, comics, artists, and other celebrities and near-celebrities to do things you think they would immediately walk away from. Here, he charmed a busy group on tour with limited time to clown in a big way.

The plucky Irish band almost single-handedly elevated traditional Irish music to the plateaus of popular music. Paddy Moloney's lead uilleann pipes—full of merriment one minute and mourning the next—and Derek Bell's delectable harp playing blend smoothly with fiddle, flute, bodhran, tin whistle, and bones. The group could sound ancient, otherworldly, and contemporary—sometimes all at once. And they had a contagious sense of humor that spilled from the stage—and in this case, to the street for this peculiar photo shoot.

Other proof of the friendly art of persuasion lies with the Chieftains' famous publicist, Charles Comer, who generated more media coverage for clients in his lifetime than a dozen PR flaks combined ever will. The Liverpool native was a natural "pitchman," a born raconteur, and simply a delightful human to talk to, although he invariably did most of the talking.

When I was on the other side of the desk writing stories, my colleagues and I often viewed publicists as a necessary distraction. These annoying interlopers would call at inopportune times pushing stories at you about "product" and groups you didn't care about. Don't get me wrong: there were, and are, a lot of smart, solid PR people out there in the music world (many of them former music writers, and I became one myself!), but some

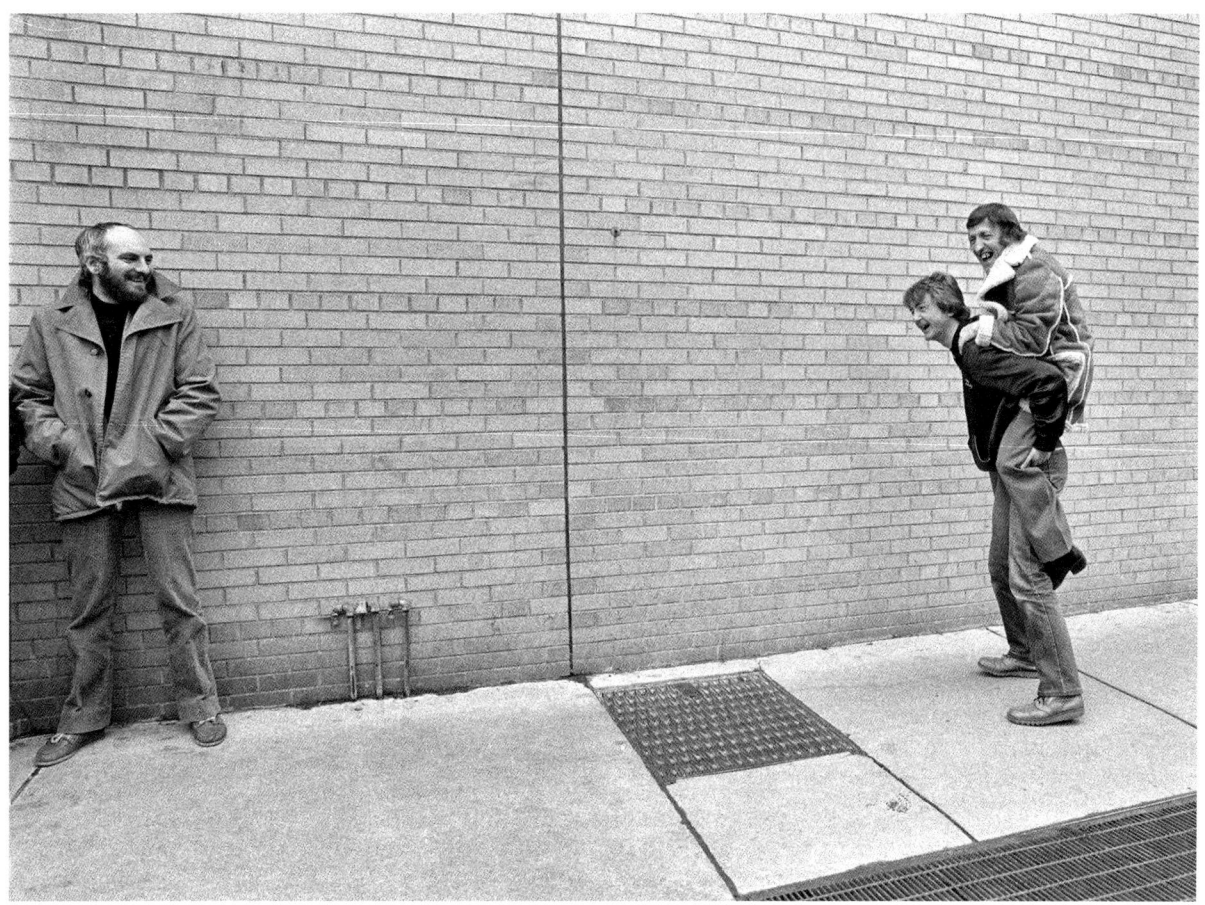

often appeared to be mere company men and women who expressed almost no passion for, or insights about, the artists they were hustling. This was not the case with Charlie.

"Well, you know, Martin, how are you, it's Charlie Comer calling. Of course, you know the lads are coming your way again. I don't know if you heard, but Paddy has been very busy, yes! Very busy! He's setting up to play with Garcia from the Dead, and that ought to be quite the session! Yes, can you imagine?!" And that was just his opening salvo. With a British accent that still had Liverpool traces, Charlie's friendly voice was one I looked forward to hearing, and if I missed his call, I always rang him back.

With his renowned joie de vivre and insider savvy, Comer shrewdly told you just enough new information that wasn't on the official press release to get you hooked. When he was finished with you, there was a pretty good chance—given the long touring itinerary of a band like the Chieftains—he would be making ten more calls like the one he just made to others around the country, probably all before noon and maybe as many or more after lunch.

The Helg convinces two of the six Chieftains—Paddy Moloney (top) and Kevin Conneff—to pony up outside the WCCO-TV building in Minneapolis in March 1980.

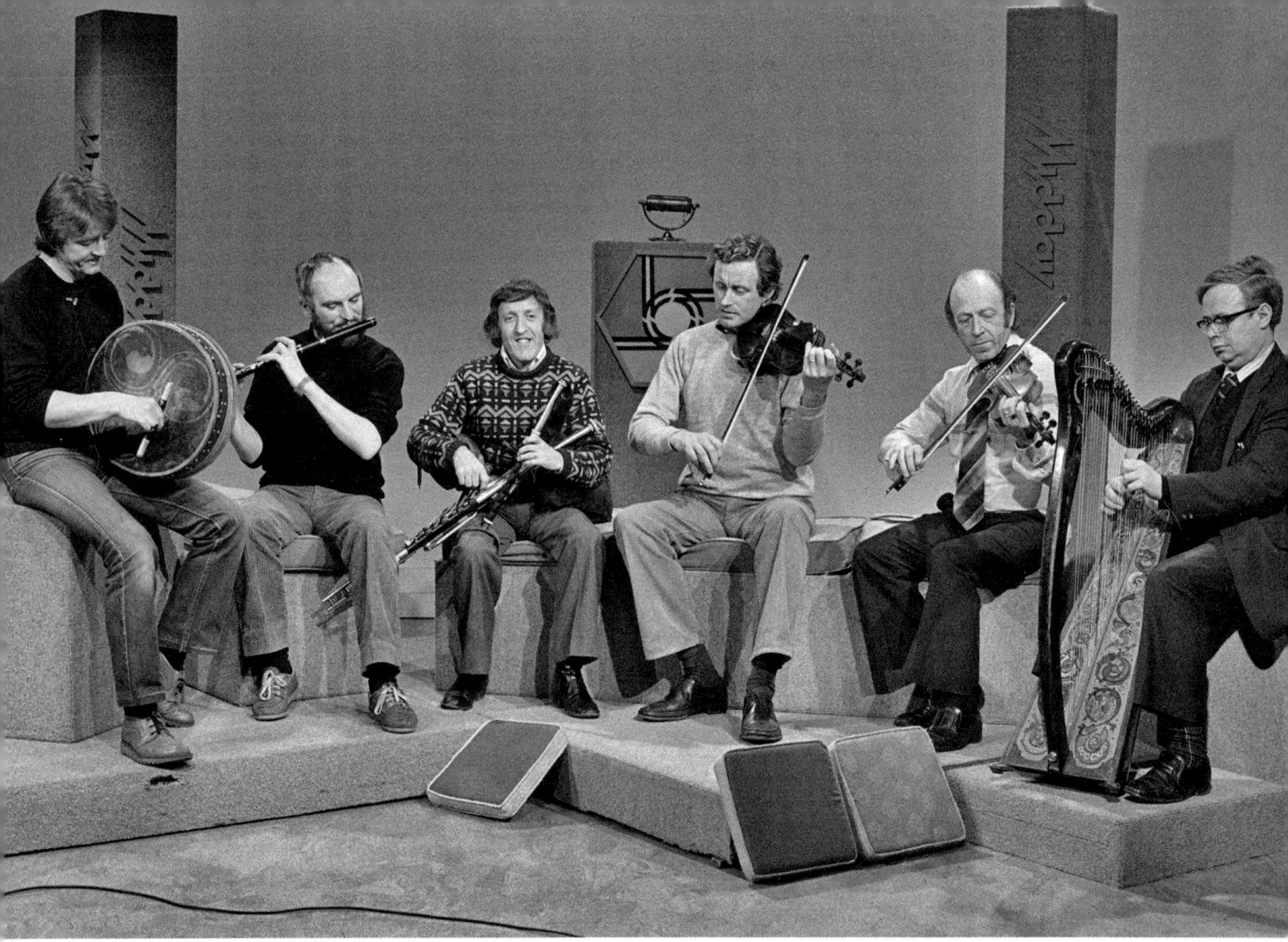

The traditional Irish folk group could sound ancient, otherworldly, and contemporary—sometimes all at once.

When Comer died suddenly in 2011 in New York at age sixty-four, the music industry lost a luminary whose work behind the scenes was known to very few outside of the biz. The writers and broadcast producers who worked with him surely also felt the sting of this loss, knowing those excitable and entertaining Comer calls would not come again.

His obituaries touted his work with an elite client list that included the Beatles, the Stones, the Bee Gees, the Who, Grace Jones, Stevie Ray Vaughan, Bob and Rita Marley, Peter Tosh, Marianne Faithfull, actors Peter O'Toole, Richard Harris, and others. *Billboard* editor Tim White quoted Chris Blackwell, founder of Island Records, Marley's label, about the role Comer played when Marley was shot in Jamaica in 1976. In his press release, Comer "termed it 'an assassination attempt,' thereby elevating Marley to the stature of presidents and popes."

The *Irish Echo*—the New York–based publication that claims to be the "oldest Irish American newspaper in USA, established in 1928"—likewise had a tidy summation of Charlie's brilliant career, noting, "Through disco, early rock and roll into reggae, and then Irish traditional music, Comer moved smoothly through the genres, as comfortable promoting the Who's 1981 first farewell performance as he was with lifting the Celtic Beats to next level."

"One of his earliest public relations coups," the paper explained, "came in 1963 with Sam Leach, when they got the job of promoting the Beatles' first album, *Meet the Beatles!*. They dubbed the band's sound 'The Mersey Beat,' a term that entered the rock and roll lexicon to describe the first wave of the 'British Invasion.'" Beatles manager Brian Epstein later hired Comer to promote their first US visit in 1964.

Was Comer as formidable as many indicated when remembering the man who often proclaimed he was in love with show business? According to the *Echo*, he was all that and more: "Mary Ryan of American Celtic Television said Comer was loved and feared at the same time, because he could make or break a career. 'He had the magic necessary for the spell of success,' she said."

He sure had a way. Decades later, I can still hear Charlie's warm voice bending my ear about the release of Peter Tosh's first album.

"Well, you know, Martin, you probably heard by now, Tosh is coming for a US tour, with the new album, and I'm sure you would like to speak with him. He doesn't like to fly, you know, he calls it the aluminum bird." He cackled heartily. "Give the record a listen, if you haven't already, and get back to me about that interview. He's only doing a few of these, you know. Okay for now."

Mr. Comer, you had me at "Well, you know."

U2

Like Hobbits Strayed Too Far from the Shire

They all fit on a queen-sized bed: Bono, the Edge (pre–stocking cap), Larry Mullen, and Adam Clayton. Barely twenty and making a stop at First Avenue (then called Sam's) during their second US tour in April 1981, they looked like Hobbits who had strayed too far from the shire. The Helg and I commandeered the second bed in the room, a rather dreary offering at the Normandy Inn. While Greg held off clicking any shots of them in the cramped space, we began talking. Rather, Bono talked mostly—born with the gift of gab, as they say, and he's never stopped. The others deferred to him on nearly all questions but occasionally jumped in or muttered agreement. They seemed extremely shy. Somehow in our hour-plus conversation, we got onto talking druids and Catholicism.

The band's debut album, *Boy*, had been released about six months earlier, in October 1980. It featured the infallible and eternal single "I Will Follow"—as great a rock tune that Ireland or any land mass has ever produced. Did U2 seem like they would become world rock superstars? Personally, I never imagined they would achieve success on the scale they have today, although that scale didn't really exist in the early eighties. Only a handful of elite rock bands, like the Stones, the Grateful Dead, and Led Zeppelin, could fill stadiums and large arenas. In many ways, the evolution of the rock arena show evolved with U2 and their inspired stage designer of thirty-five-plus years, Willie Williams. Sometimes the spectacle of the U2 stage could detract from the impact of the music, but it also could amplify the music in ways you didn't get from listening to it on record or radio.

But I wasn't thinking about the boyish lads from the isle like that as they sat humbly on the hotel bed, while punk-rock and new-wave bands were sprouting everywhere.

We wrapped up the interview session and followed the band to the club for sound check. They ran a bunch of riffs, and Greg snapped photos,

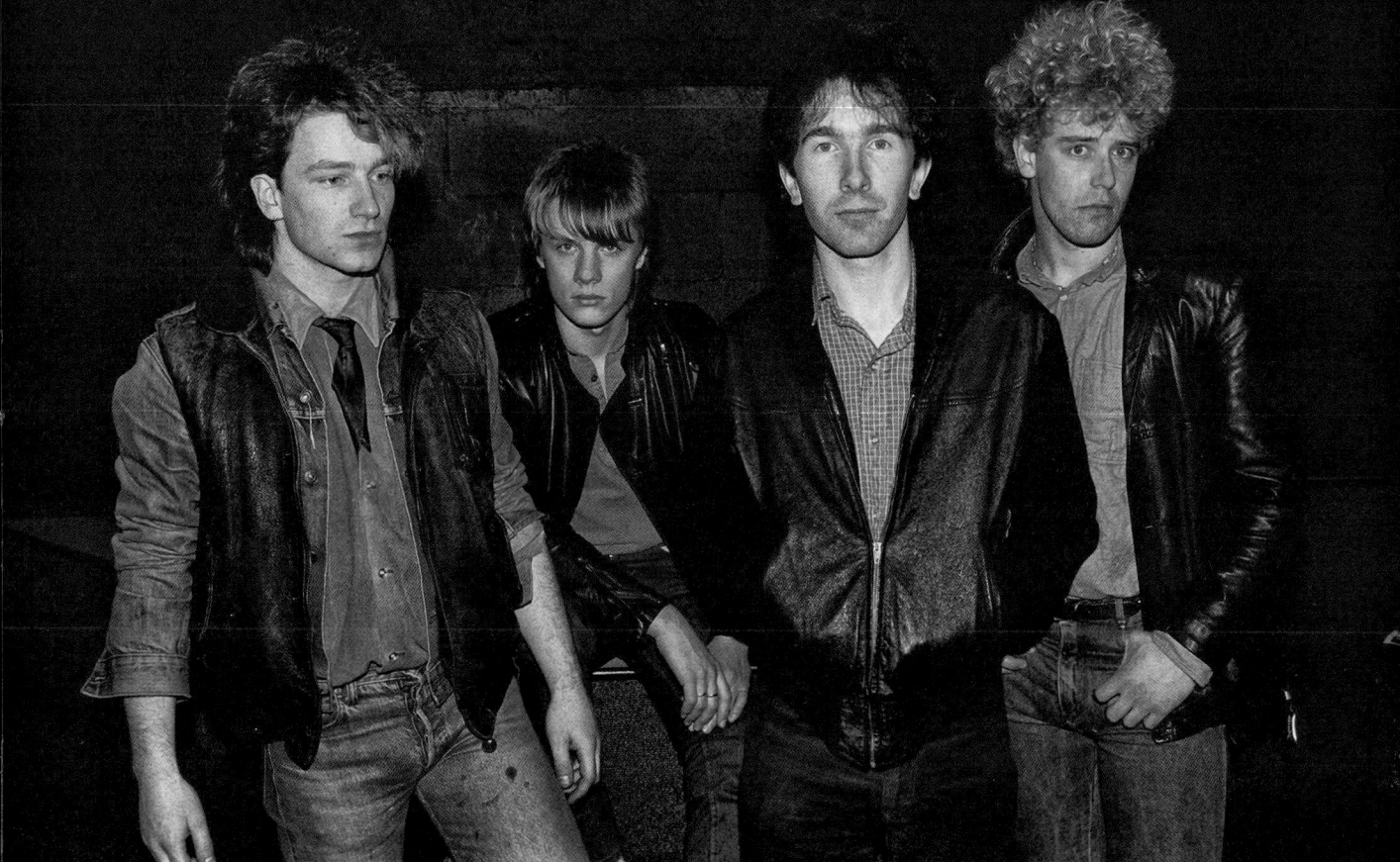

and I hung out near the main floor bar, watching and listening. That night, their set list was short, just eleven songs, plus four for the encore, including three they had already played ("I Will Follow," "The Ocean," and "11 O'clock Tick Tock"). That perplexed and bemused some in the audience, who figured that's all they knew how to play.

The sound check, though, went on for a couple hours or more as the band ran through songs from the album and then jammed on a variety of mostly instrumental numbers that were unrecognizable but sounded very good. A year later, after they released their second album, *October*, Bono told another music writer that they had written much of the new album during sound check at Sam's. Over the years, I've learned that many groups and solo artists work the same way, making good use of time on the road to build riffs, bridges, and whole tunes.

Today, Sir Bono, who is knighted, has become something of a high priest, promoting and fundraising for global causes like AIDS, poverty, education, peace, and so on. Not since Louis Armstrong has one world ambassador played the role so well. To these aging ears, Coldplay and Kings

U2 in Minneapolis during their second visit to First Avenue (then known as Sam's) in 1982

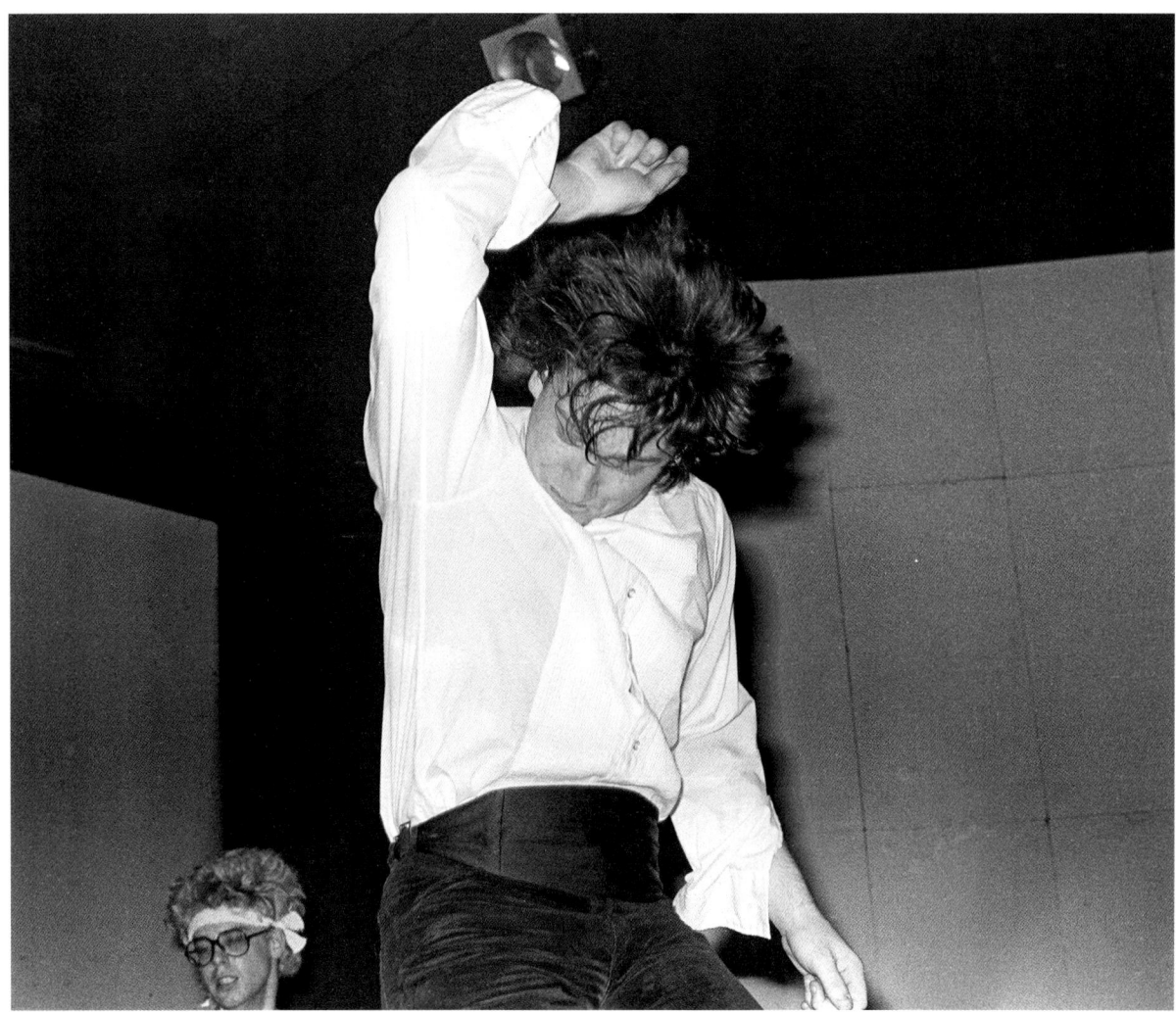

Bono gets into it onstage during a concert at Sam's—years before he became the "ambassador of everything."

of Leon have been consistently writing the kinds of downloadable-radio-stadium-friendly stuff that U2 once had a better handle on. Nonetheless, the band's trajectory remains in high orbit. Their place in the pantheon was assured long ago, well before the Spotifys and Pandoras seized on rock's algorithm.

DEVO

"The Only Hope for Us All Is Mutation"

n-store appearances at record stores seem to be a timeless promotional strategy by bands and labels that fans are still fond of, even in the age of the digital download. They have survived the Spotifycation of "the star-maker machinery behind the popular song" (thank you, Joni Mitchell), providing that increasingly rare, real-life one-on-one contact between human beings, however fleeting.

Back in 1981, a local Warner Bros. rep brought the lads from Devo to Shirley's Diner at Lake and Lyndale in south Minneapolis for a meet and greet and brief press conference. The band was kicking off a forty-city tour at the Met Center in Bloomington, and they had a few things to get off their chests first. But, a promo event at a divey Lake Street diner?

Humble, greasy Shirley's was a place the staff of *Sweet Potato/City Pages* knew well, for it was located next door to the building where the *Spud* was produced, before the paper moved downtown to the then-swanky Butler Square building.

The new-wave pioneers arrived at Shirley's wearing their plastic JFK-cum-Ronald Reagan-styled wigs and what Devo cofounder Jerry Casale called "airport-styled workers gear." They soon became engulfed by the devotees gathered at Shirley's to hear the band's pronouncements on the release of the *New Traditionalists* LP. It was a verbal picnic and a controlled lovefest. I'm not sure anyone ate, but there was plenty of platter chatter, mostly by Casale.

Devo had made its first Twin Cities appearance in November 1978 at Walker Art Center, just weeks after finding national exposure from an appearance on *Saturday Night Live.* The band's performance at the Walker was preceded by Chuck Statler's short, aberrant films that served as entertaining and edgy social satire.

Before becoming Devo, the group's founders, Jerry Casale and Mark Mothersbaugh, had embraced a book that a Kent State prof had shared

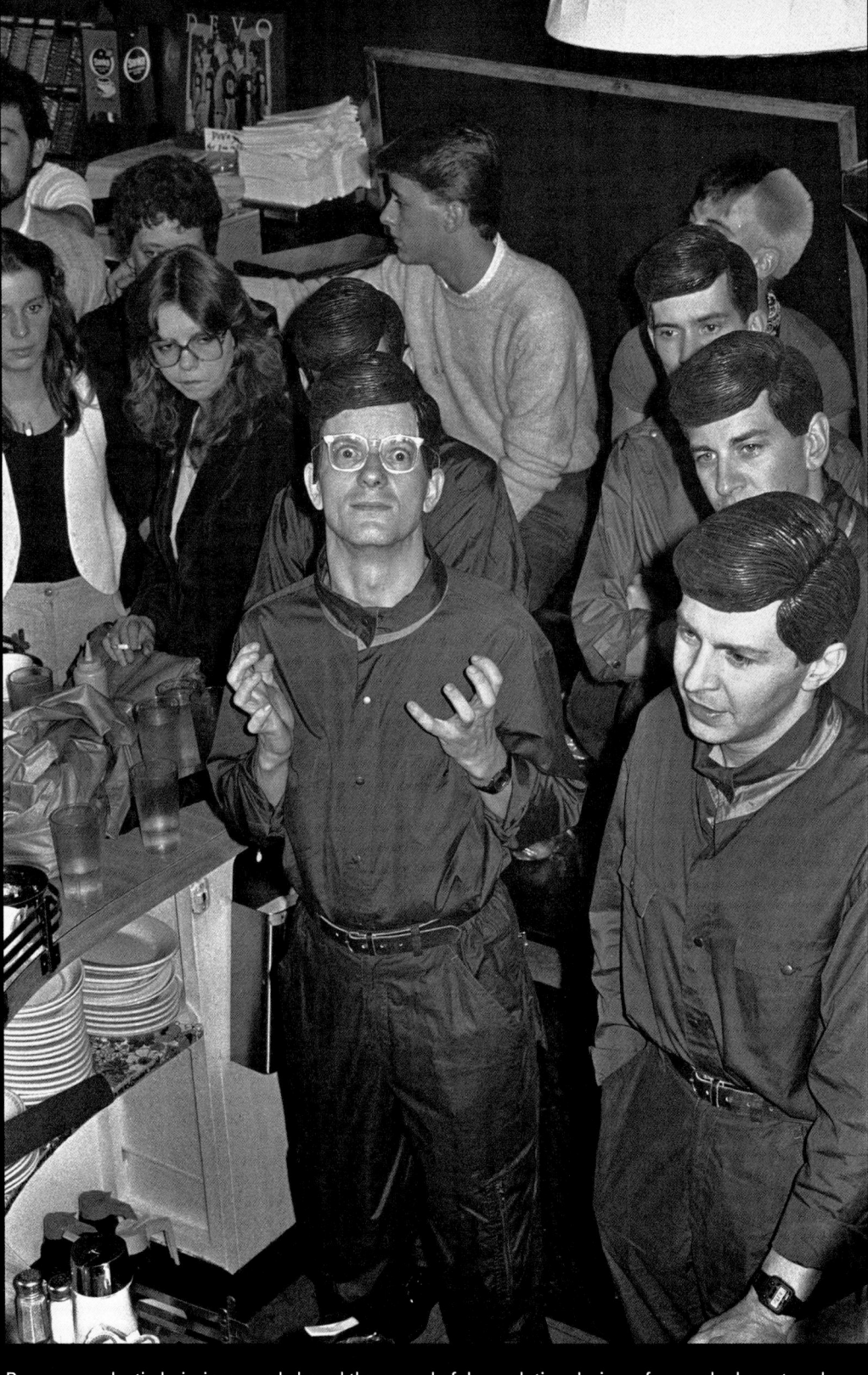

Devo wore plastic hairpieces and shared the gospel of de-evolution during a fan-packed meet-and-greet at Shirley's Diner in Minneapolis.

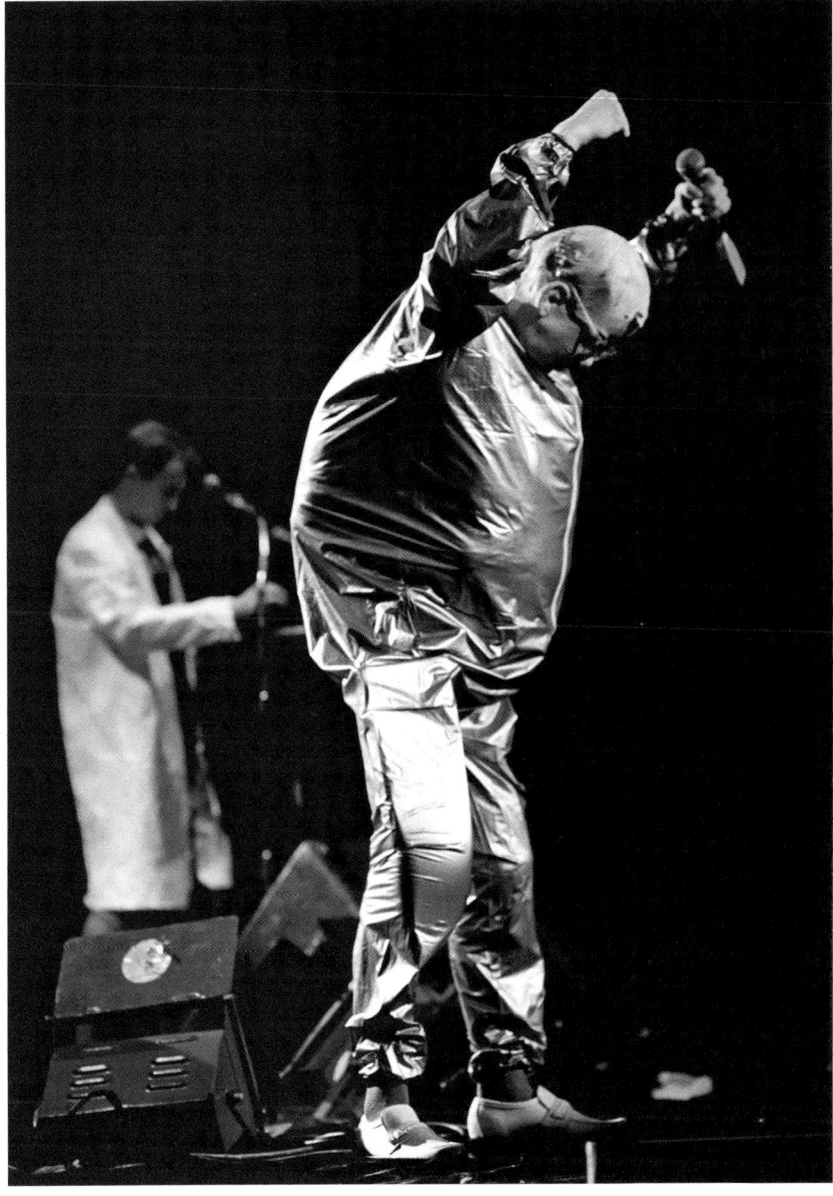

Standing triumphantly defiant onstage at a 1978 concert at Walker Art Center, Mark Mothersbaugh is dressed as the "Booji Boy" character, first introduced in the 1976 Chuck Statler–directed short film *The Truth About De-Evolution*.

with them, *The Beginning Was the End: Man Came Into Being through Cannibalism—Intelligence Can Be Eaten*, which postulated that humans evolved from mutant, brain-eating apes and were spinning backward, not progressing forward to a utopian future. The only hope for us, the book held, was to mutate into something new, something less mechanical and repressive. It was, as they say in marketing, Devo's brand message, and they've been on it with a vengeance, even to the present day.

At the diner, one-liners popped from Casale's lips, with occasional comment by Mothersbaugh and their brothers in the band, Bob 1 and

Bob 2, and drummer Alan Myers. The crowd relished his bon mots and cheered the appraisals he made, some that now seem more prescient than ever, such as his view that "there seems to be a worldwide regressive move back to bankrupt ideas of the past and romantic ideas of a past that in fact never existed. And we're just sick of it."

It got better:

"America has evolved into a corporate-feudal society," Casale said. "The middle class keeps making more money, but it doesn't improve their buying power—they're being squeezed out. They're turning into serfs, and the gap across the moat between them and the people inside the castle continues to widen. And the drawbridge is going up!"

Rolling Stone magazine? "They suck. They became the people they started out hating."

On the music biz: "The market discovered us. We didn't find it."

About using gimmicks to sell their music, Casale asserted that the band was well aware of what it was doing. "We sell our gimmicks through the music. We're the Fisher-Price toy for pop music, and we're very serious about our jokes."

Finally, Casale summed up the Devo creed and its place on the bandstand ruled ultimately by corporate overlords: "We're the court jesters" in the new corporate-feudal society. "We're on the inside. The only hope for all of us," he said with resignation, "is mutation."

It was an illuminating stop at the greasy spoon. Even the long-running Twin Cities public television affairs program *Almanac* showed up to capture fan comment and insights from Tim Holmes, a frequent *Spud* and *City Pages* contributor. Tim's brainiac wheels never stopped turning, and this was a band that accelerated his thinking. He opined that Devo was among the handful of new groups laying the groundwork for "whatever will come after rock 'n' roll." He hoped they would go on to sell a million records.

In fact, Devo went on to sell over 30 million albums, and 1980's *Freedom of Choice* reached platinum status. Looking back at their stylized sound, the singular videos, and the onstage antics, it isn't hard to imagine them in *The Hunger Games* as the house band for the ruling elites in the capital city of Panem, secretly working for the resistance. Poster boys for dystopian rock, they were in on the joke that the joke was on us.

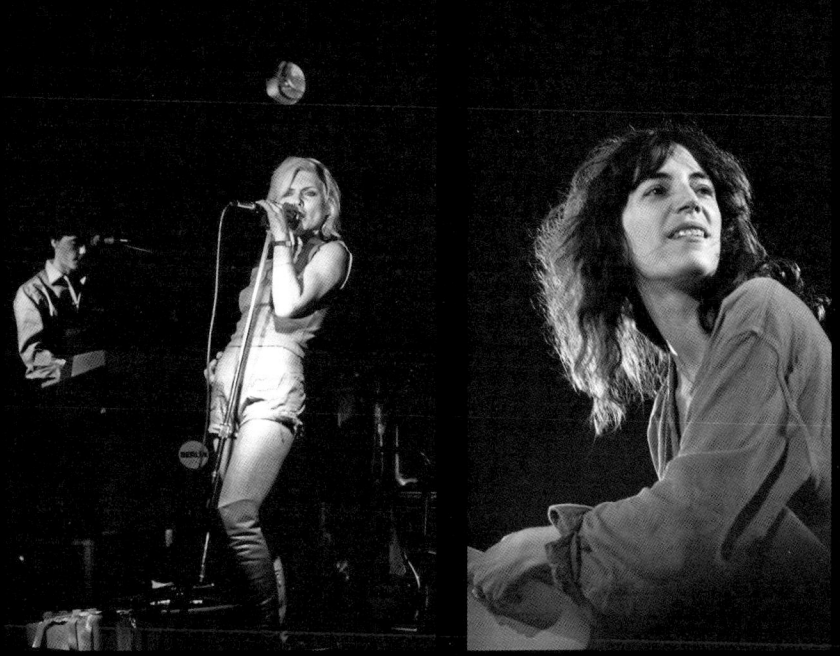

(far left) Probably the most pop-driven band ever to blow out of New York's punk/new-wave scene, Blondie made its Twin Cities debut at the Longhorn Bar. Lead singer Deborah Harry commanded the stage, as per usual.

(left) Rock high priestess Patti Smith takes a rare turn at the piano during a 1979 concert at the St. Paul Theatre. The Helg remembers that she was in a combative mood at the show, throwing beer at the crowd at one point.

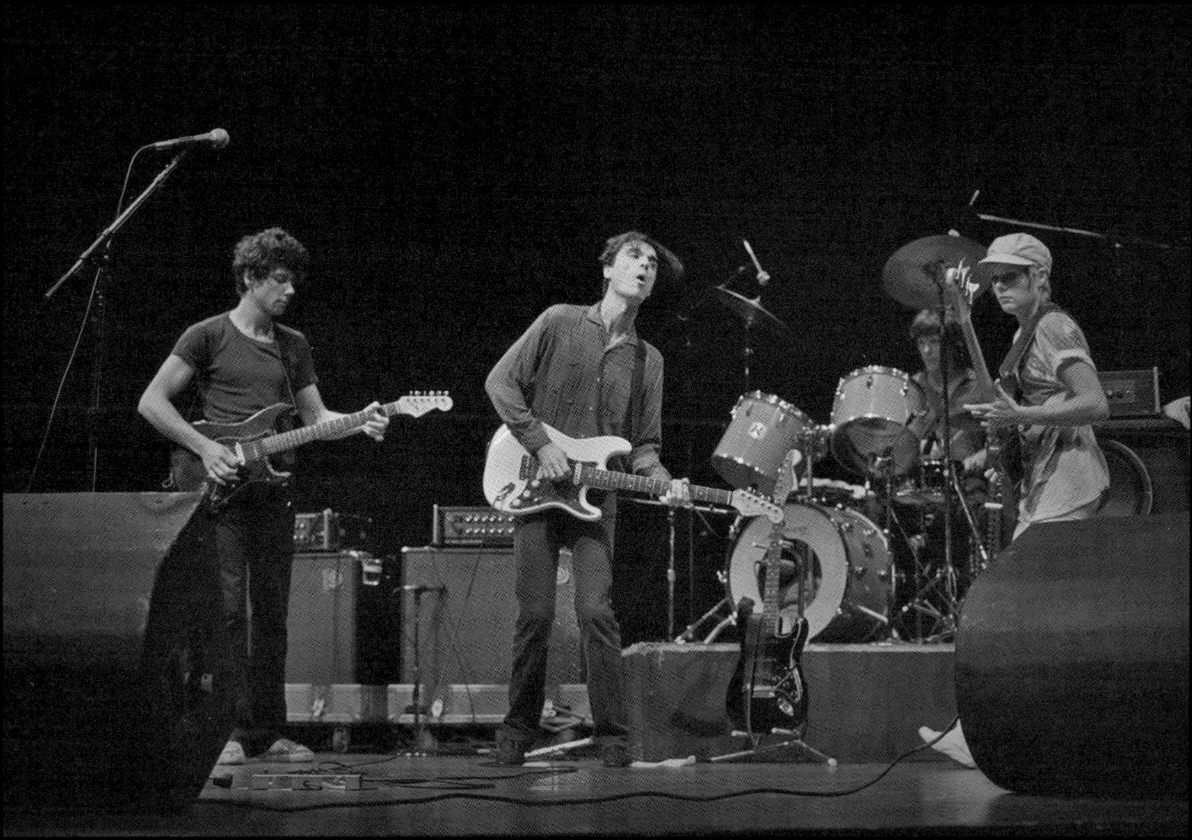

Talking Heads, another pioneering act to emerge from the New York new-wave scene orbiting around CBGB, performed at several Twin Cities venues in the late seventies and early eighties. This image is from their Guthrie Theater gig in October 1979.

Formerly of the seminal rock band the Velvet Underground—also featuring Lou Reed, Sterling Morrison, Moe Tucker, and Nico—John Cale performed with his own group at the Longhorn Bar in 1979. The multi-instrumentalist and heavy personality demonstrated why he may have clashed with Reed during his VU years—he was book smart, musically adventurous, and just as dark.

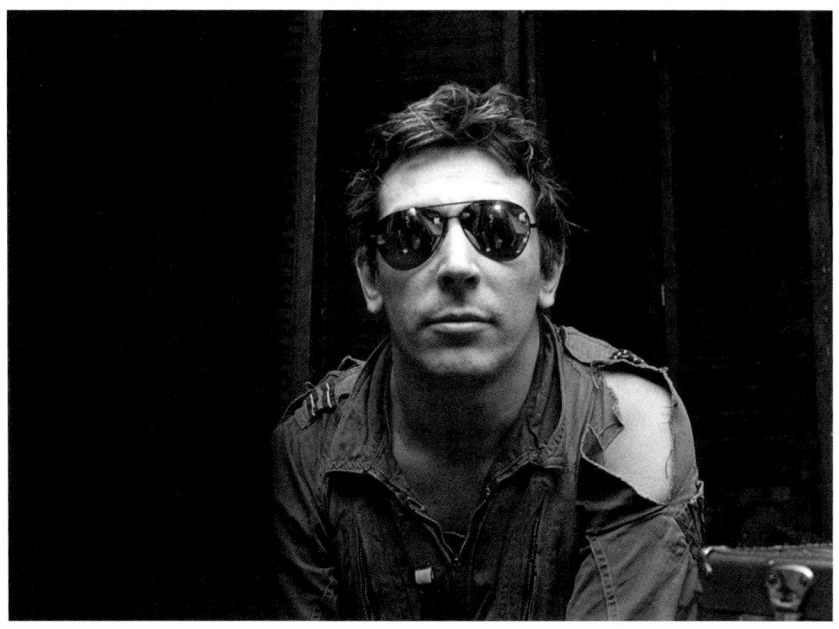

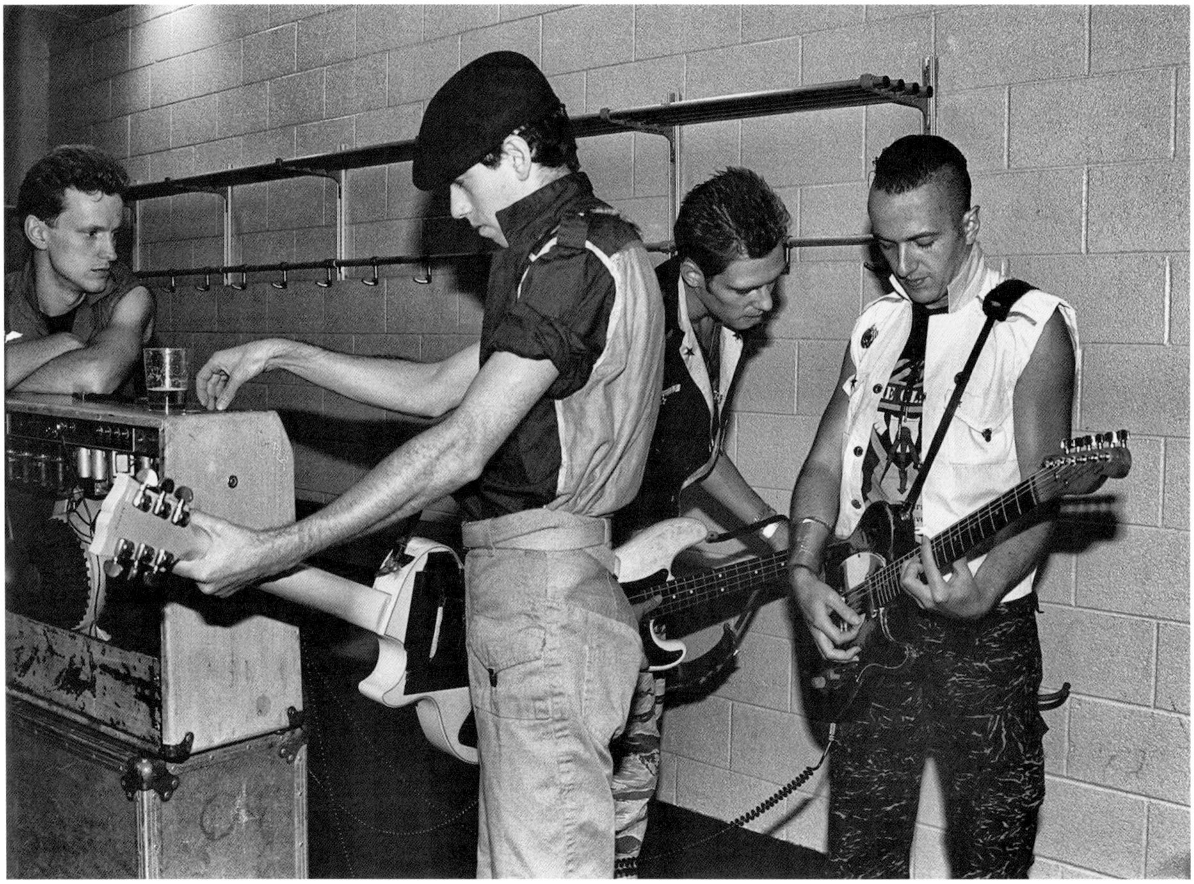

The Helg shot this photo of the Clash backstage at the St. Paul Civic Center while the band rehearsed against the clamor of kids pounding on the doors to be let in. Joe Strummer eventually asked the security team to let the crowd in. The group also allowed Helgeson to shoot onstage, which was rare then and now.

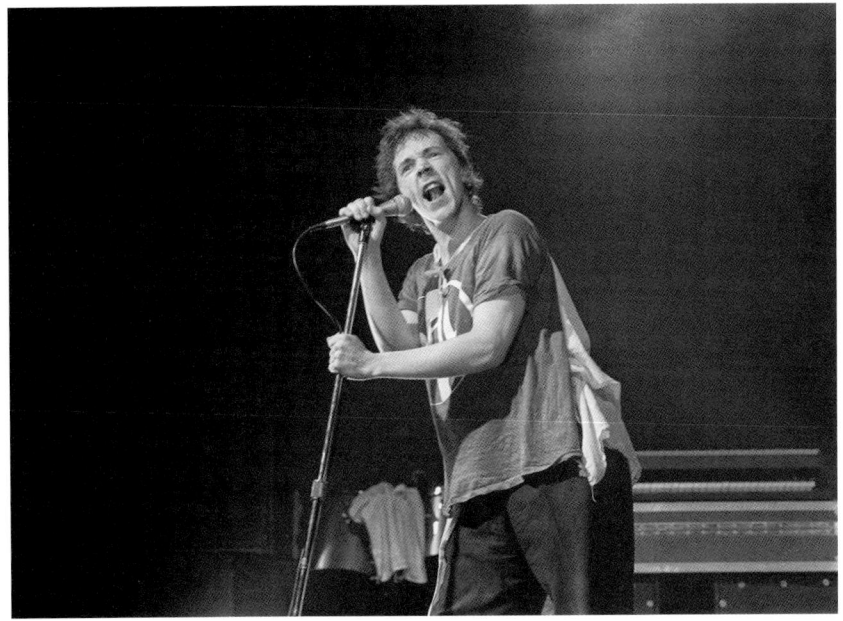

John Lydon of PiL (Public Image Ltd.), and formerly known as Johnny Rotten of the Sex Pistols, plays to the camera at First Avenue in 1982. According to the Helg, "their manager encouraged me by saying, 'Go ahead and shoot as much as you want. John likes you!' He also asked me to shoot some video. Never was quite sure what he meant by that."

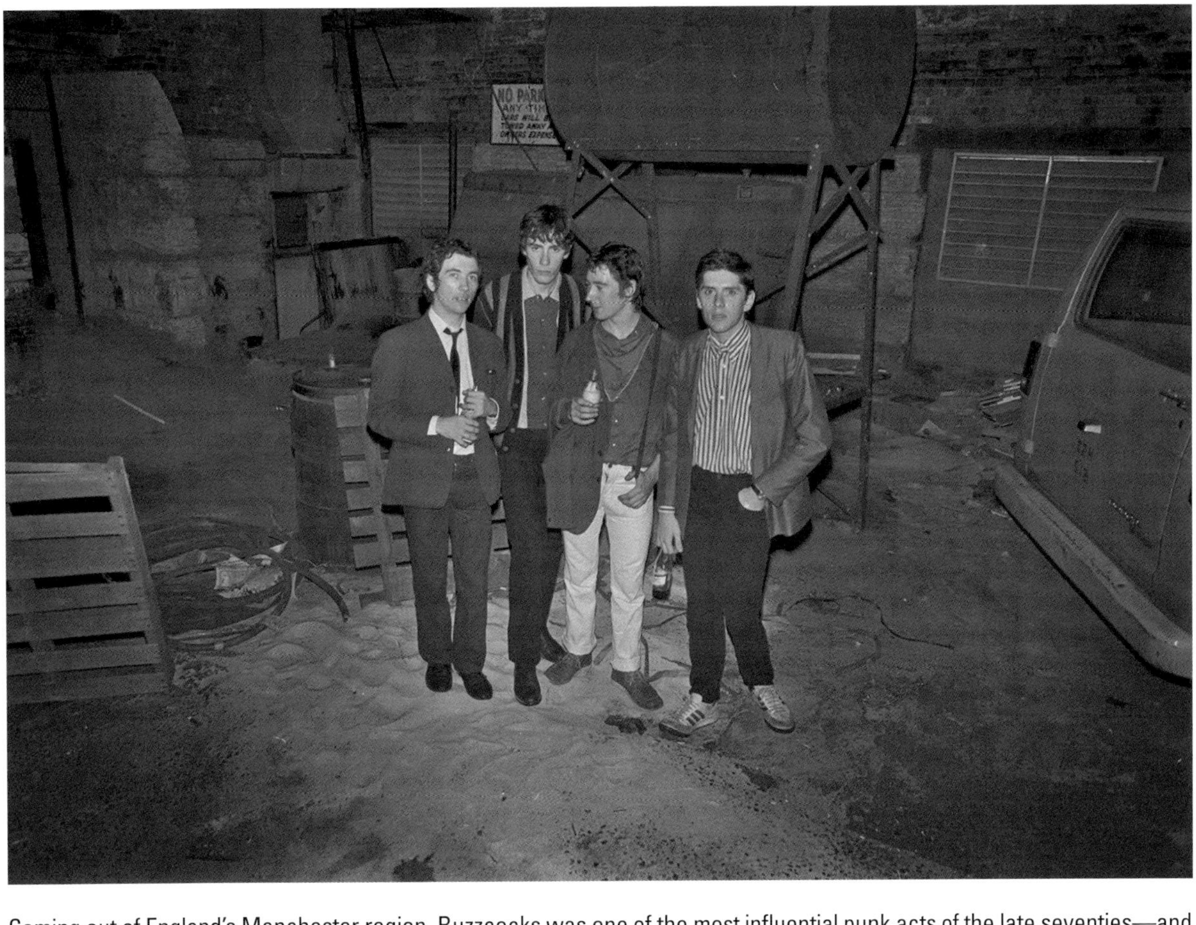

Coming out of England's Manchester region, Buzzcocks was one of the most influential punk acts of the late seventies—and one of many punk and new-wave bands to play Minneapolis's Longhorn Bar, as they did in September 1979. Pete Shelley, the group's main singer-songwriter, passed away in 2018 at age sixty-three, sparking much sorrow in the music community.

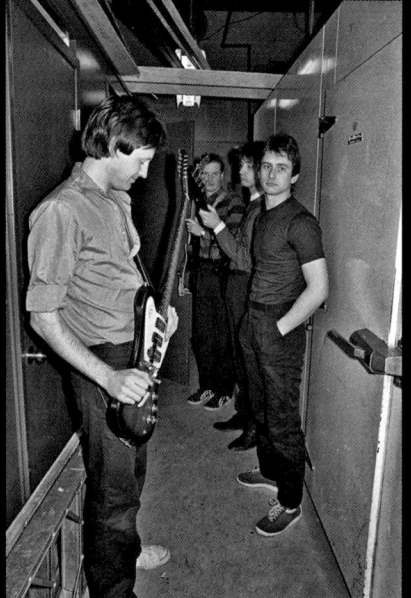
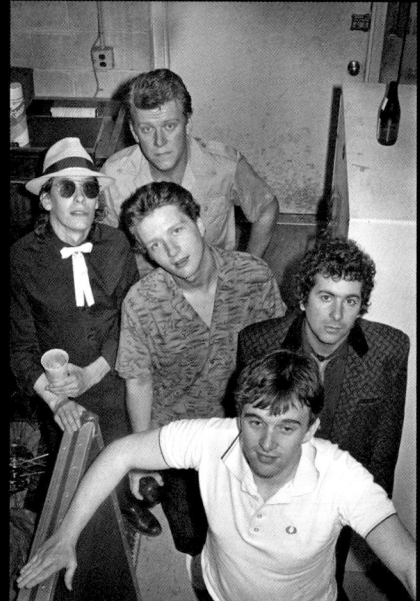
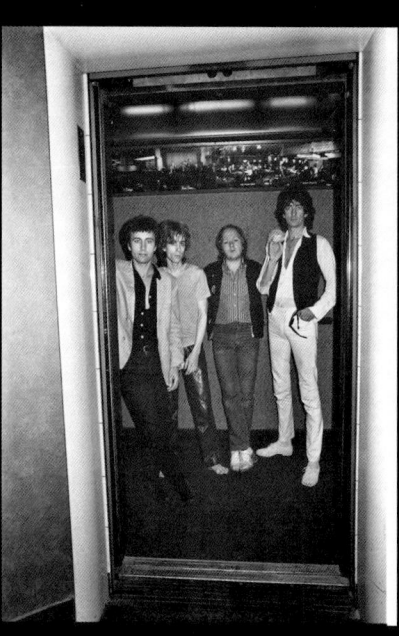
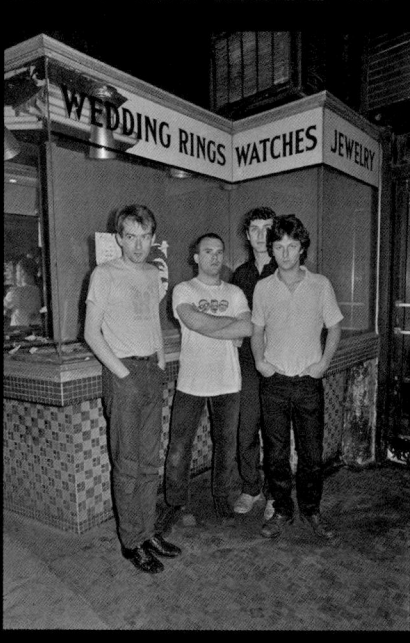

(top left) The English band XTC played Minnesota twice during a world tour in 1980, including a turn at Duffy's in February, where the Helg captured this shot. The extensive touring took a toll on band cofounder, songwriter, and guitarist Andy Partridge; "his stage fright and mental health were so bad," recalled Helgeson. **(top right)** This photo of the original Squeeze at Duffy's in June 1980 was taken prior to the departure of keyboardist Jools Holland from the beloved English band. The group persevered behind the Lennon-McCartney-esque pop-rock tunes by co-songwriters Chris Difford and Glenn Tilbrook. **(bottom left)** The Only Ones played Jay's Longhorn for two nights in August 1979, largely due to Peter Jesperson, the future Twin/Tone Records cofounder, who convinced Longhorn owner Hartley Frank to book the British rock band. This photo was taken at the nearby Radisson Hotel. "I was thrilled to meet their drummer, Mike Kellie," exclaimed Helgeson the fanboy. **(bottom right)** "This is some of what you get strolling along Hennepin Avenue in Minneapolis with a band that has plenty of time to kill before a show," Helgeson recalled of his afternoon with England's Gang of Four in 1979. The band's political edge and riotous live performances influenced many American groups, including R.E.M., according to Paul Lester's 2008 book about the band, *Gang of Four: Damaged Gods*.

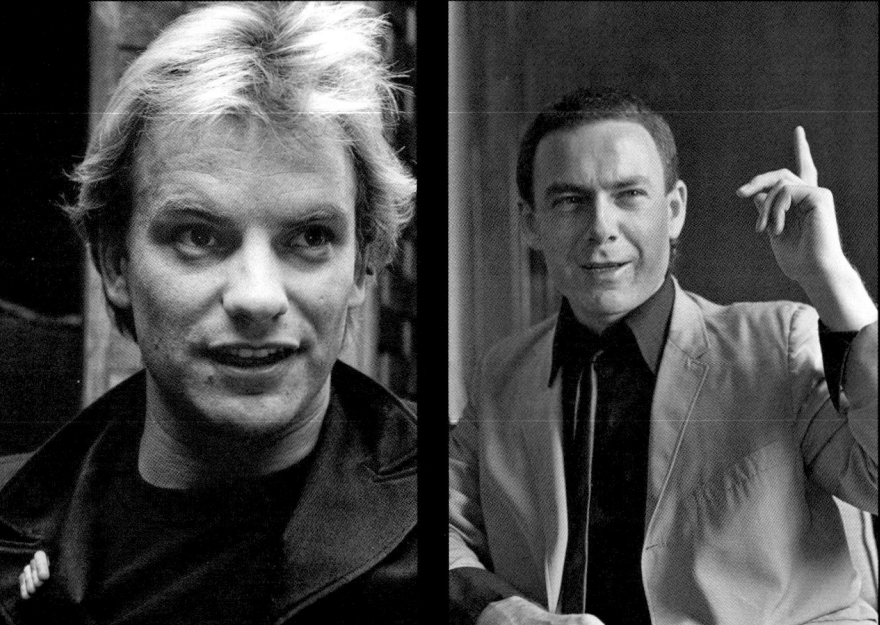

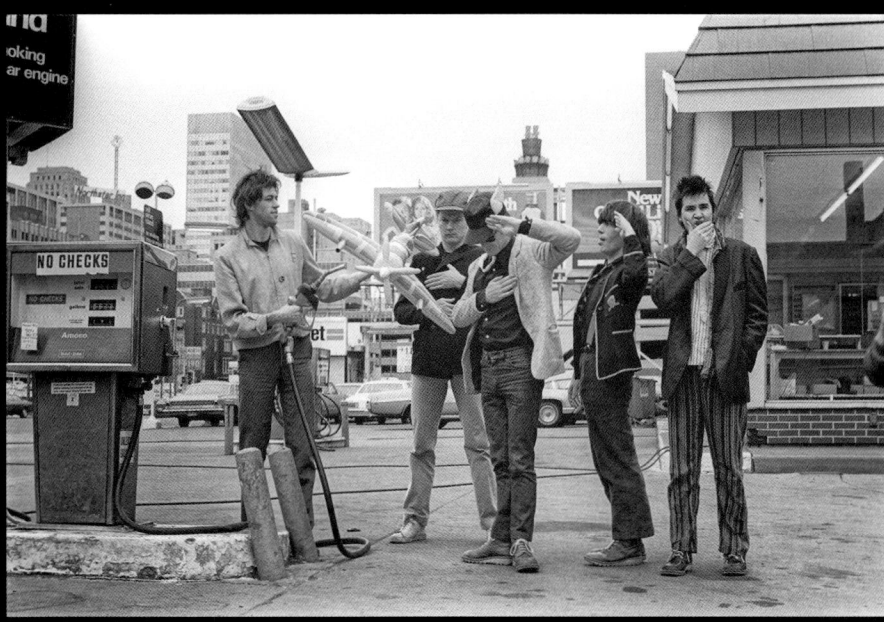

(top left) Sting and the Police had a gig at Jay's Longhorn in May 1979. At the time, the trio played a mixture of reggae-inspired originals and straight-ahead rock tunes that would catapult them to big arenas in short order. For the group's Twin Cities debut, however, turnout was light and the set list short. **(top right)** Perhaps best known for his work with prog rock pioneers King Crimson, guitarist Robert Fripp also explored sonic adventures in collaborations and session work with artists ranging from Brian Eno and David Bowie to the Roches, Blondie, Talking Heads, and more. Fripp is pictured here during an appearance at Walker Art Center in 1979, indulging his audience in music and discussions about Frippertronics and other crafty electronic techniques he deployed. **(above)** Fill 'er up, mate! Ireland's Boomtown Rats clown around at the petrol pumps during their first visit to Minneapolis–St. Paul, in 1980. While the band had several hits on the UK charts in the late seventies and early eighties, lead singer Bob Geldof would go on to earn greater fame, and an honorary knighthood, for his charity work, most notably organizing the supergroup Band Aid and its Live Aid concerts to provide relief for starving children in Ethiopia.

ELVIS COSTELLO

Elvis, Leaving the Building

Bruce Springsteen. The Band. Dusty Springfield. August Wilson. The Reverend Al Green. Brian Wilson. Robin Williams. Marty Stuart. Stevie Wonder. Frank Zappa. Patti Smith. Paul Simon. Iggy Pop. Abbie Hoffman. Jim Carrey. Grant Hart. Joel and Ethan Coen. Joni Mitchell. Tom Hanks. Archie Bell. J. K. Rowling. The Pogues. Emmylou Harris. Ray Davies. Tammy Wynette. Walter Cronkite. J. D. Salinger. Oprah. George Harrison. Bill Monroe. Isaac Hayes. Elvis Costello.

In the "writer's regrets" column, the preceding list reflects a more-than-handful of people I never got the chance or good fortune to interview but who were always high on my wish list. Some were clearly out of reach, like Salinger and the Big O. But you'd think Springsteen, Stuart, Simon, and Costello would have been relatively easy for me to get to, given the right channels and connections and the few degrees of separation between them and my circle of friends and colleagues in the biz. It just never worked out. But I did encounter Costello twice in social settings (see Dylan and Statler chapters), where I might have gotten a friendly word or two.

As the Helg reminded me recently, Elvis's management guarded him fiercely early in his career. That is, Jake Riviera did, and his reputation preceded him. Cofounder of the influential British Stiff Records label and manager of various bands and recording artists, like the inimitable Ian Dury, Graham Parker and the Rumour, and Nick Lowe, Riviera has been described as a pit bull. He wouldn't allow Elvis to be photographed at his Northrop Auditorium gig in the early eighties, when Costello was still mostly a critic's darling with a small but growing fan base. Bollocks, as the Brits say. Greg shot him anyhow.

I wasn't nearly as taken with Costello's own work as I was with his deep interest in and knowledge of music, reflected in part in his voluminous autobiography. It's hard to gauge which is greater: Costello's abundant,

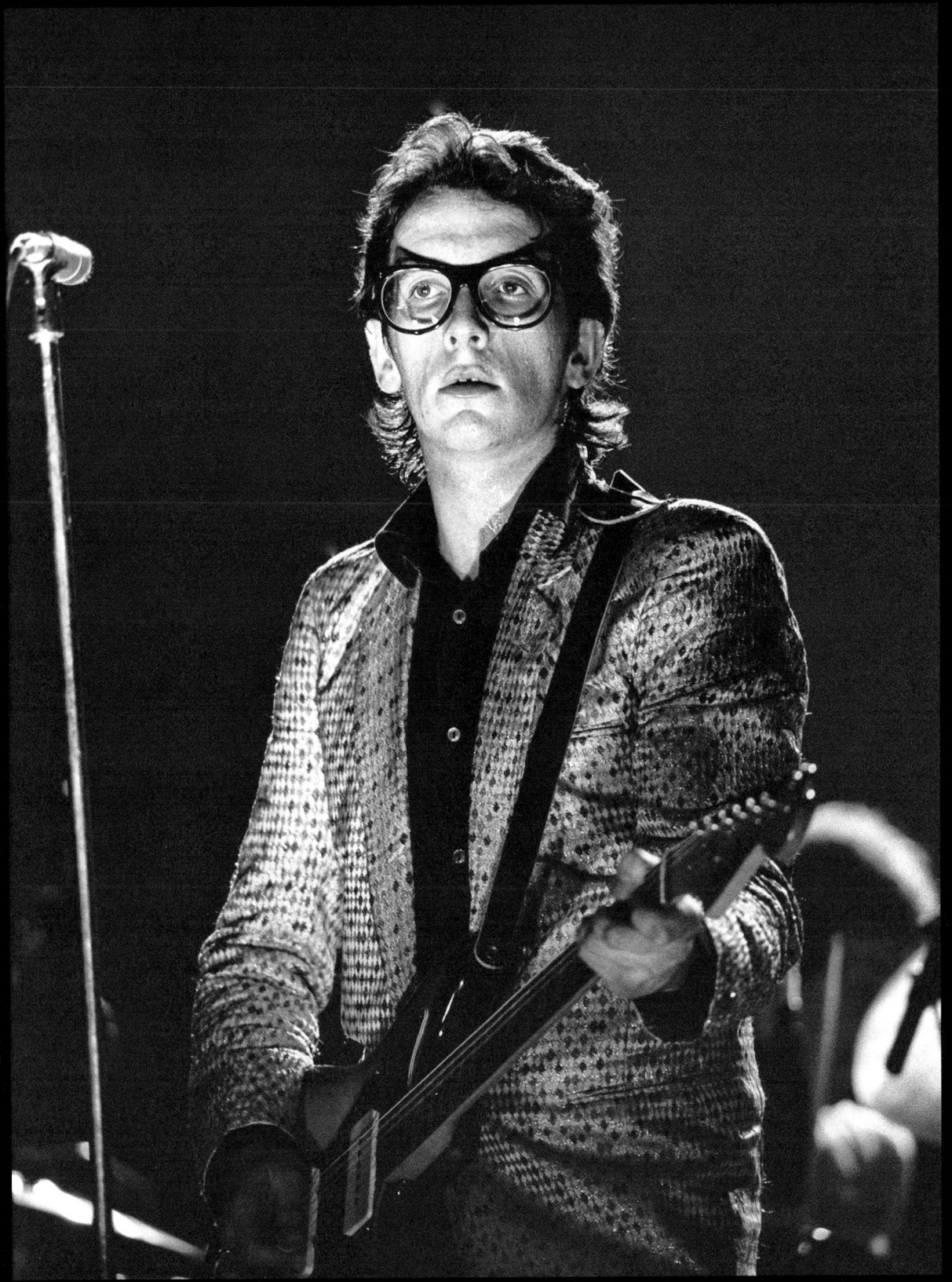

Elvis Costello, onstage in 1979 at the St. Paul Theatre, where no photos were allowed, but the Spud Boy got one anyhow.

well-informed opinions about pop music, or his staggering output of material, including noteworthy collaborations with Paul McCartney, the Chieftains, and the Brodsky Quartet.

In 2011, he and his band, the Imposters, played the State Theatre in downtown Minneapolis as part of their Revolver Tour. Matt Quast, the sound guy in Chuck Statler's film crew, called me and said he had comps from the Costello camp, and he asked if I wanted to go. I asked if the "old man" was going (our code name for Chuck, who was older than us by quite a few yardsticks).

"He says he'll go if you go."

"Hmm, that old trick."

"Come on, it'll be fun."

It was, even though the two filmmakers who shot Elvis's first music videos insisted on having a drink before we went into the theater, making us no less than forty minutes late by the time we got inside. The band had its big "Spectacular Spinning Songbook wheel" onstage, revisiting the spinning format first devised in 1986. Fans and occasionally a pretty, retro-looking "showgirl" would come out and give it a whirl. Whatever song it landed on, that's what they'd play. I'm not sure if "Purple Rain" was on the wheel ("Pop Life" was), but the fellas played the song passionately in an encore before the night was through.

Afterward Matt and I joined the band in the basement dressing rooms, while Chuck and Elvis headed off to Costello's more private space, where Statler pitched him on a film project he wanted the English rocker to be part of. Matt caught up with keyboard player Steve Nieve and drummer Pete Thomas, two of the original Attractions, as if they were lost cousins from across the pond.

Outside, the bus was already loading for Milwaukee, the band's next stop, and the road manager soon yelled that it was time to wrap it up. Elvis eventually strolled into the band's space to greet Matt, who asked how things were going.

"Well, I'll probably never make another album," he offered. The economics just didn't work anymore, he added wistfully, musing about the state of the industry that he used to know and the chaotic calculus that he and everyone like him were still trying to figure out. Coming from one of the most prolific rockers of the previous thirty years—whose fans were still buying CDs—it sounded shocking. You had to wonder if Mr. Costello, thirty-nine years after his breakout debut album, was feeling like something was happening but didn't know what it was.

Costello's first album, *My Aim Is True*, which came out in 1977, had relied on the old distribution model, in which product went from record labels (and their manufacturers) to retail outlets via big distributors, or rack jobbers, such as the Twin Cities–based Lieberman Enterprises. In the late seventies, artists were slowly exploring new revenue streams like "merch," and it didn't take them too long to discover what a cash cow it was. Merch became more widespread in the eighties, due in part to the efforts of another Twin Cities company, Nice Man Merchandising, as well as a small handful of other companies around the country. Merch's go-go years arrived, leading to the cornucopia of pricey goods and swag we all find at concerts these days.

The eighties were also the long goodbye for the 45 rpm, the cassette, and the vinyl album format (before vinyl's astounding resurrection in the 2000s), and for the album-and-singles strategies used by major and independent record labels in all eras prior to the nineties. With the arrival of downloadable media to deliver songs via MP3 devices and, later, Apple's iPod and iTunes, the music business suddenly turned into a perplexing labyrinth where dead ends loomed on the pathways to making a living.

The value of songs became more ambiguous as the internet became a major music distributor, and the relationship dynamics between fans and artists morphed into a screen-driven mystery dance in the digital matrix. It promised new artist-consumer-fan intimacy like never before, but in the early days of the World Wide Web, it seemed that people just wanted free stuff, as overt piracy became rampant. Meanwhile, the once lucrative after-market for used CDs plummeted, affecting indie record stores the most—and anyone trying to downsize their CD collection or trade up on their oldies for respectable in-store credit. It was enough to render major artists, to paraphrase Elvis, into men and women out of time.

Back in the State Theatre basement, the road manager herded everyone toward the stairs, and our little Elvis Costello meet and greet was over as quickly as it began. Dressed in a black jacket, tasteful scarf, and hat, Elvis looked like a rock 'n' roll count as he and his viceroys emerged from their dressing rooms and began exiting the building.

Elvis did make two more albums, one with the ubiquitous Roots in 2013 and another one with the Imposters in 2018. But the spectacular spinning wheel of songs began to resemble more of a symbolic roulette wheel in a smoky casino, making real wins for artists harder and harder to realize against the overwhelming house odds of the internet.

JAMES BROWN

A Tale of Two Interviews

The Godfather of Soul kicked off what was hoped to be a comeback tour with a two-night stand at the Cabooze in Minneapolis in April 1981. Over the previous two decades, James Brown ruled R&B, created funk almost single-handedly, and showed his future successors, like Prince, the blueprints for the school he built. Onstage, he was unstoppable and untoppable. Between the soldered tightness of his Famous Flames band, the drop-down splits and fast-dance spins, and the legendary cape routine, no one could touch him for live performance.

Disco, though, cut into his groove thang and eroded his fan base, despite the now-classic JB hit from the period, 1979's "It's Too Funky in Here." The album that produced the single and proclaimed King James as *The Original Disco Man* was a tough sell. But he was still putting it out there. During a low-key interview with me before his Cabooze show, he asserted, like an aging boxer ready to get back in the ring, that he wasn't done yet. At the interview, Brown was courteous and surprisingly quiet for someone so flamboyant onstage. Despite losing some of his key players, Brown still induced funkamonium at the Cabooze with his many dance hits and soulful ballads.

Our JB story could end right here with Helgeson's cool, cold-sweat performance shots. Except that a wild James Brown tale from 1966 by a well-known Twin Cities journalist and a famed photographer demands telling, for the record if nothing else. Steve Kaplan published, edited, and wrote for the underground Twin Cities *In-Beat* magazine, which was produced largely in his living room. It featured photography by a hot young shooter and aspiring filmmaker named Danny Seymour, who made some early short films with a young Jessica Lange and their mutual friend, and Lange's first husband, Paco Grande, a Spanish photographer and moviemaker.

"*In-beat* was completely lacking in class," Kaplan recalled with a laugh in 2018, remembering as best he could details from a bygone time. The

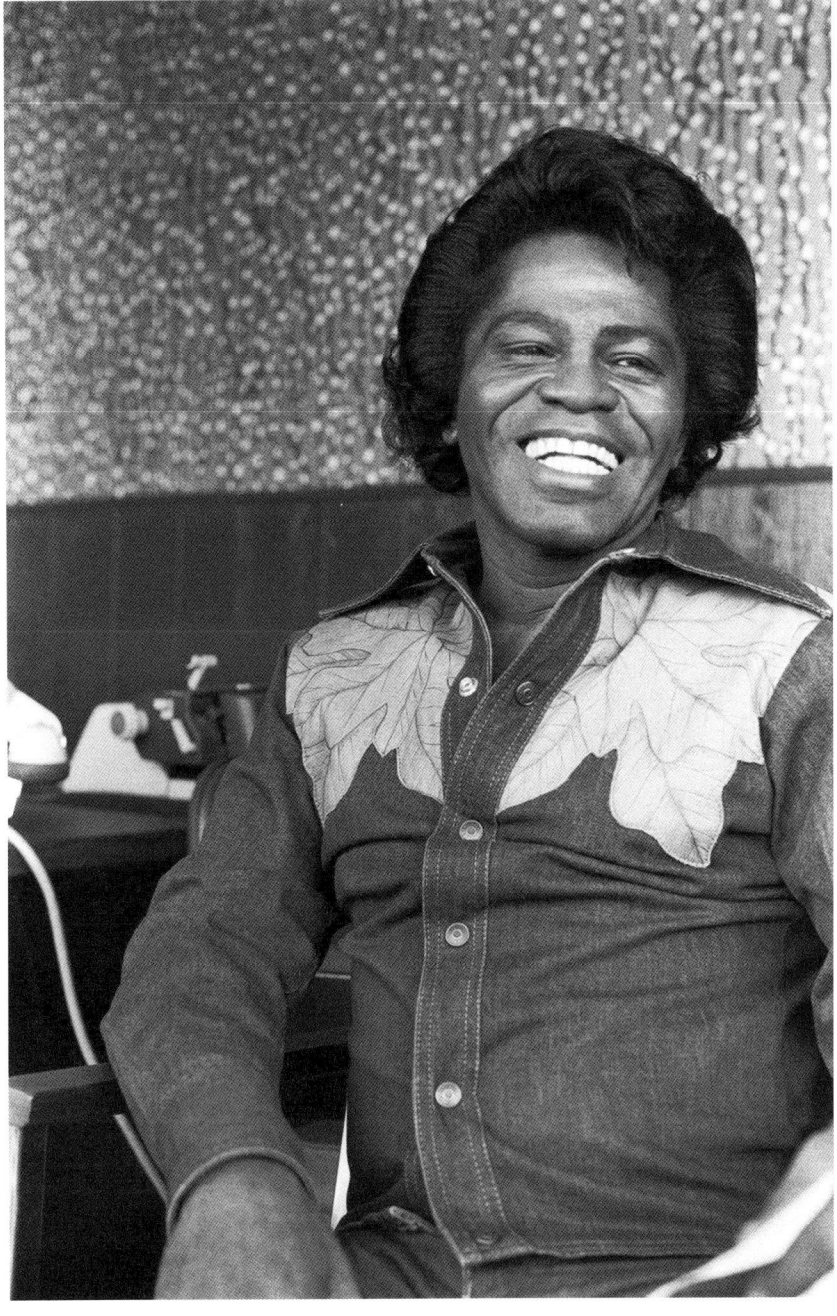

James Brown gets on his good mood during a 1981 interview.

magazine lasted only a year, because he, Danny, and some friends left to "see the New World in San Francisco" and the Monterey Pop Festival, and they never returned. But the publication reached its zenith when Kaplan and Seymour set out to see and interview James Brown at what Kaplan says was "probably" the Minneapolis Auditorium. "Wherever we were, Danny and I and a couple others were the only four white people in the place. But I had to see James Brown, and I was dying to interview him. He was my idol!"

The two hippies got their wish, and more. Kaplan and Seymour were ushered backstage, where Brown was collapsed in a chair, "exhausted from the performance," Kaplan noted. "He really was the hardest-working man in showbiz!" They tried to talk to him, but there were numerous interruptions, and Brown finally said, "This is no place to do an interview." He invited them on his Learjet and flew to Cincinnati, where he put them up in a good hotel, then gave them a tour of King Records in the morning, before putting them on a commercial flight back to Minnesota, all at Brown's expense.

"We talked a good couple of hours before taking off, while Vivaldi's *Four Seasons* played in the background, and we talked some more after the flight and at King Records the next day, but not during the flight," Kaplan said. "Danny and I were transfixed by the whole thing, the Lear. I mean, they're not very big; it was like sitting at a restaurant table."

"Were you stoned at the time?"

"I don't remember. I imagine we could have been cuz we were always stoned in those days."

While touring the record label company where Brown had an office—"with a bunch of white guys and only one other black guy running around there"—Brown played them his version of the old spiritual "Mary Don't You Weep," which he called "Oh Baby Don't You Weep" and released as a two-part single in 1964. (Coincidentally, that spiritual was the same song Prince recorded in 1983 and was released by his estate in 2018 on the *Piano & a Microphone 1983* album off of an old work cassette tape. While Prince's version is truer to the original, Brown's is more classic JB R&B, full of his open-throated snarls and screams.)

Kaplan eventually returned to Minnesota following his stoned soul picnic out in northern California. He carved out a pretty good place in Twin Cities journalism as editor of *Minnesota Law & Politics*, a monthly publication that was really about culture masquerading as a good read for the legal profession and Minnesota politicos. He later worked at *Mpls. St. Paul Magazine*, wrote for the *World Press Review* and other print media in New York, and had a ten-year stint freelancing.

The extremely talented Danny Seymour, however—full of promise but also strung out on junk at one point—met with an unknown fate. A friend of filmmaker Robert Frank, Seymour worked with Frank on the infamous documentary film about the Rolling Stones' *Exile on Mainstreet* tour, *Cocksucker Blues*. Seymour later disappeared on his boat in the Caribbean and was presumed murdered. Bruce Rubenstein wrote an account of his life and times for *City Pages* in 1986. A documentary film about Seymour is apparently still pending.

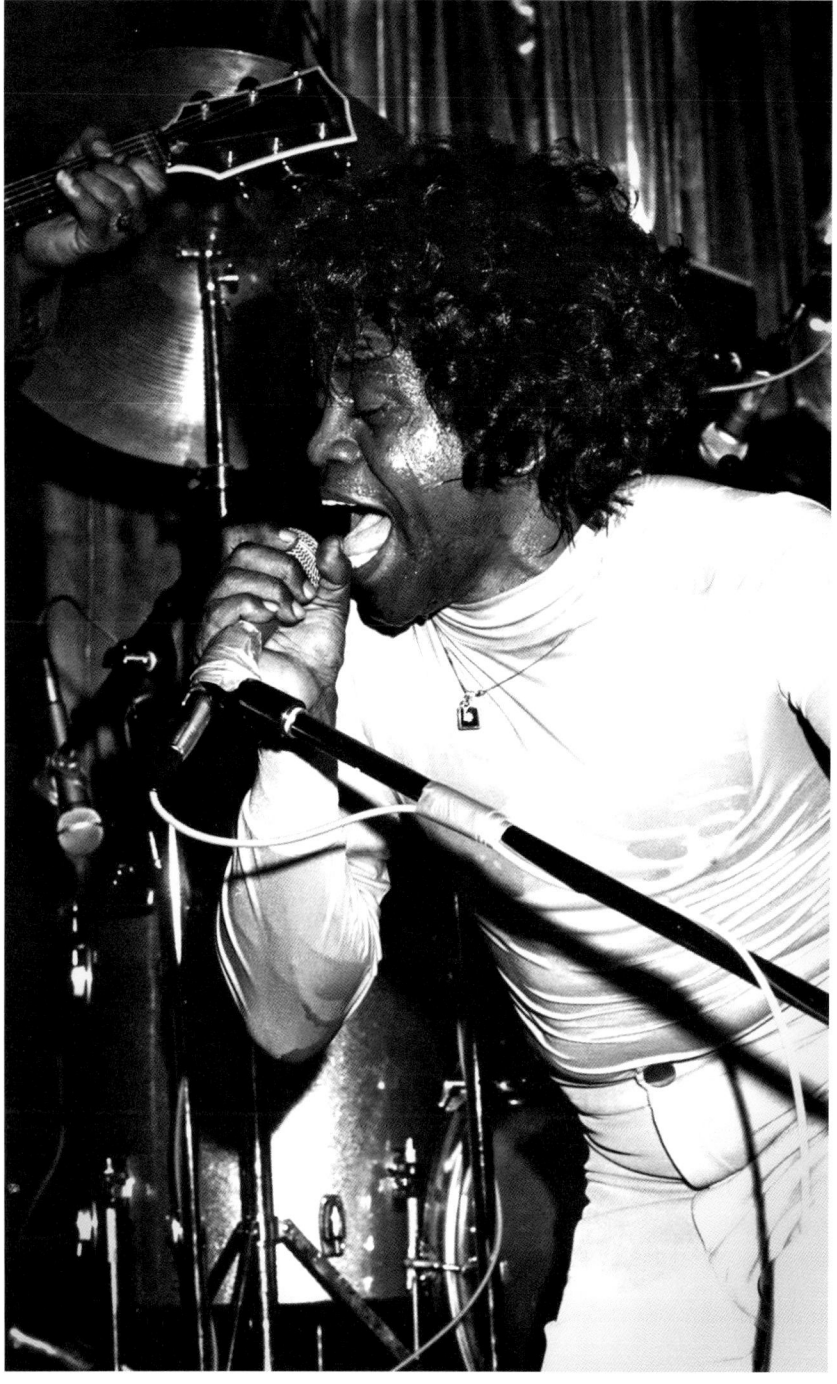

The Godfather of Soul, JB works it at the Cabooze during a comeback tour that began in Minneapolis in April 1981.

Also apparently still pending is closure for James Brown and his family and friends. Although he died on Christmas Day in 2006, his heirs—and their lawyers—are yet fighting over his estate and where to bury him. Right now, he's still in a vault. Baby don't you weep, indeed.

(right) Tina Turner cutting loose at First Avenue

(far right) Gladys Knight in soulful repose at the Carlton Celebrity Room

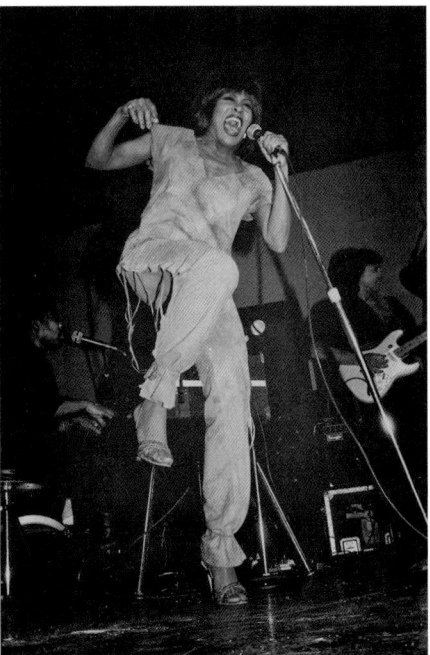

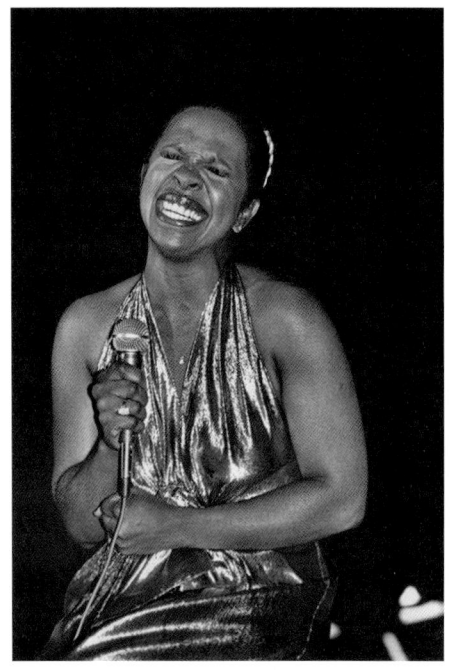

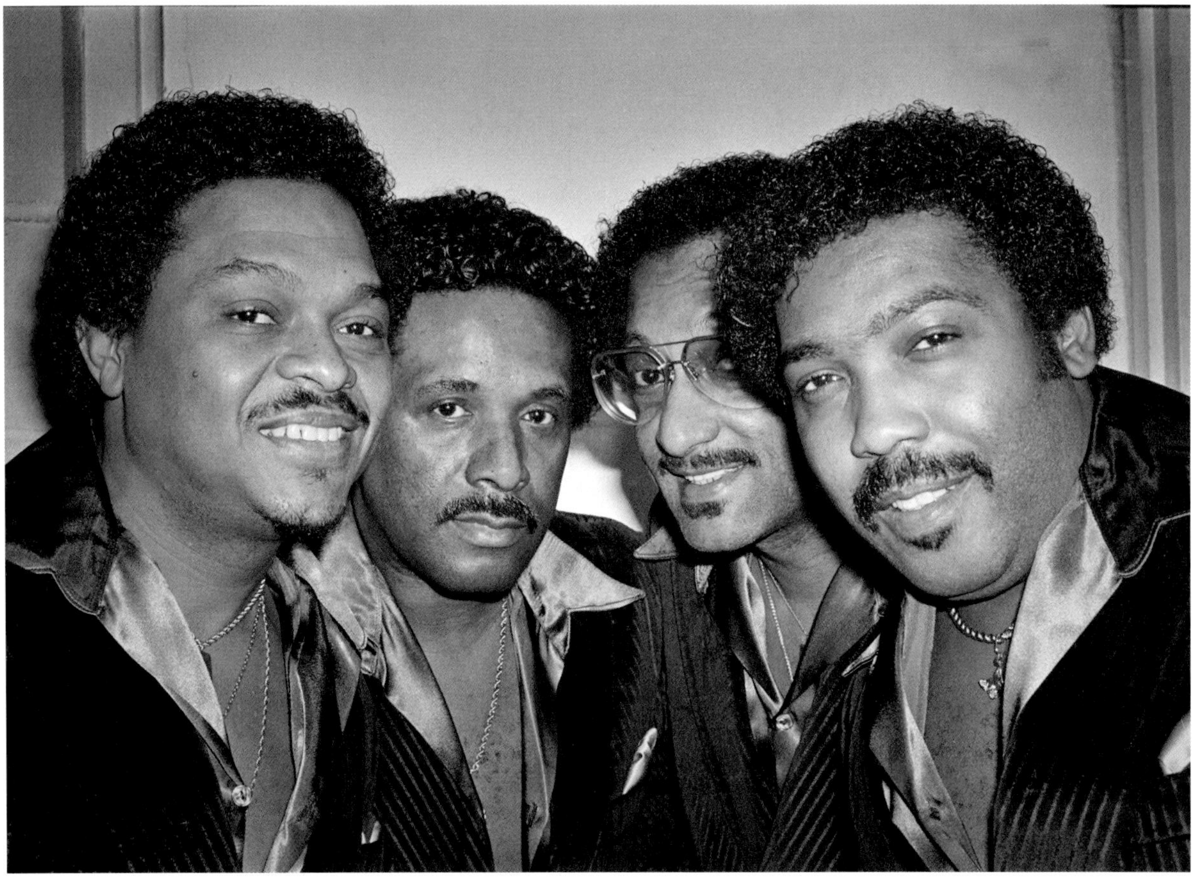

The chart-topping Motown powerhouse the Four Tops, backstage at Duffy's in 1981

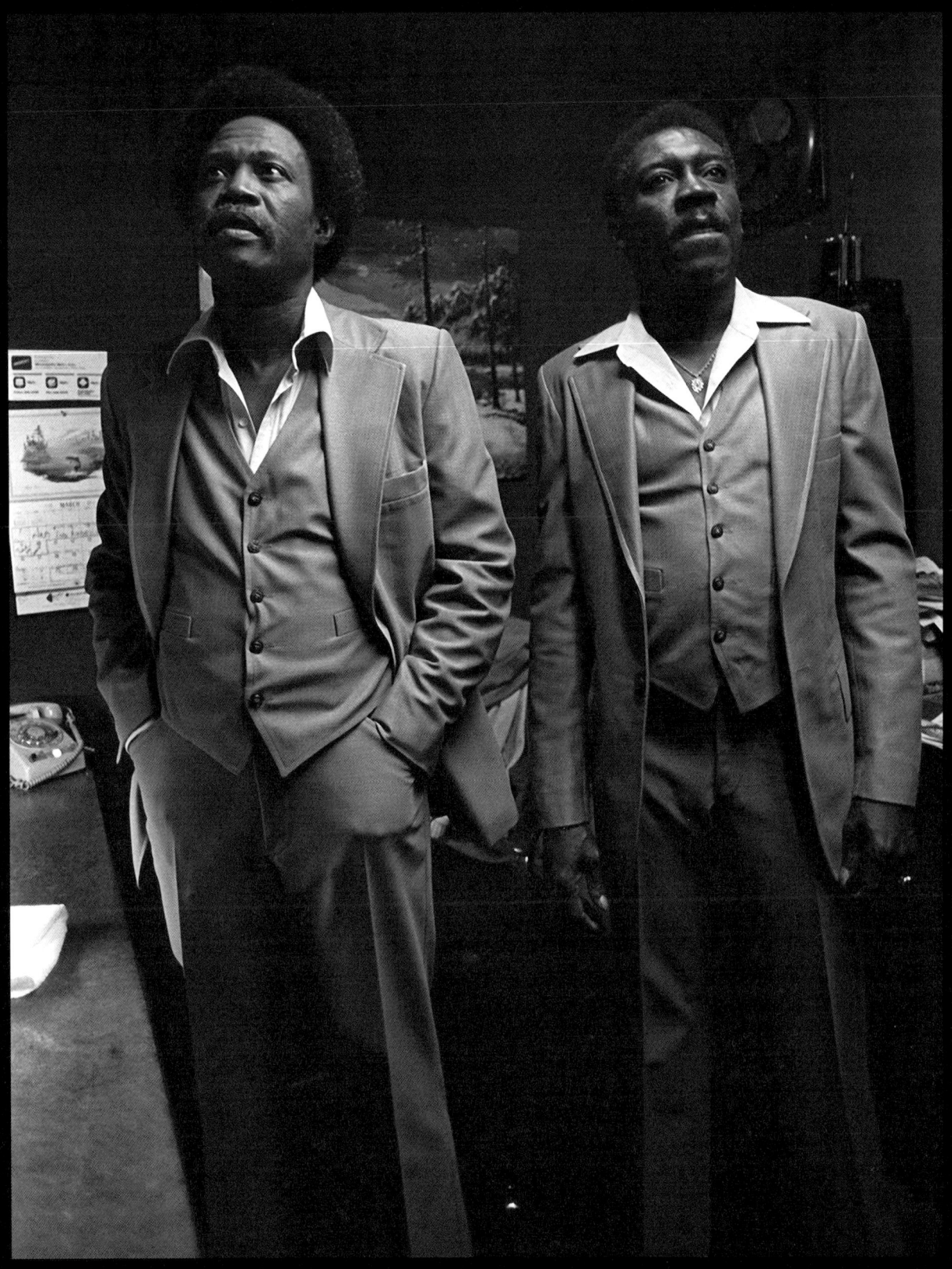

Soul men Sam and Dave, who rarely spoke to one another offstage

FAB 5 FREDDY

Hip-Hop Drops in the Mill City

Hip-hop culture made its quietly spectacular debut for wider (and whiter) Twin Cities audiences in 1982 at First Avenue in conjunction with Walker Art Center. Fab 5 Freddy—the same cat Blondie referenced in the new-wave group's 1981 song "Rapture" and who later hosted MTV's first hip-hop program, *Yo! MTV Raps*—came into the old Mill City along with DJ Spy and Rock Steady break dancers Frosty Freeze and Crazy Legs. Together they showed the crowd how to bust a move through their Bronx break dance work, Fab Freddy's rapid wordplay, and Spy's record mixing and scratching. It was a big-bang moment for the Twin Cities.

In 2009 (the same year Crazy Legs died), Jeff Chang—esteemed journalist and author on hip-hop music and culture—wrote in *Foreign Policy* magazine that hip-hop is "serious business," noting that it "sells an estimated $10 billion worth of trendsetting luxury and consumer goods every year—not just in movies, shoes, and clothing, but in everything from snack crackers and soda drinks to cars and computers." As Chang wrote a decade ago—and it's even truer today—"From *xi ha* in China to 'hip-life' in Ghana, hip-hop is a lingua franca that binds young people all around the world, all while giving them the chance to alter it with their own national flavor."

In the early eighties, the *City Pages* offices didn't receive a lot of promo "rap records" in the mail, but the ones that did arrive—mostly Sugar Hill Records from New Jersey by Grandmaster Flash and the Furious Five, the Sugarhill Gang, the Funky Four Plus One, and a few others—got snatched up quickly by staff arguing over who would get to review them. The local hip-hop scene had yet to become one. And while venues did, very occasionally, book a live rap act—like Grandmaster Flash and Kurtis Blow at Duffy's in 1982, and Run DMC at First Avenue the following year—hip-hop music made its way to Twin Cities ears mostly through local deejays. Guys like Cowboy, Alan Freed, Freddy Fresh, and Farrow Black could be heard on KMOJ and in straight and gay downtown clubs spinning twelve-inch discs on wheels of steel. It was a natural progression from the not-so-distant disco era.

Before the First Avenue gig in '82, Helgeson had to help bridge the cultural and linguistic gap between Minnie and da Bronx. Frosty Freeze had read the critic's choice preview of their show and took some offense at the expression "spin on their noggins." He had never heard it before.

The Helg explained that "noggin" meant, simply, "your head."

"You know, you're spinning on your head, your noggin. That's what you guys do, right?"

Frosty gave him a look of disbelief. But it is what he went out and did—and so much more.

I got to review the show, and I'm conflicted, and slightly embarrassed, about what I wrote. When the paper's editor, Randy Anderson, looked at it the next day, he shot me a strange look. I shot him one back.

"You didn't review it in rhyme, did you?" he asked.

Yup, I nodded. *Don't shame me, bro.* Anderson read it through, chuckled a few times, and said, "Okay. But next time, let's do it straight." Although I can't recall what, exactly, I wrote—nor can I find it, nor do I want to—I know that the review was favorable, and there were quite a few verses to it. I signed it "Capricorn" something, because there seemed to be quite a few horoscopic references in early hip-hop and the pop R&B stuff I liked. So, yeah, I stepped out of my comfort zone in search of my inner rapper.

The ever-observant Curt Wenzel, one of our ace freelancers (despite always being late with copy), wrote a longer feature story on the show that hit all the right notes. It drew historical parallels between the new African American genre and the black street dancers of the thirties, forties, and fifties, and with the witty double entendres in blues lyrics and the jazz "cutting sessions" in which players would try to one-up each other, where improvisation was imperative if you were gonna be somebody. African American culture was about to create another great, truly American cultural asset that the world would embrace.

After the issue hit the street, Capricorn got a friendly letter, approving of the rap review, from an early fan of hip-hop that we happily published in the next issue. Writers like to get letters, the screeds as well as the props. It keeps us on our game. And it reminds us that all the noise rattling around inside our noggins that spills onto the printed page really does make sense to other people and communicates something—an idea, an observation, a cultural connection, an emotion, or sometimes a great notion. At the end of everything in the communications world—and arts and entertainment in general—that's all that really matters.

Despite the buzz that First Avenue generated with the first formal

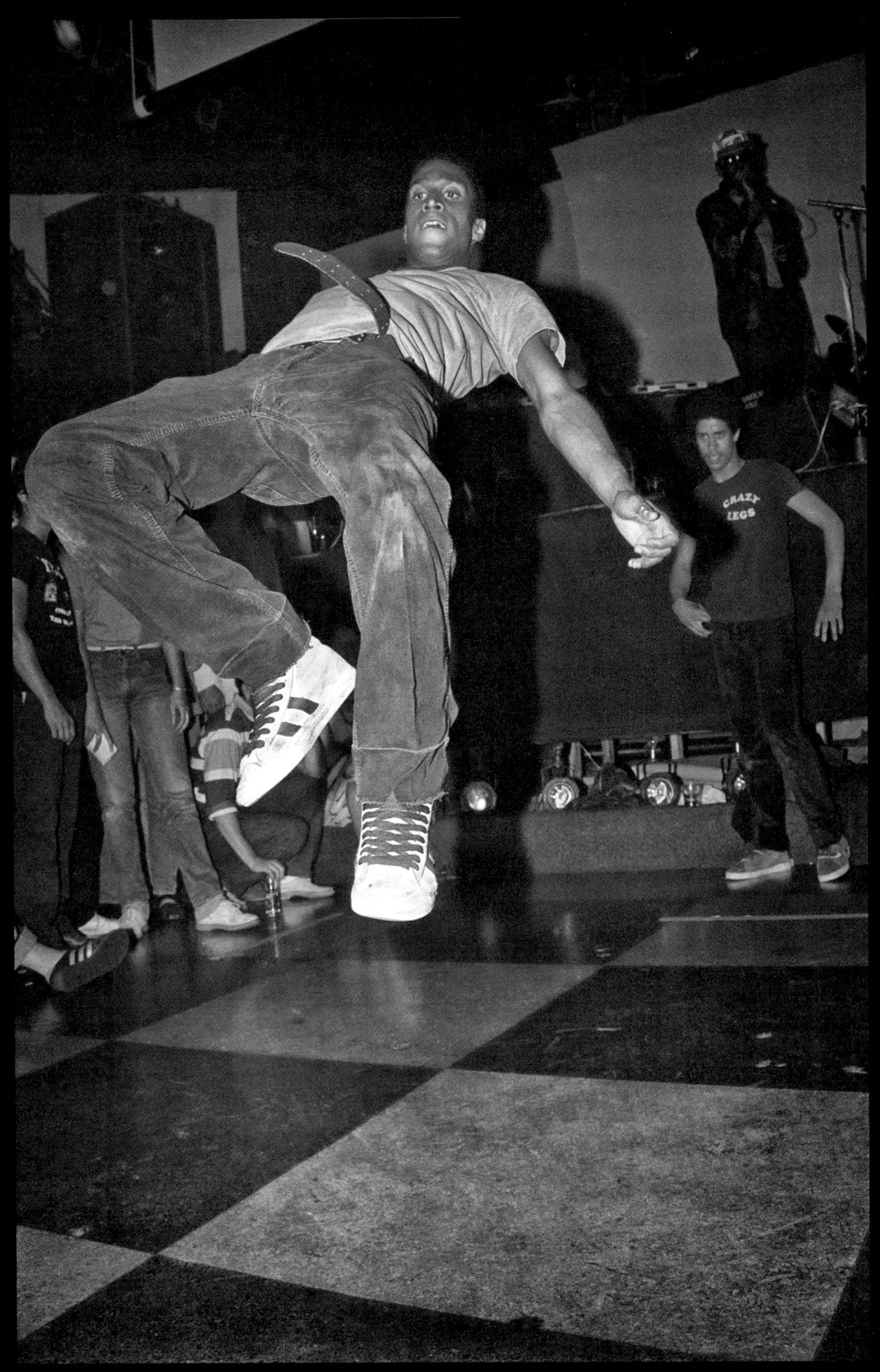

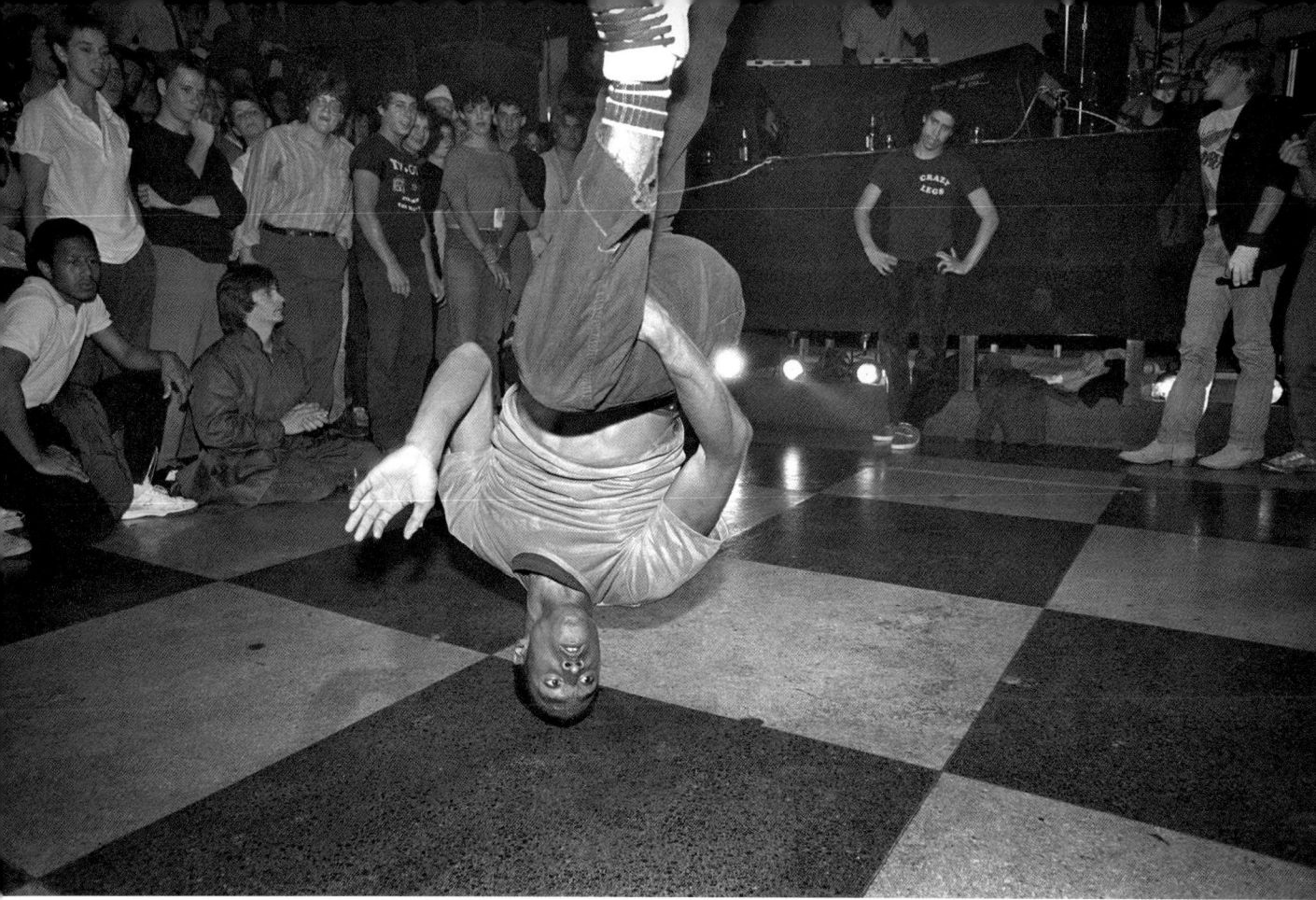

hip-hop gig to hit the Twin Cities, the local hip-hop scene saw a snail-slow build over the rest of the decade. In my "Frank Talk" column at the *Reader* in '86, I touted the appearance of north Minneapolis's own I.R.M. Crew (Immortal Rap Masters) at the Fifth Annual Minnesota Black Music Awards, masterfully produced every year by Pete Rhodes and Kimberly Bedell. The five rappers—Devastating Dee, TLC, Kel-C, I.B.M., Cuttin' Kal—had just released an EP on the indie St. Paul label Cchill Productions Inc., and made an impressive appearance above the Saturday Night Jukebox club downtown, complete with their own deejay. The creation of Rhymesayers Entertainment, with its trendsetting roster that would include Atmosphere, the redoubtable Brother Ali, and many more, was still nearly a decade away, and Doomtree and Dessa needed a few more years beyond that to percolate before they burst on the scene. And yet the hip-hop vibe had been loosed on the world and in Prince's backyard in the early eighties. Seismic and transformative, the African American phenomenon would reinvent youth culture and rejuvenate mass culture just as early rock 'n' roll did in the fifties.

(above and opposite) Frosty Freeze helped bring hip-hop culture to the Twin Cities when he showed off his break-dancing moves at First Avenue while touring with Fab 5 Freddy. Crazy Legs looks on in the background.

LIPPS, INC.

This Town Is Too Small, Part 1. Or, Which Exit for Funkytown?

Shortly after he moved from Nashville to Los Angeles, David Z got a text from his old friend and client, Steven Greenberg, asking why he was relocating after a fairly successful stint in Music City. Z simply wrote back: "Gotta make a move to a town that's right for me." He was of course quoting the first line of "Funkytown," the hit song that Greenberg penned for his group, Lipps, Inc., and which David Z (née Rivkin) produced at Minneapolis's renowned Sound 80 studio in 1980.

Despite his work on one of the most enduring one-hit wonders ever recorded and subsequent work with the Fine Young Cannibals, Etta James, Billy Idol, BoDeans, Buddy Guy, Sheila E., the Family, Jonny Lang, Leo Kottke, Neneh Cherry, and many others, David Z will probably always be best known for arranging and producing Prince's third US number-one hit, "Kiss," a stripped-down funk track that defied gravity—it didn't have a bass line. Who makes a hit funk single without a bass line?! Those guys! Still, Lipps, Inc. beat Prince to the top of the charts in the summer of 1980, which didn't sit well with the young, budding superstar out in suburban Chanhassen, Minnesota, according to Owen Husney, the man who discovered him (after Chris Moon) and landed the legendary Warner Bros. contract.

Singer Cynthia Johnson, on the other hand, will most likely always be known as the soulful vocalist on "Funkytown," despite a long résumé that included work as a solo singer, as an actress, and with acts like Aretha Franklin, Maceo Parker, Sounds of Blackness, and others. She was also the singer in the original Flyte Tyme band in the late seventies that included Terry Lewis and Jimmy Jam, Monte Moir, and Jellybean Johnson—the core group that became the Time.

But in 1977, the most I knew about Cynthia—aside from her being "Miss Black Minnesota" for 1976—was that she was hired as the new receptionist at the Urban League Street Academy, where I also was employed, the

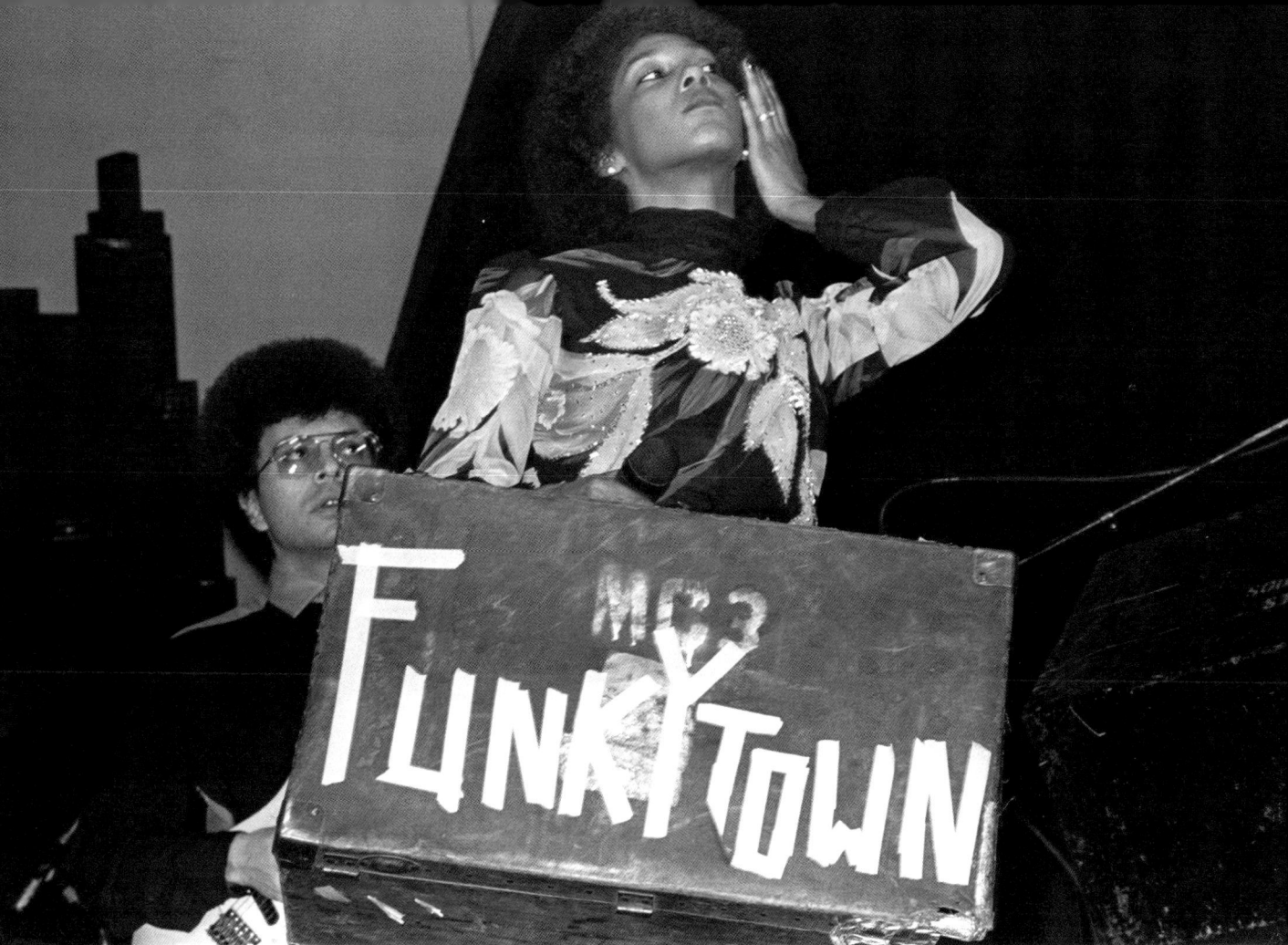

only white person among otherwise African American teachers and staff. The Street Academy was a small, alternative high school for students who struggled in bigger settings and for tougher kids who were court-ordered to attend as an alternative to jail. Since I didn't have a teaching degree, I was assigned to a teacher's assistant role. One of my tasks was to fill the study hall period either with individual help with homework or by showing short films from the public library, usually performance clips of legendary jazz, blues, and R&B artists.

"Man, Marty, man, don't be showing us all this old stuff. Where are the P-Funk movies?!" demanded Johnny C., who passionately dug Parliament Funkadelic. "Where's the Earth, Wind and Fire films?!" Despite the small student population, Cynthia, the other staff, and I had our hands full on most days. Ralph, a linebacker-sized kid who loved words and devoured my copy of Ralph Ellison's *Invisible Man*, often had epileptic seizures; another kid wanted to whale on the white boy for what his ancestors had done. That student lasted a week.

Singer Cynthia Johnson preens during a Lipps, Inc. concert at First Avenue. It was one of only five live performances by the group during the first peak of their hit song, "Funkytown."

After a year, the job's funding ended, and the next time I saw Cynthia, she was onstage at First Avenue in one of only a handful of live Lipps, Inc. shows (the rest were in Mexico) as "Funkytown" took off on the charts in 1980. It shot to number one not just in the States, but around the world, earning numerous gold and platinum records before becoming a licensing juggernaut in subsequent decades. "Funkytown"—that mythical place that is nowhere and everywhere—imprinted itself on the world map like few singles ever to come out of Minnesota.

Trying to capture lightning and platinum again, Greenberg recorded three more albums with Lipps, Inc. for Casablanca Records. Following 1980's *Pucker Up*, they released *Designer Music* in 1981, featuring the single "Hold Me Down." That same year saw the debut of the new cable television channel MTV, and suddenly any contending single needed a music video. So, in the fall of that year, Greenberg and Johnson turned to Chuck Statler, a fellow homie who had done pioneering music video work with Devo (who were his clever college pals from Akron, Ohio), among others. The Helg and I got typecast in the Lipps, Inc. video, playing members of the press. But the video never came out, for reasons we may never know.

After recording one more album, *4*, under the Lipps, Inc. moniker in 1983, Greenberg moved on. In 1984, he produced the Suburbs' major label debut, *Love Is the Law*, for Mercury, giving the former Twin/Tone band its best shot at the brass ring (and a lasting single of the same name that decades later became an anthem for same-sex marriage in Minnesota). Greenberg went on to establish his own indie label, October Records, in the mid-nineties. Not content to rest on his creative laurels or "Funkytown" royalties, he made a rockumentary movie, shot between 1995 and 1998, about five bands trying to make it. Naturally, he called it *Funkytown: The Movie*. It originally featured Tina and the B-Sides, bar-band super-favorite Greazy Meal, the Iya Rik Band (whose lead singer was gunned down dead over a pot debt before the film was finished), the Delilahs, and the Honeydogs. The H-dogs were pulled from the movie when their manager reportedly gummed up the works, and they were replaced with a short-lived pop-rock combo, the Found, lessening the movie's musical impact and cinematic appeal.

Greenberg later started with two associates an early and successful digital agency, called Designstein, that built branded websites and later also became a digital ad agency. But in the background, through all his entrepreneurial endeavors, the "Funkytown" song took on a life of its own, spinning gold through the decades in licensing deals almost too good to be true. When the song became part of the *Shrek 2* soundtrack in 2004, an entirely new generation of fans made it a gold record once again.

Having worked with Greenberg as a publicist, I was privy to some of the unimaginable placements the song got, and the obscure places that

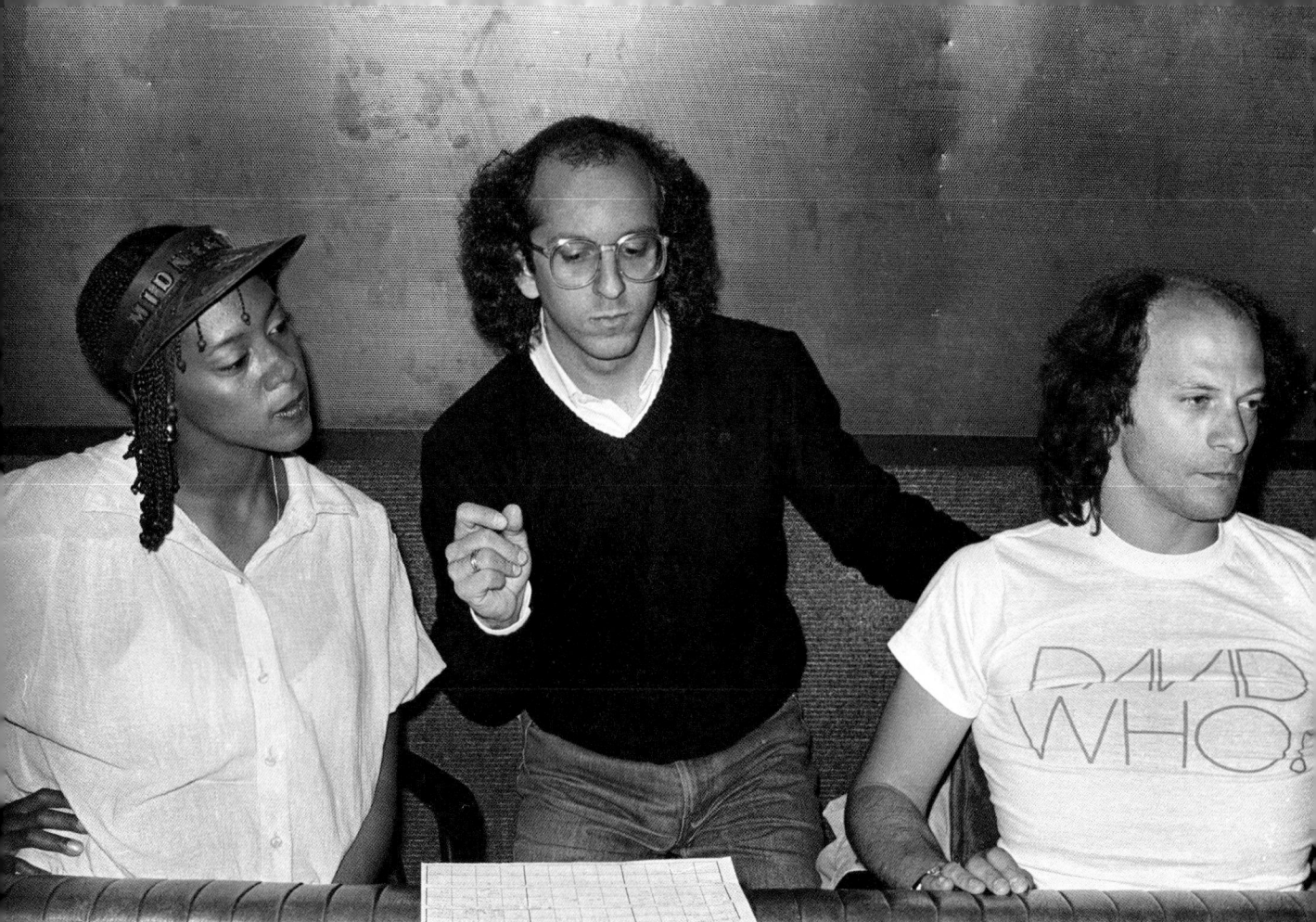

occasional royalty checks would come from. The antiquated, but somehow always current, dance tune refused to say "uncle" (actually that was Greenberg's nickname, "Unc," a handle given to him by his multi-instrumentalist and producer nephew, John Fields, which some employees and musicians started calling him, as well).

"Funkytown" has been used around the world in hundreds of movies and TV shows, for special events like the Olympics, and even on a New York Yankees–branded compilation album. Greenberg's favorite use of the song is the version produced by a French nuclear energy company, Areva, which hired the London Symphony Orchestra to record a string version at Abbey Road Studios. My favorite doesn't even include any music: a Nissan advertisement featuring a tasteful black and white photograph of an elegant-looking car pulling off the highway at night onto an exit ramp marked "Funkytown." But the most endearing "Funkytown" artifacts were the heartfelt fan letters to the song that were posted for a time on a dedicated website describing how it had been used at weddings, funerals, and other rites of passage. The letters from fans in the former Eastern Bloc,

Cynthia Johnson, songwriter-producer Steven Greenberg, and producer David Z at work at Sound 80, the legendary studio where "Funkytown" was recorded.

where western music was criminally prohibited, were particularly tantalizing and underscored how important music could be in a person's life, especially in repressive regimes.

Not only is it one of the most licensed one-hit wonders in recent times, "Funkytown" might also be one of the most covered songs, too, either live, sampled, or on record: RuPaul, Henry Rollins, U2, polka bands, New Orleans–style brass bands, Cokehead Hipsters, Pseudo Echo, bluegrassers, a Russian soul band—the list is long and loopy. In 2016, after collecting as many interpretations of the song as he could over the years, "Unc" brought together a cross-genre A-list of producers, singers, and musicians to reimagine and rerecord the hit in wide-ranging and eclectic styles. Called, simply, *The Funkytown 15*, the record is a good, multicultural primer to the song for new and future generations.

The producer-musicians contributing to the record include Ed Boyer (*Glee, Pitch Perfect*, and many others); Steve Lu (Shakira, Christina Aguilera, and others); Aaron Alexander (numerous jazz and klezmer groups); nephew Fields (Nick Jonas, Miley Cyrus, Switchfoot, and Demi Lovato); and more. These creative minds reinvented "Funkytown" in ways you wouldn't think possible. The record opens with a swopping a cappella/doo-wop treatment from Boyer, followed by a marching-band version by rising jazz and foodie stars the Potash Twins (whose debut album Greenberg executive produced with producer and musician Cory Wong). There's a classical arrangement with real strings, no synths; versions ranging from klezmer to jazz, folk to heavy metal; and even a magical Christmas mash-up arranged by the irrepressible Wong. After you hear it, you'll never ask directions to Funkytown again.

Over the years, I have often wondered what happened to those Street Academy kids and how they may have fared in their own Funkytowns. As for their former receptionist and the vocalist who sent "Funkytown" dancing up the international charts as *the* big summer hit of 1980, the last time I saw Cynthia, she was on TV and social media in early February 2018. There she was, former Miss Black Minnesota, taking a ragged run at "Funkytown" outside in the crippling cold with the reunited, original Flyte Tyme, her old band—including Jam and Lewis—during the Super Bowl shows on Minneapolis's Nicollet Mall. Call it the wicked windchill version. Some things it seems—like hearing this old warhorse in places and times you least expect—are just inevitable.

TERRY LEWIS AND JIMMY JAM

The Cool, Chili-Sauce Sounds of the Men in Black(ness)

Sometimes a snowstorm is a good thing. In 1983, Terry Lewis and Jimmy Jam (née James Harris III) were fired from the Time by Prince when a blizzard prevented them from getting back to the Controversy tour, where the Time was opening for him. Jimmy and Terry had slipped away from the tour on a day off to produce a record for the S.O.S. Band in Atlanta. The wintery wrath of Mother Nature and Mutha Prince had gold, platinum, and diamond linings, however.

The two friends, who met in junior high school and formed the band Flyte Tyme, went on to become one of the most successful songwriting and producing duos of all time. Built on Jam's love of the pop R&B hits of the Philadelphia Sound (spawned by two similar songwriting producers, Kenneth Gamble and Leon Huff), and Lewis's penchant for the edgy and groovacious Parliament Funkadelic, it was an ideal partnership formed at the dawn of the so-called Minneapolis Sound.

Although their work with S.O.S. netted a slow burner of a hit record, "Just Be Good to Me," the song might just as well have been an early plea or a paean to the gods of the music industry. Whatever it was, it seemed to work.

Jimmy and Terry's creativity with the Twin Cities' own Alexander O'Neal, Mint Condition, and the Sounds of Blackness; England's George Michael, the Human League, Spice Girls, and Rod Stewart; and other major stateside stars like Michael and Janet Jackson, Boyz II Men, Cherrelle, Mariah Carey, Patti LaBelle, New Edition, Bruno Mars—well, you get the idea of how long the ultimate Jam and Lewis credit page is. They elevated Janet Jackson nearly to the level her more famous brother achieved, launching and then shaping her career, first in Minneapolis and later in Los Angeles after they made the move west in 2003.

Going beyond all the A-list names, try some of the big industry numbers: Together, Jimmy Jam and Terry Lewis have earned more than one hundred

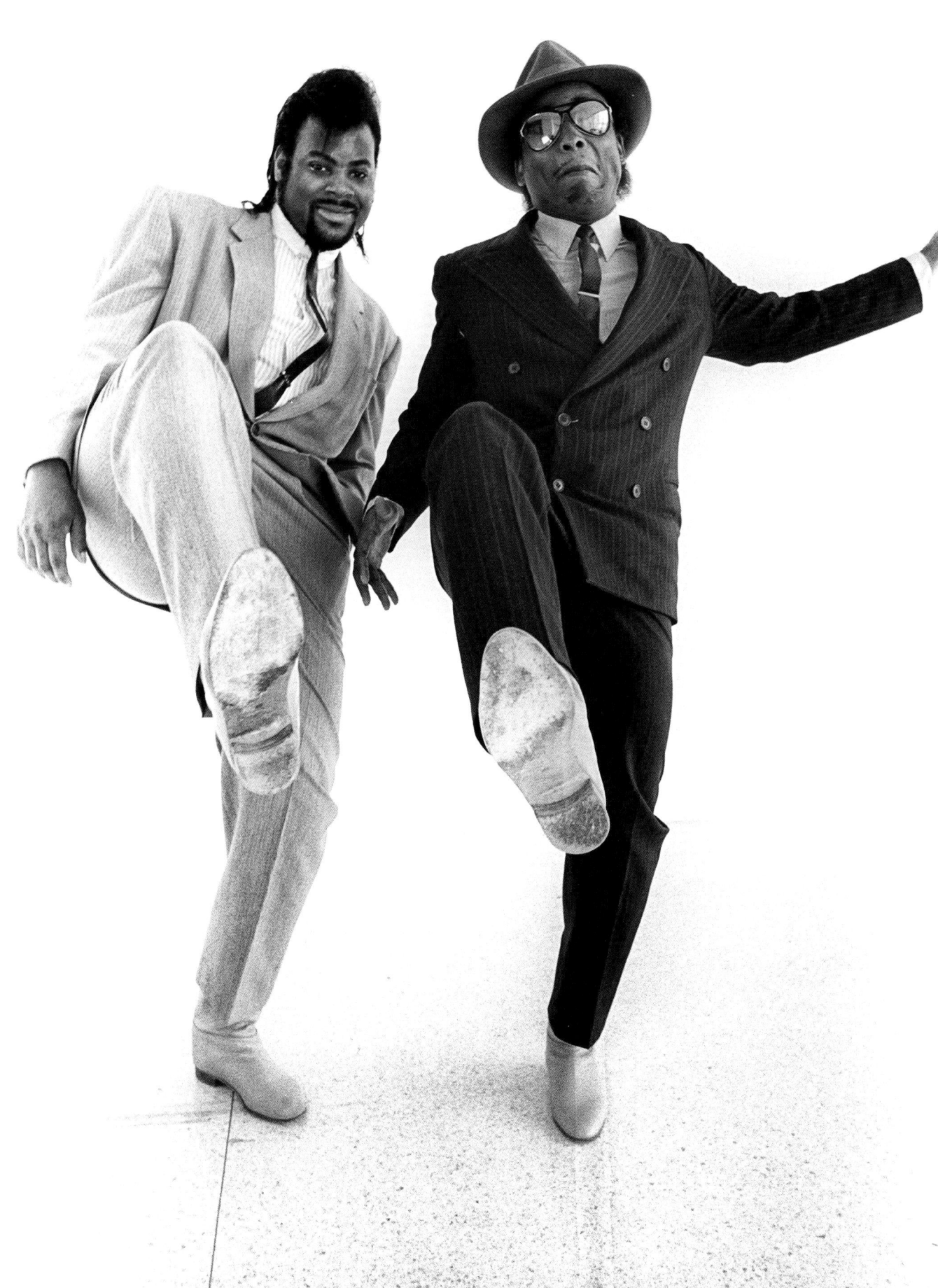

gold, platinum, multiplatinum, and diamond albums. They've cranked out forty-one *Billboard* Top 10 songs, including twenty-six number one R&B smashes and sixteen number one Hot 100 hit records—and counting.

"Their music has so much attitude," jazzman Ben Sidran once remarked while recording in Minneapolis in the eighties. So does their signature sartorial style. Always handsomely dressed, these "men in black" usually sported smart designer or custom, tailor-made black suits, white shirts, black hats, and dark shades. The rhythm-and-blues bros created an elegant persona to match their vaunted songwriting, musicianship, and studio production skills—what Lewis famously termed "the chili sauce."

The recipe has not lost its kick through the years. Jam and Lewis are rivaled only by Prince for their musical sensibilities and production techniques. After getting axed from the Princely court, the duo kept apace of music trends through the nineties and into the next century, employing what Lewis once described as a three-dimensional approach to music making. It rested on strong melodies, a good story, and a healthy respect for each artist's history and style that would be reflected in any new material written and produced for the singer or group, whether Gladys Knight or Luther Vandross's former band, Change. Jimmy and Terry also worked hard during sessions. Creation Audio engineer and owner Steve Wiese once remarked that their work ethic was impressive, "clean and meticulous." And they didn't waste time; Wiese said they always came into the studio knowing what they wanted. You get a sense of that MO listening to how seamlessly they sample Joni Mitchell's "Big Yellow Taxi" and punch in Q-Tip rap motifs over an incessant rhythm track with Janet's sweet vocals riding a lovely melody in 1997's "Got 'Til It's Gone."

In person, Jimmy has always been the more outspoken of the two, while Terry is typically the more introspective one, but his funny one-liners will catch you off guard and deliver the money quote. The Helg and I caught up with them for a cover story for the short-lived *Nightbeat* monthly music rag, published by the *Twin Cities Reader*, in 1984. (David Carr, who was working there at the time, snidely called it *Night Soil*.) During the interview, Lewis noted that making successive hits presented its own challenges: "Producing hit records all of the sudden puts a lot of pressure on you. You don't like to see your work rise up one week into the top twenty and the next week watch it fall below seventy. We ain't been off the charts for almost a year. That's more pressure."

(opposite) Record-breaking, high-stepping mega producers Jimmy Jam Harris and Terry Lewis, photographed at the original Guthrie Theater in April 1984. "They were great fun and very cooperative and understood immediately what I was trying to do," the Helg said of this shoot. "I had an impulse for some reason to ask them to high step me. As usual, I had no preplanned agenda; I just felt things out as I went."

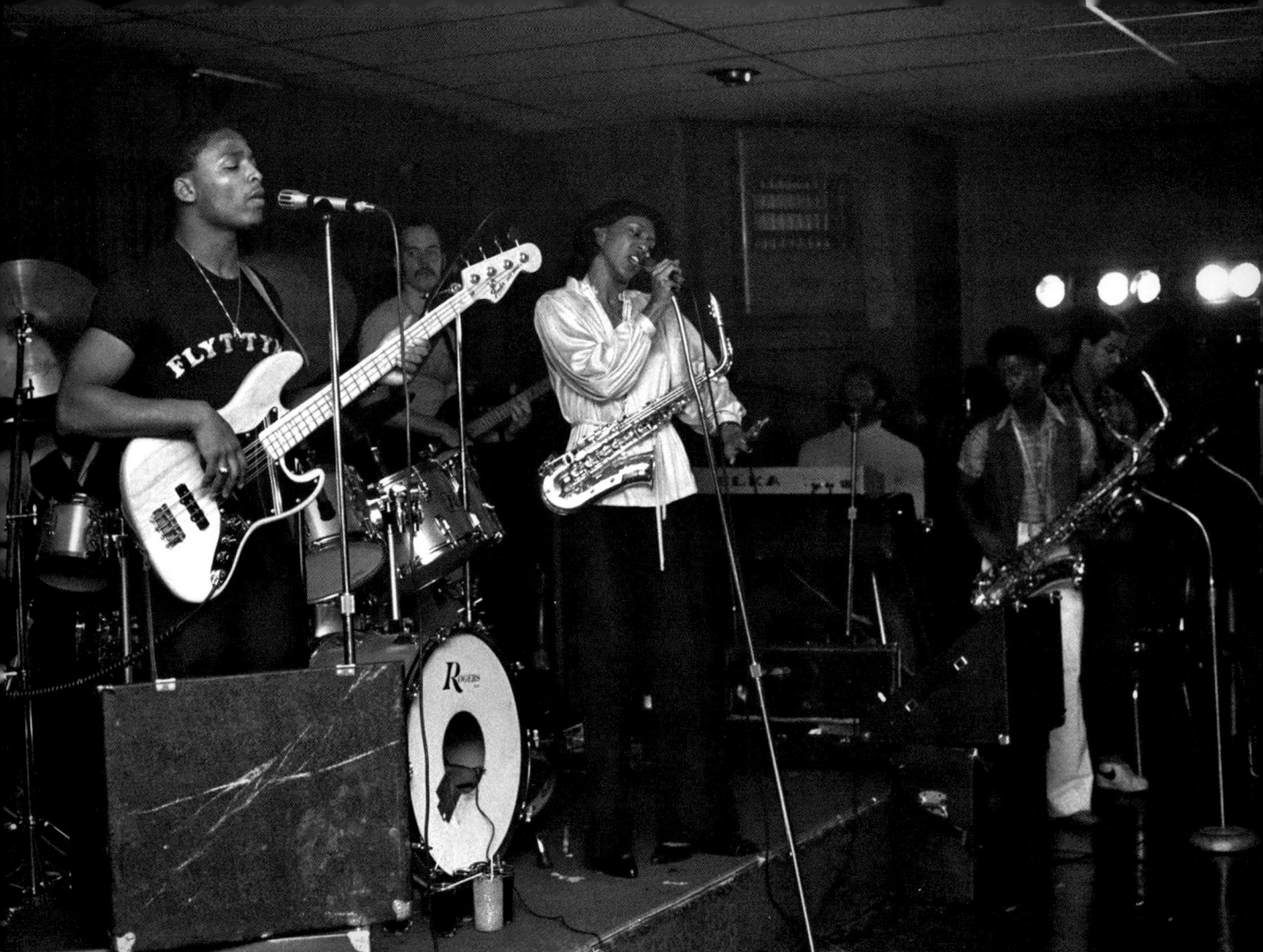

Flyte Tyme, featuring vocalist Cynthia Johnson, was Jam and Lewis's original band and would later become the Time with Morris Day.

"This ain't no glamor job," Jam chimed in. "It makes a man out of you." Finishing the thought, Lewis added, "You got to have a one-track mind to keep on it." Sadly, because of the racist programming of the radio business, much of what they wrote and charted was not heard locally except on the northside African American community station, KMOJ, or in clubs as they began conquering the industry.

In 1987, I revisited them at their first Flyte Tyme Studio, located on Nicollet Avenue and Forty-fourth Street in south Minneapolis, where a home renovation company resides these days. It was terribly small by the standards of their next studio in suburban Edina, and of Paisley Park, for example. But it was big enough to house their growing collection of cars: two Ferraris and two Ford Explorers ("better in the snow," Jimmy drolly noted later) were parked in the back of the building. Up front, trumpeter, bandleader, and A&M Records cofounder Herb Alpert, and his wife, singer Lani Hall, waited for the guys to arrive for their session. Their secret sauce worked again for the legendary mogul, sending his singles "Making Love in the Rain" and "Keep Your Eye on Me" (also the name of the album) to the high ends of both the pop and R&B charts. The album blasted to the eighteenth position.

Jam and Lewis later moved Flyte Tyme Studios to Seventy-seventh Street and France Avenue in Edina. It was here that they would record with both Janet and Michael Jackson, among many others. The state-of-the-art studios were fitting work spaces for the two mega-producers, and their individual offices offered insights into each one's personality. Jam's was strewn with music industry trade magazines, albums, gold records, memorabilia, and loaded bookshelves. Terry's sparse room made it look like he was well out in front of the decluttering trend; there were but two books on the shelf, one of which was titled *How to Be a Billionaire*.

When Jam and Lewis returned to their hometown during Super Bowl LII in early 2018 for the free Super Bowl Live concerts on Nicollet Mall they curated, they had a good laugh about that memory of their old studio. (Sadly, the building met the wrecking ball later that year.) Despite their runaway success, Jam and Lewis seemed pretty much the same. Never one to shy away from talking about "the biz," Jimmy started debating the artistic merits of Bruno Mars with me the minute his name came up.

One argued that Mars was a chronic imitator of the Police and/or Sting and the Time, asserting that he was a gifted performer who was too derivative and had not really gotten to his true Bruno-ness artistry. The other, the guy with the black hat and shades, quickly rebutted the claim, pointing out that Bruno's millions of fans were too young to know those influences, and he was merely keeping them vital while also paying homage. Game. Set. Match.

Still soft spoken and stoic, Lewis was equally friendly. We spoke quietly about a Prince Scholars program he was interested in participating in, should it come to fruition. Then Dessa and her group blew off the stage just as it started to snow hard, with two more acts left to go, Mint Condition and the New Power Generation. Posing for selfies backstage, the dynamic producing duo struck their classic poses in black hats and dark shades with Dessa and her band.

As the night wore on, the two frequently took the stage to announce the bands and also record the event on their phones. Standing off to the side, Jam looked like an otherworldly presence, a half-lit shadow presiding over the funk. Snow often blew up into their faces and those of the musicians onstage. It was almost as if they had never left the cold Minnesota winters.

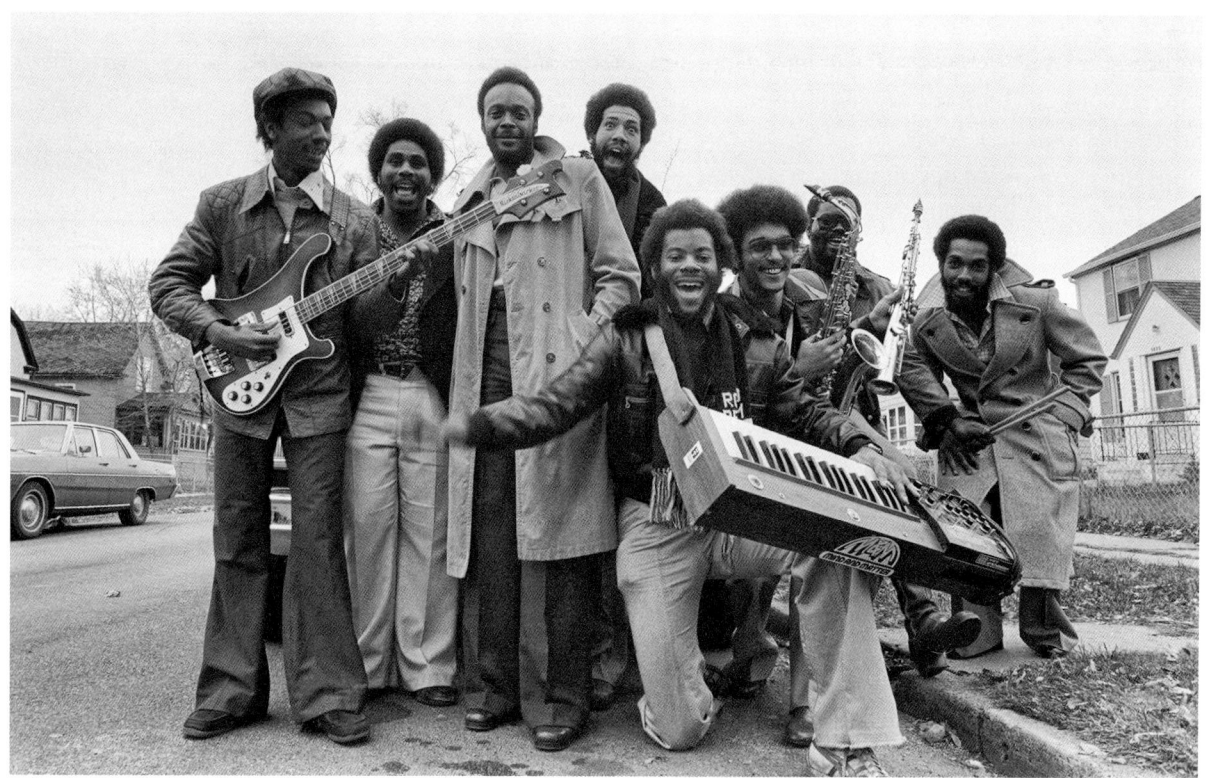

(above) While still a teenager, Jimmy Jam formed Mind and Matter, featuring two keyboards, robust horn and rhythm sections, multiple vocalists, and ample quantities of the funk and soul that would define the Minneapolis Sound. The band's recordings from 1977 were finally shown the light of day in 2013, thanks to a release by the Chicago-based Numero Group. Entitled *1514 Oliver Avenue (Basement),* after the location where it was recorded, the album featured this photo by Helgeson on the cover; the image also appeared in a story by Keller for the *Musician's Insider* in the late seventies.

(right) Singer Sue Ann Carwell, photographed here in her Minneapolis apartment, emerged on the Minneapolis scene in the late 1970s and soon caught the attention of Prince and André Cymone. With help from Prince's first manager, Owen Husney, Carwell signed a record deal with Warner Bros., but her career never really took off.

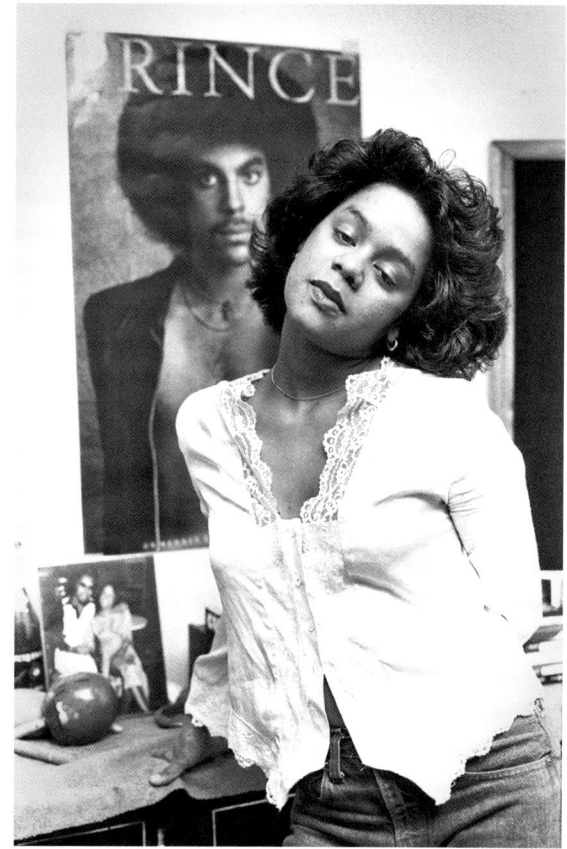

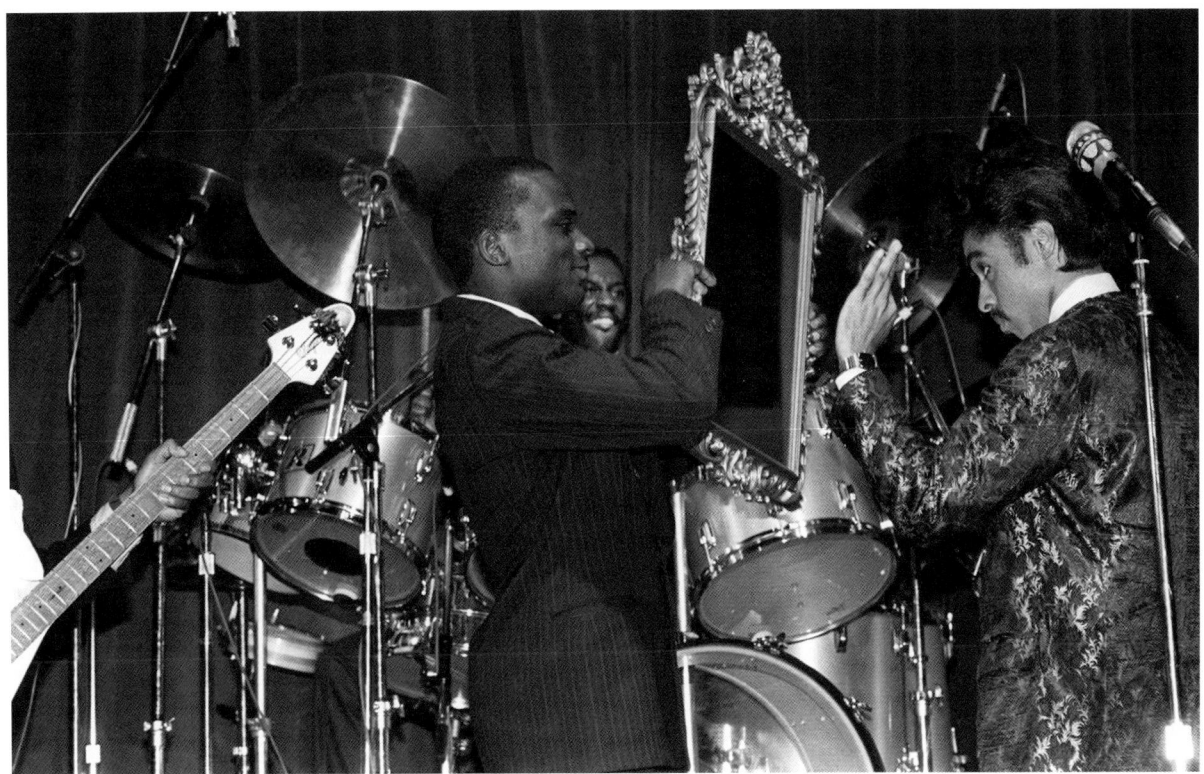

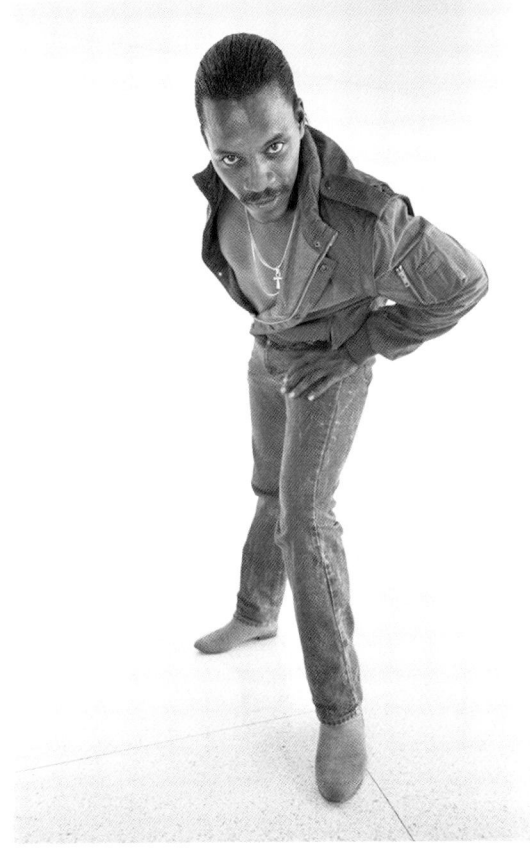

(above) What a time it was! Jerome Benton image checks Morris Day in one of the Time's trademark antics.

(left) Alexander O'Neal always predicted that he would become a big star, and he did, with the help of Jimmy Jam and Terry Lewis and a huge R&B fan base in England, where he lived for many years. He was a member of Flyte Tyme with Jam and Lewis, but he left shortly after the band was reconfigured as the Time and was replaced by Morris Day. As a solo artist, O'Neal has recorded ten studio albums and enjoyed numerous hits on the R&B charts.

STEVE KRAMER

"Lawrence Welk Meets James Brown Meets Captain Beefheart" Meets ... World

He had a thing for mice. (He drew them often in pencil and paint.) And music. Art. Theater. Advertising and branding. Laurel and Hardy. And maybe for being too hip for the room. He also had a "way of saying the perfectly wrong thing at the right time," according to friend and artistic collaborator—and storyteller—Kevin Kling, which "helped me with my bad mood by making it worse. But then I'd see the absurdity of myself and the laughter would come."

There were a lot of so-called original characters doing cool things in the Twin Cities in the eighties, but there was only one Steven Kramer. Even in 2019, six years after his sudden death at age fifty-nine while attending the Sundance Film Festival, you'd still be hard pressed to find anyone like him—and we are talking about two cities that have produced more than their fair share of ferocious pop life originals.

Kramer is best known for leading the Wallets, his band with Jim Clifford, Max Ray, Rod Gordon, and Erik Anderson. The group made three albums for Twin/Tone Records. The first, *Take It*, was produced by the legendary New Orleans songwriter and producer Allen Toussaint, in what was one of the more head-scratching culture combos of that or any other era. Onstage, the Wallets had a devilish penchant for performing in front of handmade sets and dressed in costumes like nun habits, cardboard cutouts, and other outrageous getups.

On record, the combo was nearly indescribable. But rocker Jody Hanks, from the band Raggs, took a pretty good cut at defining Kramer and the Wallets after Kramer passed away: "Lawrence Welk meets James Brown meets Captain Beefheart."

If you're up for a scavenger hunt, seek out the band's debut EP, released on Spiffola Records in 1983, *Catch a Falling Star*. The title track explodes like one of those fireworks that looks like it's petering out only to burst into a giant sparkling palm tree. The band's equally rare singles

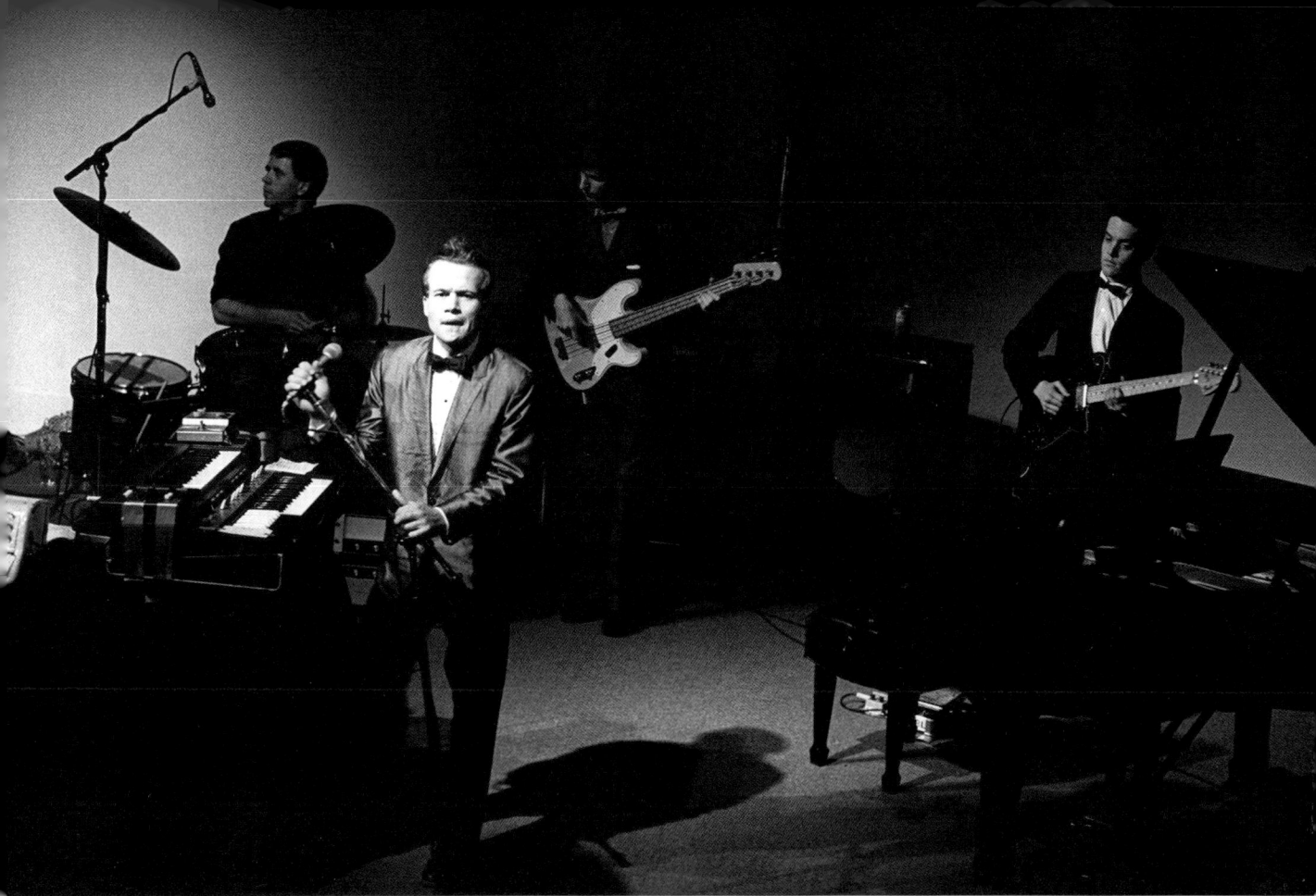

have their own kind of Kramer-magic that made the Wallets' currency valuable: a rapped version of "Twas the Night Before Christmas" over a manic keyboard figure (also on Spiffola) and "Totally Nude," released on Vermillion in 1984. The video for "Totally Nude," directed by Craig Sinard, beautifully captured the band's eccentric edges, its soulful musical center, and Kramer's ironic showmanship.

The Wallets also exhibited elements of the New York–based no-wave jazz group James Chance and the Contortions, for whom Kramer played keyboards, until he fell three floors from a Manhattan building, landing on the sidewalk on his face. He came home to Minnesota to repair and recover from addiction, and his creative life soared.

In addition to his keyboard skills, Kramer was a solid accordion player. During one gig at the 7th Street Entry with the Wallets, David Byrne of Talking Heads sat in on guitar and vocals as Kramer wielded the squeeze box for a droll rendition of Dean Martin's "Houston" (referring, in this case, to Houston Street in New York, not the city in Texas).

By 1989, the Wallets were done; they played their final set at the Guthrie Theater that January. Although the band folded up their tent, Kramer

Led by Steve Kramer, the Wallets were the biggest wild card on the Twin Cities new-wave scene of the eighties. The combo embraced a mélange of styles and performed occasionally in costume and against handmade sets.

was just getting started, pursuing an entirely new creative adventure with the band's manager, Bob Hest. They opened Hest + Kramer, where the two worked together as equal partners for thirty-three years doing music and sound design for television and radio commercials—building their own gleeful corner in the world of advertising.

"Can you imagine Steve Kramer sitting in a first client meeting to talk about a new project?" asked an incredulous friend of mine, Emily Scott, who was a writer at the Martin Williams agency at the time. Actually, I could.

Around the same time that Kramer and Hest crossed over into the "dark side," I did, too, going to work in public relations. When I set out on my own after a couple years at an agency we called Welts and Millstones, I went to work for Bob and Steve to help expose them to the wider world. They were great clients. Neither one of them blinked when I presented them with their bios for the media kit; each one was only five or six sentences long, and both ended with the sentence, "He brings his dog to work." Jeff Baenen from the local bureau of the Associated Press seized the story. Soon it was syndicated in newspapers across North America.

Hest + Kramer flourished, long after my small role in helping them publicize their talents. The agency made a point of hiring local singers and musicians whenever they could, if it fit the creative concept they'd hatched. Their music for broadcast, including commercials, jingles, and other musical signatures, brought to life major brands that included Target, JCPenney, Converse, Budweiser, and countless others. Among the firm's most memorable local work was for Erik's Bike Shop, in which Kramer's voice roars, "Erik the bike man!" The ad is still playing in this market after many years.

Despite his success in the audio ad world—a high-stakes realm every bit as challenging as the music business—Kramer never gave up on other creative ventures. He served as a special guest soundman on *A Prairie Home Companion*, and he teamed up with Kling in 2011 for a Minnesota Public Radio special presentation called "Of Mirth and Mischief" at the Fitzgerald Theater. Around the time of his death, Kramer and the master storyteller were at it again, working on a musical for the Children's Theatre Company, titled *The Best Summer Ever!* Kramer had already written four songs for the production.

Kling delivered a memorable eulogy for his departed pal to a full church in south Minneapolis that mixed as many metaphors and low-brow, high-brow strokes as Kramer did in his rich creative life. "Goethe said people should go to the theater like they were visiting a foreign country, open to new experiences and reveling in connections. This is how Steve entered a room," Kevin intoned.

Kling recalled how, on the first day of what would become regular Monday morning coffee meetings to work on the MPR show, Kramer "walked

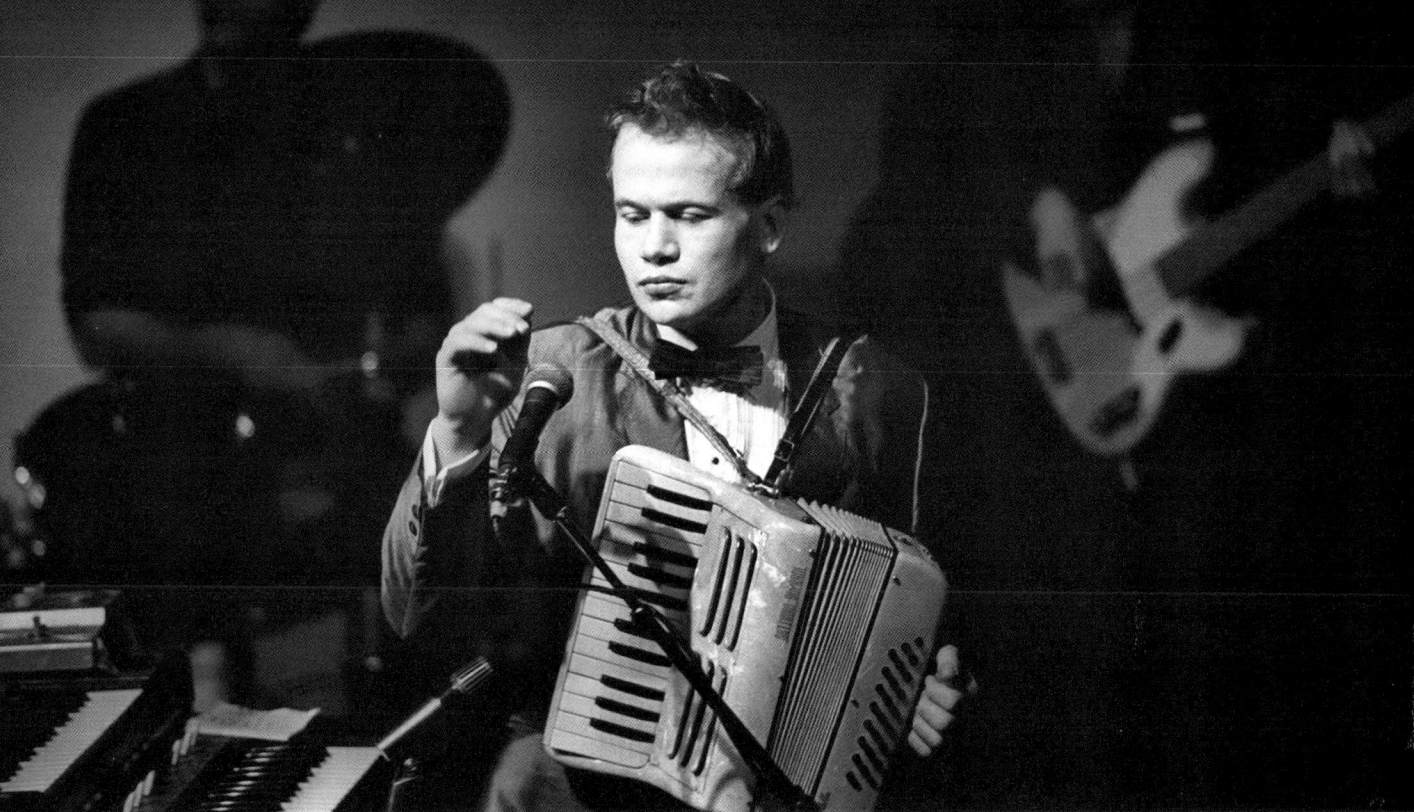

in and the whole place turned to see what the commotion was, only to find Steve staring back. There was a brief pause, then Steve announced, 'I'm from the home office and you're all fired!' The place was stunned for a second, then, like often happened, everyone cheered."

Inside the church, that story got a huge round of laughs and applause, the first of many. But Kling, possessing a seasoned story maker's sense to know when enough is enough and how to leave them wanting more, saved the heart-tugging best for last:

> When I think of Shakespeare connecting the lover, the fool, and the poet in imagination all as one, I think of Steve. His language was music. It could be nuanced, emotional, bold. But it was how he communicated. There was a simplicity to it that revealed hidden depths. He let the listener's imagination fill in and round out the layers and colors, but they were all there. In every laugh there was a tear, a note that promised depth.
>
> I know it's said that some of the stars in the sky have stopped burning but still send their light. That's true with Steve. The effect he had on us will remain.

Steve Kramer was an accomplished keyboardist, accordion player, percussionist, singer, songwriter, and visual artist who eventually took his diverse creative skills to the art world, commercial radio and TV, and theatrical endeavors with renowned storyteller Kevin Kling.

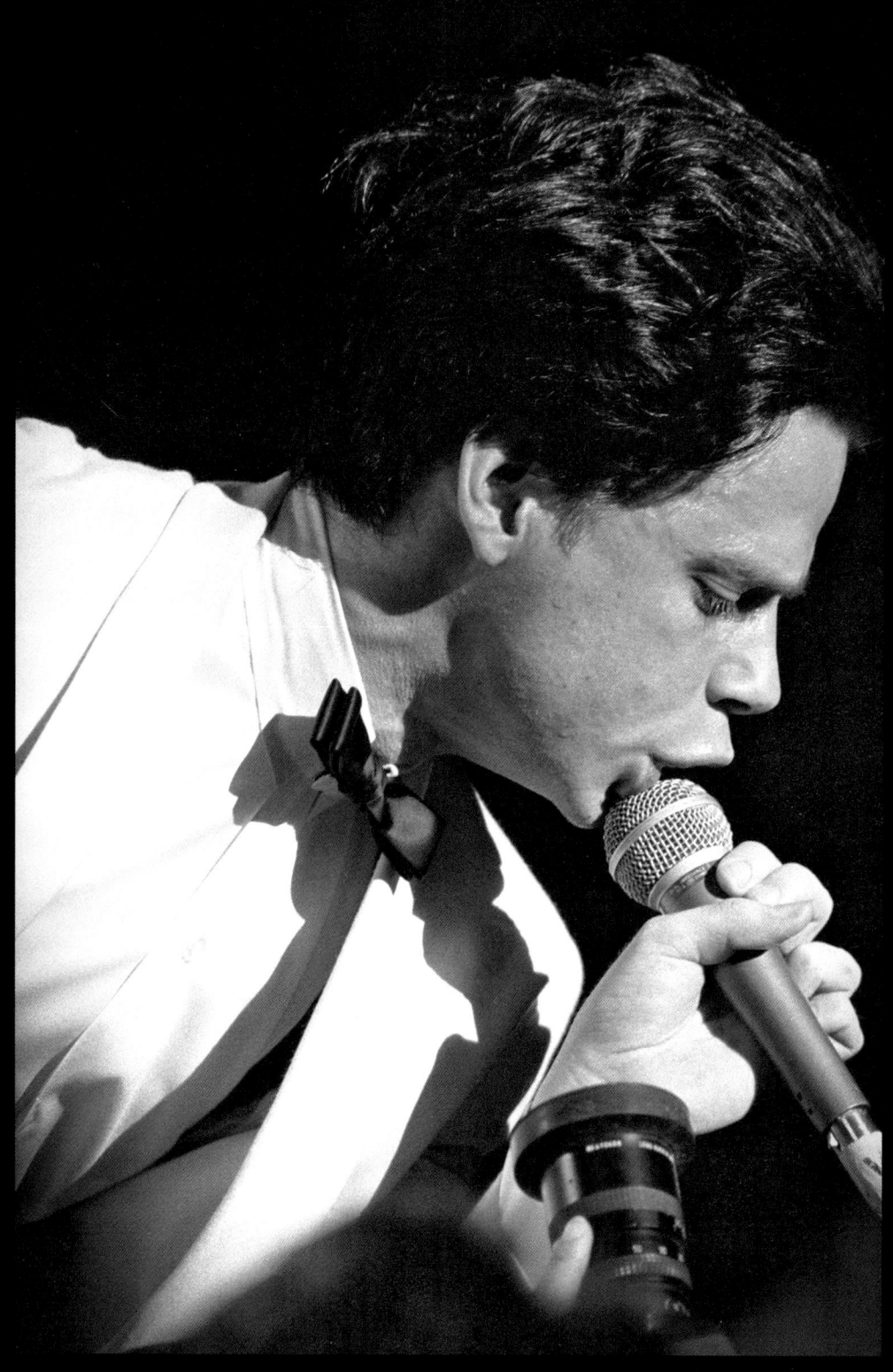

Steve Kramer began his music career in New York City in the late seventies and early eighties as a member of the no-wave jazz band James Chance and the Contortions.

TÊTES NOIRES

The Island of the "All-Girl Band Misfits"

Jennifer Holt was a Miss South Dakota beauty queen, but by the time she assembled the all-female alt-rock-folk-punk-pop band Têtes Noires, all that was left of the quaint all-American pageantry was Holt's loquacious violin and her leader-of-the pack instincts. This band of women, all with black or brown hair (*Têtes Noires* is French for "black heads"), emerged in an overheated, all male, and mostly straight music scene in Minneapolis in the early eighties, making them anomalies and pioneers. Along with the Clams, a straight-ahead classic rock band of four female players, the six-member group helped set the stage for the arrival of Zuzu's Petals, Babes in Toyland, and others later in the decade.

The Têtes' keyboardist, Angela Frucci, noted in 2014, "To be honest, we were from the island of all-girl band misfits locally." Tons of attention was geared toward the testosterone-fueled likes of Hüsker Dü and the Replacements, she noted. Frucci said the group "had the feeling that we were someone's irritating little sister who wouldn't go away. For all the press and attention we received, I think we felt everything from acceptance to resistance to envy to awe."

With support from clubs like First Avenue and fellow oddball bands like the Wallets, the sextet earned their way in with deft three- and sometimes six-part harmonies, sparse instrumentation, and topical songs that often squarely kicked the patriarchy in the pants. Critics around the country cheered and swooned while their fan base seemingly blossomed overnight. Têtes Noires' music was like listening to a parallel universe in which the Andrews Sisters (another Minnesota all-female group) had read Camille Paglia and listened to a lot of Woody Guthrie, Violent Femmes, Suzanne Vega, the Roches, Phranc, and Ferron. The *Trouser Press Record Guide* wrote humorously but succinctly about them: "This Minneapolis sextet shows what can happen when a demented Girl Scout singalong turns into a pop band."

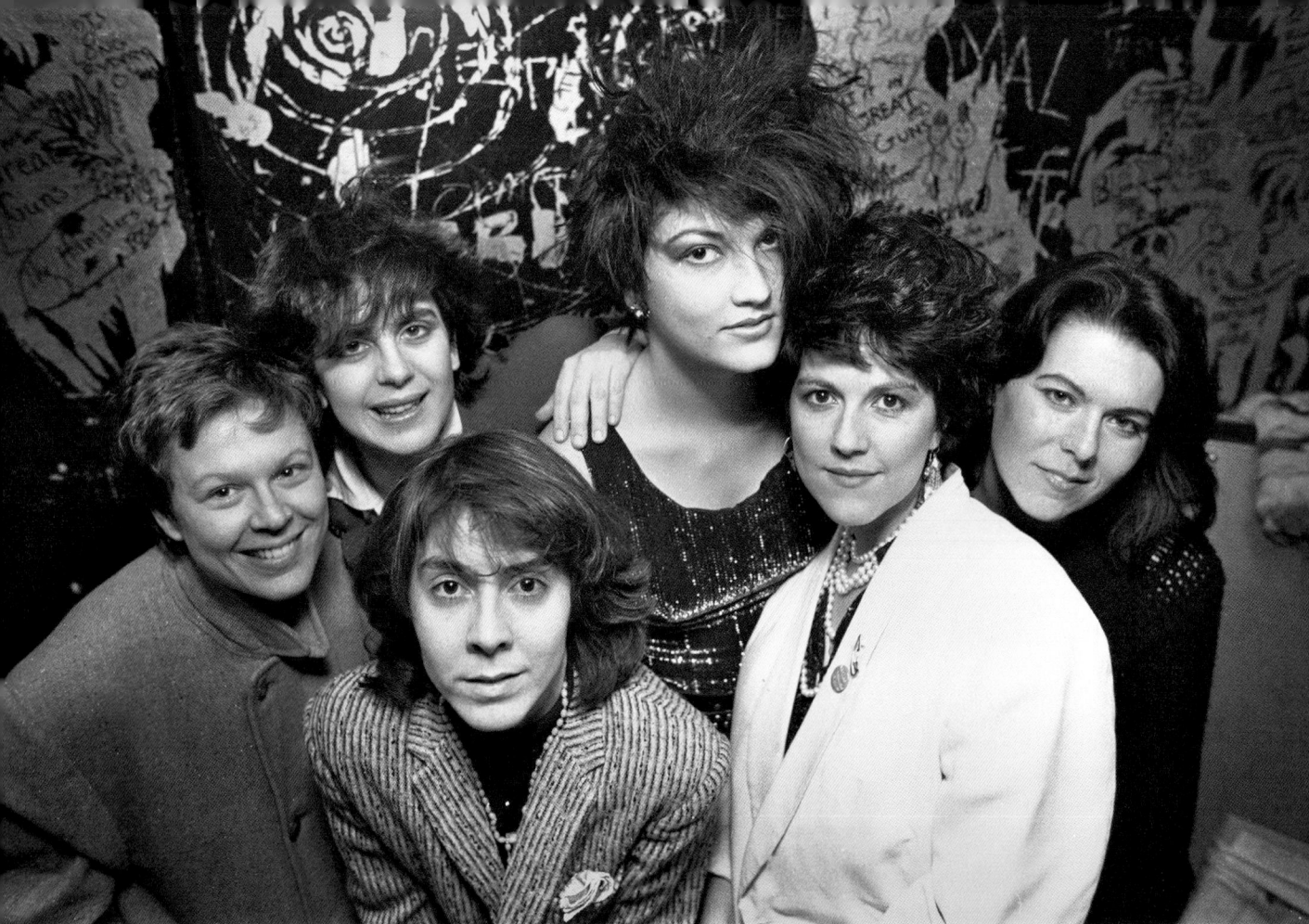

Têtes Noires sounded like the Andrews Sisters in an alt-rock-folk-punk-pop parallel universe. Or, in the words of *Trouser Press*: "This Minneapolis sextet shows what can happen when a demented Girl Scout singalong turns into a pop band."

Always outspoken, Holt bad-mouthed the term "all-girl band," pointing out that no writer ever called the 'Mats or Led Zeppelin an "all-boy band." While she had a point, it's doubtful she lost any sleep over coverage that used the expression. The widespread use of "riot grrrl" didn't come along until the nineties, and the doubling down on gender politics and language wouldn't dawn till well into the new millennium.

Whatever you wanted to call them, Têtes Noires wrote catchy, atypical tunes about such topics as gay male prostitutes, the Moonie Unification Church, and other subjects from off in the margins. Still, the band's more benign numbers like the simple, handclapping ditty about a "Recipe for Love" sounded like it sprang from Betty Crocker's cookbook out at General Mills, with a bunch of Doris Days serenading the Pillsbury Doughboy around the mixing bowl.

Whatever they put in the mix, it proved to be the right stuff. Writing in the *New York Times* about the band's July 1985 live set at the legendary Folk City and the group's acute musical sensibilities, Jon Pareles noted: "For its dark character studies, Têtes Noires writes blithe melodies and builds mock-sweet arrangements, featuring Cynthia Bartell's percolating bass lines, Angela Frucci's punchy keyboard licks, and up to six-part vocal harmonies. The fiddler Jennifer Holt writes observant, casually mocking lyrics; occasionally, Têtes Noires denounce a target outright while maintaining bright, Andrews Sisters–style harmonies. Like the Roches, Têtes Noires are virtuosic patter singers, but they bolster their songs with arrangements that suggest soul, garage-band rock, country, and even, in *American Dream* [their 1984 album], a hora."

Nearly three decades later, the allure had not worn off as Frucci—with the group's wrestled blessing—went to work in 2013 to remix and sonically improve *American Dream*, the Têtes' second of three albums. Jim DeRogatis, of the nationally syndicated *Sound Opinions* radio program, picked Frucci's remixed album as one of his "Desert Island" discs and championed the band on his WBEZ *Pop N Stuff* blog: "Têtes Noires were yet another of my favorite devotedly eccentric and startlingly original indie-rock acts from an era when weirder really was better in the underground. The six-member, largely a cappella, all-female troupe was for me as beloved as their male Twin Cities peers the Replacements and Hüsker Dü." He added that, while the band, "may not have survived past its '80s heyday…its spirit lives on in the new remaster."

A newcomer to the Têtes' sound had an even more enthusiastic reaction. Ben Apatoff wrote on his *Apatoff for Destruction* music blog that he "can't get enough of" the remixed and reissued *New American Dream*: "Years before anyone was called a riot grrrl, this irreverent sextet was re-imagining punk rock (new wave? folk rock? help) with keyboards, violin, non–drum kit percussion, acoustic guitars, hand claps, and up to six-part harmonies graced by brash, subversive lyrics. It's rare to hear authentic punk music that you could put on a mixtape for your parents, which makes *The New American Dream* more dangerous than your brother's hardcore."

Like their songs, the lives of the band members took unexpected turns after they broke up in 1987, just four years after their formation. Bartell became a lawyer and eventually a partner at Foley & Mansfield, which was ranked in 2016 as the fifteenth best law firm in the country for women, according to Law360, a law news service. Vocalist and keyboard player Camille Gage, who also wrote some of the band's songs, went on to become a successful mixed-media artist and a founding member of the Form + Content Gallery. Gage's sister, vocalist and percussionist Renée George, is a filmmaker in LA. Guitarist Polly Alexander died in 2005 at age forty-seven. Frucci has split her time between copywriting in the Bay Area and occasionally reporting stories for public radio, the *New York Times*, and other media outlets.

Holt's post-Noires transformation was the most profound. Today she works as a counselor, healer, musician, and "mystic agitator" (as one

The "all-girl" Têtes Noires made a name for itself in the testosterone-heavy world of the Minneapolis music scene of the 1980s.

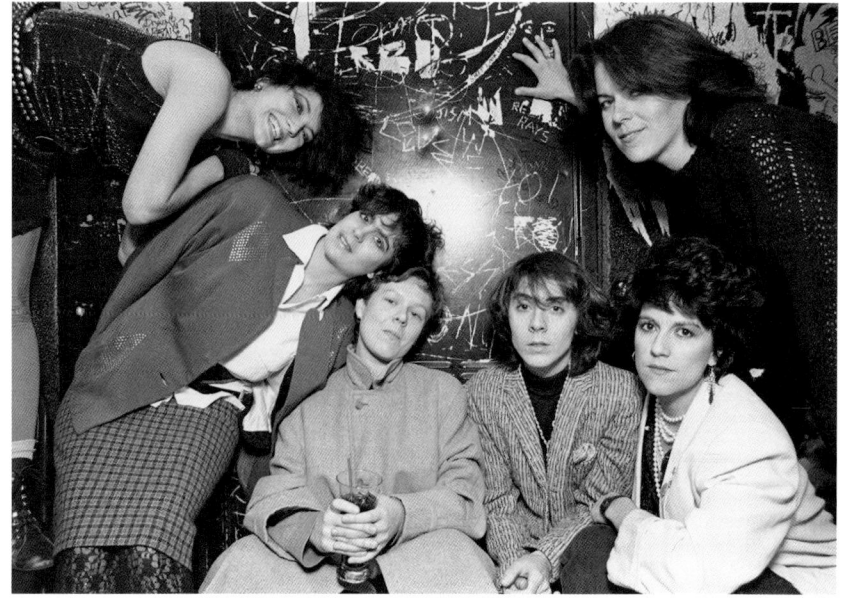

longtime colleague calls her), after earning a doctorate in educational psychology. She went into private practice in Minneapolis and, later, Los Angeles. She also became a self-described "New Thought Muslim" and worked for years with women prisoners on grief and loss issues. That life-changing experience for Dr. Jennifer Salima Holt, PhD, and her incarcerated subjects yielded a compelling book, *Sacred Gateway of Grief and Loss: Freeing the Imprisoned Soul*, and an accompanying album, *Ecstatic Groove: Sacred World Chant Infusions.*

Holt's contemporary collection of traditional hymns, chants, and sacred songs is one of the most tantalizing post-eighties albums ever produced by anyone from that torrid period. Her spiritually rooted songs relied on many traditions, from Sufi forgiveness chants to Christian invocations, such as the Kyrie, to the Hawaiian practice known as Ho'oponopono. It will give you pause. *Ecstatic Groove* infused these sacred sounds with techno and hip-hop elements, giving new relevance to the devotional music known throughout the world.

With it, Holt showed just how far she'd come since the days when she and her Têtes mates used to sing me the last line from an old Walt Disney TV show theme song, "The Ballad of Davy Crockett," whenever I approached them for a friendly printed word. They'd change Davy Crockett's name to mine—"Marty, Marty Keller, king of the wild frontier." It's a sweet little earworm that has traveled over the years just as well as the recorded work of those lovably irritating little sisters of song. In the meantime, Frucci is still hoping to stage a Têtes Noires reunion one day. Light a candle so that it truly happens.

HÜSKER DÜ

Remembering Hüsker Dü in 1984 and Beyond

Running debates among scenesters are as old as music making. But when the one about how the rivalry between Hüsker Dü and the Replacements resembled the alleged Beatles-Stones competition surfaced, I shrugged it off. Didn't see it. Or maybe I missed it altogether. That was the case when the three-piece hardcore punk band from St. Paul issued its 1984 double album, *Zen Arcade*, widely believed to be a classic across a broad spectrum of discerning fans, smart critics, and loyal, punkish headbangers.

I wrote a hastily composed review of the album for the *Twin Cities Reader*, missing just about every important aspect and nuance—its massive sense of alienation, the growing influence of Grant Hart's fun pop sensibilities, Bob Mould's maturing guitar work, and even some experimental use (at least for them) of reversed tape sounds in production. David Fricke, whose work I admired in *Rolling Stone*, even though he often wrote about bigger rock stars, not punk bands, noted, "*Zen Arcade* is probably the closest hardcore will ever get to an opera. A kind of thrash *Quadrophenia*." Gulp. (Because I carried this writer's guilt—and that Hüsker's gap—around with me, I had to turn down the enticing offer from their attorney, Dennis Pelowski, to write the liner notes for the band's *Savage Young Dü* box set in 2017.)

The *Reader* was delivered early enough in the day on Wednesdays for clubs, restaurants, bookstores, street boxes, and other drop spots to provide their patrons and occasional readers the issue in plenty of time for nightclubbers and concertgoers to make weekend plans. Sometime before noon on the day my review came out, I stopped in at Oar Folk for something, only to see the name of the new album and the band's name, plus an excerpt from my review, xeroxed on a four-by-six-inch piece of paper and taped to the front door glass. My name and *Reader* affiliation were highlighted in bold. At the bottom it read: "...transitional at best...."

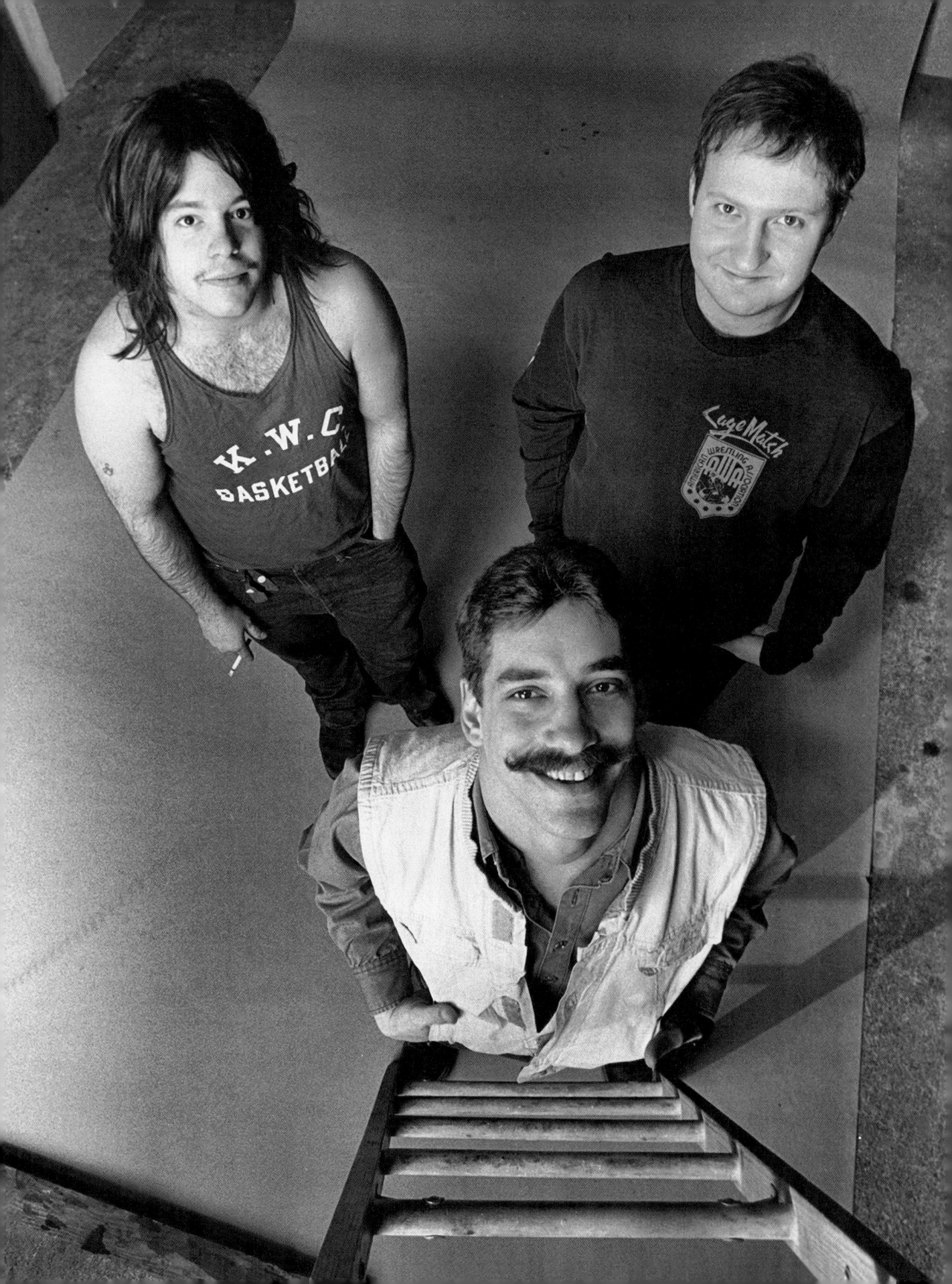

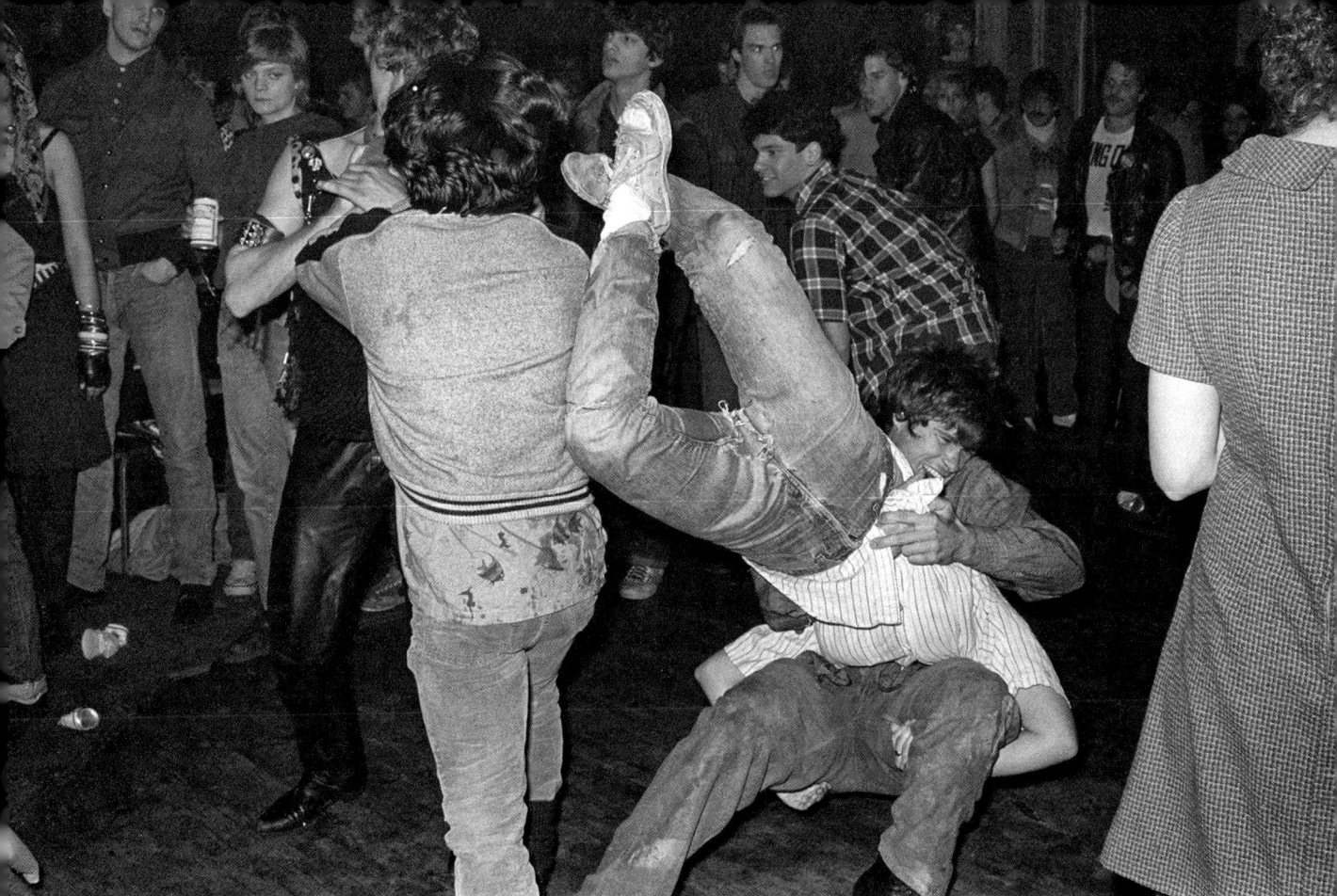

I passed Mould on my way in as he was on his way out. He was carrying a handful of these fresh new flyers in one hand and a tape roll in the other, a man on a mission. Blindsided, I think my expectations for *Zen* were too much colored by the many live shows I'd seen and by their first album from 1982, a live set recorded at the 7th Street Entry and appropriately named *Land Speed Record.* Slammed with seventeen songs, the record was over faster than the time it took to drive five blocks up and back from Oar Folk to Hum's Liquor Store on Lyndale for a cold six-pack—twenty-six-some fast, loud minutes.

My back-of-the-brain notion that the Hüskers would never move beyond the hardcore landscape, in which they were worshipped as the holy trinity, was fatally flawed. They didn't just thrive in the niche; they were the niche. But a mosh pit apparently was not their idea of heaven on earth. They had shit to say, and although only a three-piece, they possessed the advancing musical vocab to get it said. And in 1984, that was saying a lot! So many critical five-star albums—that still hold up more than three decades later—came out that year that you had to wonder what kind of cultural karmic buildup had been fomenting to release the tectonic energy

(above) The mosh pit at Goofy's Upper Deck and elsewhere truly came to life under the loud, fast sounds of Greg Norton, Bob Mould, and Grant Hart.

(opposite) Heroes of hardcore punk, Hüsker Dü developed a broader rock and pop vocabulary over its short but influential eight-year run as a band.

that exploded in 1984: Springsteen's *Born in the USA*, Prince's *Purple Rain*, REM's *Reckoning*, the Replacements' *Let It Be*, Run DMC's self-titled debut, Linton Kwesi Johnson's *Making History*, the Pretenders' *Learning to Crawl*, Stevie Ray Vaughan's *Couldn't Stand the Weather*, Los Lobos' *How Will the Wolf Survive*, Talking Heads' *Stop Making Sense* (film soundtrack), Sade's *Diamond Life*, George Strait's *Does Fort Worth Ever Cross Your Mind*, Têtes Noires' *American Dream*, Nanci Griffith's *Once in a Very Blue Moon*, Ali Farka Touré's *Ali Farka Touré*, Womack and Womack's *Love Wars*, Leonard Cohen's *Various Positions* (featuring "Hallelujah")—it was a feast.

Zen Arcade was the first of two double albums by Hüsker Dü; the second, *Warehouse: Songs and Stories*, came out in 1987 on the major label Warner Bros. The band had truly broken out of the hardcore ghetto and the land of DIY. It was also their last album as a band.

Regrettably, I rarely crossed paths with the Hüskers while they were together, as compared to musicians from other bands like the 'Mats, the 'Burbs, Trip Shakespeare, Flamin' Oh's, and sundry others, perhaps because they lived in St. Paul and were on the road constantly. Hüsker bassist Greg Norton was a guy with whom I shared barely more than a handful of words. There was also widely known internal friction in the group; why disturb a wasp's nest? The palpable tension was exacerbated by heroin use and alcohol abuse, and it reached a nadir when their manager, friend, and maybe their biggest fan, David Savoy Jr., threw himself off a bridge in 1987. He was just twenty-four years old.

The day after Savoy's suicide, a small, sad gathering took place in the Twin/Tone offices (because it was available) with Mould and Hart, scene maker and music lover Abbie Kane, and a few others, trying to decide how to break the news to fans, media, and the public at large. Kane had called writer P. D. Larson and me to help with a news release, even though either he or I would be reporting on it in some fashion that week. Understandably, people had a hard time talking. Slowly it emerged that Savoy had suffered from depression, but one wondered what trigger event or events, if any, led to his fatal decision.

Before their implosion in 1987, the punky power trio had pulled some nice surprises along the way. Besides integrating other musical tongues into their original hardcore aesthetic, they covered *The Mary Tyler Moore* TV theme song, "Love Is All Around," and the Byrds' "Eight Miles High," perfectly ironic and fitting choices for them. In the space of just three years, Hüsker Dü made an astonishing five albums, all pretty much without flaws or many hiccups. In their land-speed evolution, Hart and Mould demonstrated they were complex alpha rockers. They were also curious fellows. I often wondered how Grant got to be friends with Patti Smith and William Burroughs; it didn't seem far afield based on his interests and songwriting subjects, but it did seem wildly unpredictable.

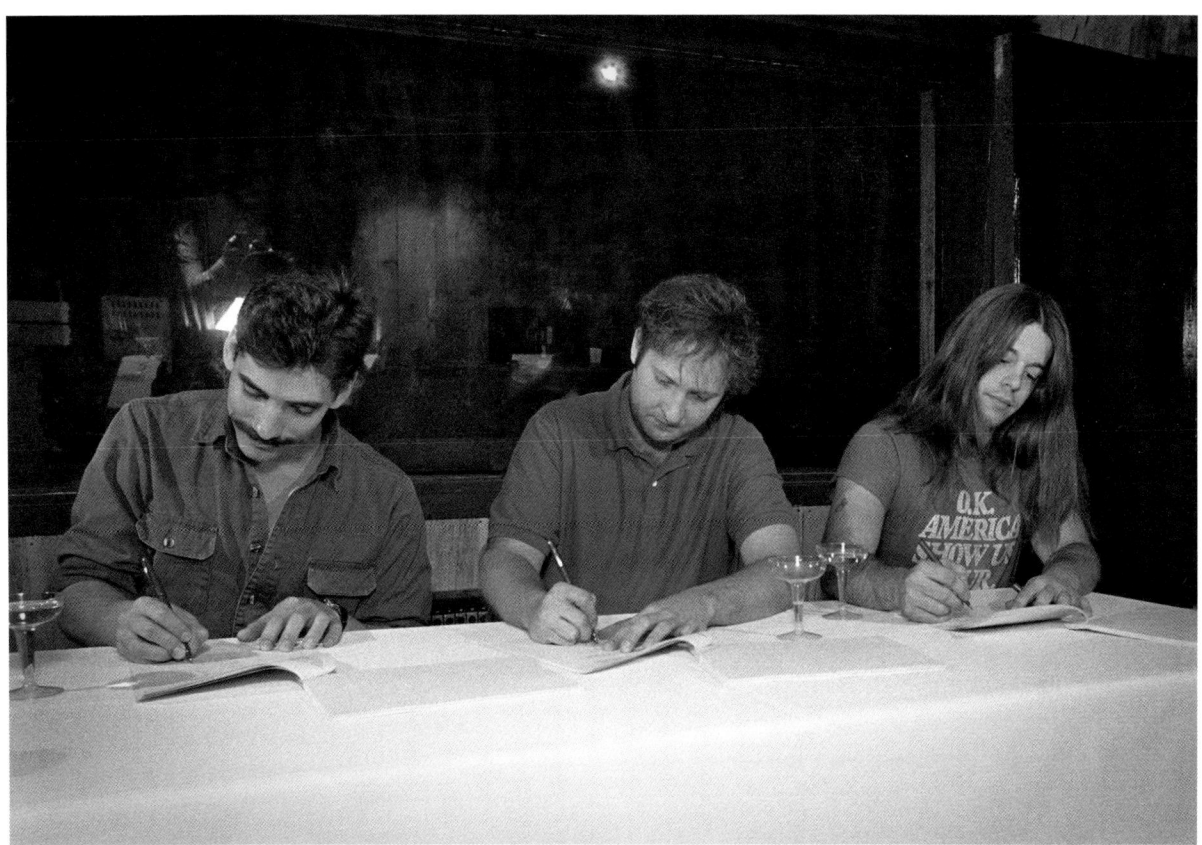

Both Hart and Mould were also openly gay. That would have been a good storyline to explore, but I felt it intruded on their private lives, so I dropped it in the same stroke that I dismissed doing a story on heroin use in the local rock world. Or maybe I just pushed both aside, as I began to feel an increasing sense of burnout—and worse, indifference about what I was covering—after roughly ten years at it.

Mould wisely warned us in 1983 in an album title and song of the same name, *Everything Falls Apart*. And as Hüsker Dü cratered in '87, I remember feeling "transitional at best" myself, wondering—to quote the Clash, another one-time punk band that grew into a stylistically diverse rock group—"should I stay or should I go now?"

When the Hüskers inked their deal with Warner Bros. in 1985, the band seemed on the verge of a much wider breakout. In fact, internal friction, drug use, and an unforgiving touring regimen led to the band's demise just two years later.

Greg Norton (pre-moustache), Grant Hart, and Bob Mould joke around as young hardcore punks.

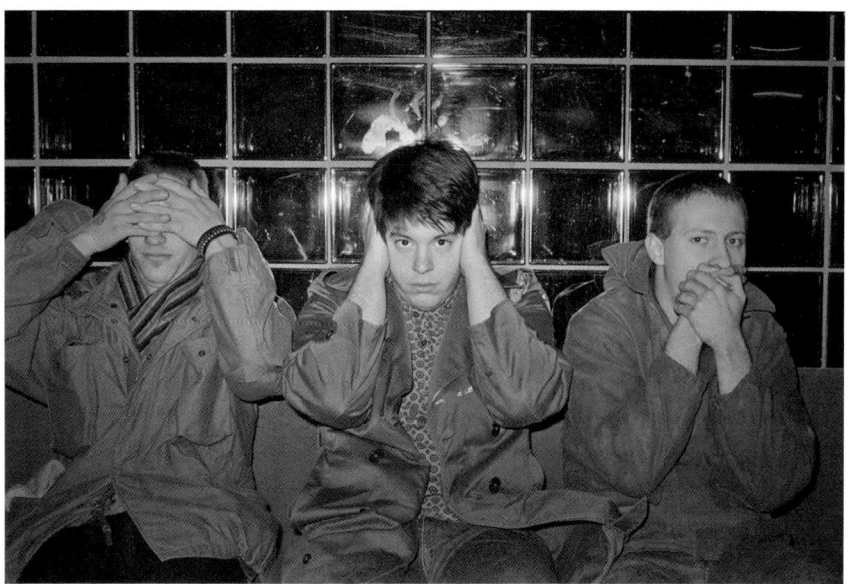

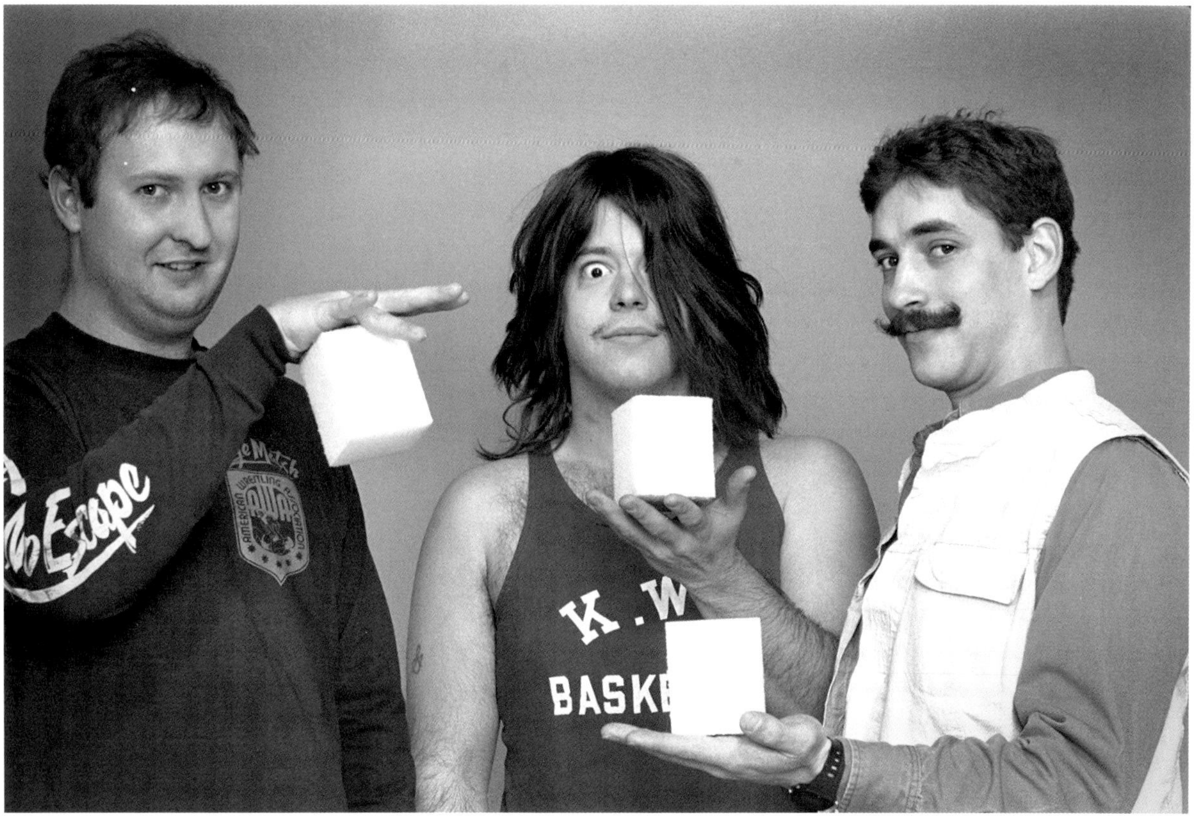

The Hüskers in 1985 at their office below Northern Lights record store in St. Paul

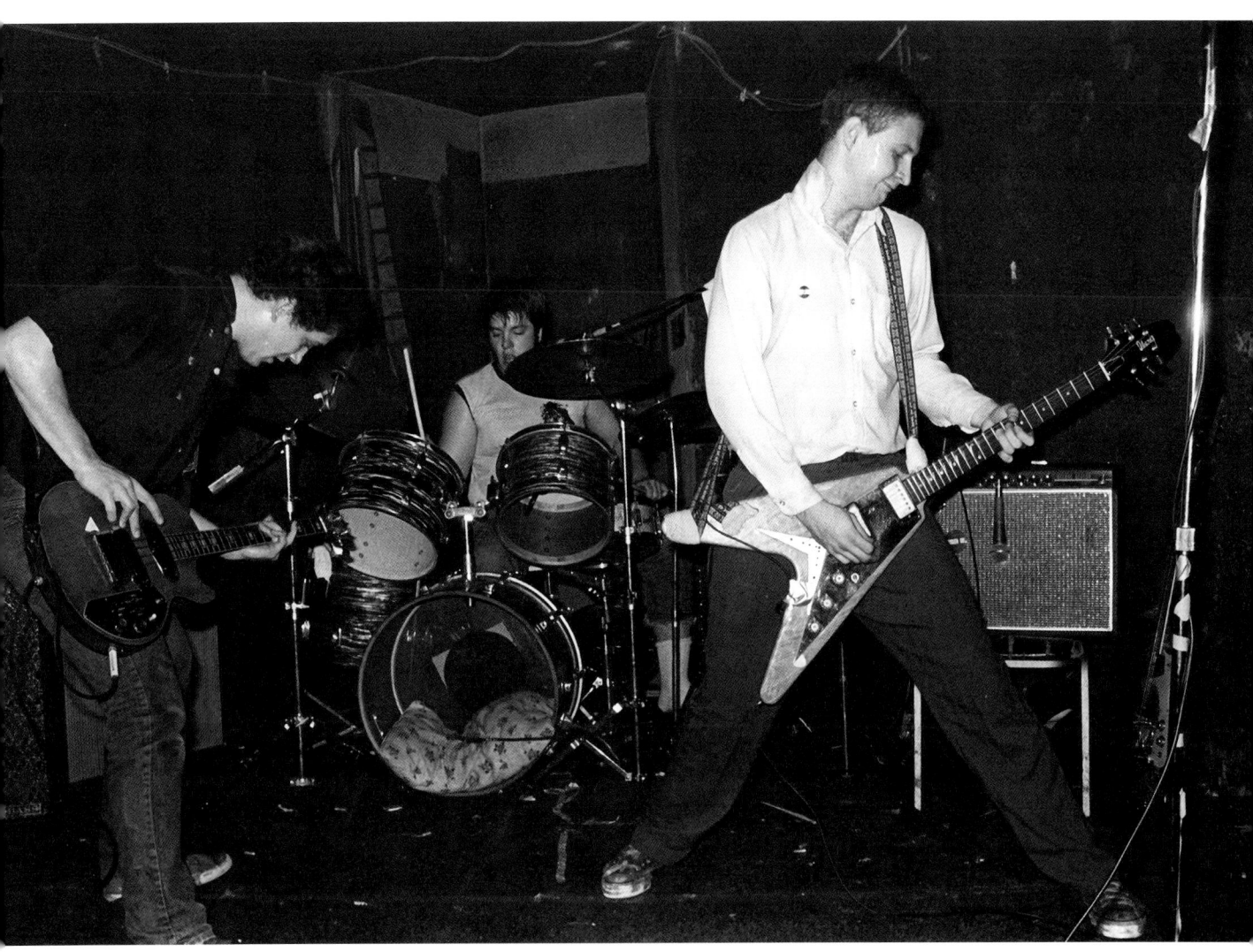

Known for their energetic and pronounced live performances, Hüsker Dü also cranked out six albums, including two double LPs, from 1982's live *Land Speed Record* to 1987's *Warehouse: Songs and Stories.*

THE REPLACEMENTS

This Town Is Too Small, Part 2. Or, "Go Team!"

The vastly overlooked, underrated, nearly unclassifiable Twin Cities–based guitar shaman, improvisor, and international recording artist Steve Tibbetts liked to harangue me whenever possible about being "a cheerleader for *the scene*." His good-humored digs, though, gave me pause. Music journalists, especially those covering local scenes at alternative weekly newspapers around the country, did become supporters of those they covered just by virtue of covering them.

But we did write critical reviews of their recorded work and stage performances. And in my case, as the first music gossip columnist in town, rumors and reality about musician news, antics, and foibles also fell under scrutiny on a weekly basis.

In the burgeoning music capital of Minneapolis–St. Paul in the late seventies and early eighties, it was easy to cheerlead for the Replacements, no matter if they were stumble-fuck lousy or giddy brilliant. Fellow scribe P. D. Larson, who road manages the Jayhawks these days, approached me (in my music editor capacity) about the band. He said the Replacements tape he'd heard at Oar Folkjokeopus record store was "pretty good," and Peter Jesperson, who went on to sign them at Twin/Tone Records and manage them, was going ape over the band. So the first 'Mats story ever, anywhere, got written and published at the *Spud*. Not simply because Peter—the biggest music fan on planet rock—was batshit about them and a huge tastemaker, but because the tape—raw, biting, and nervy as hell—hinted at something more to come.

I filed one of my own feature stories about them, "Mythunderstanding the Replacements," at the *Reader* a few years later following the release of *Tim* in 1985. The legendary David Carr was a fellow staffer at the time, covering news. He wasn't the brilliant writer and penetrating thinker he later became at the *New York Times*, but he left his mark on me as a scribe. Even before he died, I often relied on the "Carr Solution"; it was a

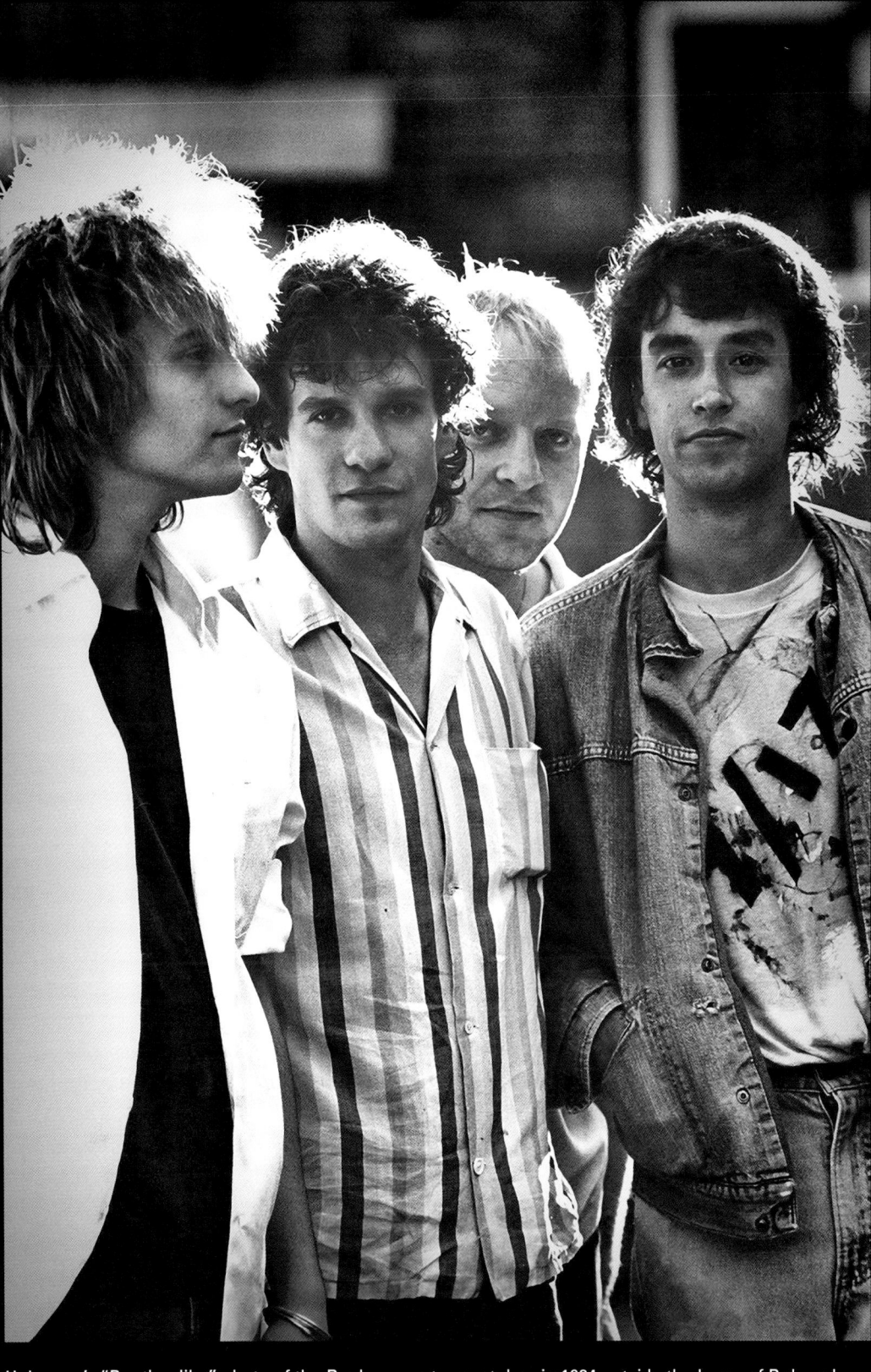

Helgeson's "Beatles-like" photo of the Replacements was taken in 1984 outside the home of Bob and Tommy Stinson.

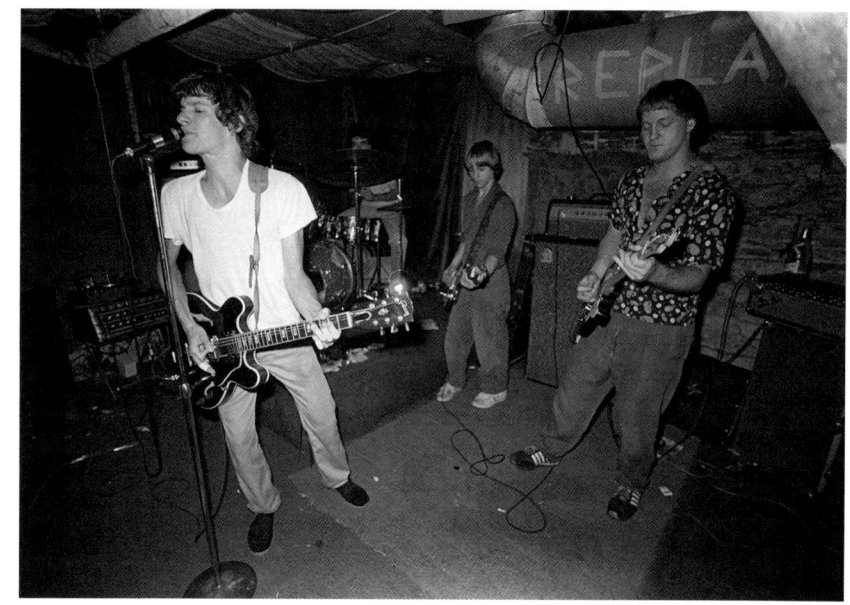

Basement rockers: The Replacements circa 1980 in Tommy and Bob Stinson's house. "You couldn't push these guys," said Helgeson. "I did a lot of waiting around for them. They were also ear-splitting loud during the basement rehearsal. The cops showed up at two in the afternoon to tell them to turn it down!"

question I would ask myself if I got stuck writing a sentence or forming a paragraph or was struggling to convey what I was trying to say. "*How would Carr do it?*"

At the *Reader*, Carr often offered compliments and trash talking. Sometimes both simultaneously. He nudged me in the hallway after the 'Mats piece ran and said it was the best thing he'd seen written about them. Carr later wrote his own Replacements stories for the old Gray Lady, and he's pretty funny discussing them in Gorman Bechard's *Color Me Obsessed* film documentary about Replacements fans.

There's no need to rehash more of the same Replacements tales here. You can get your fill of them in the 2018 book *Lemon Jail*, by their roadie, Bill Sullivan. It's a horrific and hilarious account of a young, broke, bored, and unleashed band in a van, grappling with the demands of the road, the pressure to play the game, and the pissed-off passion required not to play it, plus all their personal quirks and excesses balled up like five-week-old laundry stuffed inside a smelly duffel bag.

Still, there were saner moments in their lives. Paul Westerberg's son and mine were in the same grade school class and Cub Scout troop in south Minneapolis. There were school, scouting, sporting, and social functions where my brood invariably socialized with Pa Westerberg, his wife at the time, the former Zuzu's Petals member and writer Laurie Lindeen, and the kid. Those episodes seemed a galaxy removed from the rock world.

You haven't got a complete picture of the anti–rock star rock star if you've never seen him digging in the dirt for fossils at Lilydale Regional Park, up on the limestone bluffs of St. Paul, during a scout trip.

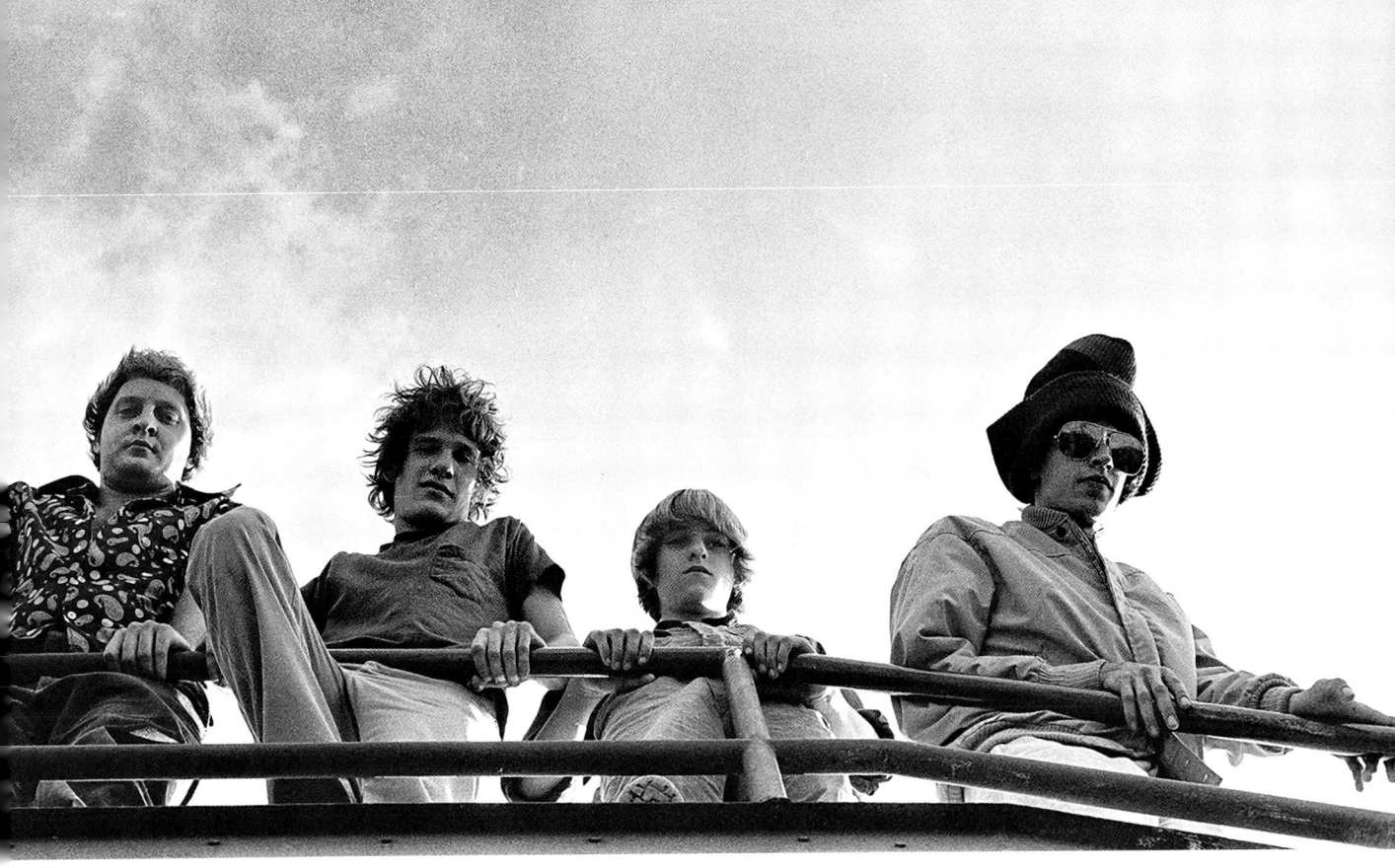

Or jamming with the kids in his basement (where he often wrote and recorded music himself) during the annual Westerberg-Lindeen holiday party, making a charitable, happy noise with youngsters, some of whom still believed in Santa. Upstairs, other notable guests like Dan Wilson, John Eller, Westerberg's sisters, including Mary Lucia, his mom, and others noshed and tipped a glass so old acquaintances would not soon be forgot. Down in the cellar, there was the guy whose songs will outlive his band's ragged reputation, creating a God-rock-us-everyone diversion with a bunch of fourth graders.

For all that's been written about Paul, Tommy and Bob Stinson, and Chris Mars, the best thing I've seen about them still are Helgeson's early photographs—including the 'Mats' noir-style image on the cover of this book—and the later ones with the replacement Replacements, Bob Dunlop and Steve Foley. Greg's pictures of the group have been seen often (and some not often enough), including on the cover of Bob Mehr's definitive tome on the hometown rockers, *Trouble Boys*. The series of photos he did with them at the Walker and elsewhere captures something true about their rock 'n' roll snarkiness and combustible energy. But they also reveal an innocence that's just starting to unravel, like a favorite old flannel shirt that will put on many more miles in high and low places.

Helgeson's photos taken at Walker Art Center and the Guthrie Theater in 1980 have become part of the Replacements' iconic history, capturing them at a defining period in their rise from the basement to become one of the most influential—and notorious—rock bands of the past four decades.

Another photo from the Walker/Guthrie series, the first of two major sessions the Helg shot with the band

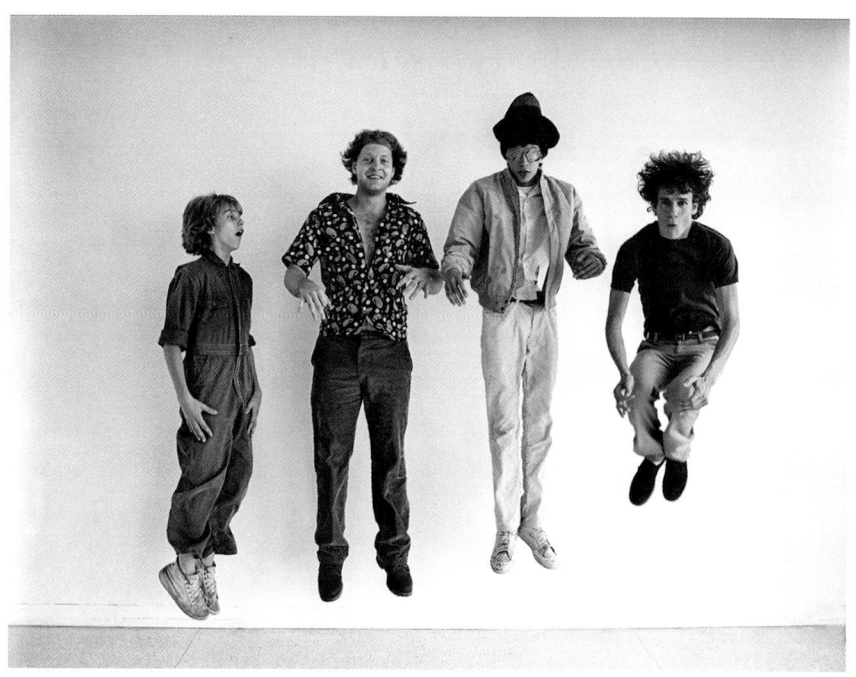

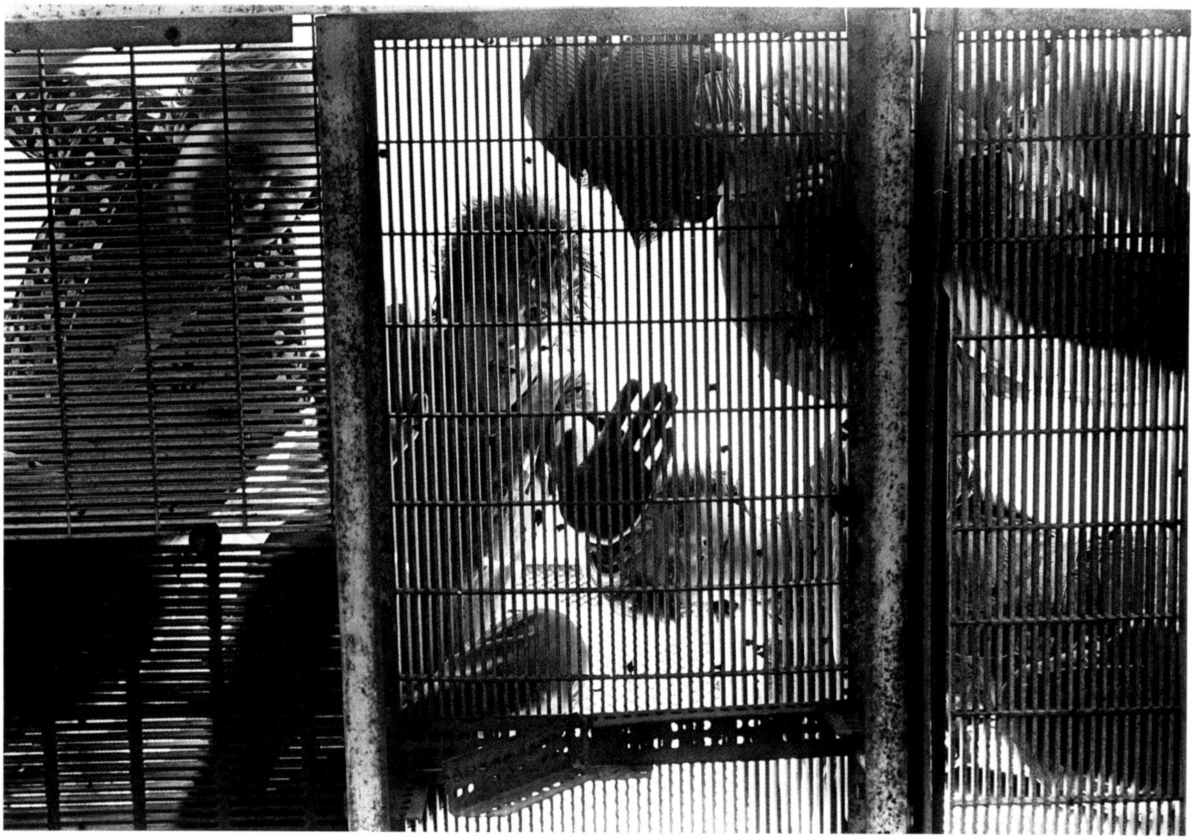

Through a grate darkly: Minneapolis's most influential rock band peers into their future, or is it their past?

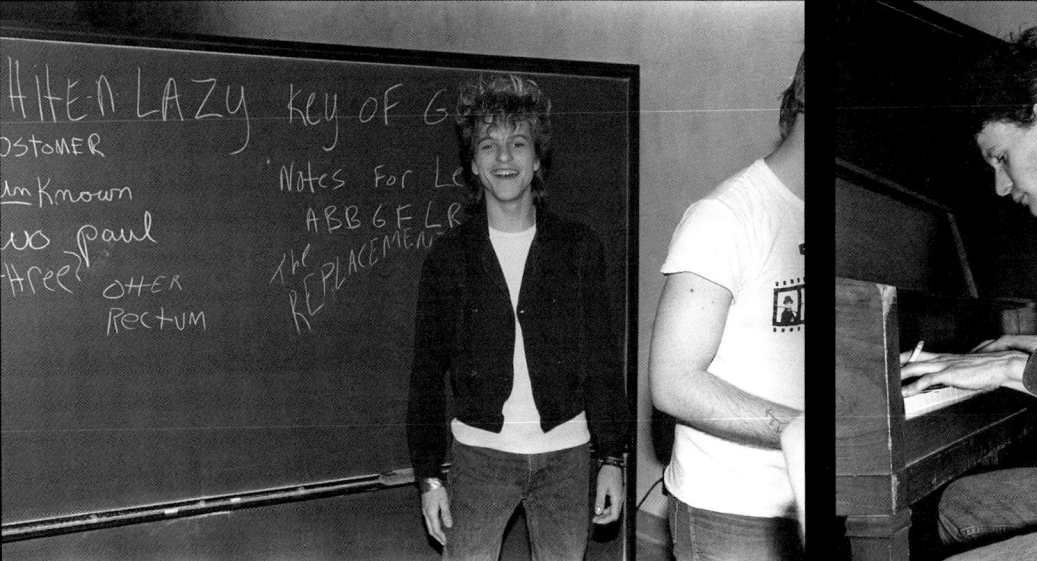
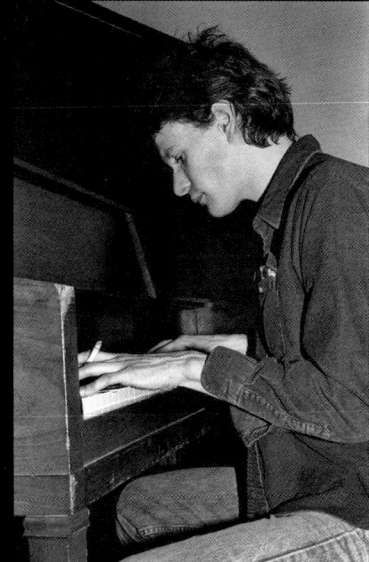

(above left) The naughty schoolboy who always plays in the "lazy key of G"—Tommy Stinson in Willey Hall.
(above right) Paul Westerberg finds a piano in the basement of Willey Hall.

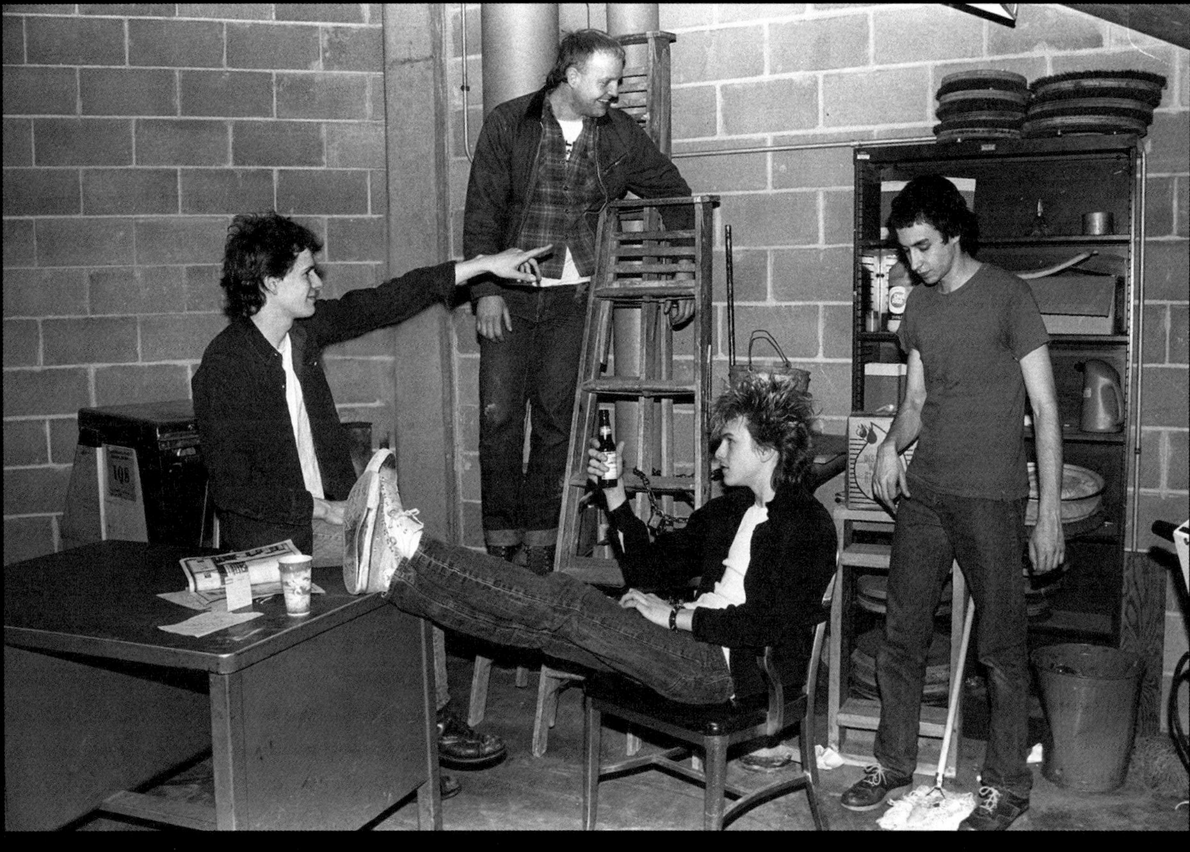

The Replacements in Willey Hall at the University of Minnesota's West Bank campus, in 1982

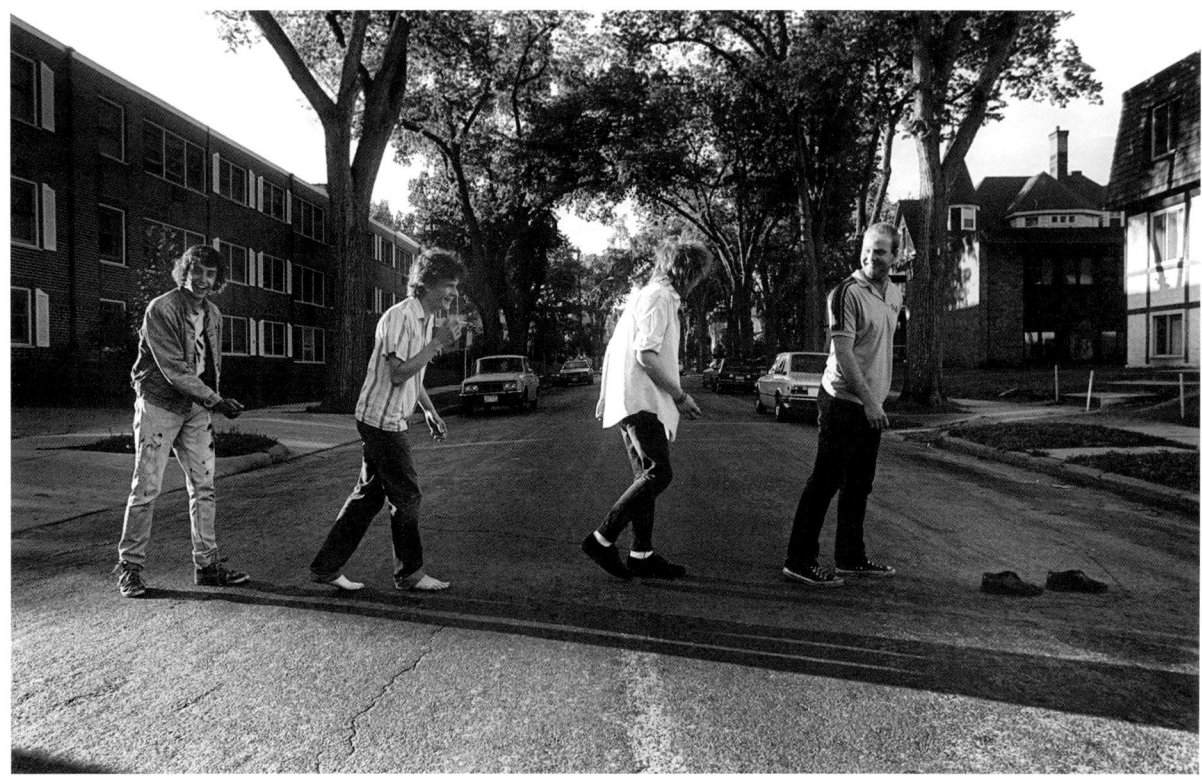

(above) Spoofing the *Abbey Road* album cover outside the Stinson home in south Minneapolis, July 1984

(right) Chris Mars, Paul Westerberg, Tommy Stinson, and Bob Stinson at the Stinson home, July 1984

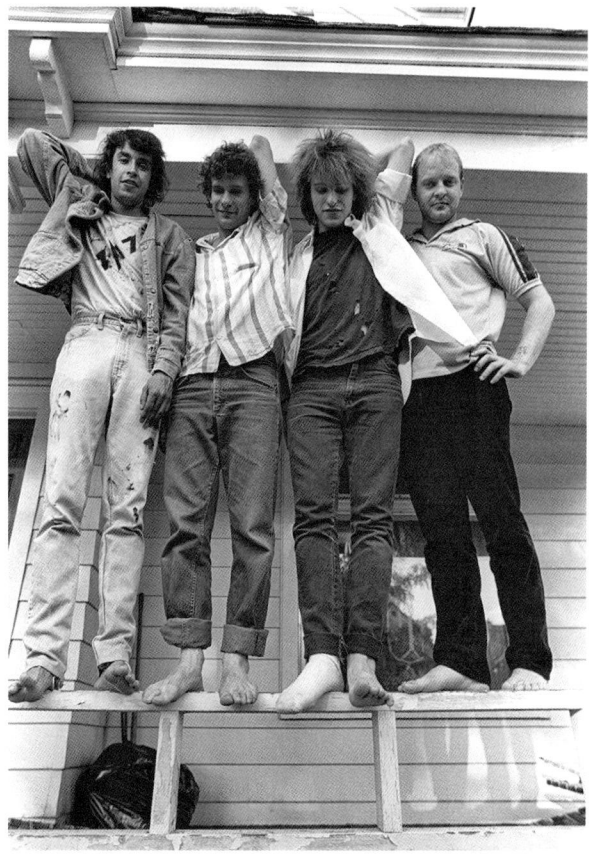

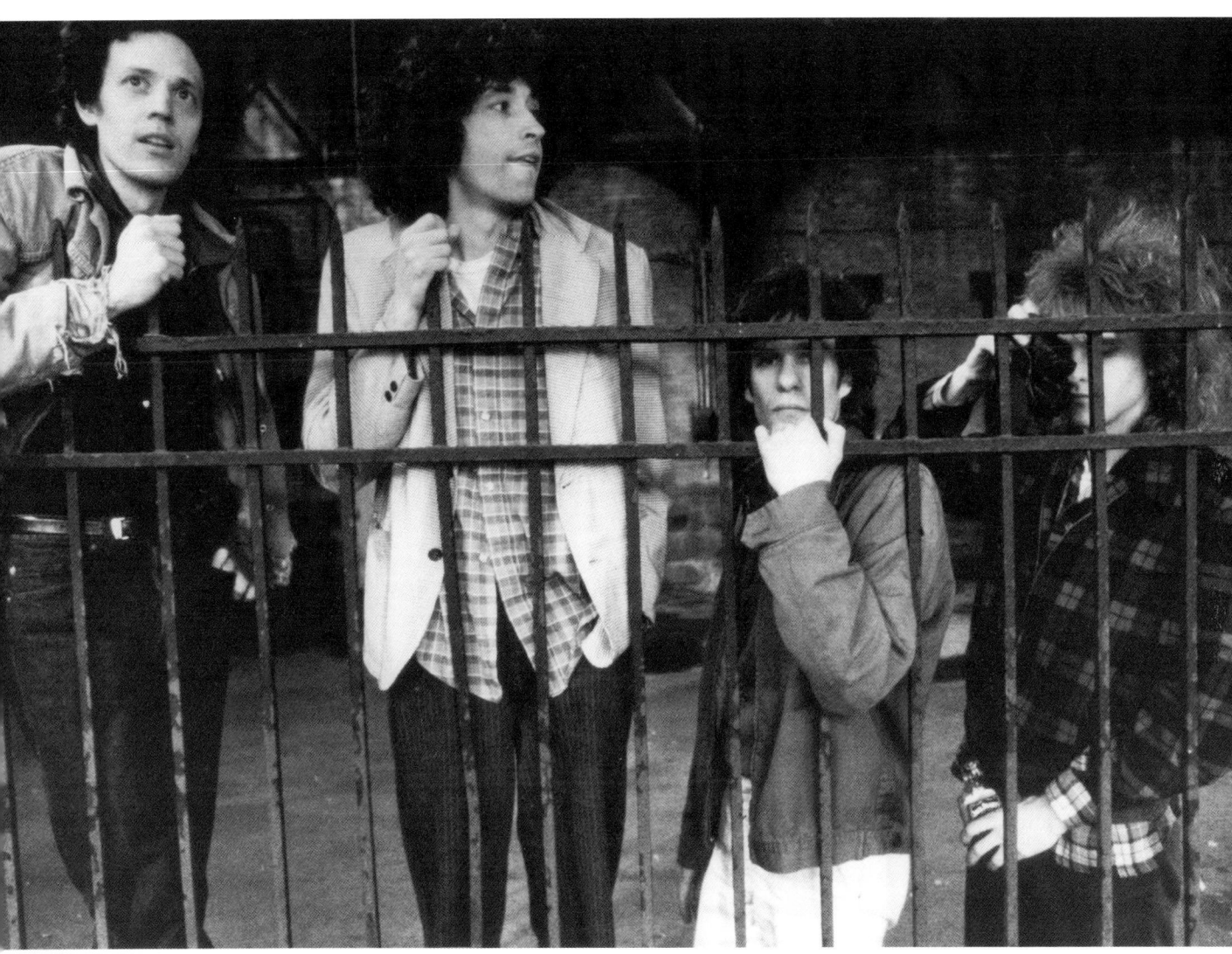

The band at the Milwaukee Depot with replacement Replacement Bob "Slim" Dunlap (left), with Mars, Westerberg, and Tommy Stinson. Dunlap replaced Bob Stinson as guitarist in 1987.

CURTISS A AND BIG AL

Dear Diary: A Recording Session at Twin/Tone

Curtiss A (née Curt Almsted) has always been "good copy," as they say in the newspaper world. He rocks. He'll put a spell on you with cool original songs and ripping covers. With heart and soul, Curt can somehow transform into Howlin' Wolf, Hank Williams, or Elvis—not so much by way of simply paying tribute but by shape-shifting to *become* them. He honors John Lennon every December 8 (since 1980) at First Avenue with a huge ensemble of Twin Cities musicians in a spirited marathon of Lennon songs that magically jump-starts the holiday season. The four-plus-hour event resurrects early Beatlemania, Beatles psychedelia, and Lennon's post-Beatles work.

His musical nom de plume comes from a long-gone Minneapolis hotel. He has taken a vow of poverty. He's a fab grandpa. He works one day a week at the Comic Book College in south Minneapolis. He makes daunting art collages from comic books full of good-vs.-evil conflict, ironic humor, and sheer craziness. He's for pot. He has sung that modern, Lennon-penned requiem "In My Life" at so many memorial services for fallen fellow rockers and others that he ought to be called the "Funeral Singer" as often as he is called the "Dean of Scream," a tag New York rock critic Bob Christgau once hung on him that stuck.

Curt's basement is a life-size pop-culture diorama full of superhero and rock-star figures, assorted memorabilia, lava lamps, board games, a blowgun, a Louis Armstrong autograph his mother got him while waiting on Satchmo at the old Leamington Hotel, newspaper clippings about his career, and other stuff. Rock instruments reside there. It must be seen to be believed. UFOs? Don't get him started; it's one of the many so-called paranormal interests we share and have both "experienced." Only he wears his obsession on his sleeve; mine I keep in my back pocket and another manuscript.

Curtiss A was one of the original acts on Twin/Tone Records. The *1980–1990* seven-inch EP with his band the Spooks was released by the

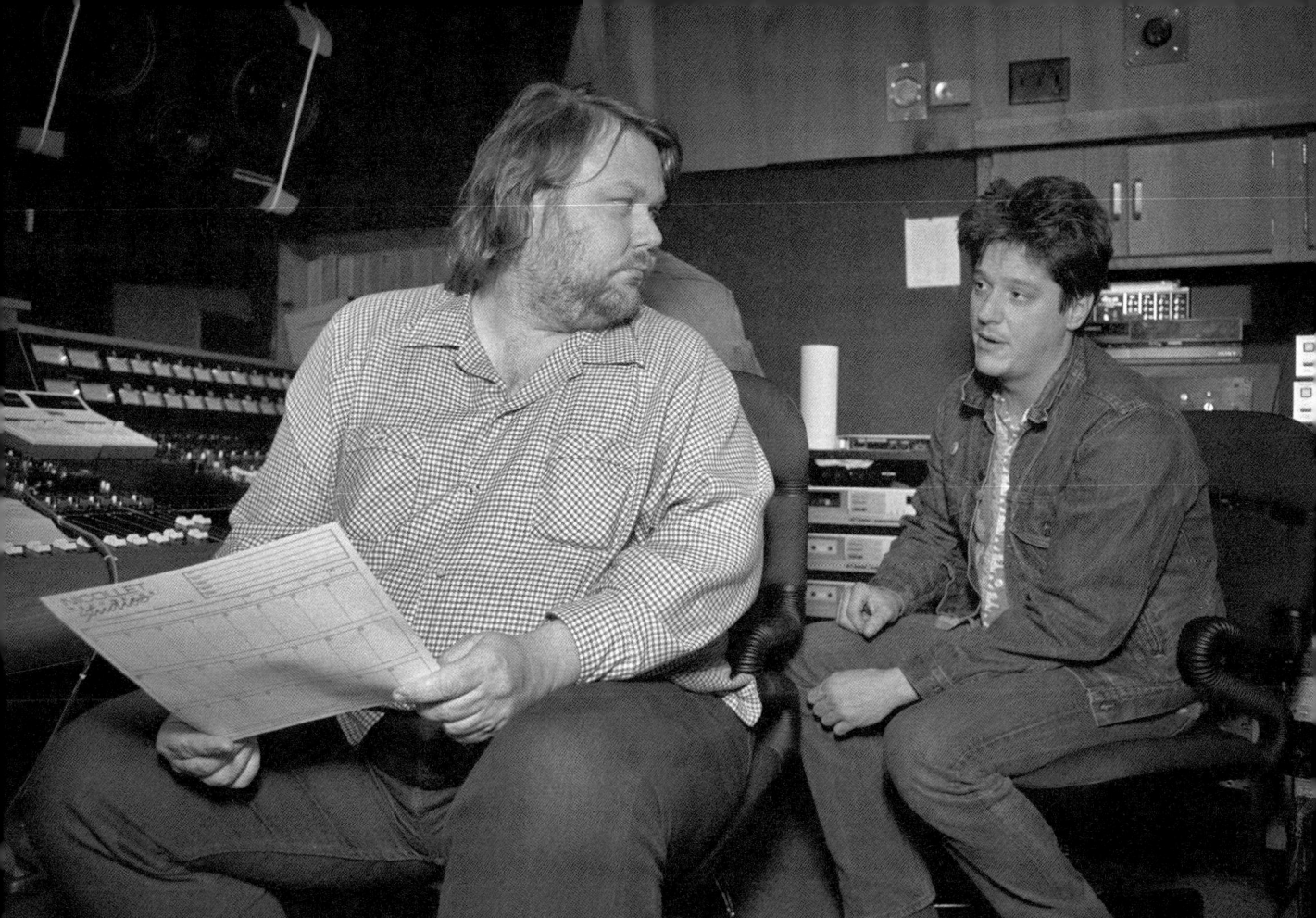

local label in 1978, along with eponymous debuts from the Suburbs and Fingerprints. Curt would go on to record three full-length albums with Twin/Tone, culminating with 1987's *A Scarlet Letter*.

In May of that year, Twin/Tone hired Big Al Anderson, the writer, guitar wrangler, singer, and master of drollery from NRBQ, to produce Curt's album. NRBQ is the band that Mr. Almsted and I both believe—along with legions of other fans and many swell rock artists, like Elvis Costello and Bonnie Raitt, who are far more successful than "the Q" will ever be—is as great as the Beatles, and ten times more fun live. How could I not write about these two rock masters—who were about to be locked in either musical combat or collaborative blissfulness, or perhaps both, for the recording of Curt's latest creation?

At the time, Big Al was rumored to be leaving NRBQ, and he was planning to release a solo album with Twin/Tone. There was tension around him, like static electricity. He was also a man of few words—and you could never be sure if he was putting you on or not when he did speak. When Helgeson told Anderson he had shot a photo of NRBQ that became one

Curtiss A (right) confers with producer Big Al Anderson during the recording session for Curt's Twin/Tone release *A Scarlet Letter*, at Creation Audio.

of their publicity photos, he shot back, "Fuck you!" He kinda reminded me of a combination of W. C. Fields and a wrestler from the WWF.

Curtiss A was recording his new album at Nicollet Studios on Twenty-fifth and Nicollet Avenue South, which was the legendary space where everyone from Bobby Vee to Dave "Six Days on the Road" Dudley recorded. When Helg and I popped over there for the session, it was relatively quiet. Some players had already laid down their parts; others, such as Willie Murphy and Maurice Jacox from the Bees, were expected in later that night. Dave Ayers, Twin/Tone's A&R guy and publicist (and a rock writer before that), was minding the store.

After Tom Bartel, the co-owner of *City Pages*, whom many called "Black Bart," fired me in the fall of 1983 over a few key differences, I went to work for the competition, the *Twin Cities Reader*, which was located right across the street. Besides doing the usual entertainment coverage and managing freelancers, I was also writing a weekly gossip column called "Diary of a Free-Lunch Writer," under the pseudonym Frank "Big Ears" Schwartz. It was based on the clichéd idea that there was no free lunch. Recording sessions can be a lot like film sets; there's plenty of waiting around time until a scene catches fire, or a song becomes a song in its fully realized song state. This session was no different. At any given time, it was hard to know where exactly this session was at, but after nearly four days, they seemed to be "almost finished." Frank Schwartz profiled the scene in the *Reader* with his conversation with Curt and Big Al.

> **FRANK:** Tell the folks in *Readerland*, why are you working with Big Al, big Curt?
>
> **CURT:** I wanted the best man for the job. At first, I thought I'd go with one of the dB's [a New York City–based power pop group from Winston-Salem, North Carolina] but that fell through. Al was the best man for the job. He's my biggest fan.
>
> **BIG AL:** Literally.
>
> **FRANK:** How's it going then, eh?
>
> **CURT:** It's fun. We're almost finished. At the tense moments, somebody would crack a joke. That's better than being mad in the studio. Working with Al taught me how little I knew about music. It coulda been like Joni Mitchell producing the MC5, but it hasn't been like that at all.
>
> **FRANK:** How does the record sound?
>
> **CURT:** The whole album is pretty hard hitting. I was surprised how much Al liked it that way. I thought we'd have conflicts over how it should sound. You know he's a pretty tasty guy who really listens to stuff, but

he likes to rock out. There is this one part in a song we were doin' where I wanted a staccato blues lick, like Freddie King. Al objected. And I said, "But Al, I *am* the blues." Al said, "No, you're mod now." Anyway, there's no electronic drums or synthesizers on the record.

BIG AL: Not yet anyway.

CURT: Yeah, not yet. We might have Willie Murphy play some bagpipe parts on a synthesizer. Maybe. Al, think bagpipes, think sax.

FRANK: Talk about some of the songs, would ya?

CURT: There's this song I wrote . . . actually I wrote all of the thirteen we've recorded. We'll probably use just ten. One is called, "These Aren't Teardrops in My Eyes." It's one of the greatest songs ever written in the Twin Cities—next to Prince's "Why Don't You Call Me Anymore?" Al plays the guitar parts, and it's like having Les Paul, Chet Atkins, and Santo & Johnny on your record.

Then there's "I've Got a Bone." That's about the Jordan sex scandals. And there's one song about happiness on every album I've made, and this is my third album. It's called "I Want You to Be Happy." It's to my girlfriend. On my last record, I did, "Oh How Happy We Should Be." I dedicated it to Larry Williams. He died suddenly, and they didn't know if it was an accident or he killed himself. Anyway, he wasn't very happy when he died.

FRANK: Big Al, I've heard you've done national Toyota commercials with NRBQ. But there's also lots of talk that you're leaving NRBQ, and I've already heard that you've been saying, "They can find somebody else to play my parts but they can never replace me." What gives, are ya actually leaving, or what?

BIG AL: I don't know yet.

CURT: How could you break up a group like that? What would it take?

BIG AL: It would take two more commercials.

FRANK: You'll be here recording this summer for Twin/Tone, doing your own solo LP. Are you going to play everything on it or work with some local people?

BIG AL: I don't know yet.

DAVE AYERS: He doesn't even want to play on his own record!

FRANK: (sarcastically) Aside from the huge amount of money Twin/Tone is paying you to do Curt's record, what else interests you about this project?

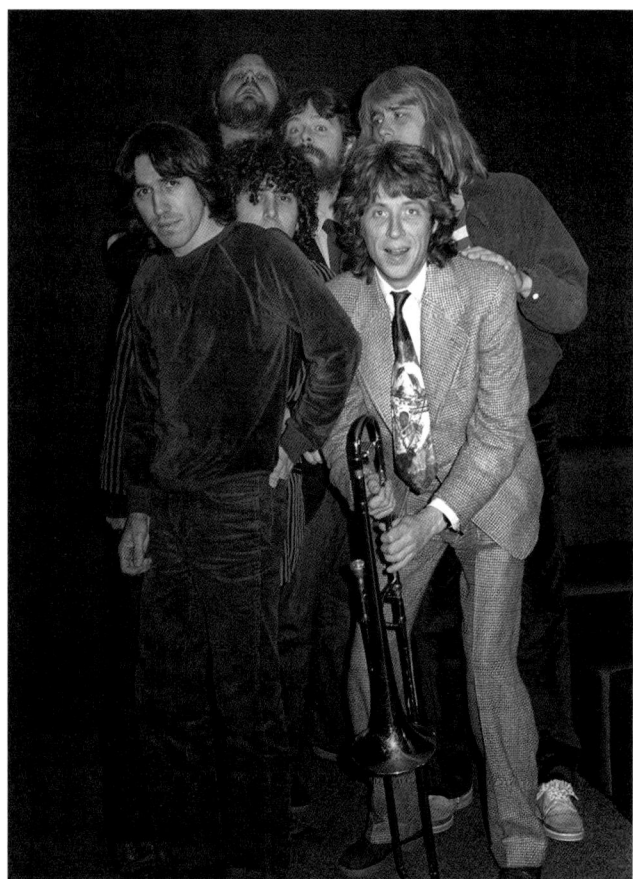

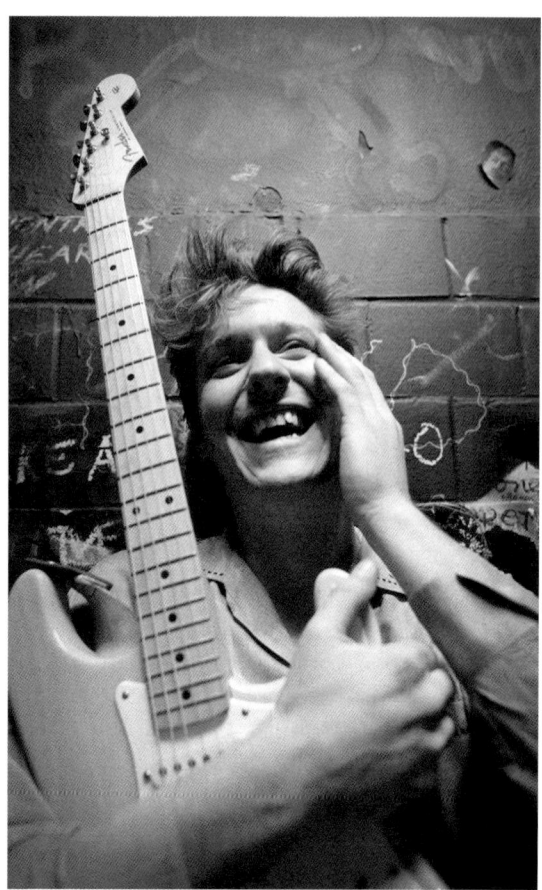

(above left) This photo of NRBQ, shot by Helgeson at the U of M's Coffman Union in 1980, became one of the band's publicity shots.

(above right) The many facets of Curtiss A include collage artist, comic book expert, UFO experiencer, grandfather, ranter, and shape-shifting rocker able to do Hank Williams, Howlin' Wolf, and Elvis—for starters.

BIG AL: Just the huge amount of money.

FRANK: When's Curt's album being released?

DAVE AYERS: Maybe in the fall. We want both Curt's and Al's records to come out at the same time.

BIG AL (stretching his arms, cracking his knuckles, and giving a big mock yawn): And *mine* could take a lot of time. Which reminds me, I said we wouldn't work past six today. I wasn't supposed to work past six, boys. That was my personal deadline. We should be done with business.

CURT: I had a personal deadline fourteen years ago. You've had *four* days!

BIG AL: I don't care. I ain't producing another goddamn thing tonight!

Twin/Tone released Curtiss A's *A Scarlet Letter* later in 1987. Big Al's *Party Favors* followed in 1988. After twenty-three years with the band, Anderson finally left NRBQ in 1994. He went to Nashville, where he's since become a hot songwriter and cowriter for a variety of artists, including

Jerry Lee Lewis, Tim McGraw, the Mavericks, Carlene Carter, Trisha Yearwood, Bonne Raitt, Alabama, Jimmy Buffett, Vince Gill, and many others. NRBQ is still together, despite one death and two more departures of core members from the Big Al days. And they're still fun, still capable of making you believe in the magic of rock 'n' roll.

More than three decades after *A Scarlet Letter*, Curtiss A still plays small clubs, worthy benefits, his annual Lennon tribute, and a monthly residence with his band, the Jerks of Fate, at the Schooner, one of the Twin Cities' oldest taverns and the current stomping ground of former First Avenue manager Steve McClellan, who has probably booked Curtiss A for more gigs than anyone in Curt's near half century of performing. Any time I call Curt, or he calls me, I know to set aside at least sixty minutes. Topics are wide ranging, but usually come back to music and ufological matters, like the impact of the December 2017 *New York Times* bombshell about a secret Pentagon study of UFOs—a first for the old Gray Lady of journalism—without once using the lazy and odious expression "conspiracy theory."

It's uncertain what will happen to Curtiss's amazing basement and all his cool stuff when, you know. . . .

Originally known as Flamingo (until a band of the same name got them to change it), the Flamin' Oh's could have kicked the Cars' asses in a battle of the bands and had just as many hits, but the fates never allowed the big break or the right management to make it happen.

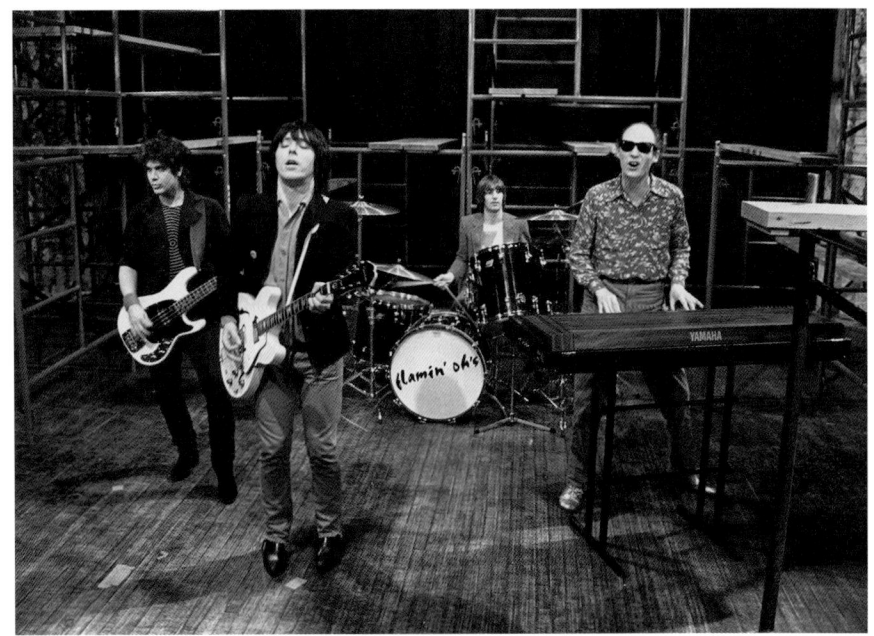

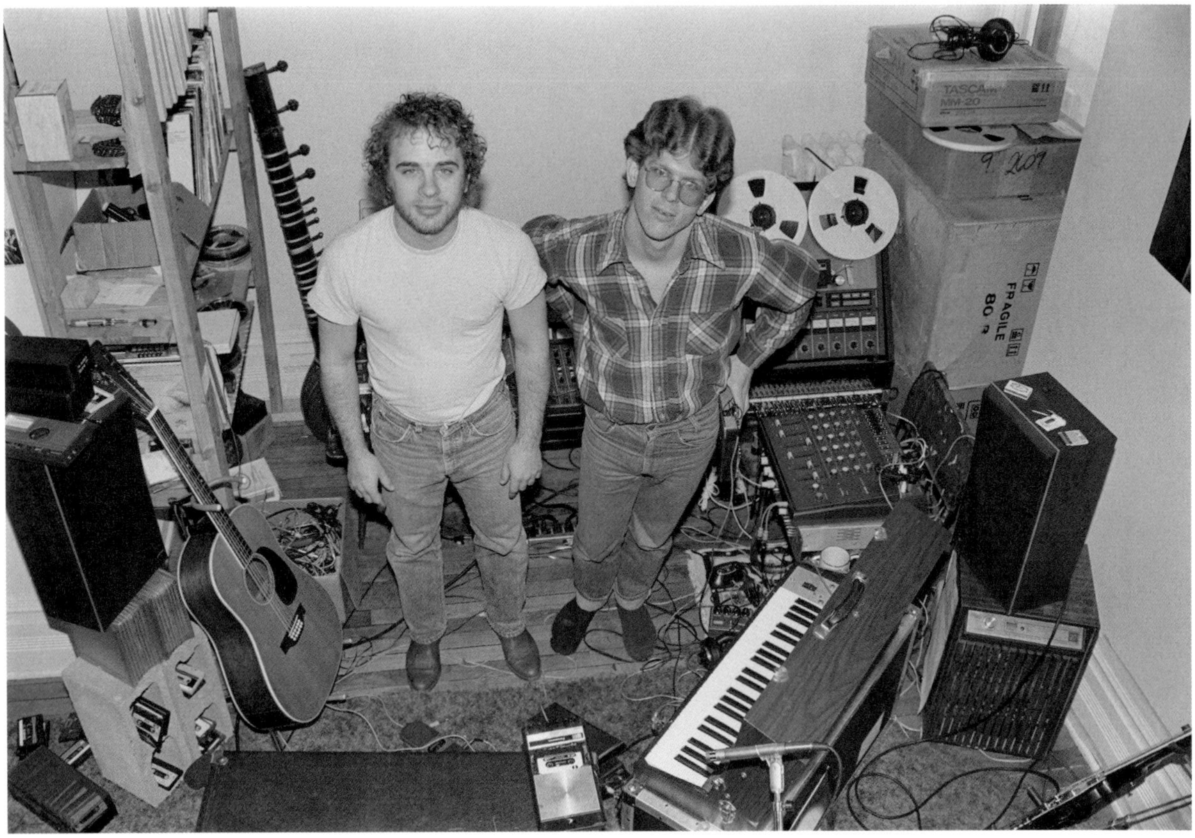

Recording artist and guitarist Steve Tibbetts (right), posing here with percussionist Marc Anderson, began composing music during the new-wave/punk and Prince-funk explosion of the eighties, but his instrumental work is frequently labeled as jazz and can also be described as ambient, incidental, and imbued with ethereal subtlety. The critically acclaimed artist has long been an inspired outlier.

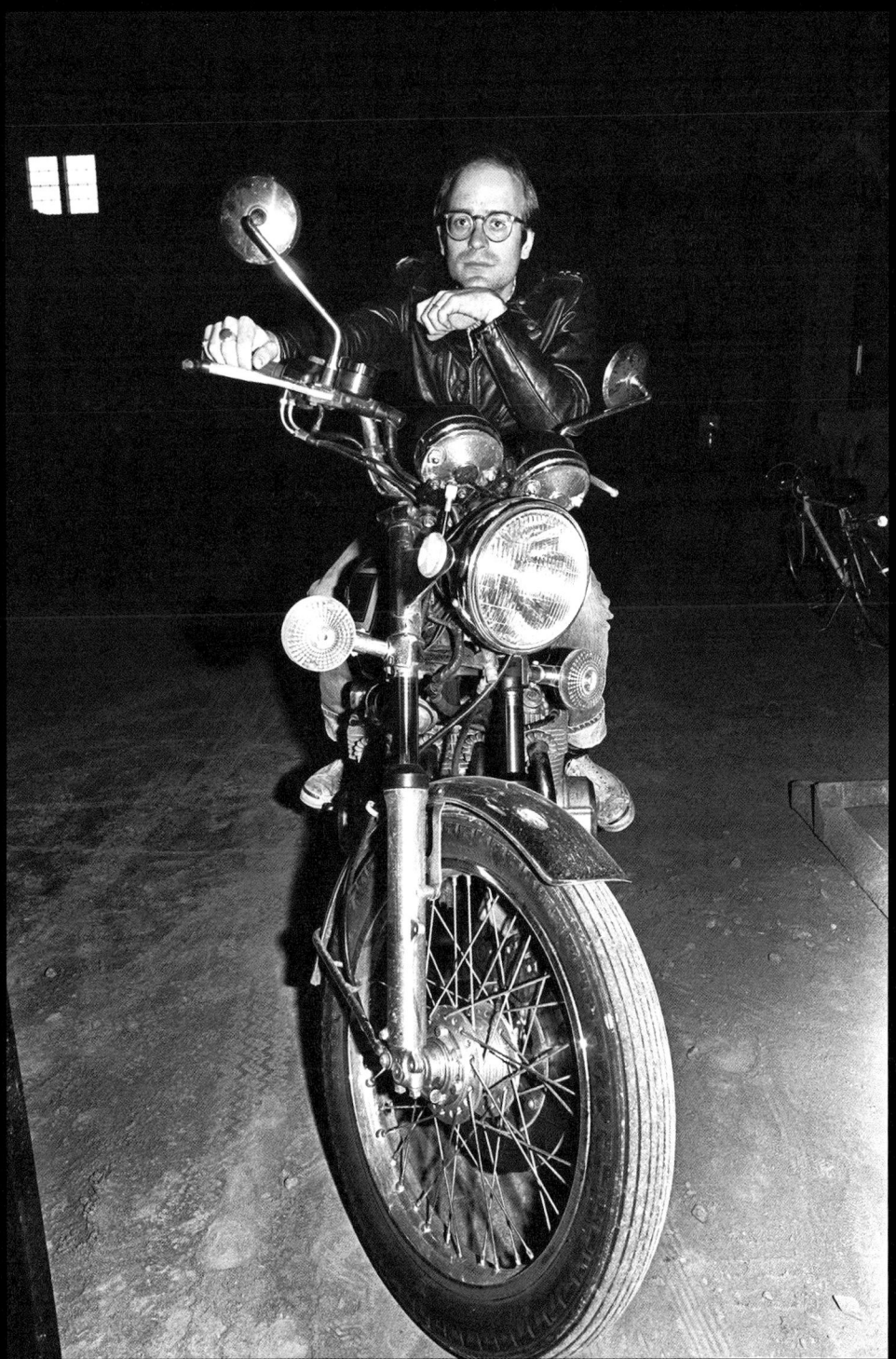

Chris Osgood of the punk trio Suicide Commandos helped to start it all on the Twin Cities scene in the late seventies. Following their 1977 debut *Make a Record* and the live *Suicide Commandos Commit Suicide Dance Concert* of 1978, the Commandos recorded a third album in 2017, *Time Bomb*, following a four-decade silence. Commandos bass player Steve Almaas had a good run with the New York–based Beat Rodeo in the early eighties and several subsequent solo albums, while drummer Dave Ahl has become a master studio craftsman.

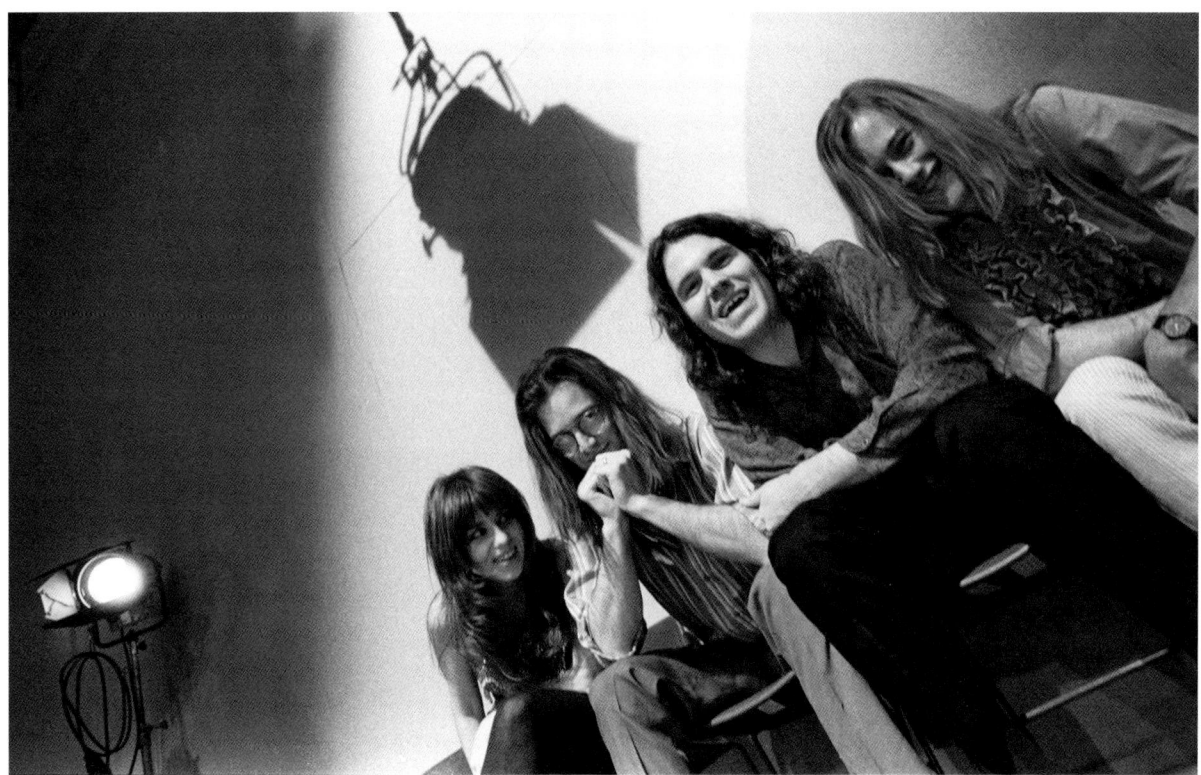

(above) Featuring (left to right) Elaine Harris, Dan Wilson, John Munson, and Matt Wilson, Trip Shakespeare built a loyal local following in the late eighties and early nineties and created a cult classic with the song "Toolmaster of Brainerd." The band later gave rise to Semisonic (of "Closing Time" fame), featuring Dan Wilson and Munson. Dan Wilson also went on to an amazing solo songwriting career, penning Grammy-worthy tunes for the likes of Adele, the Dixie Chicks, John Legend, Taylor Swift, Pink, and many others.

(right) Latter-day descendants of Poco, the Flying Burrito Brothers, and the Byrds at their country apex, the Jayhawks helped to kickstart the alt-country and country-rock movement in the Twin Cities beginning in the mid-eighties. Despite a few hiatuses and the prickly departure of songwriter and cofounder Mark Olson, the Jayhawks continue to soar with Gary Louris at the helm after several decades.

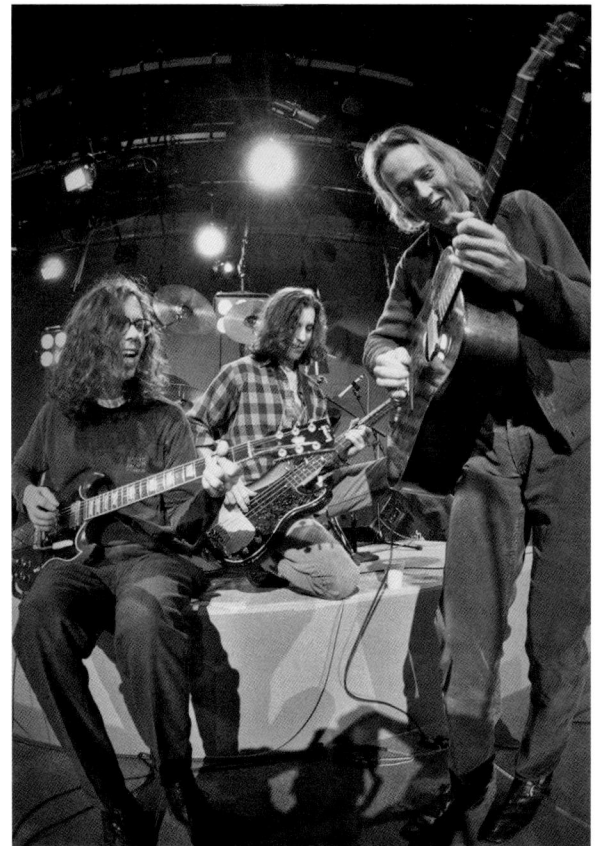

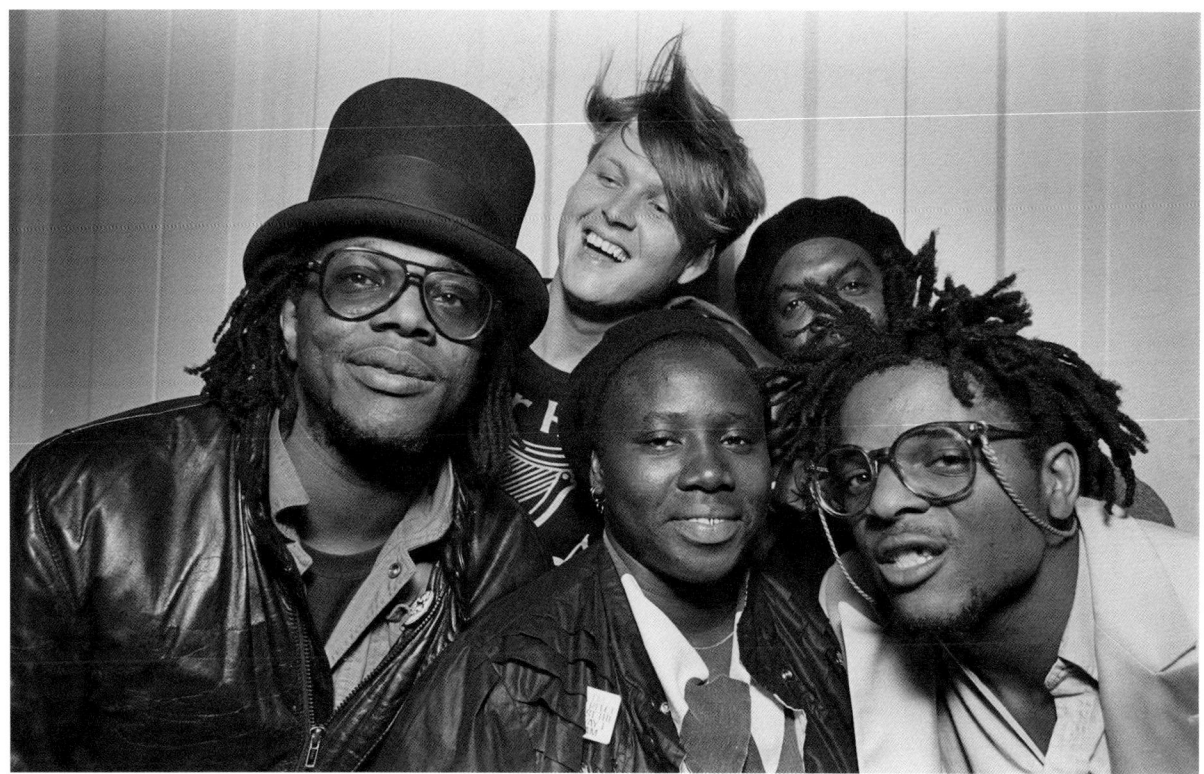

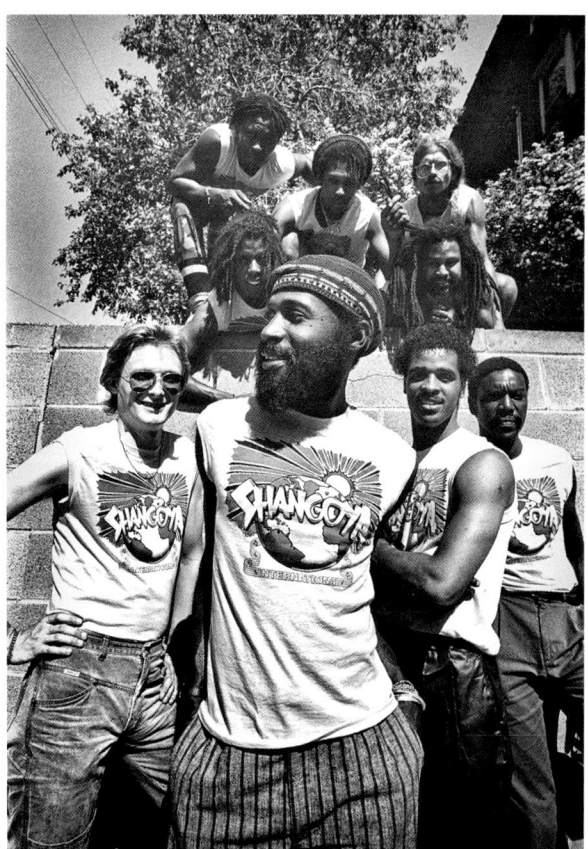

(above) Minneapolis reggae stalwart Ipso Facto was established in 1986 by former Shangoya member Wain McFarlane and his brothers Juju and Greg. Ipso Facto continues to perform politically charged, reggae-rooted work more than three decades later.

(left) Trinidad native Peter Nelson combined the sounds of soca, calypso, and reggae in establishing Minnesota's most rhythmically grooved band, Shangoya. Formed in 1972, Shangoya remained active and influential for more than thirty years, until Nelson's death in 2004 at the age of fifty-nine.

CHUCK STATLER

Another Mother of Invention

t's hard to say what was more fun: watching Chuck Statler's pioneering music videos or watching him process incongruous images from the human comedy that fed his creative impulses. Even before MTV became a widely viewed video jukebox after it launched in 1981, Statler had set the tone, if not the style, for the slate of music film shorts that followed with his ten-minute promotional Devo film from 1976, *The Truth About De-Evolution*.

That early piece, complete with a woozy, mechanical remake of a 1966 Johnny Rivers hit, "Secret Agent Man," offered delicious glimpses of the Statler school of filmmaking. His crazy cutaways, in particular, proved to be a trademark—such as the monkey-masked guys in boxing shorts swatting the behind of a masked woman in a funky bathrobe with ping-pong paddles embossed with the images of Mao and Nixon. It was almost like a scene from *A Clockwork Orange* recast as a comic nightmare. Rock 'n' roll had not seen this before, at least not this level of WTF-ism. But then rock hadn't met the offbeat filmmaker from Akron, Ohio, the so-called godfather of the TV music video, and the unofficial sixth member of Devo.

Many more films for Devo—all with funny, absurdist edges—would follow into the Reagan years. But it was the handful of simple celluloid shorts for Elvis Costello and the Attractions that ensured that Statler and his Location Services crew were on the new budget lines of major and indie record labels vying for airtime on the hot, fresh vid channel.

The list of clients would eventually include the J. Geils Band, Nick Lowe, Graham Parker, City Boy, Pere Ubu, and many others. Statler's music video res included high- and low-profile locals like the Suicide Commandos, Flamin' Oh's, Alpha Consumer, the Time, and Prince (including footage that has never been seen from the *Controversy* period). In a true and surprising departure from previous work, his video for the Jayhawks' "Comeback Kids" in 2016 featured front man Gary Louris futilely

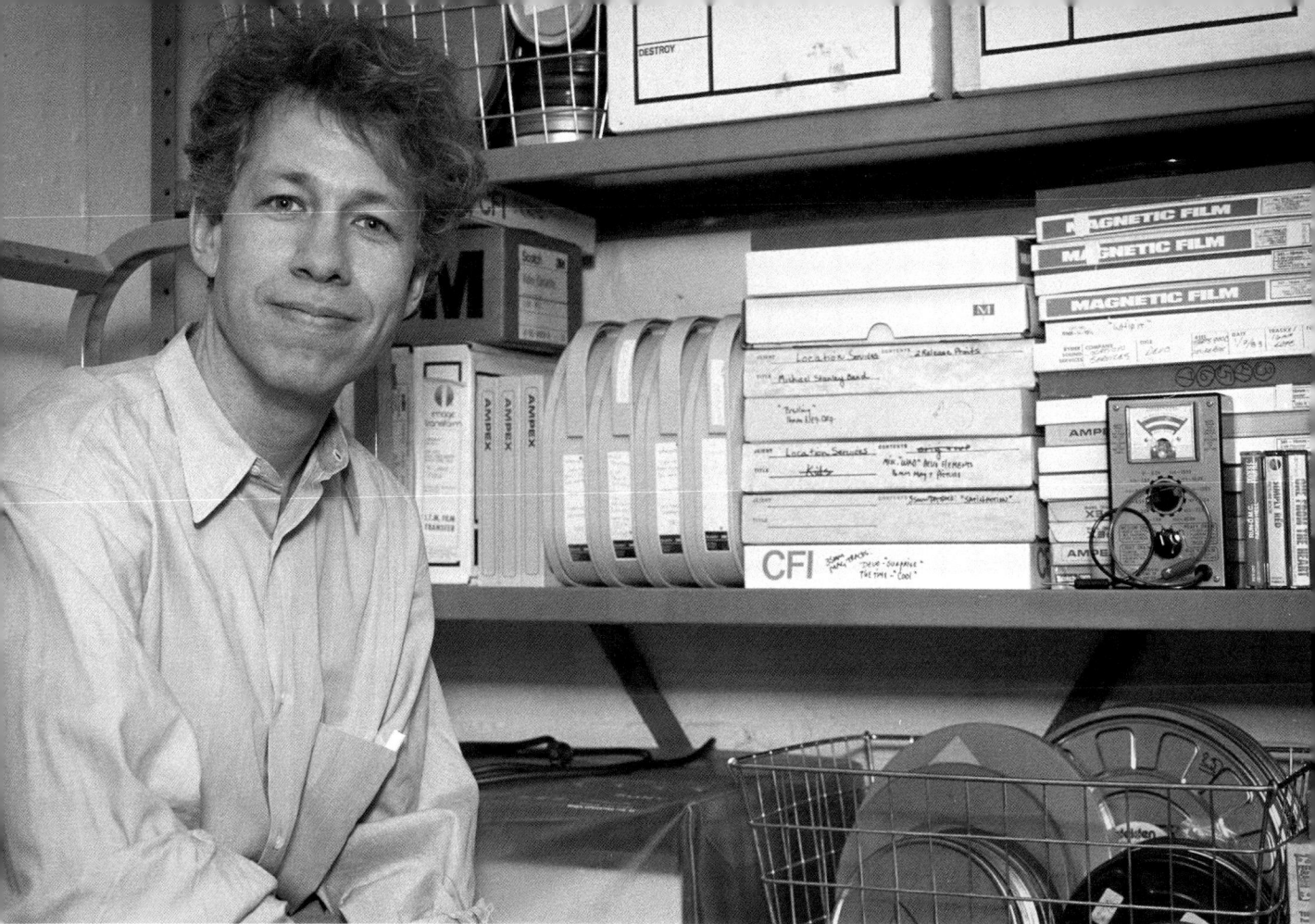

searching for something, or someone, perhaps his bandmates. Shot in stark black and white, it's a visually beautiful inner and outer journey by train, bus, car, and dark imagination, again with wild, occasionally creepy cutaways, most of those in color.

A mutual friend whom I'd met at college introduced me to Statler one night at the Cabooze. We discovered that we shared common passions: music and movies, late nights in clubland, and light and black humor—the kind you find in a comedy joint and the kind that finds you, the reality quirks that goose your senses and assail your sensibilities. We found a lot of that in the Wallets, whom we tried to catch as often as possible. (It was Chuck who first called to let me know that Steve Kramer had died.) We also both owed some of our work breakthroughs to serendipity, mine with Bob Dylan at the Cabooze, his with Elvis Costello at the Longhorn.

Statler met Jake Riviera, Costello's manager, by chance one night at the 'horn when Nick Lowe was playing there. Statler almost didn't go since he felt a cold coming on. Sitting in the bar lobby, he was approached by Riviera, also Lowe's manager, who wondered why he wasn't in listening

The man on the other side of the camera: Chuck Statler in his studio. Statler is considered the godfather of the modern music video, starting with his work with Devo. Statler fancied "talent" from day labor pools, deployed absurd cutaways in his films, and had a good eye for the human comedy.

to the band. The conversation turned to introductions. When Statler told him who he was, Riviera was taken aback. He'd been trying to figure out how to get a hold of the filmmaker ever since he saw the Devo films and wanted Statler to do something similar for Elvis.

It wasn't long after that that I started badgering Statler to let me shadow the film shoot with Elvis Costello and the Attractions in Hawaii for "(What's So Funny 'Bout) Peace Love and Understanding," "Oliver's Army," and "I Can't Stand Up for Falling Down." I would write individual stories about Elvis and him, complete with interviews and coconut trees. Riviera put a quick end to that pipe dream. Chuck later got to work on four more.

Still, we forged a solid, long-lasting friendship that has transcended the rifts in our careers and our rock 'n' roll carousing and our personal lives. I served as Statler's best man at his second wedding. And I joined the Statler family and a few close friends to celebrate his first kid's tenth birthday. Unfortunately, it was the same night that George W. Bush launched the second Iraq War, and the thing was televised on network TV as if it were the season premiere of a new military drama. Even the birthday boy was mesmerized and put off by the images of missiles flying through the night sky, the sanctimonious newscaster voiceovers, and guest generals pontificating about the imminent fall of Baghdad and the demise of the "tyrant Saddam."

"Blow out yer candles, son."

The demand for Chuck's music video work eventually cooled off, but he never lost his edge. Looking back, he was well suited to his trade. Statler had killer casting instincts, often hiring people who had "good looks"— and he didn't mean handsome—as extras from day labor places like Employers Overload. It was his version of general casting in the Twin Cities. He likewise drew occasionally from the ranks of local rockers, such as former Things That Fall Down player and record-shop owner Dave Foley (in the Jayhawks video). He also wasn't averse to putting family members in scenes, including his wife, who is seen wielding a paddle against the backside of a guy eating a hamburger and wearing a Burger King crown in the video for Alpha Consumer's "The Eat."

Although I only watched him and his crew in action for a full day one time, for the Flamin' Oh's "Stop" video, which served as the basis for a cover story in the *Spud*, I always dug his finished product. Statler's videos had a guerrilla-filmmaking quality that synched up nicely with the often screwball storyboards he concocted, giving them an original and juvenile and antiauthoritarian authenticity that was often missing once ad agency–styled music video divisions, Statler copycats, and other players got in the game.

An avowed fan of Russ Meyer's sexploitation films, slippery B-movie celluloid that was wildly over the top, he was still a pretty down-to-earth and practical filmmaker in many ways. When hired by Riviera to do a video for Lowe's song "Cruel to Be Kind," Statler had only a limited window in which to shoot the celebrated British rocker and his band, since Nick was getting ready for his wedding with Carlene Carter. No problem.

It was agreed that Statler and his crew—Matt, John, and Dale—would film the wedding ceremony and incorporate it into the video. In preparation, Statler did what any virgin wedding photographer would do: he went out and bought a how-to handbook on shooting nuptials. No one was the wiser.

When the Minnetonka home and practice space of the Suicide Commandos was condemned and slated to be burned in a training exercise for the local fire department, the Commandos' Chris Osgood quickly wrote a song called "Burn It Down" and enlisted Statler to film the band playing in front of the inferno. At the end of the video, one of Statler's street-cast characters yells, "Burn it down! Or burn it up! Or both." The last bit was totally unscripted, as were the burning embers that floated down onto Dave Ahl's drum set.

Despite long-overdue retrospective shows of his work at prestigious museums in New York, Denver, LA, and the Twin Cities, and having major filmmakers champion his work, the curtain or the Netflix stream has yet to rise on any full-length Chuck Statler projects. Perhaps it's because he's never been a flagrant self-promoter, and that's one of the things I like about him. But it's not for lack of trying; Chuck has a couple of features on his drawing board and one or two worthy documentaries he's pitched. Maybe it's just a matter of time.

The long pause on his more ambitious film work hasn't slowed him down, however, nor has it dampened his passion for music, especially live music. His soundman, Matt Quast, calls Statler the oldest teenager in the Twin Cities. Only recently did he start cutting back on going out to see bands of all sounds and shapes. I gave up long ago trying to keep up with him, or even trying to vet the groups he recommends I see. He did successfully drag me out to the 7th Street Entry for the exotic psychedelic drone music of Acid Mothers Temple from Japan. "They'll blow your mind," he predicted. They did!

I've also goaded him over the years to try a few things, such as five-star flicks I've seen like *Bang! The Bert Berns Story*. After talking "Bobism" at him forever, he finally came around on Dylan with *Blood on the Tracks*, which he couldn't stop listening to in his car. In our approaching twilight years, we've indulged our mutual movie joneses a lot more than the music side, even trying to schedule semi-regular Friday matinees. But these weren't your standard popcorn flicks.

Before our work schedules and family obligations got in the way again, we watched obscure, challenging movies like *Lobster Boy* and an

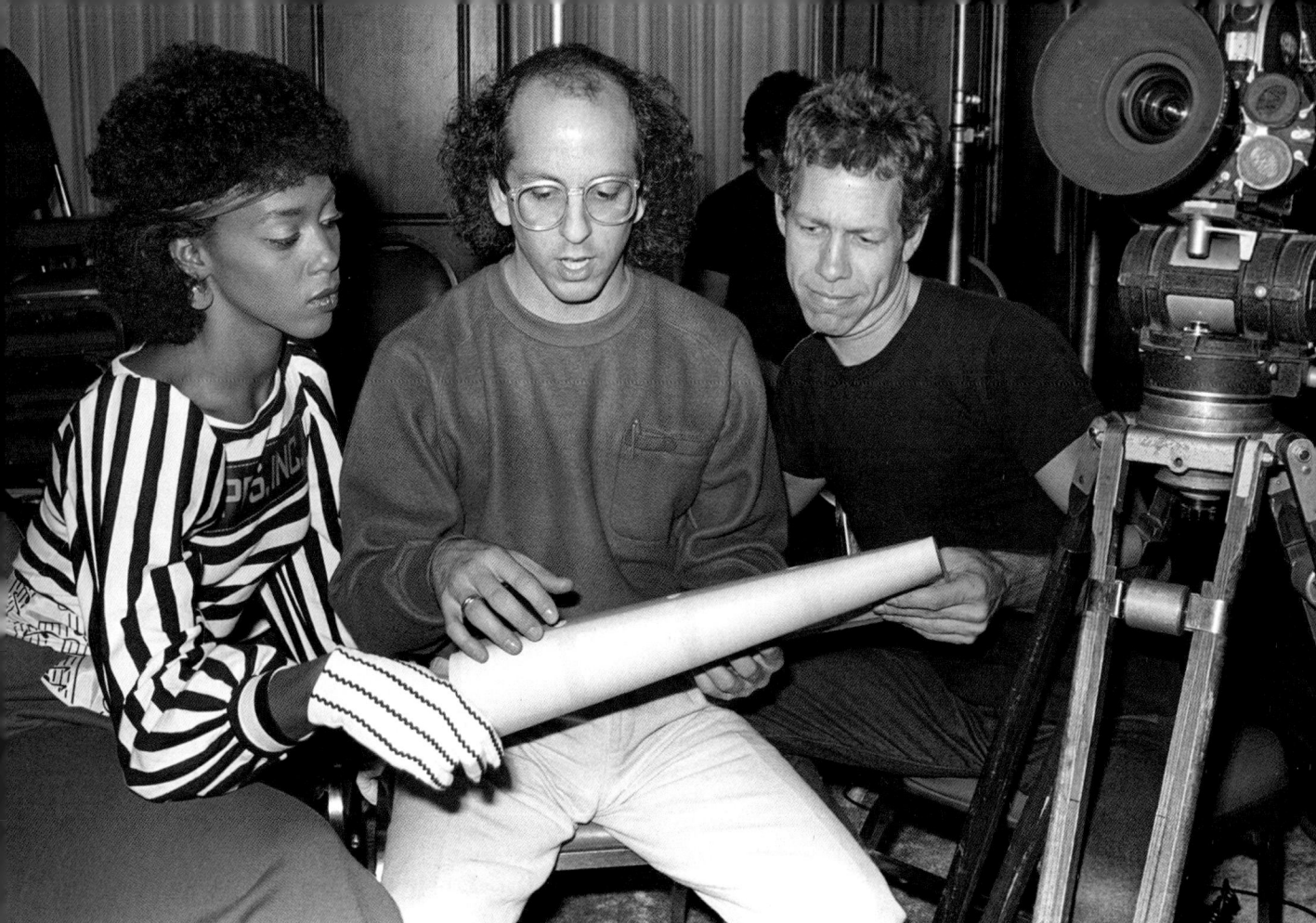

Lipps, Inc.'s Cynthia Johnson and Steven Greenberg look over the storyboards of Statler's music video for the band's 1981 release, "Hold Me Down." Mysteriously, the video was never released.

insightful and entertaining documentary about Frank Zappa, the timeless Mother of Invention. Up on the screen, Frank's erudite social observations and sarcastic sense of humor reminded me of one of my favorite running buddies: the guy sitting in the next seat, absorbed in the movie and eating his M&M's. If there's any peace, love, and understanding left in Minnie, perhaps someday he'll get his long overdue star on First Avenue.

STEVE MCCLELLAN

Stark Raving Steve!

T here was tongue-in-cheek speculation that the small barbershop on the main floor inside the Produce office building, where Target Center now sits, was also a numbers-running operation. Although no one ever proved it, the rumor persisted, since there seemed to be so few actual customers getting a haircut.

Right across the street from First Avenue, that same building housed the *Twin Cities Reader*, *City Business*, and *Corporate Report*—all on one floor, all part of MCP, Inc., owned primarily by Mark and Deb Hopp. When it was announced in 1988 that our building would come down to make way for the new basketball arena, some staffers also wondered if this spelled trouble for the beloved night club that had become an international destination ever since *Purple Rain* hit movie theaters in 1984. Why not set up a little betting pool with the barbershop, create some odds, and let the numbers fall where they may?

Gaming aside, the other joke was that the club's two managers, the legendary GM/booker, Steve McClellan, and the mostly behind-the-scenes bean counter, Jack Meyers, would be found barricaded in their offices amongst the rubble should the club ever be hit with the wrecking ball. In Steve's case, he might have never been found.

Within his dimly lit cave/office, Steve was barely recognizable the first time I met him. A bit disheveled, gracious, complimentary, and manic, he seemed comfortably perplexed in there—with its piles of vinyl, overflowing garbage cans, newspapers, trade magazines, and press kits strewn about, posters and photos hanging or slipping on the walls, files open, desk drawers askew, a phone someplace, maybe a few personal belongings. I dug it. It was a perfect storm.

This was sort of how I had imagined the office of the man—and the man himself—who booked exotic Afro-pop, speed metal, funk, reggae, punk, pop, folk-rock, country rock, hip-hop, and the occasional jazz and comedy acts to perform at First Avenue and its offshoot 7th Street Entry. Of course, he had help from trusted advisers like Chrissie Dunlap, Maggie Macpherson (before she jumped to the Uptown Bar), Leann Weimer, and house deejays Kevin Cole and Roy Freedom. But Steve was the face of the club.

Although it soon became apparent that the former Greyhound bus depot would not fall like a domino with the construction of Target Center, other challenges would come along. A Hard Rock Cafe franchise opened across the street on the north side of Seventh Street in 2002, a glorified gift shop with marginal food and predictable music images on the walls—in many ways the antithesis of First Avenue. From a certain angle, the chain restaurant's guitar-shaped sign out front looked like a tombstone for the big black building across the street with the white stars name-checking the greats who had played and worked there. It felt even more ominous when the club faced severe financial problems over the next two years and temporarily closed after the owner filed for bankruptcy in early November 2004.

I imagine Steve and Jack were rattled to the core by the tumult that followed. Steve's emotional state may have resembled the Jack-Nicholson-from-*The-Shining*-like portrait that Greg shot in the early eighties.

In my experience, McClellan was one of the smartest, most enthusiastic music lovers ever to run a joint. He had earned the respect of industry veterans, writers and reporters, and legions of musicians and music fans from across the diverse spectrum he brought to the stages of the main room and the Entry. He wasn't fondly called "Chainsaw" by rock writer P. D. Larson for nothin' either: Steve's buzzing manner could silence the unaware.

David Carr from the *New York Times* called me when the club's money troubles started, looking for an appraisal as to whether our dark, former rock 'n' roll neighbor from across the street at the *Reader* was going to make it.

"Do you think it's all over for the club?" he asked.

"Well, no one seems to know for sure. It's like that situation with Arafat—is he or isn't he gone?" I replied, referencing the famous, or infamous, Middle East figure who was rumored to be dead, or near death, that same week.

"Nice."

We bantered a bit more, and I emphasized that I probably wasn't his best source, since I had moved on from the pop culture beat through most of the nineties. He didn't care; he had a list of other people to call, as well.

The house that Steve and Jack built survived, obviously. Hard Rock shut down in 2011, removing its tombstone from the fabled First Avenue

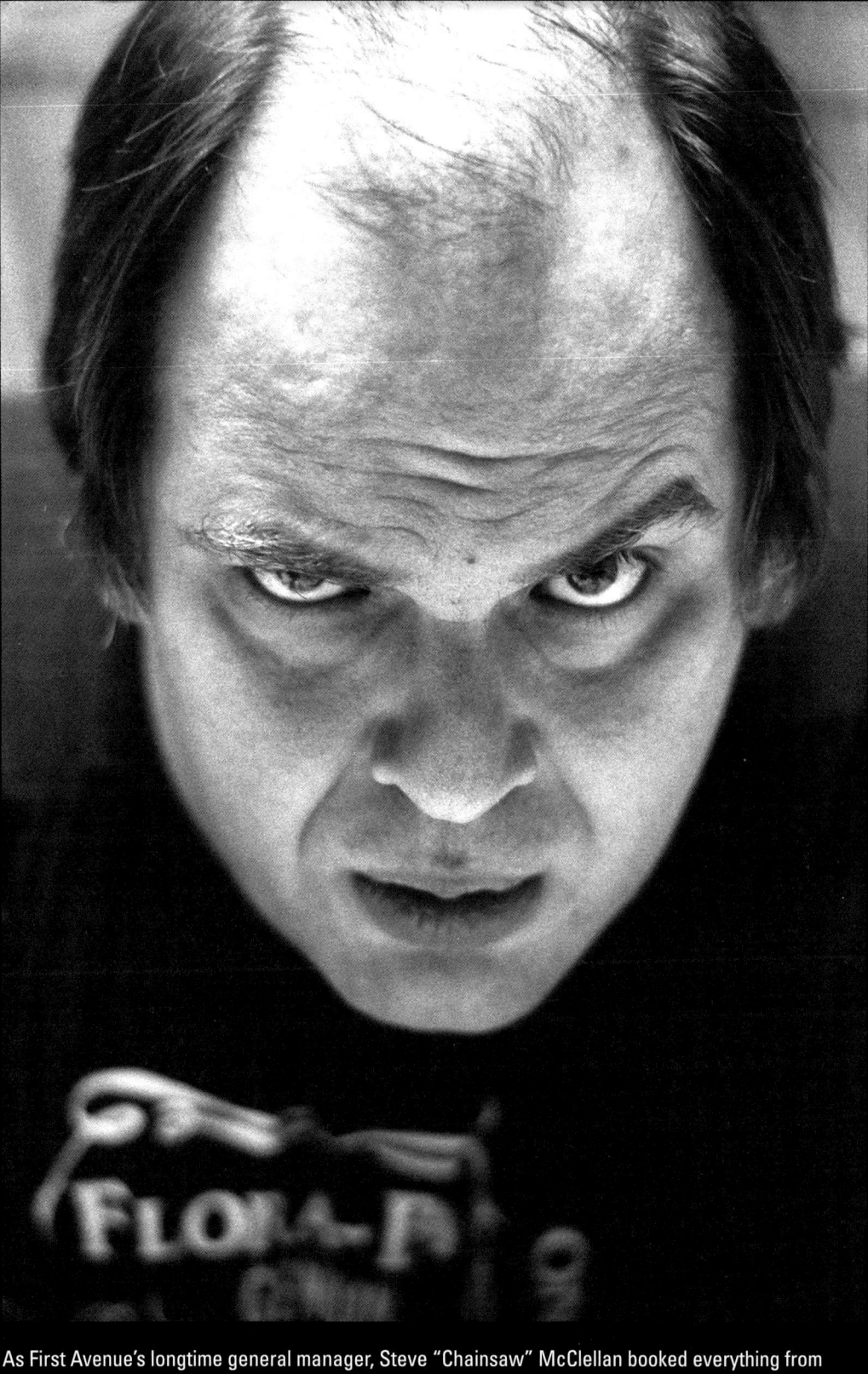

As First Avenue's longtime general manager, Steve "Chainsaw" McClellan booked everything from exotic Afro-pop, speed metal, funk, reggae, punk, pop, folk-rock, country rock, and hip-hop to the occasional jazz act and stand-up comedians.

and Seventh Street crossroads. But both of First Avenue's longtime managers were overthrown in a later buyout of their minority shares, which looked mostly like a soft palace coup to those on the sidelines.

These days I run into McClellan fairly frequently at the Schooner, a hundred-plus-year-old watering hole not far from the location of the old Duffy's and Mr. Nib's clubs in south Minneapolis. There, an increasing number of self-deprecating geezer-hipsters and other music fans take in a robust mix of groups, a lot of the same gang that would pay to see King Sunny Adé and his African Beats from Nigeria at First Avenue and return a couple nights later to hear Têtes Noires, the local all-women punk/new-wave band. We had Mr. McClellan to thank for those inspired bookings.

He bartends at the low-fi tavern part-time and hangs out to catch the likes of the Hula Peppers, Ernie and Billy Batson's King Kustom & the Cruisers, the fabulous Meteor Boys, and others. His lovable rough edges have not been sanded down. He's got his own star on First Avenue's wall of fame, although he could tell you in a twenty-minute burst who else deserves to be up there. Or who doesn't. And why some certifiably mediocre bands make it in the business while other, more deserving groups suffer in obscurity. Harangues about whatever else is crossing his mind on a given day might catch the unacquainted off guard. The Twins, the city council, TV shows, his health, your health, favorite reminisces of days gone by, and recent pet peeves never properly cleaned up—it was all open season.

But frankly, we'd all be a lot more worried about him if he wasn't raving about something.

TIM CARR

A Nearly Unstoppable Force of Scenesterism

He talked fast and moved even faster. But the only time I ever saw Tim Carr speechless was when he was sitting in my lowly walk-out apartment in south Minneapolis on Colfax Avenue staring into the cover of Bob Dylan's *Slow Train Coming* as side one ended. The intensity and passion of the songs that marked the beginning of Dylan's "born-again" or gospel period momentarily rattled the normally quick-quipping lapsed Catholic from Hopkins, Minnesota.

Finally, he shook his head, stood up, and announced, "Let's go out." He glanced up into the house next door, checking to see if Steve Almaas from the Suicide Commandos might be home, or if Robert Wilkinson from the Flamin' Oh's might be visiting. Almaas rented a room there and Wilkinson was dating the young woman who lived next door with her rock 'n' roll fan mother who taught public school. Nobody was home.

Smart, capricious, and sometimes conniving, Carr rose rapidly out of the *Minnesota Daily* student newspaper, which was as good as any other local newsprint organ at the time. Especially notable was its arts and entertainment coverage under Allan Robinson and then Randy Anderson, who groomed two of the best writers of the era: Debby Miller (née Bull) and Lisa Hendrickson, the latter being the first ever to interview Prince. Both ended up in New York working for publications like *Rolling Stone* and *GQ*. Anderson went on to take *Sweet Potato* from a monthly music rag to a competitive weekly news and arts alternative newspaper called *City Pages*; its archrival, the *Twin Cities Reader*, was also full of former *Daily* staffers.

Carr wasn't a quick study; he was a buzz-sawing scenery chewer, as they sometimes say in the film biz. When Michael Anthony took a sabbatical from the *Minneapolis Tribune*, Carr took on his classical music beat for the paper. "It's not that hard," he offered, when asked how he could sit through so many orchestra and chamber music concerts—and write

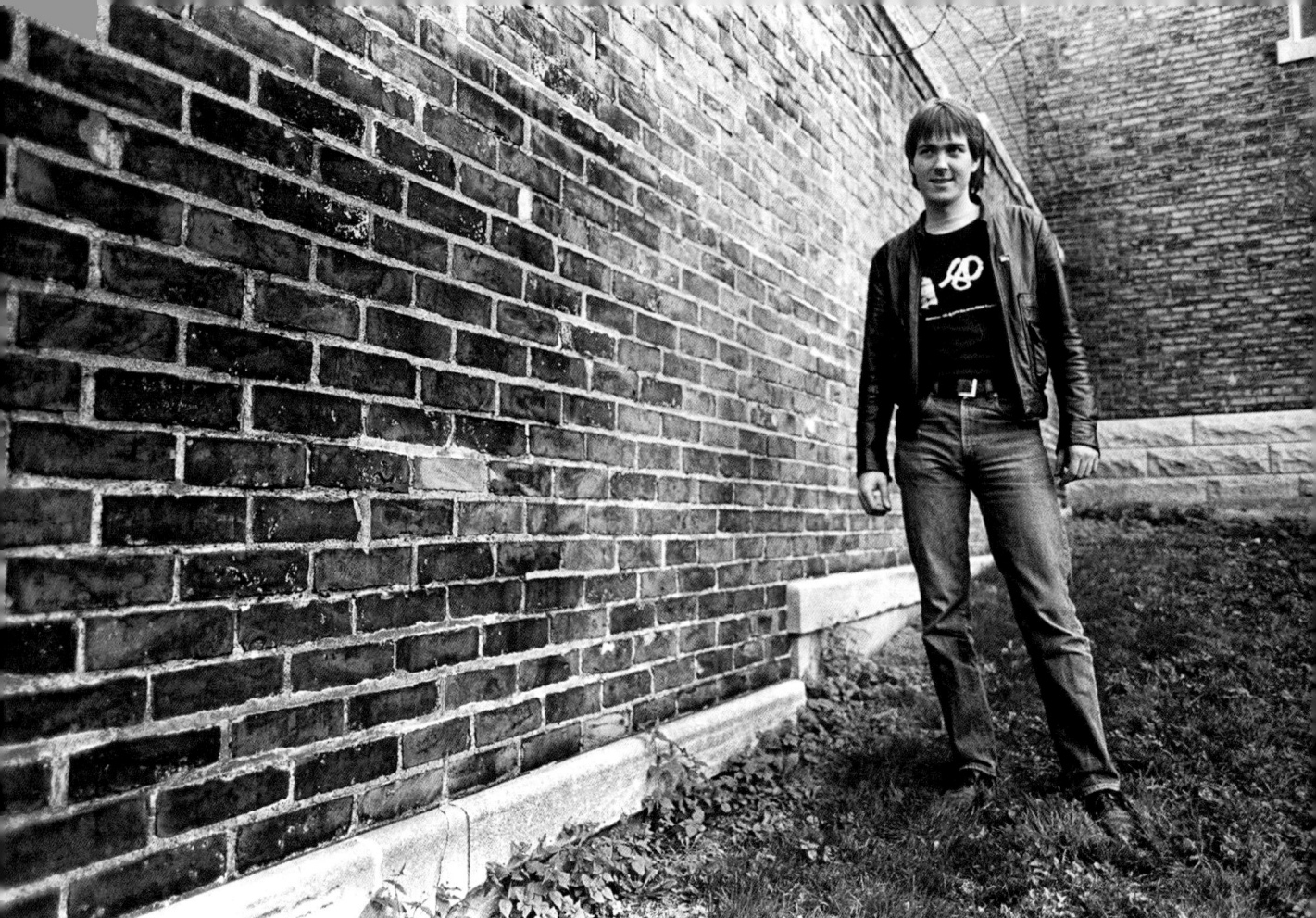

Tim Carr was a fast-moving journalist turned impresario who later scored high-flying gigs at the Brooklyn Academy of Music and at DreamWorks Animation in LA.

about them—since he was a rocker at heart whose passion for all variations of the music was outdone by hardly anyone in either city.

From there, Carr went on to Walker Art Center for the highly coveted role of performing arts curator. He next jumped to the Brooklyn Academy of Music (BAM). Although his writer's voice was missed in printland, his inescapable machine-gun-fire vocal assault would ring in your ears when he called you on the phone about some of the adventurous programming he was doing at the Walker, or if you ran into him—or with him—in the clubs or concert venues.

The rest of his résumé would eventually read: A&R guy at Warner Bros., Capitol, and DreamWorks labels, with deals made for David Byrne, Laurie Anderson, the Beastie Boys, Megadeth, the Twin Cities' own Babes in Toyland, and others. Despite these accomplishments, many remember him most fondly as the driven impresario who hoped to capture the new-wave, no-wave, punk, and noise-rock artists of the late seventies by putting on a festival at the University of Minnesota Field House in September 1979. He called it "Marathon '80: A New-No-Now Wave Festival"—known more

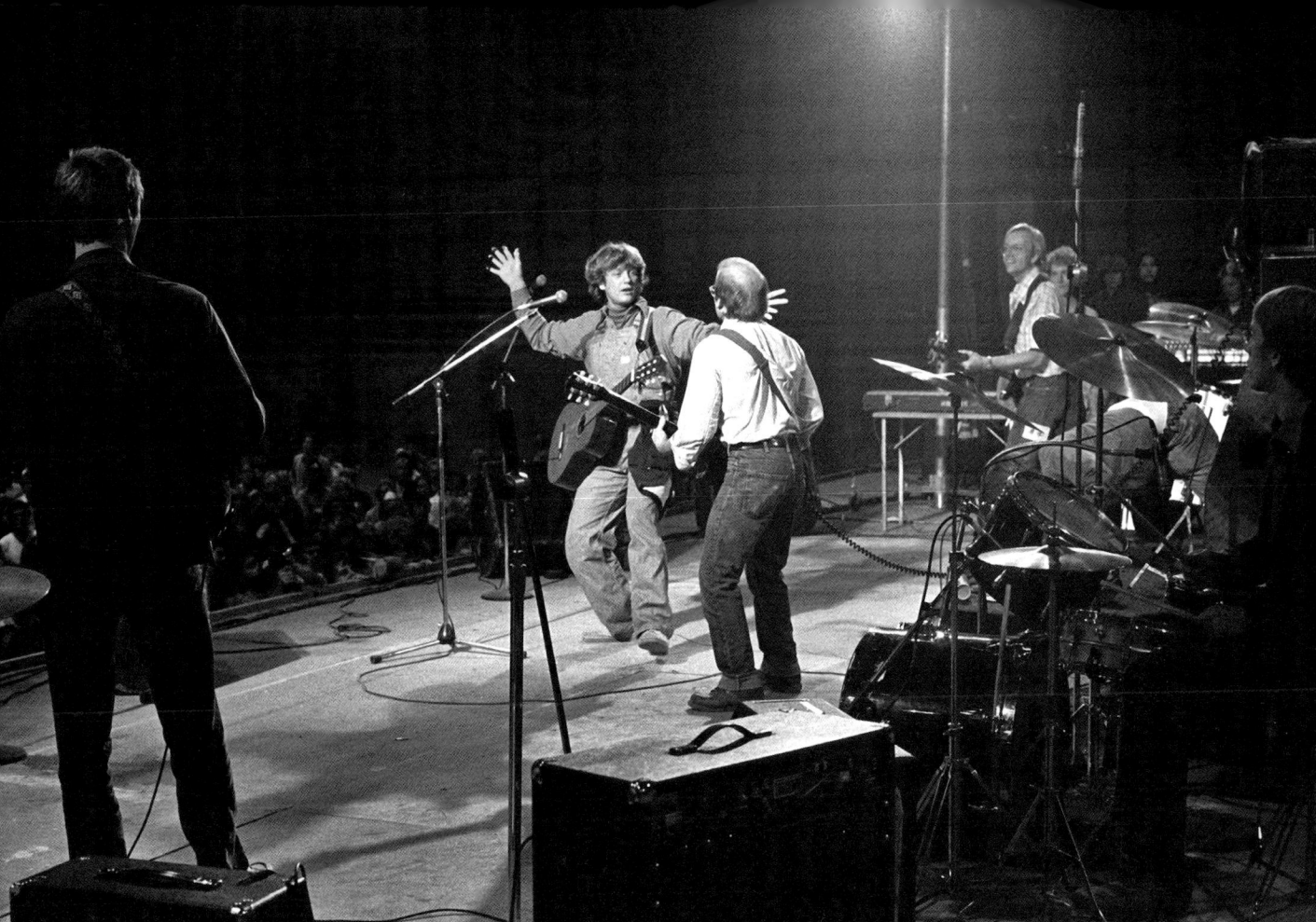

familiarly as "M-80"—the number 80 indicating it would be a musical preview of the coming decade. Maybe this was Tim's way of tossing a New Year's Eve party three months early and on the Walker's nickel.

As he threw the event together, Carr commented that "it would be like Woodstock, only for what's happening now in music." He invited known quantities, as well as some lesser known: James Chance and the Contortions (with Minneapolis's own Steve Kramer on keyboards, pre-Wallets), the Fleshtones, Chris Stamey and the dB's, Joan Jett, the Feelies, and many others. The two-day festival featured a good representation of local acts, as well, like Curtiss A, the Suburbs, Flamingo (before they became the Flamin' Oh's), a rare set by NNB, and an all-star mash-up, the Minneapolis Rockestra, led by Chris Osgood of the Suicide Commandos. There was even a freak workup by Devo, who performed as a religious combo known as Dove, playing off Dylan's recent pivot to Christianity, as only the de-evolved band from Akron could. M-80 was a scene unto itself, created by the nearly unstoppable force of scenesterism, Tim Carr.

M-80 didn't quite live up to the explosive power of the firecracker of

Marathon '80, or M-80, was billed as a "new-no-now wave festival" and featured local, national, and international acts. Suicide Commando Chris Osgood (center, with his back to the camera) commandeered a supergroup of local musicians under the Minneapolis Rockestra moniker.

the same name. Turnout was light. A lot of the same people you saw at the Longhorn Bar you saw on the dirt floor of the university building that also had a slight whiff of livestock in the air. Attempts to get the two-day marathon professionally filmed by Chuck Statler's video crew, Location Services, fell flat due to lack of financing. The festival was nonetheless a benchmark event in the land of ten thousand rock 'n' roll moments.

After Carr lived in New York and then LA for a time, working for major labels, he vanished. Or at least he fell off the radars of friends he might have considered "close." Whatever the case, he maintained a long period of radio silence to the point that wild rumors started taking wing: Tim had OD'd on drugs; Tim was running an art gallery in a foreign land; Tim had joined a monastery in Asia. That last one reminded me of Thomas Merton, a New York bon vivant from the fifties, who swore off the fast life, converted to Catholicism, and became a contemplative Trappist monk, poet, mystic, and later a published writer, social critic, and activist who began studying Buddhism in Asia, looking for a bridge to his own faith.

Merton died accidentally—some contend mysteriously—near Bangkok, Thailand, while attending an interfaith conference of Christian and Buddhist monks. Carr, it turns out, didn't quite follow the same path as Merton. He eventually resurfaced after almost a decade of being missing in action and was trying to leverage various arts and entertainment projects in the same country.

Carr died in 2013 at age fifty-seven, in South Pattaya, Thailand, where he had been living for eight years. The first news from the tabloid press was sensational and troubling, claiming he'd been stabbed and even showing a pixelated photo of a naked body in a kitchen, with alleged drugs thrown about. It was later dismissed as hyperbole; he most likely died of heart failure. He was buried after a traditional Catholic mass in Hopkins.

The church was filled with family members, rock musicians, and longtime music fans, many of whom had been to M-80. David Carr, a cousin of Tim's, attended the service. Fellow scribes, such as David Ayers—another fine writer minted at the *Daily* who later went into the music side of the business in New York, much like Tim—rounded out the rows of tables in the church basement for a predictable church ladies' lunch after the service.

Comparing notes on Tim Carr's life over cold pasta salads, Ayers offered his own assessment. He quipped that no matter how he died, Tim would have loved the swirling controversy and rank gossip about it and shrugged it off, ready to move on to the next Tim thing.

WILLIAM BURROUGHS

The Beat Goes on in Minneapolis

Strippers in the late afternoon. Assorted local and national rock groups and imported new-wave and ska bands from the UK, and unforgettable and sometimes intergalactic jazz shows like Sun Ra and His Arkestra at night. There was an appealing pretzel logic to the kind of acts booked by club owners Leslie and Dan Johnson at Duffy's in south Minneapolis in the eighties. But when ads appeared in *Sweet Potato* announcing a reading by the sixty-seven-year-old writer and visual artist William Burroughs at the club in March of '81, all logic was tossed aside.

The addled and brilliant godfather of the Beats, occult practitioner, and self-confessed junkie wielded an uncanny influence on many rock bands—the group Steely Dan was named after a dildo in *Naked Lunch*, and the name for Grant Hart's post–Hüsker Dü project, Nova Mob, was based on wild Bill's book *Nova Express*. Burroughs inspired in diverse ways an even wider range of musicians, from guitarist Bill Laswell to Patti Smith to Lou Reed, David Bowie, and many others.

The Twin Cities have always been a literate and literary outpost. Two years after the Burroughs gig, the Minnesota Center for Book Arts opened in the McKesson Building in the pre-groovy warehouse district of Minneapolis. Decades later, you didn't have to look far to find either city on the top ten lists of America's Most Literate Cities (Minneapolis was number 1 in 2015 and St. Paul 4, falling to 3 and 9 respectively in 2017). Active local libraries tell the rest of the story. But the Burroughs booking in a funky nightspot—you'd expect that in lower Manhattan, not in a quiet, working-class neighborhood near a bowling alley.

The local literati expected good book coverage from the *Spud* and its weekly successor, *City Pages*. Beyond the Burroughs cover story, a regular quarterly book section became a standard feature. Its debut included an exclusive two-page interview with Tom Wolfe, written by Debby Miller, that really turned heads. Miller could have easily sold the piece for a lot more to a magazine or newspaper in New York, where she eventually landed, but editor Randy Anderson was well practiced at the art of persuasion.

Had it been one of the Beat poets like Allen Ginsberg or Lawrence Ferlinghetti coming to Duffy's, I would have eagerly volunteered for the interview. But I could never get past Burroughs' "cut-up" method, in which he would deconstruct sentences and then reformulate them. Ginsberg's "Howl" is the most powerful poem I have ever read, and *A Coney Island of the Mind* by Ferlinghetti is a small collection of illuminating poems that I have poured over more times than any other works by living or dead poets from any century—and it has sealed more than a handful of long relationships with friends.

I had experienced a close encounter with Ginsberg in college when I was taking a complete semester study of William Blake. Ginsberg's celebrated poem about having a vision of Blake while reading his poems always fascinated me, and I asked him about it following a reading by the "bard of the Beats" at St. Cloud State. Surprisingly, he hemmed and hawed and backpedaled, saying maybe after all it really wasn't, you know, "a vision." Maybe it was just, you know, his imagination running away with him, this poet with clay feet and disappointing second guesses. Or maybe he was just putting me off.

With Burroughs, however, only one or two people were cut out for the job of interviewing him. Tony Glover, of the Koerner, Ray, and Glover folk-blues trio, was a fan. He owned an imported British copy of *Junkie*, which, like other early Burroughs works, had been banned as obscene in the freedom-loving USA. Tony's friend, Bruce Rubenstein, an occasional features contributor to the paper, had read even more—if not all—of Burroughs's stuff, and they shared a byline in an engaging and in-depth question-and-answer format.

The interview took place at the Curtis Hotel before the Duffy's reading. Like Glover, Burroughs brought a friend along, poet and artist John Giorno, who collaborated with Burroughs beginning in the 1960s. Both men imbibed while Bruce and Tony worked through their long and insightful list of questions.

Reading the nearly four-decades-old interview again recently, I was struck by how prescient Burroughs was, saying the Democratic and Republican parties were really no different from each other (an argument still debated today); calling for the legalization of heroin to take the taxpayer dollars out of the hands of corrupt law enforcement and drug dealers; and amplifying what a sex change means, a theme that appears in his work fairly consistently. Discussing his writing process he said, "a writer writes more than he knows. . . . In any serious writing, there's always an element of prophecy." He also said he used cannabis while working but never psychedelics. He touched on his favorite novelists (Joseph Conrad,

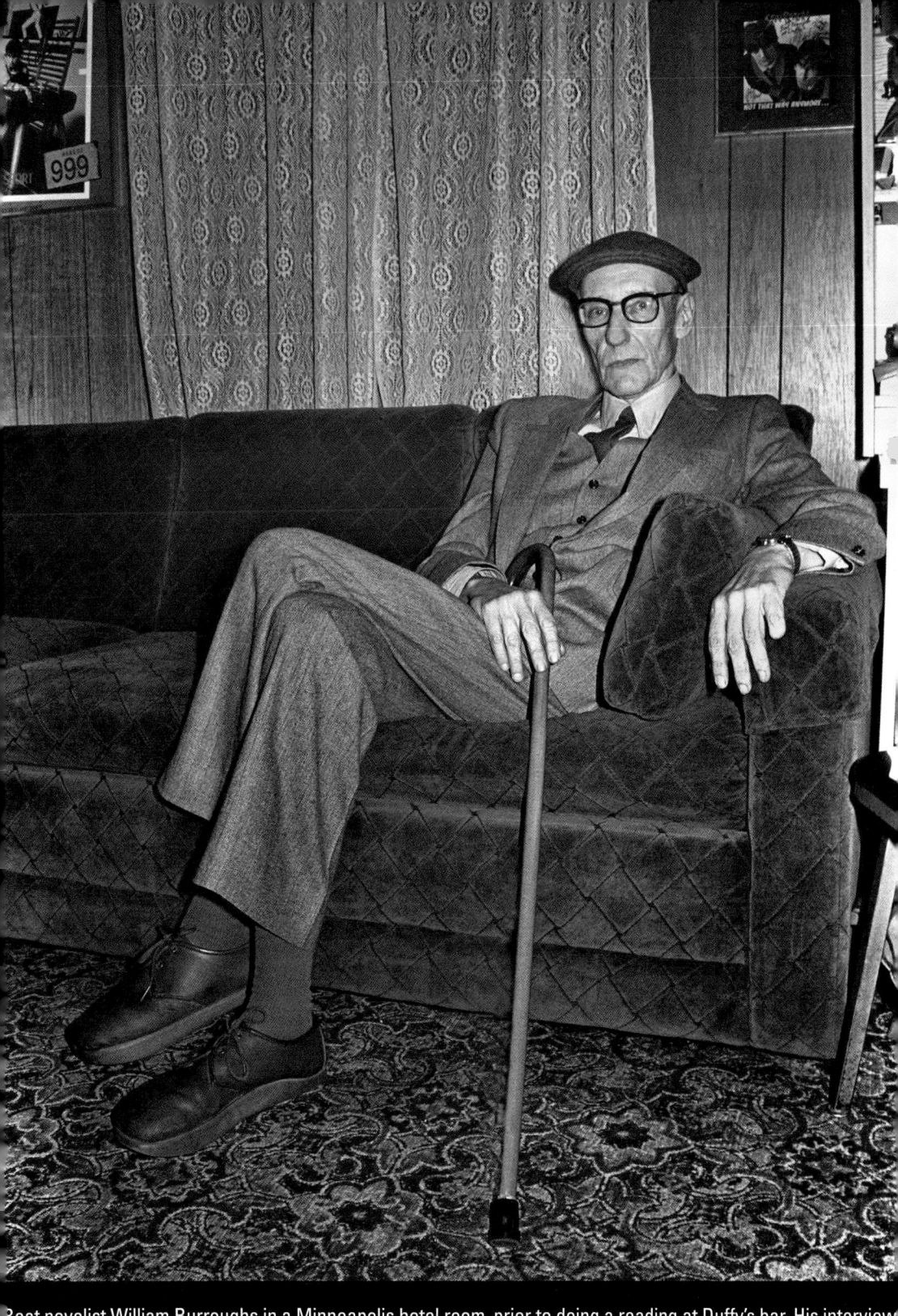

Beat novelist William Burroughs in a Minneapolis hotel room, prior to doing a reading at Duffy's bar. His interview covered his thoughts on subjects ranging from life after death to poets, drug use, and human evolution.

Graham Greene, F. Scott Fitzgerald, Louis-Ferdinand Céline), while disparaging poets ("a poet is a lazy prose writer"). And he admitted he had to tour for financial reasons, despite coming from a very wealthy family: "*Naked Lunch* brings in maybe $1,800 a year."

Bruce and Tony left no stone unturned. Before they were done, they asked whether Burroughs believed in an afterlife ("Of course. . . . It'll be very much like the dream state") and the viral theory of evolution, which argues that mutations occur not over a long period but within one generation ("Darwin's theory is less and less credible. . . . The only hope for humanity is mutation. Change is the only hope for any species."). Glover's most surprising question, "Have you ever had any UFO contacts?" elicited an even more surprising answer: "Never, never seen any. I'd love to see one, love to get in one, love to leave. There's nothing to keep me here. . . . I desire to leave the solar system, yes indeed."

But Burroughs's escapist saucer desires were eclipsed by a larger, darker statement: "I'd like to kill somebody 'fore I die." Of course, most know that he had already accomplished this deed; when he was living in Mexico in the early fifties, he accidentally shot his wife while playing a botched game of William Tell and the apple. Glover and Rubenstein didn't press him on it, and William Tell-All went on to talk about his current writing projects to end the piece.

Looking back, it's too bad there wasn't one of those annual supercilious literary surveys in 1983 when Burroughs was on the cover of the *Spud*. Minneapolis–St. Paul might have picked up a bunch of bonus points for exposing the isolated Beat prose writer and his curious and caustic thoughts to a wider readership.

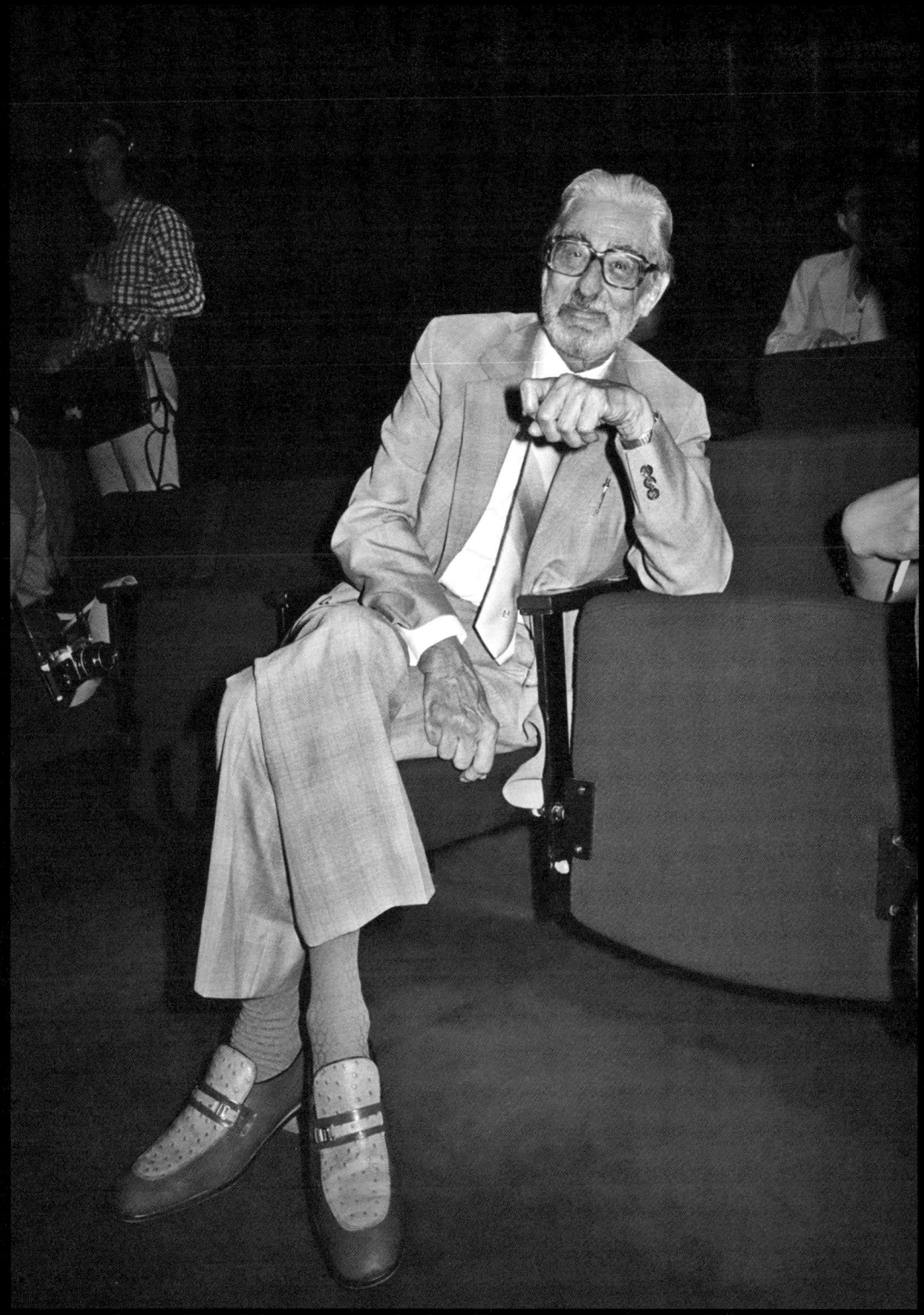

Theodor Seuss Geisel, better known Dr. Seuss, poses in his seat before the world premiere and first stage adaptation of his work *The 500 Hats of Bartholomew Cubbins*, at Minneapolis's Children's Theatre Company in 1979. He also obliged Helgeson with autographs for the photographer's two daughters. "He was one of those rare people who had a great calming influence, just by the way he talked and moved," the Helg recalled.

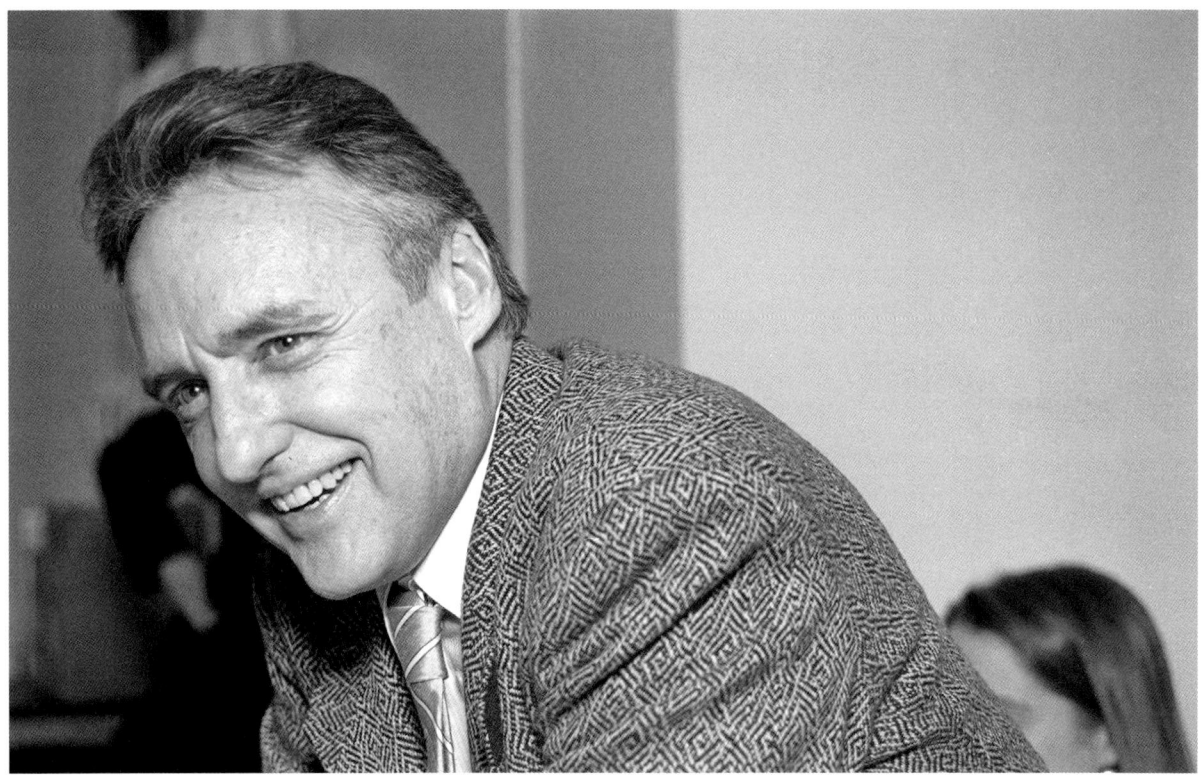

(above) Actor and director Dennis Hopper—whose breakout role came in the classic sixties movie *Easy Rider*—attends an exhibit of his photo work at Walker Art Center in 1988. Helgeson was told no photos were allowed, but Hopper agreed to it. "He was a damn good photographer, too."

(right) Graphic artist Doug Henders in his funky apartment near Goofy's Upper Deck bar in downtown Minneapolis. Among his many credits, he created the art for Prince's *Around the World in a Day* album in 1985: "Even though he did the art, Henders didn't even have a copy of the album!"

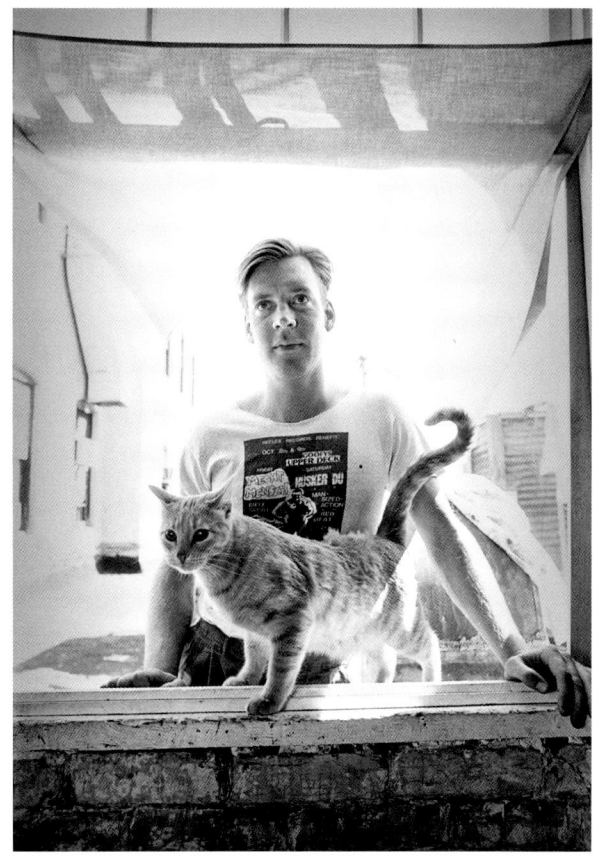

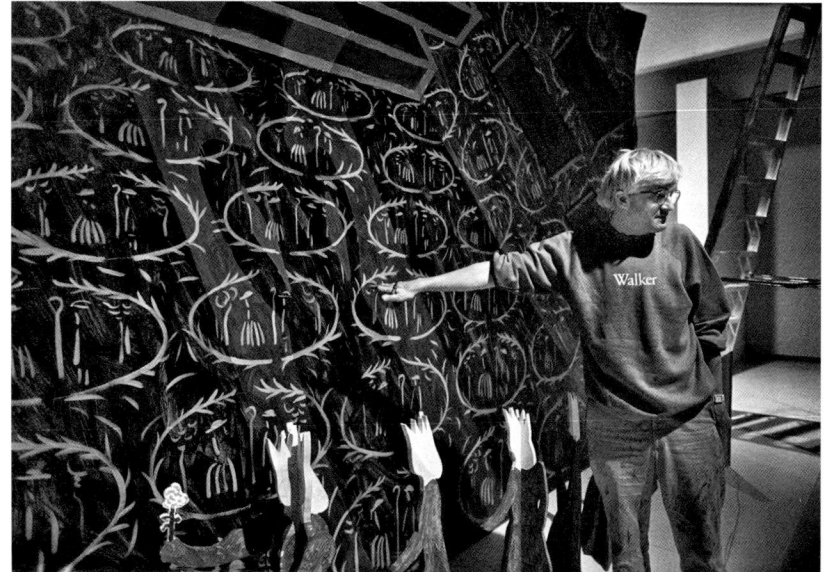

Painter David Hockney prepares his exhibit at Walker Art Center in 1983. "One of my better journalistic shots that I've always liked," says Helgeson. A few images from the shoot ran in the *Twin Cities Reader*.

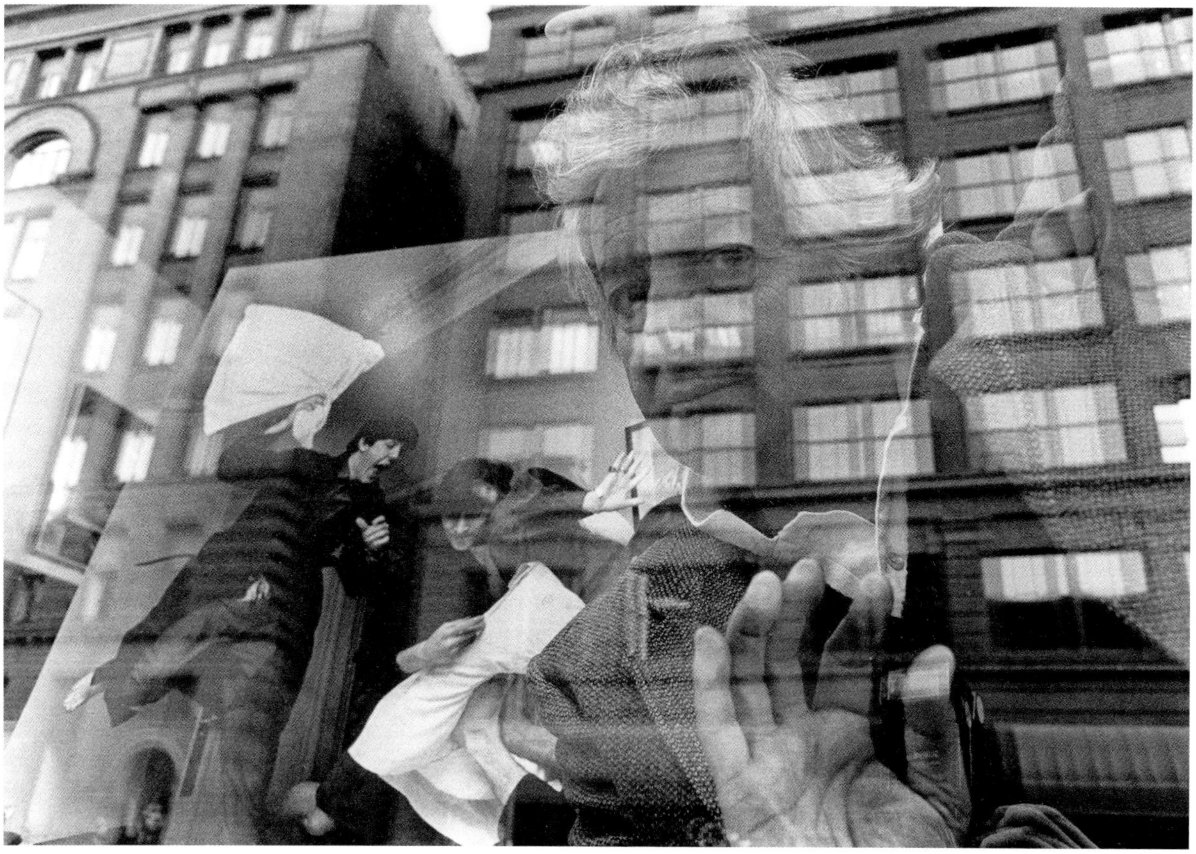

One of Spud Boy 1's favorite photographers, Scotland native Harry Benson shot the famous early Beatles pillow fight photo (visible in the background), as well as many others. The Helg captured him through the window of a downtown Minneapolis art gallery where Benson's work was being exhibited in 1986. Over his long career, Benson has photographed A-list Hollywood actors, US presidents, rock stars, high-profile authors, and, according to Helgeson, "probably any famous person you can mention. And he's still at it!"

GARRISON KEILLOR

This Town Is Too Small, Part 3. Or, If the Statue of the Unknown Norwegian Falls in Lake Wobegon, Does Anyone Hear It?

n 2010, *The Zombies of Lake Begotten* appeared, followed in 2011 by *The Twilight of Lake Begotten.* Both books were written by Harrison Geillor. You know your art and craft have risen to oxygen-thin cultural peaks when they are blatantly cannibalized by the zombie zeitgeist. Over the decades, Garrison Keillor's work, voice, and radio show have been satirized on everything from *The Simpsons* and *Saturday Night Live* to *Portlandia* and in other media. But these raw parodies lie so close to the comforting and stylized storytelling of the fictionalized Lake Wobegon tales by the self-described "Old Scout" that you wonder if it wasn't GK himself pulling those strings.

Of course, parody and satire lie at the heart of many things Keillor, along with prose, poetry, political punditry, and public broadcasting. Lake Wobegon is one of the most famous rural American places that never was, a small town somewhere in central Minnesota whose city fathers might have been Thornton Wilder, Will Rogers, and James Thurber, its mothers Tammy Wynette, Edith Bunker, and Willa Cather. There, the town's common folk and Norwegian bachelor farmers face life's daily challenges and the unintended consequences of the weather, religion, work, romance and sex, family, and the unchecked foibles of others.

In 2014, Amy Goetzman, a one-time fellow scribe at the *Twin Cities Reader*, reviewed the newly published *Keillor Reader* for MinnPost. Commenting on Keillor's radio show, *A Prairie Home Companion (APHC)*, and its weekly "News from Lake Wobegon" segment, Goetzman wrote, "that News bit is sort of a singular work of American letters. . . . But watch the show live and you're seeing an original story essentially told from memory, with the teller only occasionally glancing at notes as he wanders around the stage, even though, as we learn in this book, he wrote it just that same morning, after procrastinating long enough. What other writer can do that? And still, that story is so complex and nuanced, with its insights into human nature and turns of phrase and plot twists, that those of us not yet seventy-one can only hope that we'll be so sharp one day.... There are people who will dismiss the News as the nostalgic ramblings of an old fart, but those people aren't paying attention. It's something more."

Keillor's radio show ran for more than forty years. Its origins lay in the country music mecca of the Grand Ole Opry, broadcast in Nashville and still America's longest-running radio program. But as Keillor's *Companion* show evolved, it seemed more like a satisfying combo of the old Ed Sullivan TV variety show from New York City and Keillor's own short-lived *The Morning Show*.

Beginning in 1969, *The Morning Show* beamed out from a few small rooms in the tower of the Quadrangle of what was then the only Minnesota Public Radio station in the state, KSJN-FM in Collegeville on the campus of St. John's University. I was there and tuned in faithfully. And my fellow Johnnies and I often saw the tall, bearded man, usually wearing a big hat, walking toward the Quad or having a brew in nearby St. Joseph on cheap-beer nights.

In place of Sullivan's plate spinners and acrobats, sketch comedy bits were transformed into memorable, well-spun yarns at *APHC*, thanks to marvelous sound-effect guys Tom Keith and then Fred Newman. Keillor's talent roster on *The Morning Show*, and subsequently on *A Prairie Home*, ran from low-brow to high-brow artists. He was fond of showcasing class-crashing mash-ups, like the Beach Boys followed by a performance of one of Vivaldi's *Four Seasons*. For quirky, nearly free-form radio, it didn't get much better than that. And with some modifications, it would translate well to the six hundred public radio stations and 2.5 million listeners that *Prairie Home* had at its peak, before Keillor left the show for good in 2016, after several false stops.

In 1981, I interviewed him for a *City Pages* cover story on the publication of his first book, *Happy to Be Here*. Smoking a cig in his St. Paul MPR office, he said I looked too young to be interested in what he was doing. When I told him that I'd been a fan of *The Morning Show* since my Collegeville days and was a regular listener to *APHC*, he darted sideways and offered that it was a great thing I had the opportunity to do this kind of writing and reporting without having to go to New York.

I didn't bring up the fact that, because our names fell one after the other alphabetically, we had facing poems in the spring edition of the St. John's literary publication, *The Lower Stumpf Lake Review*, eight years earlier. His sweet, compacted verse, "Vernal Equinox," expressed childlike wonder that the Earth's rotation occurs "simply because an orange representing the sun / Reaches the right relation / To a pea held by our teach in fourth grade." It even quoted "Here Comes the Sun." Mine, "Spring Storm on the Ewegowan," meditated on the indifferent cruelties of a spring

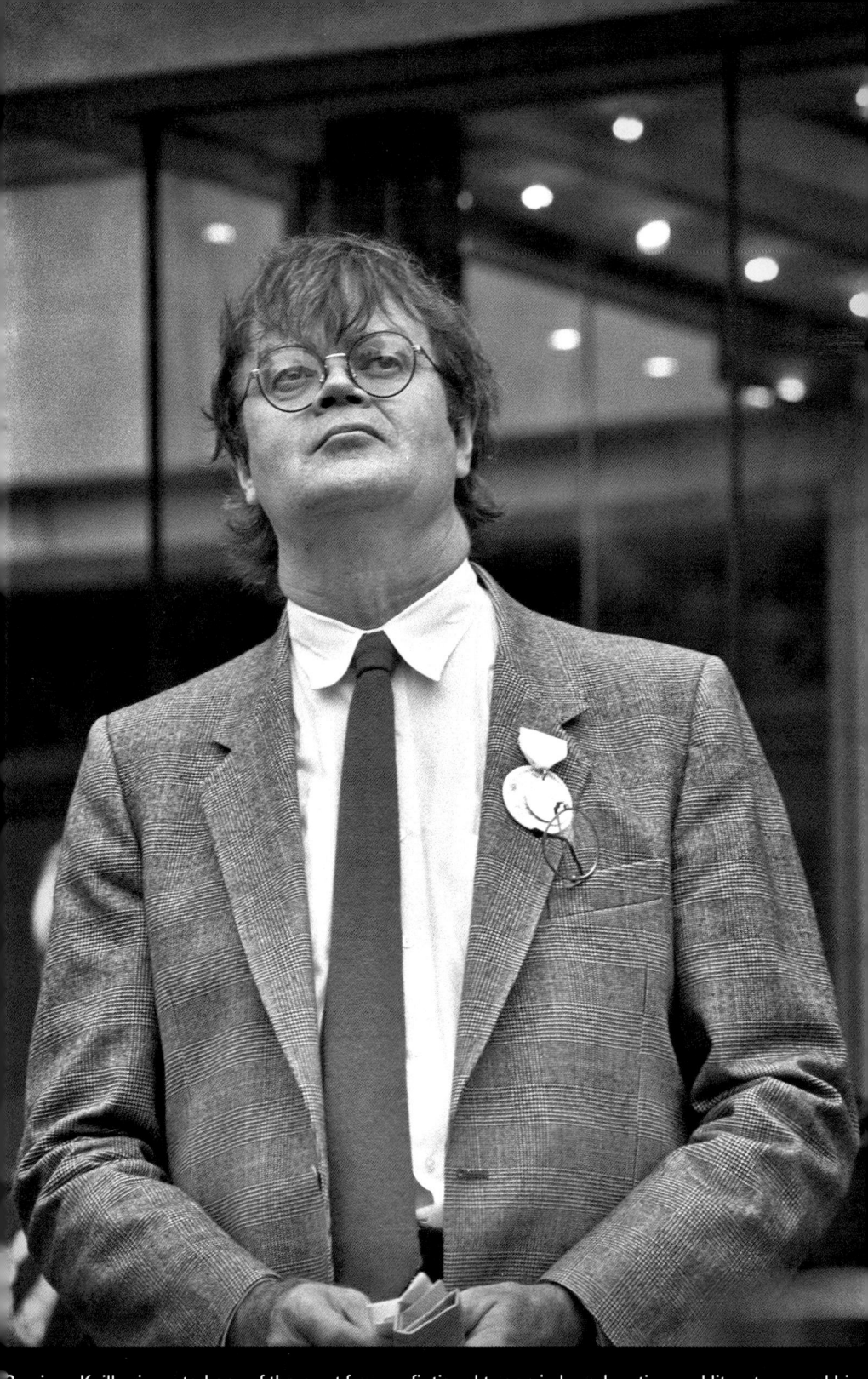

Garrison Keillor invented one of the most famous fictional towns in broadcasting and literature, and his acclaimed (and highly satirized) *A Prairie Home Companion* show ran for more than forty years.

blizzard in which an unborn lamb and its mother are lost in "a horrible economy of death." (Okay, I was just a college kid from the Dakotas under the influence of the Naturalists I was studying at the time, while the older, wiser bard of the pen and microphone simply and more effectively namechecked the Beatles and his own Anoka childhood without angst.)

Keillor provided ample personal and professional insights for the story. Then he turned the tables and interviewed me for a while, offering some curious advice at the conclusion: I should go back to attending Mass regularly and start reading *Mad* magazine again.

We exchanged a few short letters over the years as he became more famous, more published, more broadcast, more nationwide. In one, he hoped I would write something good in advance about country music legend Ernest Tubb, who was going to be on *Prairie Home* and also do a concert. He noted that Tubb's record label at one time had refused to issue his new album, so Ernest earnestly told them where they could stick it. "A Great Man!" Keillor wrote.

Helgeson's photo of Keillor was taken at the official opening of the restored Fitzgerald Theater in St. Paul in 1986. The refurbishment of the Fitz was the result of an almost single-handed fundraising feat Keillor had achieved on the strength of his celebrity status. He loathed the idea of celebrity, however, and he often went after reporters who wrote front-page stories about his personal activities, such as buying a new house. He would not be ascribed to that C-realm, as if it were one of Dante's levels of hell where only bad but popular writers like Jackie Collins belonged.

Then, in 2017–18, the headlines grew more serious: Keillor's alleged inappropriate deeds with members of the opposite sex, coming to light at the height of the #metoo era. The accusations divided people, rallying supporters and enflaming detractors, and put the celebrated broadcaster and writer and MPR staff and execs through the wringer. The reported incidents and the subsequent public intellectual property fight with MPR over his rights to *A Prairie Home Companion*, *The Writer's Almanac*, and other brand assets became a public spectacle with far-reaching implications. The allegations likely will prevent him from ever receiving the Mark Twain Prize for American Humor or a Kennedy Center Honor.

Meanwhile, in that place where "all the women are strong, all the men are good-looking, and all the children are above average," it has grown deathly quiet since *A Prairie Home Companion* was reborn as *Live from Here with Chris Thile*. Still, just the other day, idle Collegevillians from Keillor's old stumpfing grounds wondered aloud over spendy craft beers whether if the Statue of the Unknown Norwegian fell like a Confederate effigy in Lake Wobegon, would anyone still care to hear about it?

JOEL HODGSON AND JERRY SEINFELD

Big Talkers

J oel and Jerry. The former made it okay to talk during movies, especially really bad movies, and created an entirely new way of film watching. The latter elevated the prosaic talk of everyday life among four friends into a comedic art that transformed the TV sitcom. Both shaped a modern conversational comedy world that continues to reverberate. But in 1987, neither Joel Hodgson nor Jerry Seinfeld were bona fide household names, even though Fate was breathing heavily down their necks. Their friendship, however, was airtight. And you can glimpse it in the wonderful shots Greg captured near the DoubleTree hotel parking garage in downtown Minneapolis.

At first a Twin Cities stand-up comic who relied on an array of weird props, Hodgson was on the verge of developing *Mystery Science Theater 3000* (aka MST3K) for an obscure local cable channel, KTMA-TV 23, with Best Brains, Inc.; the show would debut in November 1988. A seasoned New York comic, Seinfeld had successfully plowed into the television talk show circuit, appearing on shows like *The Tonight Show Starring Johnny Carson* and *Late Night with David Letterman*, and left a deep impression. But his self-titled show—first airing a year later in 1989—was still being hatched inside the shared craniums of Seinfeld and cocreator Larry David.

Hodgson often compared the local comedy scenes around the country during the late seventies and throughout the eighties to the punk rock or new-wave scenes that sprung up in that same period. Unfettered creativity and an independent spirit were hallmarks of both. The long-running Second City in Chicago, Carolines and the Comedy Cellar in New York, Ding Ho and Comedy Connection in Boston, Comedy Works in Denver, the Improv and the Comedy Store in LA—you name it, nearly every major metropolis had comedy joints. Seattle had four at one time, about as many as the Twin Cities had at the peak of the comedy renaissance that swept the country.

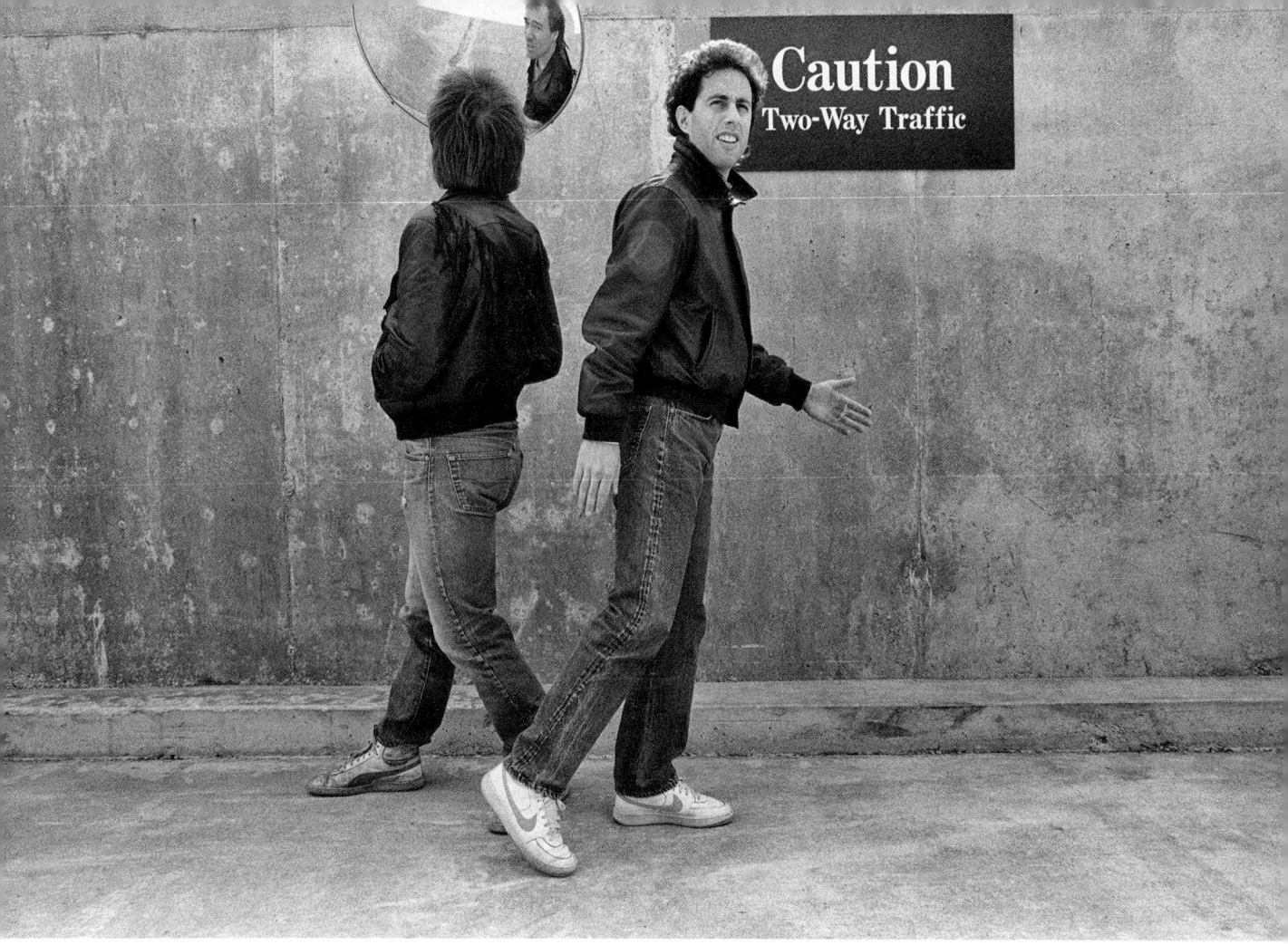

Caution
Two-Way Traffic

Hodgson's solo act was understatedly brilliant. He had a deadpan look that could kill, and that's what comics wanted to do: *kill!* Making people laugh could mean lucrative TV and movie contracts, book deals, and good paydays at clubs. When Hodgson started talking with his robot buddies over some of the best worst B-movies ever made, he and his team of acutely sharp writers struck a new kind of comedy never before seen. By interacting with bad dialogue, insulting hokey story premises, blasting cheap cinematic effects, and mocking frame after frame of anemic acting, the crew carved out a new corner of comedy that utilized the improvisation of stand-up and the semi-scripted structure of sketch comedy. MST3K tickled audiences and critics in a new way and maybe even freed endorphins we never knew we had. Thus the art of "movie riffing" was born.

As for *Seinfeld*, I saw only a handful of episodes when it was on prime time for nine triumphant seasons. TV was not a priority beat of mine and the DVR had yet to be invented. I have caught up with it over time and admired its elevated state of irony, the cozy chaos of the unpredictable

Joel Hodgson, creator of *Mystery Science Theater 3000*, and Jerry Seinfeld, cocreator of *Seinfeld*, both changed the shape of comedy. Here they joke around for a photo shoot with Helgeson.

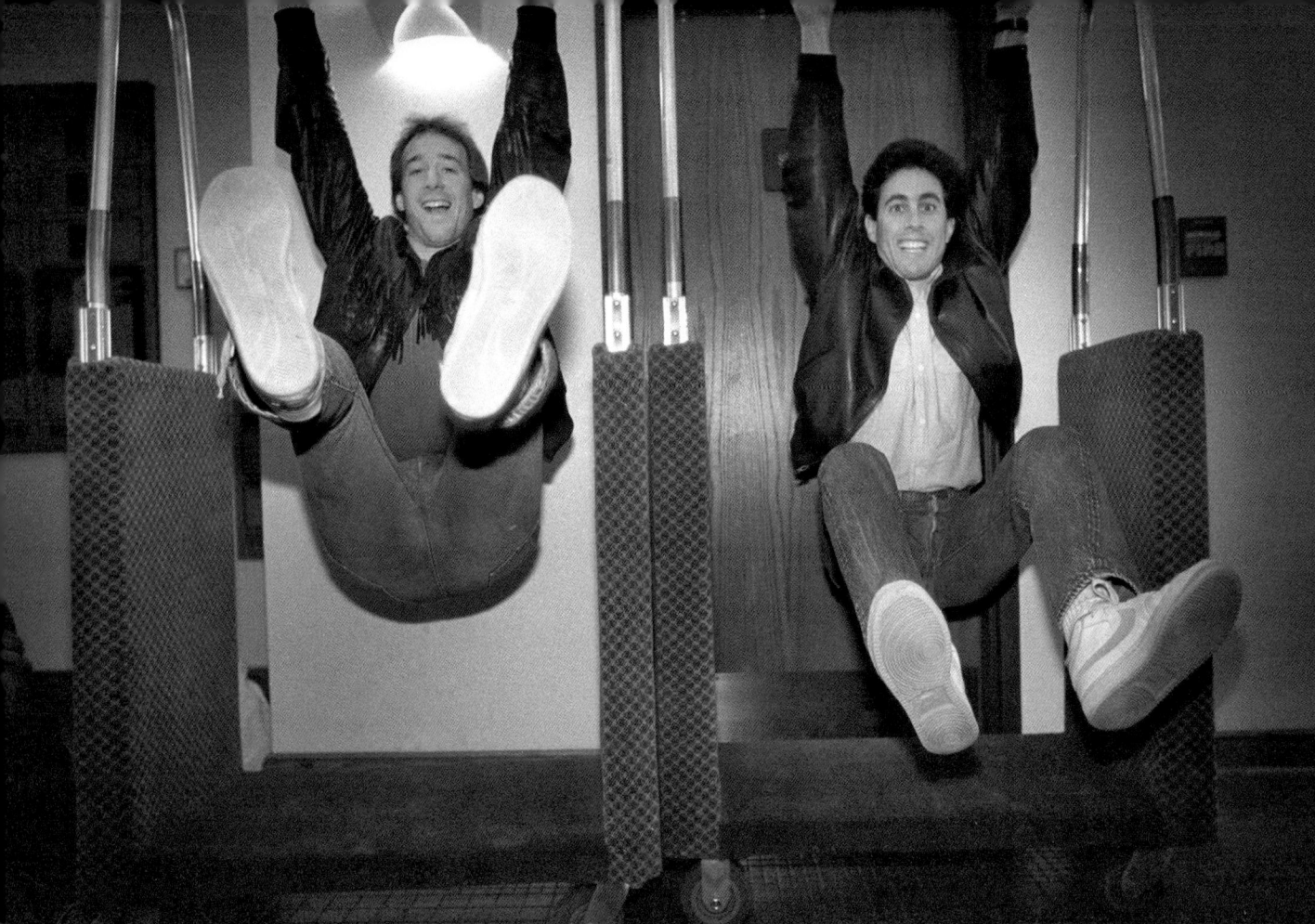

Hodgson and Seinfeld: killin' it on a luggage cart

friendships, and the minimalist New York apartment set that seemed to trap them in time and endless, occasionally absurd conversation as they waited for Uncle Godot to visit, or for Chinese takeout. *Seinfeld*'s world captured everyday life, the mundane and the maddening, the little victories and looming defeats, that made perfect comic (non)sense, no matter who you were. While the show is often described as a show about nothing, that might not be entirely accurate. Matt Goldman, a Minnesota native and part of the early stand-up crowd, went west and wrote for *Seinfeld* and other TV shows. Although he was never able to define precisely what the show was about, he did venture that maybe at the bottom, it was really about "selfishness."

Probably around the time that Greg photographed Hodgson and Seinfeld, I shared a Mexican lunch with them at Pepitos in south Minneapolis. It was a fairly ordinary conversation about what each of them was doing, some talk about bands and other comics; I don't recall even having a notebook, let alone a tape recorder. The restaurant—owned and run by the family of Joe Minjares, who was also a celebrated stand-up comedian, actor, and writer—placed tiny, gold plaques on tables, saying so-and-so celebrity ate here. And Pepitos commemorated the spot where Joel and Jerry crushed their queso, tacos, and frijoles.

Years later, while planning for the twelfth season of MST3K in late 2017, Hodgson graciously came back to Pepitos and the adjacent Parkway Theater to do a benefit for Minjares with other comics, including Mary Jo Pehl (one of his early MST3K writers), Kristin Andersen-Anderson, Tom Baumgartner, and Karen Pickering. Minjares was awaiting a lifesaving lung transplant after pulmonary fibrosis had ruined one of his lungs. Adding to the family's woes, financial setbacks stemming from the Great Recession of the late 2000s had led them to announce that, at the end of the year, the restaurant would be closing after forty-one years in business.

Hodgson's cray-cray show that night—part stand-up act, part absent-minded-professor lecture, complete with slides—explored the roots of his comedy, going back to his Green Bay, Wisconsin, childhood, when he aspired to do a ventriloquist-and-dummy act. The black-and-white screenshots of dummies from the catalogs that he ordered from, and which he had meticulously preserved, were both funny and frightening. He was upstaged only by Minjares, who appeared in a surprise FaceTime feed from his hospital bed. He had just gotten a lung, but he was already telling newly minted dirty jokes.

As for Joel's longtime and highly successful friend, these days Jerry is driving around with other comedians on his laugh-and-caffeine-fueled buddy-fest streaming series, *Comedians in Cars Getting Coffee*. He and his famous guests simply ride around places talking about stuff—offering a similar feel to *Seinfeld*, only set in uber-cool vintage cars instead of a tiny New York apartment. His old buddy Hodgson was featured in the show's first season.

Talk about longevity, both Hodgson and Seinfeld are still indulging the deep passions of their youth when many have put theirs into memory boxes in a storage space someplace.

LOUIE ANDERSON

A Stardust Memory

He wasn't the funniest kid in his sprawling, classically dysfunctional family of eleven siblings, raised in the St. Paul projects by a comforting mother and an abusive, alcoholic dad. Louie Anderson insisted that Roger, the oldest, was. And until I went to an Anderson family picnic one day many long years ago, fortified with more chicken wings than a Tyson chicken factory, I seriously doubted it. But it became clear every time Louie's big brother opened his mouth, Mountain-Dew-through-the-nose laughter on all sides would spray the air. Rog was as quick as Louie with an improvised line, a smart-aleck crack, or a witty comeback or put-down.

The difference is Roger never took the dare Louie did to perform at an open mic night at Mickey Finn's in 1978. By day, Louie was doing social work at St. Joseph's Home for Children. But that open mic night would lead to appearances on *The Tonight Show Starring Johnny Carson* and other late-night yak fests, three Emmy awards, four books, including a *New York Times* best seller, game-show hosting, comedy specials, an acclaimed cartoon series, film roles, and being designated by Comedy Central as "One of the One Hundred Greatest Stand-Up Comedians of All Time."

Anderson's most recent TV triumph is *Baskets*, in which he plays Christine Baskets, the overburdened mother of another dysfunctional family whose main problem adult child is played by Zach Galifianakis. In reality, *Baskets* is Louie Anderson playing his own mom, Ora, and channeling all his audience-pleasing stand-up bits about his beloved mama and many sisters into the quirky and comical persona of Christine.

Has it all been easy? Hell, no!

Anderson's dance card of demons has included food, weight, weight-loss programs that didn't work, weight-gain cycles that did, booze, gambling, and deep self-doubt about his work. His odds of "making it" in show business were formidable, his personal saga humbling.

In the early eighties, the Comedy Store on Los Angeles's Sunset Strip,

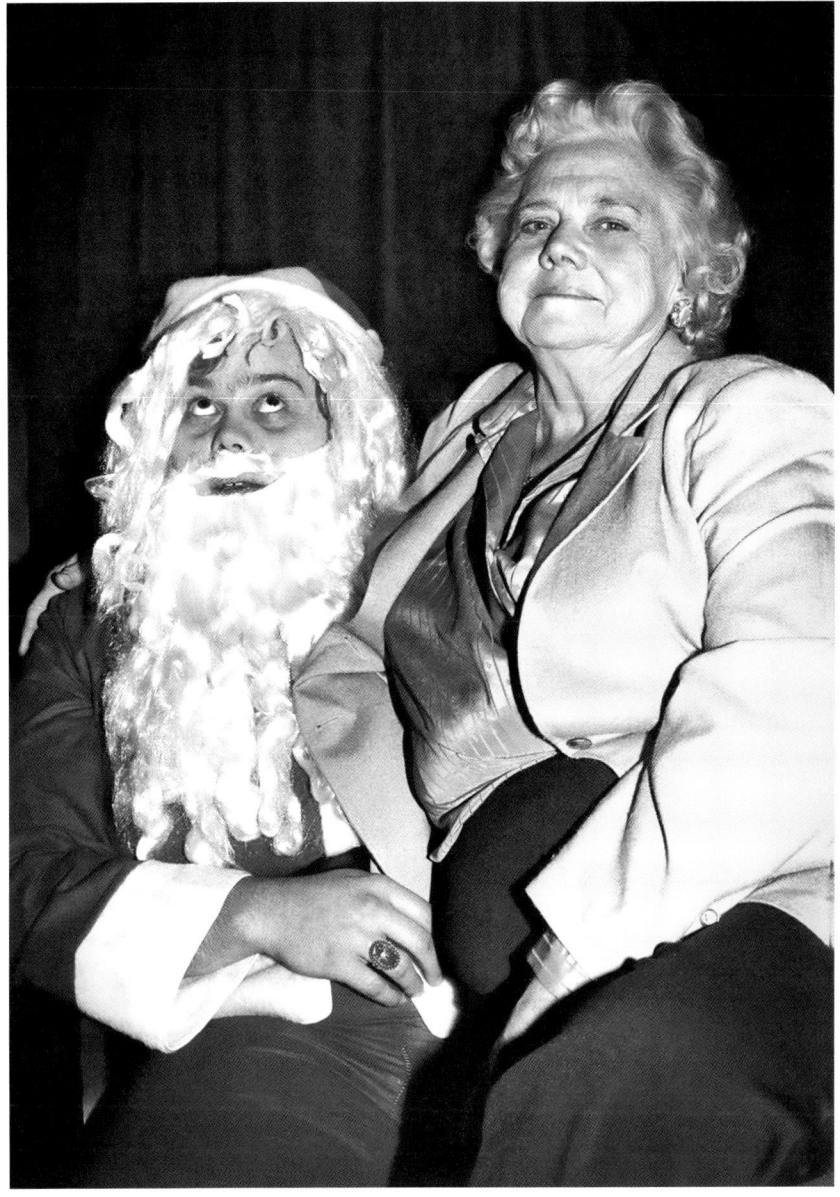

Louie Anderson went from playing Santa with his mother, Ora, in 1981 to playing a mother in an Emmy-winning performance on the show *Baskets*. Anderson says he channels his mom, as well as some of the quirky mannerisms of his sisters, for the role.

and other clubs in the area, was where Anderson and his peers went to get discovered by TV show bookers, high-powered agents, and other showbiz kingmakers. And the scene was bursting with talent. His class of Hollywood wannabes included such established stars and then-unknowns as Eddie Murphy, Robin Williams, Roseanne Barr, Jim Carrey, Garry Shandling, Sam Kinison, Andrew Dice Clay, and Whoopi Goldberg. That old "tough act to follow" adage might have been invented for any one of them.

The Twin Cities comedy scene of the early eighties that produced Anderson and others was as inspired as the emerging rock and funk bands of that era, and seemingly came out of nowhere. As both editor and writer, I shifted coverage in order to capture what was happening with these rising stand-up comics in makeshift "comedy clubs," who were suddenly rivaling the five-star sketch comedy offerings of Dudley Riggs's Brave New Workshop. In the process, a long friendship started with Anderson. Journalists are warned not to become friends with the people they cover. It's smart, good advice, and moreover an ethical pillar of the profession. It helps separate the holy church of journalism from the washed and unwashed state of humanity. But sometimes it's inevitable that friendships form.

My friendship with the St. Paul native goes back more than thirty-five years, starting with the Minneapolis Comedy All-Stars, a quartet of promising stand-up guys that Riggs branded as such once he started booking them at his workshop space. The All Stars included Jeff Cesario, Alex Cole, Joel Madison, and Anderson. The foursome also was featured regularly at Scott Hansen's clubs, when the Twin Cities was experiencing a comedy boom not unlike those in other cities around the country.

Long friendships, though, are always marked by highs, lows, occasional long absences, and, if you're lucky, magic when you need it most.

Home for a holiday visit and his annual New Year's Eve shows, Louie joined Bill Pohlad from River Road Entertainment and me on January 4, 1990, for a showing of the latest Steven Spielberg movie, *Always*, a remake of the 1943 romantic drama *A Guy Named Joe*, starring Holly Hunter, Richard Dreyfuss, John Goodman, and Audrey Hepburn in her final screen role. It's a so-so film about a firefighter pilot who dies and, as a returning spirit, becomes involved in a love triangle of sorts with his girlfriend and another pilot. Louie, Bill, and I exchanged a fair amount of snark about it afterward, mostly at the expense of the afterlife pilot.

Around six the next morning, Louie called, sobbing inconsolably. His mother had died during the night. He needed help with the obituary, and he wanted to talk. He came over to the shabby, rented Kenwood duplex I was sharing with another guy. The big living room was littered mostly with my stuff, including piles of vinyl records.

There were two or three stacks, each about ten to fifteen albums deep, facing us. Louie and I sat on the couch and started the slow, troubling, and necessary talk about Ora, the family, his big broken heart. We'd barely begun when Louie noticed a Hoagy Carmichael album at the head of one of the album columns. It featured a black-and-white picture of Carmichael's band on the cover. In it was Louie's dad, a trumpet player who died in 1980.

He gasped as he reached for it and pointed out his father in the photo. For a moment we sat silently trying to process this unsettling coincidence and emotionally loaded synchronicity. This early-morning moment of grief wasn't supposed to be about his pops on an album cover,

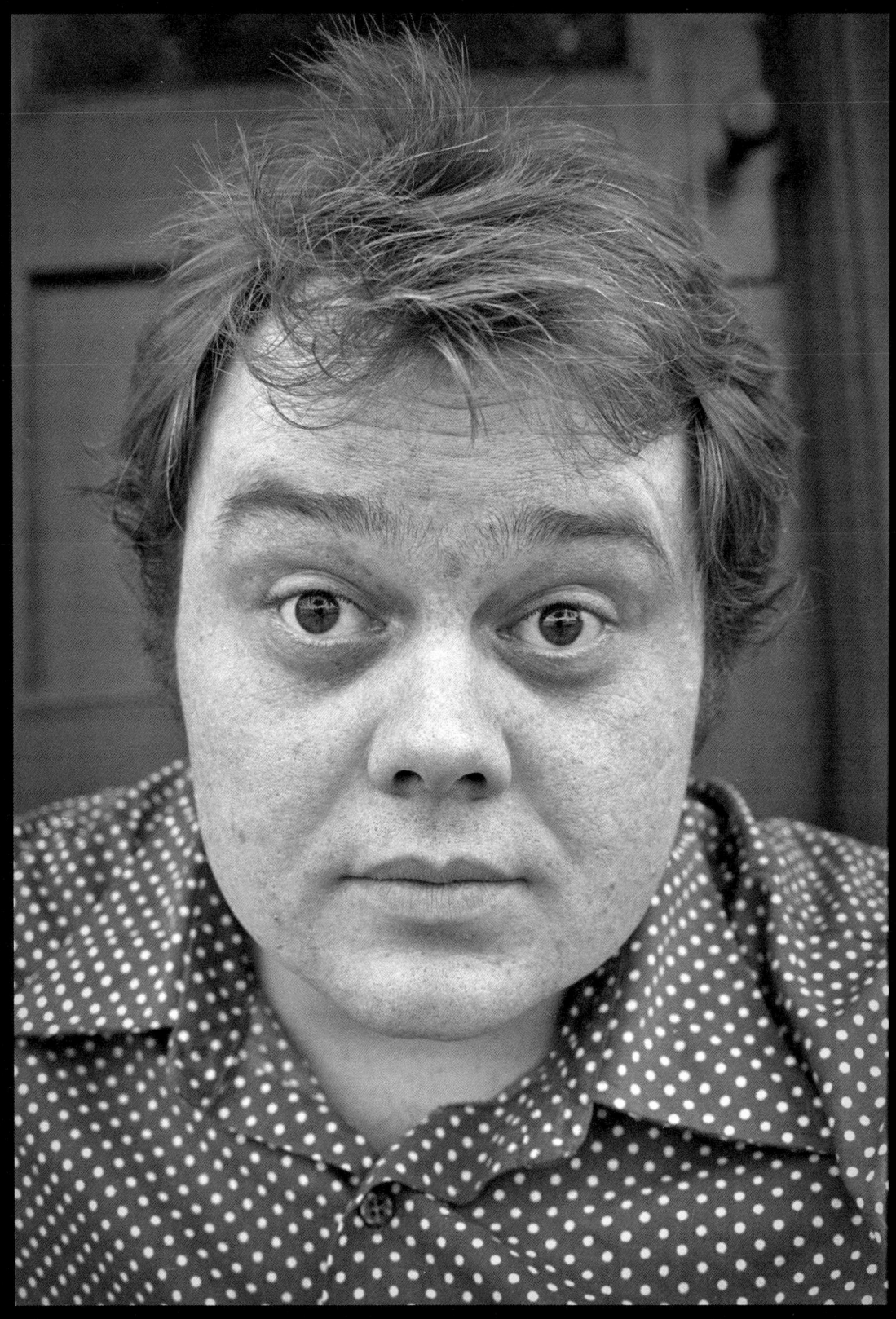

In one of his favorite stand-up routines about his dysfunctional family, Anderson described how he often taunted his little brother with the threat, "Your eyes are gonna bug out!" Here, Louie bugs out his eyes for the Helg.

was it? I assured him I hadn't put the album out for his visit, and frankly, I had forgotten his old man—the sometimes-violent alcoholic who was the subject of Louie's first book, *Dear Dad: Letters from an Adult Child*—was even in the band, let alone on the cover of the record.

One of Carmichael's biggest hits was "Stardust," a song about loss, memory, and love remaining "in the stardust of a song." Carmichael was no scientist or shrink. But I think he had an inkling of what we're made of and what we need. In 2017, science discovered what the poets and songwriters already knew: the stars in what we call the Milky Way share the same chemicals of life as human beings.

In 1952, Carl Jung introduced the concept of synchronicity as a way to explain coincidences, both deep and superficial. Jung, after whom a whole branch of psychology and parapsychology is named, defined synchronicity as "a meaningful coincidence of two or more events where something other than the probability of chance is involved." Jung's concept was inspired by a patient's case that was at an impasse due to her fierce rationalism that he felt was holding her back from using the unconscious that would help unlock her affliction. Then one night the patient dreamed of a golden scarab. The next day, during her session, a real golden scarab hit against a window pane and was caught by Jung. It served as a starting point to begin healing the patient.

Louie's grief over his mother would last a long time. But that accidental/coincidental discovery of the Hoagy Carmichael album on the floor of a friend's apartment seemed to bring comfort and relief at the right time, and it provided a pivotal moment from which he could begin to reconcile a close parent's sudden passing. It also zapped all the snark we'd exchanged the night before on the film's notions of an afterlife, putting our cynical selves in our place.

After almost four decades, Anderson acknowledges that his family-centric stand-up act can have a healing, cathartic effect on audiences. It's a feel-good measure of Louie-styled psychotherapy that he dispenses every night as fans erupt in sustained laughter at a string of one-liners or a screwy grimace he makes to put a fine point on a bit, usually about his crazy family. All the personal hardships people carry around inside momentarily melt away. It makes you wonder why stand-up comedy is often viewed as the lowest rung of the entertainment industry. The truth is, it's good medicine, and in Anderson's hands, it's as good as having ten mothers.

SCOTT HANSEN

King of the Comedy Clubs

Scott Hansen's Laff Boat on the St. Croix River celebrated its fifteenth summer in 2018. Featuring national comics like Tim Cavanagh and stay-fresh locals, such as Fancy Ray McCloney and others, the Laff Boat embarked for its annual trip on the river for an almost three-hour cruise, just like Gilligan's crew—only this boat always came back to shore.

"It's been operating longer than most comedy clubs," Hansen observed. He would know. As a founding member of the Twin Cities comedy scene, Hansen is to Twin Cities comedy what First Avenue's Steve McClellan was to music during the eighties and beyond.

The big-and-tall combo impresario-comedian has invented numerous opportunities for comics of all shapes and sizes, not only in the metro area but throughout the upper Midwest and elsewhere. If he found an empty room—or, in the case of the Laff Boat, an underutilized floating space—there was a good chance he would convert it to a comedy venue. Among his projects: the Comedy Gallery, a club he opened in downtown Minneapolis largely to showcase Joel Hodgson after a rival club kept cutting his and other comics' stage time; a second Comedy Gallery inside a Howard Johnson's in Rochester; a club tucked inside Grandma's Saloon and Grill in Duluth; the Comedy Cabaret in south Minneapolis; and Belly Laughs, inside Mandarin Yen restaurant on the 494 strip. (Working at the latter was Louis Lee, a future comic-preneur who now runs the highly successful Acme Comedy Company in Minneapolis's warehouse district.) You get the picture.

For a time, Hansen was booking occasional shows at the Carlton Celebrity Backstage Room—Bloomington's version of a Vegas club—where the Mall of America sprawls today. I don't know if he or Jeff Gerbino or both were responsible for the Rodney Dangerfield show there, in a location then still surrounded by cornfields, but it provided a trademark one-liner for one of the funniest old-school comics of all time. During an appearance on *The Tonight Show Starring Johnny Carson*, Carson asked Dangerfield where he was performing next. Rodney jerked his head, bugged his eyes out, and quipped that it was someplace called the Carlton Celebrity club—"the place is so far out in the woods, my act is gonna be reviewed in *Field and Stream*!"

After one appearance at the Carlton, Dangerfield showed up at a makeshift stage at Cork's in the Foshay Tower to take in the local acts. He even got up and did some time himself. You can hang that triumph on Jeff Gerbino, the real godfather of the Twin Cities comedy scene: "I was the original 'birther' at Mickey Finn's," Gerbino boasted. Appropriately enough, Mickey Finn's was set inside the labor union building just over the Hennepin Avenue Bridge in northeast Minneapolis. Nobody worked harder in the late seventies than Gerbino trying to make stand-up comedy a reality. "I ran around town like a madman promoting and trying to make work the dream I had inside my head since I was a little kid." It worked.

A fast-talking and furiously funny Long Island native, Gerbino opened Finn's in January 1978. Eventually, he says, "Scott took it to the next level." After Finn's, the floodgates opened. It wasn't unusual to see comics like Jay Leno, Roseanne Barr, Jerry Seinfeld, Dana Gould, and others playing in small rooms not even big enough for a wedding reception, with openers such as Louie Anderson, Jeff Cesario, Alex Cole, Tom Arnold, Lizz Winstead, Gerbino, and the true mad hatter of Minneapolis, Wild Bill Bauer (who also did the riskier, darker material Hansen wrote that he himself would never touch). It was very similar to catching the "new" bands like Talking Heads, Blondie, the Police, and the B-52s at Jay's Longhorn with local rockers as the opening acts—and limited audience numbers of a hundred or less.

In 1986, I wrote a long cover story for the *Reader* after watching Hansen's restless entrepreneurial efforts—and solid stand-up act—reach a higher plateau. On the business side, he was propagating comedy all over the place with a missionary's zeal. Working with fellow comic Tom Baumgartner and Hansen's brother Tom, Scott started sending comics into the entertainment wilderness of the Dakotas and southern Minnesota. Denver comedian Michael Floorwax described the one-nighters and weekends in Aberdeen, Grand Forks, Fargo, and Mankato as the "Rambo Tours." Hansen concurred: "You get *real* beat up by the end of it." Oddly enough, the Mankato show, featuring a different comic every week at T. J. Finnegan's—on Sunday nights, no less—ran for twenty-six years, "the longest running live comedy gig anywhere," the Hansen brothers boasted.

Tom Hansen noted that demand for funny was way high back then, from Little Rock to Winnipeg. "We could have put a comic on tour for ten weeks with only a couple days off," he said. "But we only did it a few times, as it drove them crazy." He and the comics often gave those tours

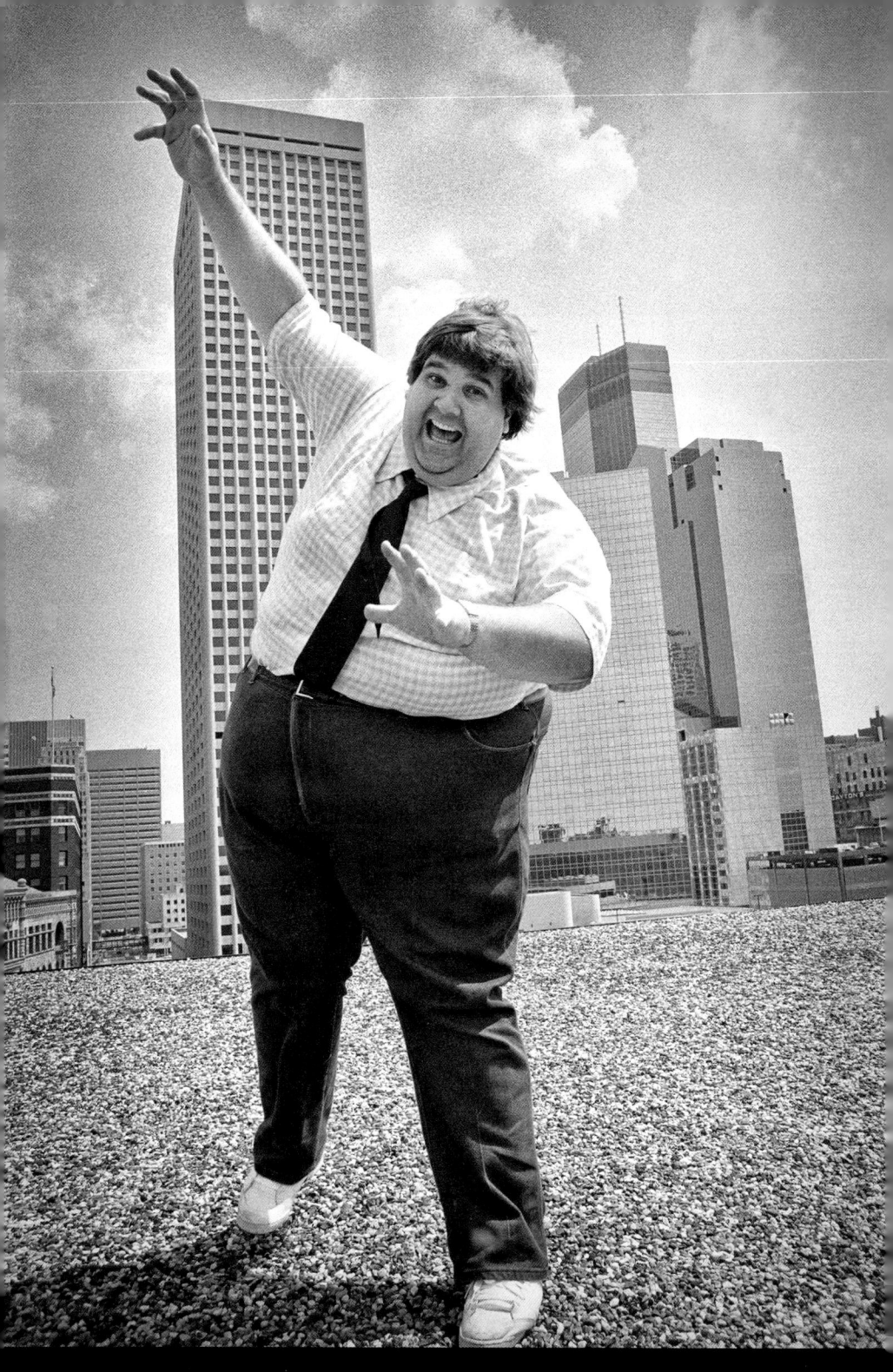

King of the Twin Cities comedy clubs, Scott Hansen poses teetering against the Minneapolis skyline. Hansen and his booking-agent brother propagated comedy from Alabama to Winnipeg with a missionary's zeal to bring the funny to the hinterlands and the home crowd.

unofficial titles like "The Cheese Curd Tour" (Wisconsin), "The Studded Tire Tour" (the Dakotas), and "The Westward Ho Tour" (for anything else points west) because "it made it easier for the comics to identify the places they were headed to." Even though they sometimes complained about the far-flung locations they had to drive to and back, the money was frequently better in the sticks. Plus, there was an upside for everybody to pushing comics to the hinterlands, Scott Hansen advised: People in those places were so hungry for comedy, the lousy stuff that died in the cities—where comedy audiences are among the most discerning in the country—killed out in the wheat belt. A stand-up act, however good or bad, is a terrible thing to waste.

It didn't take long before Hansen had seen it all, from all sides of the business, including horrible nights where there were so few people "the comics had to heckle themselves." At the peak of his business, however, Scott and company were booking thirty-five rooms a week in comedy joints throughout America, including Arkansas, Wisconsin, Iowa, Wyoming, Michigan, Montana, Indiana, and sometimes Canada. And that doesn't include colleges, corporate events, weddings, and, sadly, one funeral: a twenty-one-year-old who killed himself indicated in his suicide note that he wanted Hansen to perform at his wake. Hansen managed to do ten minutes and donated his fee to a suicide prevention organization.

But it didn't end there.

Enter *Comedy Gallery: The TV Show.* As the appetite for comedy remained high, Hansen started a television show on KMSP-TV, Channel 9, that ran on Friday nights. He and his crew would tape four shows at a stretch on Sunday nights at either the World Theater or the State Theatre. For special occasions like April Fools' Day, Valentine's Day, Halloween, and one or two New Year's Eve performances, they aired live shows. Hansen said proudly, "the Gallery TV show beat Letterman and *The Tonight Show* on many nights for two years!"

It would be easy to overlook Hansen's own stand-up career with the bulging book of businesses that he built and the influence that it had. Scott—who was taller than and as round as Louie Anderson in the old days—naturally played off his girthish figure while performing onstage, telling people near the front who were staring up into his ampleness, "What's wrong, lady, you've never seen a sweater vest before?!"

A house husband while his wife, Michelle, worked, the Twin Cities' king of comedy clubs frequently turned his daddy daycare experiences into comic fodder. One such nugget he offered to Roseanne Barr: "I figure if the kids are still alive when my spouse comes home from work, then I've done my job." Among others, over the years he penned jokes for Anderson, Leno, and Arnold—whose earliest stand-up act featured a goldfish. ("A lot of comics just starting out had crutches; that [the goldfish] was his," Tom

Hansen observed, "although I thought Arnold was the funniest comic in the Twin Cities for a long time.")

Arnold was an amusing pain in the ass every time he saw me, demanding to know when I was going to give him some ink. I wasn't averse to doing it, but there were better players in the lineup ahead of him at that point. By the time I had the space to profile him, he'd already gone off to LA to be with Roseanne (seeing them together when they came back to town, whether onstage or off, was like standing in hurricane-force winds as they loudly and manically tried to one-up each other).

Leno was a loyal Hansen fan early on, long before his ascension to Carson's *Tonight Show* throne. He later offered Scott a chance to set up in Hollywood or New York, if Hansen wanted to kick it to the next level. As far as Leno was concerned, Hansen held all the right cards: "I think he's very funny," he said for the *Reader* article. "And I enjoy working for him. Usually I don't say that about other comedians; I just cringe and tell people, 'Well, I've never seen so and so's act.'" Leno went on to add, with a little black twist, that Hansen was "funny all the time. He thinks funny, his premises are funny. . . . He was a good guy to jam with. I'm sorry he passed away."

Reminiscing for me in 2018 as I took notes for this vignette about his salad days—make that his carb-loading days—Scott said he considered the potential opportunities that awaited him in the wider entertainment world as his comedy businesses were booming. He grew uncharacteristically philosophical about why he chose to stay put. He knew the sacrifices would be big if he were to chase those dreams, and the sacrifices centered mostly around family. He would either have to uproot everyone to live in LA, or he would have to be away from his family for significant stretches of time in order to make a national career with television, touring, movies, and whatever else might come with the territory.

"I wouldn't have traded the time with my kids growing up for one *Tonight Show*," he adamantly remarked. "Well, maybe for two shows I would."

LIZZ WINSTEAD

Leader of the Lady Parts PAC

Y ou have probably seen Lizz Winstead on national cable news programs, commenting on the political potholes and Machiavellian assholes in what's left of American democracy. Or caught one of her annual New Year's Eve shows, where she assesses all the good, the bad, and the ugly the year had to offer on all sides of the political spectrum and across the glutted media landscape. You might even have a VHS tape of her performing her stand-up act on the old *Women of the Night* HBO special. There's also a rare chance you heard her on the sputtering flights of Air America Radio. And unless you have been living in a prepper bunker, or an ivory Trump Tower, surely you've caught, at least once, the long-running program that she cocreated in 1996, *The Daily Show*, which became the go-to program for political satire—and often the only source of political news for those who gave up on network talking heads.

If you read her brazenly honest, caustically funny 2012 memoir, *Lizz Free or Die*, you know she doesn't suffer fools or bullshit.

Comedian, activist, writer, producer, feminist, and south Minneapolis homegirl, Lizz Winstead has long had a ubiquitous media presence for anyone paying attention. Before she left town, first for the Left Coast in 1987 and then to the media capital of Manhattan in '90, Winstead packed a pretty steady schedule of stand-up dates and emcee duties around the Twin Cities. She was also a "rock 'n' roll chick" and mad fan of the Replacements and Prince; she helped host auditions for *Purple Rain* dancers and extras, and she was front and center stage for the Great Pretenders nights and dance contests at First Avenue. To lean on a phrase, she was on the scene, man! She was also integral to building the scene with the many

---

(opposite) Looking like one of the Bangles back in her early stand-up days, Lizz Winstead went on to cocreate *The Daily Show* and also become a champion of women's health care and reproductive rights.

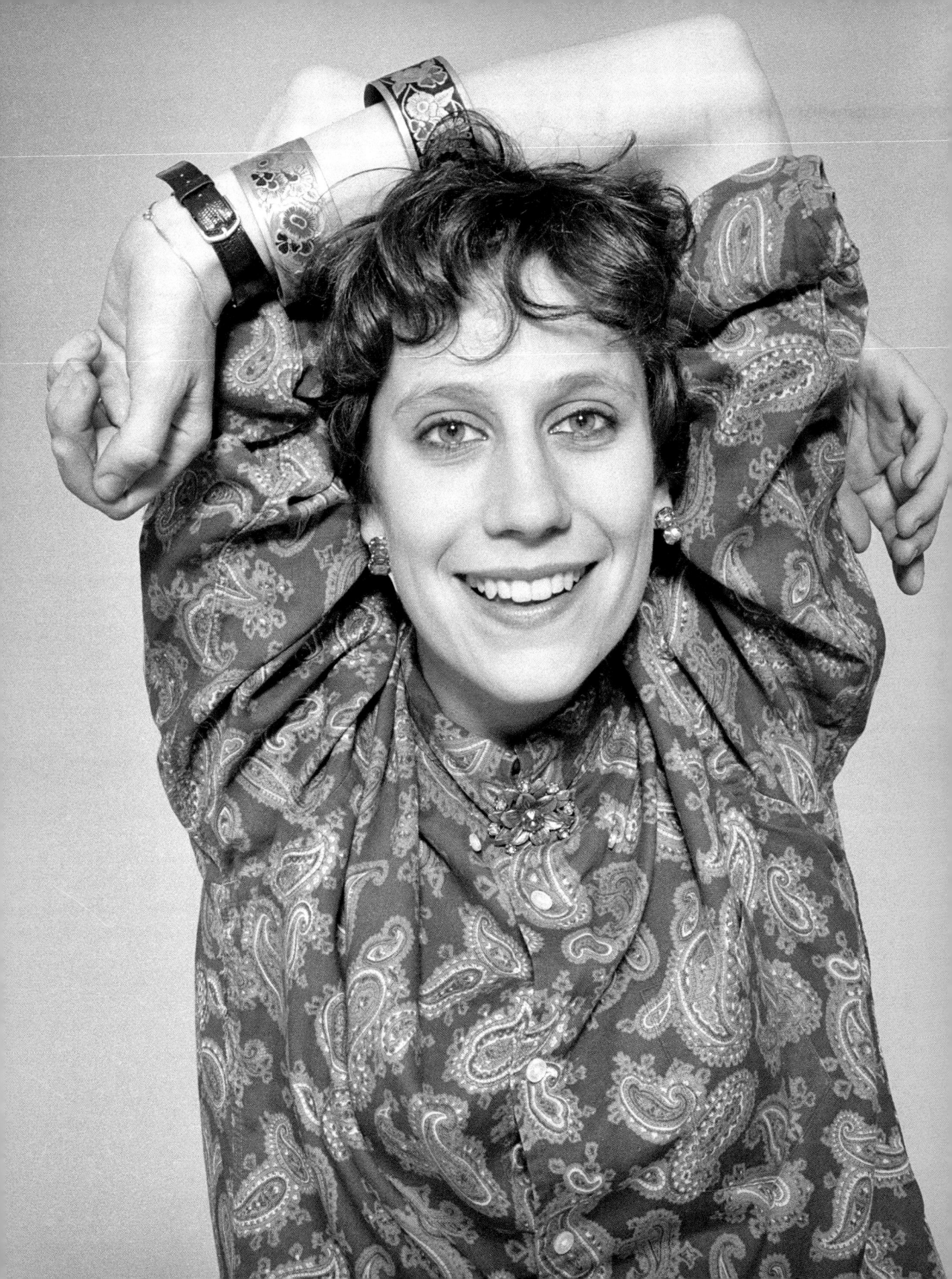

male and female comics who made comedy a viable option for a fun, and sometimes even intellectually challenging, night out in the Twin Cities.

Winstead seemed to have an enlarged camaraderie gene that many of her comedienne peers didn't. She generally hit it off with the Twin Cities comedy A-team—Louie Anderson, Wild Bill Bauer, Scott Hansen, Alex Cole, Joel Madison, Jeff Gerbino, and Jeff Cesario. The vibrant local comic scene, along with the out-of-town headliners who regularly trouped through, allowed ample opportunity for her to do quick studies of their work and provided strong contacts for when she decided to venture beyond her Minneapolitan comfort zone. Anderson liked her and her stand-up act enough to fly in from Los Angeles to *open for her* the first time she headlined at the Comedy Gallery in 1984, ensuring that she would have a good audience. Gerbino, who practically invented Twin Cities stand-up at Mickey Finn's, says Winstead would riff with the guys more than the other female comics during that burgeoning period, whether at clubs or during late-night dinners at Rudolph's Bar-B-Que in what became an after-show debriefing ritual.

Winstead's early comedy was stacked with your standard observational jokes, but it always had a feminist undertone. That undertone would ring louder and clearer as she made her way through the big leagues out east. In a brief walk down memory lane in late 2018, she offered that *The Daily Show*, created with producer Madeleine Smithberg for Comedy Central in 1996, "was a way for me to keep the media and politicians in check. I was seeing a lot of disinformation in the media, and since comedians are *the* truth tellers of society, I wanted to take that one step further and create a format where we could be the watchdogs, as well."

As the show's head writer, she took on the hard, all-consuming work demanded of a nightly platform, in a city and industry that never sleeps. I ran into her in a SoHo restaurant one night in New York, prior to the launch of her TV show, hunched over a table full of papers with another writer and a couple glasses of wine. Hard to say who was more surprised to see the other. I was in town trying to create a show myself with Bill Pohlad of River Road Entertainment and our corporate partner, Music-land, the national record retailer based in the Twin Cities. It was called *Talk Music*, a weekly critical TV look at the latest music releases and a few pertinent news items, similar to the popular Gene Siskel and Roger Ebert show, *At the Movies*—but with four critics, not two. We already had Bob Christgau from the *Village Voice* on board, but we were in search of two women and another man to fill the remaining seats. Too bad Lizz Winstead was already taken. Our pilot looked good once we produced it back in Minneapolis, but the lousy syndicator who tried to sell it could only find three-in-the-morning graveyard slots. *Talk Music* went on the shelf; *The Daily Show* took off like a rocket sled.

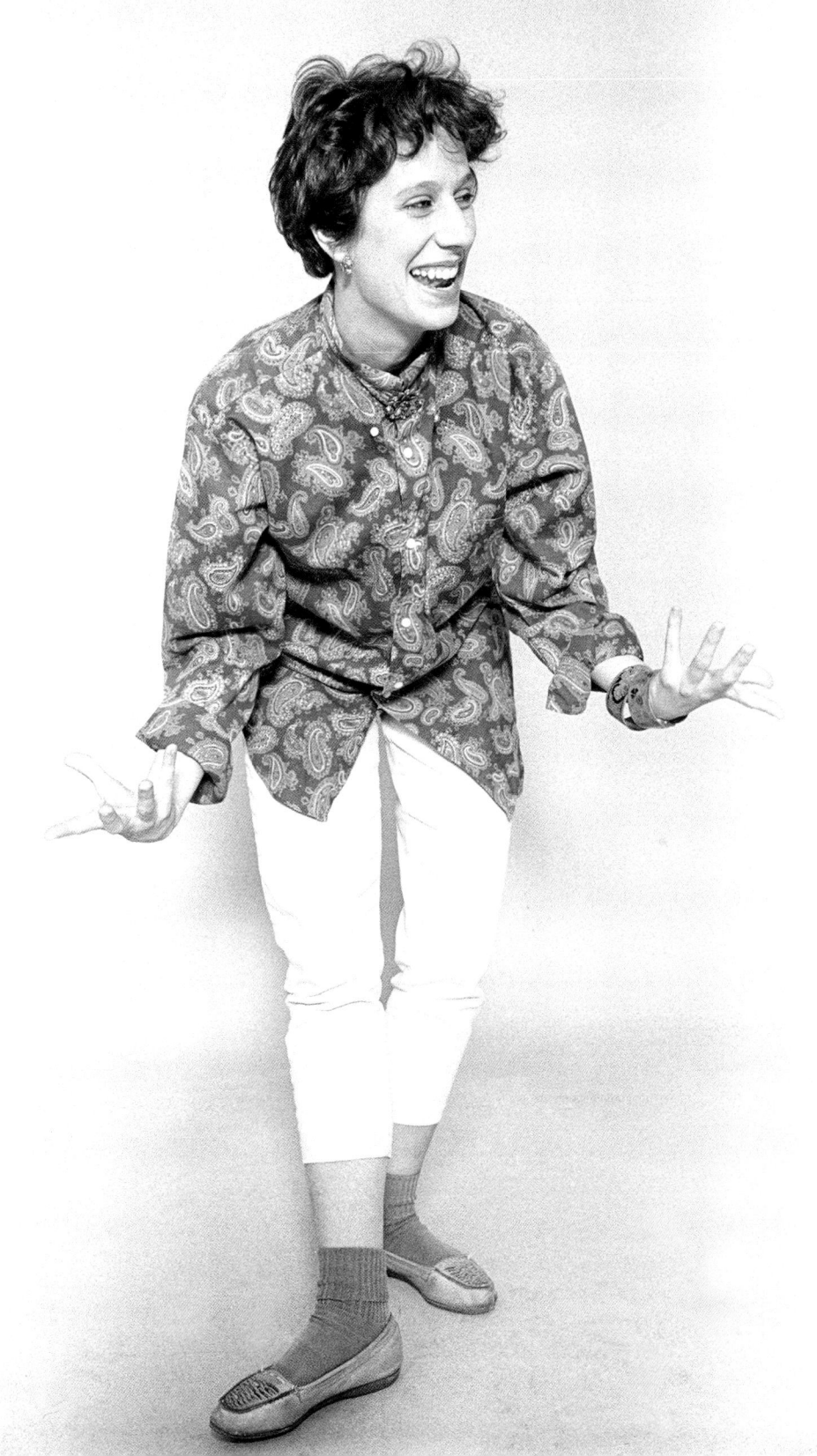

Winstead left *Daily* after two years, and she later tried to reinvent the format. Her off-Broadway show, *Wake Up World*, was a cutting and jolly ensemble-based parody of morning news shows. Winstead brought it to Minneapolis's Parkway Theater for three nights during the ugly Republican National Convention in St. Paul—starring Bush-Cheney and McCain-Palin—that turned the capital city into a heavily militarized urban war zone. *Wake Up* flirted briefly with an internet run, although it was too early technologically to relay it over the limited bandwidth of most web users.

Winstead said that she learned the power of comedy for social change with *The Daily Show*, "but I also learned that it was just one element of social change." Meaning, it didn't go far enough. She has watched federal and state lawmakers consistently go after women's reproductive rights and health care for as long as she can remember. In 2015, along with a collective of writers, comedians, producers, social media gurus, and others, change-agent Winstead helped form the Lady Parts Justice League. It's like a transparent, nonpartisan PAC for women, transgender, and male supporters who share views on many women's issues.

Four months out of the year, the League travels the country on the Vagical Mystery Tour, building grassroots activist movements through comedy and music shows. While on the road, they help other women take care of themselves and do projects at clinics, from replanting gardens and painting clinic interiors to providing meals and support to the doctors and clinic staff. They also register folks to vote at every show.

Why do Winstead and her allies do it? The answer lies front and center on the nonprofit's web page: "We do the job that the media doesn't, creating provocative and hilarious videos and social media content that educates people about the pervasive, discriminatory abortion laws that profoundly and disproportionately impact poor women and women of color."

Unfettered by the divisive and mean-spirited political paralysis that has a chokehold on the nation, Winstead is in it for the long haul. On her right forearm, she proudly wears a symbolic and straightforward tattoo of a uterus.

TWIN CITIES WOMEN OF COMEDY

What's So Funny about Being Female?

I t wasn't all about the guys during the heyday of stand-up comedy in the Twin Cities. There were about as many good-to-great female comics working the planks as there were male counterparts. Aside from Lizz Winstead (huddled in the back of this group shot by Helgeson—page 230), Phyllis Wright (on the left), Stephanie Hodge (center), Susan Vass (on the right), Linda Wallem, and others were critic-proof laugh ladies capable of garnering good followings in the clubs and a sturdy foundation on which to build their futures. Although some didn't leave to seek greater opportunity on the coasts, they left their mark nevertheless.

At a national level, the rise of female comedians to more visible and more powerful places in the entertainment empires of New York or Los Angeles in the eighties paralleled a next generation of funny, foul-mouthed, and fiercely empowered women in the Twin Cities who wouldn't settle for second-banana billing. Nor would they serve as token members of their gender in the yuk-making genre. During the sixties and seventies, stellar comic actresses like Lucille Ball, Phyllis Diller, and Carol Burnett, along with stand-up queen Joan Rivers and the groundbreaking black comic Moms Mabley, elevated themselves to true showbiz stardom. But countless other female comedians didn't even get a shot just because some imaginary quota had been filled, or there were just too many men—comics and gatekeepers—blocking their way. In the eighties, the Ellen DeGatekeepers—blocking their way. In the eighties, the Ellen DeGenereses, Whoopi Goldbergs, Paula Poundstones, Roseanne Barrs, Carol Leifers, and Cathy Ladmans of the realm made the world safer for the comic femocracy to reshape the landscape. Those same fires were burning here in the Twin Cities with a core of tenacious and talented women comics.

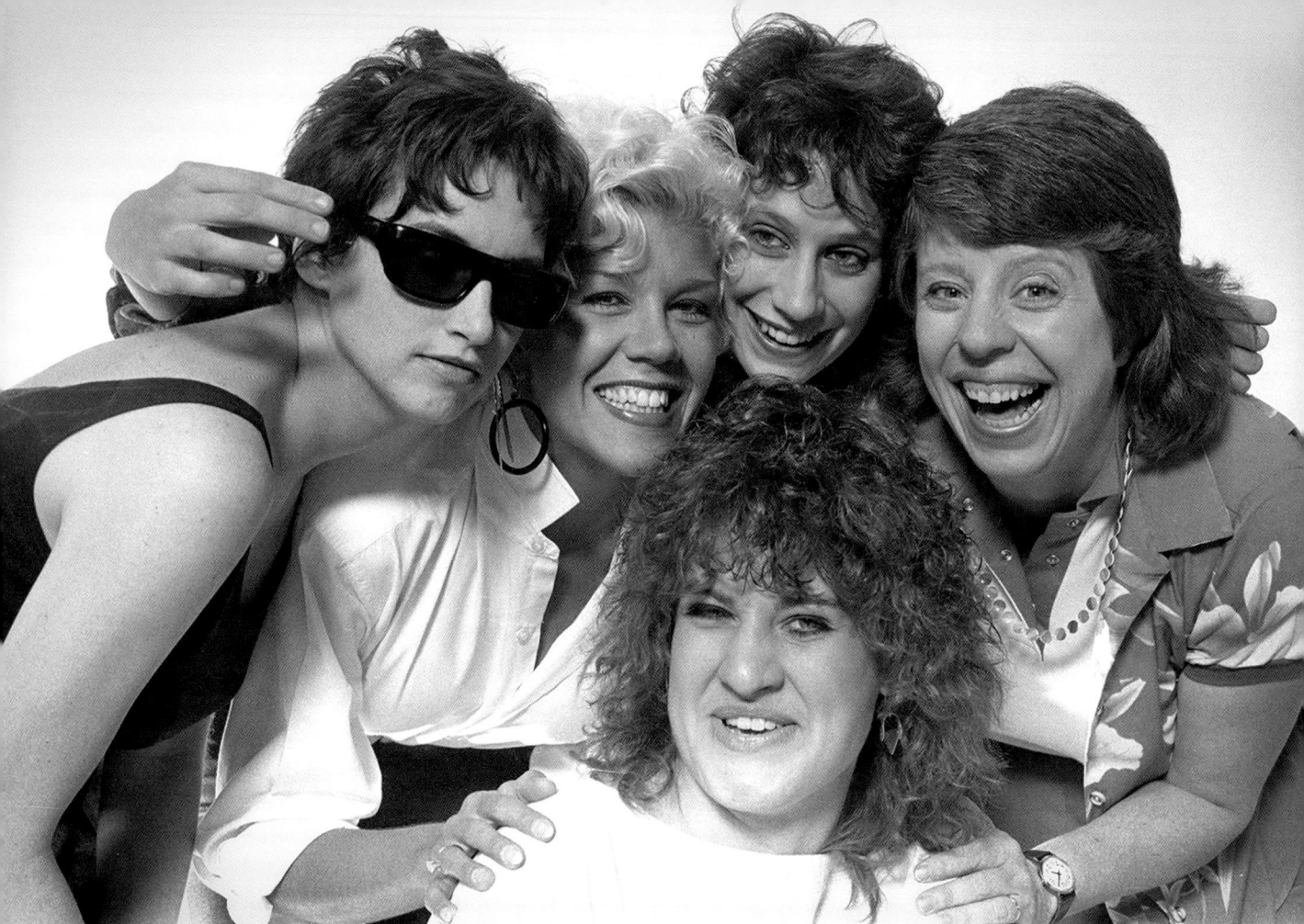

The Twin Cities comedy-scene explosion in the 1980s included a strong contingent of female comedians, among them (back row, left to right) Phyllis Wright, Stephanie Hodge, Lizz Winstead, Susan Vass, and (front) Linda Wallem.

SUSAN VASS

The Maplewood mother took a chance that Louie Anderson might like some jokes she had written especially for him. Instead, he kindly told her she should be doing them herself. Once Susan Vass found her way to the stage—first at Dudley Riggs's Brave New Workshop, then at the Guthrie Theater, *A Prairie Home Companion*, and a variety of stand-up stages outstate and elsewhere—it was clear which jokes she had intended for the big man. I still think of her bit about eating an entire chocolate cheesecake for breakfast whenever I shamelessly reach for a sweet morsel before the proper hour.

Older than many of her comic peers, Susan staked out her turf without resorting to blue language or prurient jokes. Like Anderson, she played off her "chubbiness," claiming she was too short for her weight and that marriage was fattening: "I gained twenty-five pounds at my reception." She was also about thirty years ahead of the redefinition of the plus-size women theme, bemoaning the stuff they sold at the "House of

Large Knockers" and the horrible quality of lingerie for women her size "at nice places like Sears."

Vass and Merrilyn Belgum, who was considerably older than Vass and made the move to comedy when she was in her sixties, were refreshing because they played smartly and hilariously against ageist and female stereotypes. Belgum offered a more bookish humor laced with the burdens of Lutheranism. Both appeared on the local TPT special *Land o' Loons* in 1989, and you can find clips of the show online; you might even see some funny men you recognize.

From 1986 to 1991, Vass, Winstead, and other comediennes were part of a show at Brave New Workshop called *What's So Funny about Being Female?* (the Helg's photo was shot for this long-running gig). In many ways, the aptly named show and its wise-cracking women comics perfectly summed up the breakthrough era.

PHYLLIS WRIGHT

Equally at home on a stand-up or theatrical stage, at a TV or film set, or in front of a radio mic, Phyllis Wright was a loud omnipresence in the Twin Cities culture zone wherever she chose to tread. During the eighties, it was most often within the confines of the comedy clubs.

In another example of these cities being too small, I met Phyllis first as the sister of Marcia Wright, the steadfast, usually cheery designer and layout person during the first few years of *Sweet Potato*. (Their brother David had started the original *Sweet Potato* back in Maine and convinced his Minnesota friends, Tom Bartel and Kris Henning, to start one here.) The Wright sisters were also active music fans that you might run into frequently in the clubs. These days, Phyllis has become something of the fourth Suicide Commando with her semi-regular cameos with the band.

Phyllis also had the acting bug, and a versatile voice that could peel paint or purr like a sleeping bobcat. It was put to good use on radio commercials. It also served her well on the big screen after securing bit parts in Dan Appleby's *Bound and Gagged* and the Arnold Schwarzenegger Christmas movie, *Jingle All the Way*, both filmed locally.

Her impressive résumé includes acting gigs across all the main Twin Cities theaters, and she was a member of Riggs's renowned Brave New Workshop touring company for a time. She schlepped her stand-up act to Chicago's legendary Second City, New York City comedy clubs, and other places. She appeared in "Martian's Chronicles" from time to time. I'm pretty sure I wrote something about her opening set for gonzo journalist Hunter Thompson at the College of St. Catherine in St. Paul, although my most accessible memory of that night was Thompson blatantly flirting with a Katie during the Q&A.

STEPHANIE HODGE

Another pioneering force on the home front, Stephanie Hodge did head to the West Coast after her early stand-up foray in the Twin Cities. There she has established a successful career acting in a string of television shows, sitcoms, and series, as well as movies. For a time in Minnesota, she was married to comedian and comedy club operator Scott Novotny. Until Tom Arnold and Roseanne Barr tied the knot, they were something of a showbiz rarity, at least in these parts.

At the time of Helgeson's photo, Hodge was sporting a striking bleached blonde façade that under a spotlight almost required sunglasses. She's made fun of it in subsequent years (older, wiser, less blonde, if at all), proving once again that self-effacing humor is not only a great survival hack but also a good way to say oops.

LINDA WALLEM

Another famous Dudley Riggs alumnus, Linda Wallem teamed with fellow Riggs writer and funny man Peter Tolan early in their careers as part of the troupe and, later, as a duo. Both did very well after relocating to Los Angles, where she became an A-list writer, producer, and actress. She has had a trusted hand in such television shows as *Cybill*, *That '70s Show*, and the Emmy Award–nominated *Nurse Jackie*.

Having never seen her work before she blew town, I can't qualify or quantify its potency. But if one can judge her by the company she keeps—and the company she was keeping in this photograph—she obviously had the goods to do what she's done.

Since the 1980s, women have made tremendous and widespread gains in comedy, as well as in politics and other professions. But progress is soooo slow. A lot of meat-and-potato guys I know can't wait until the day when "they" take it all over and hopefully run things in a new way, cuz the errant higher mammals currently in charge and sporting the Y chromosome are either blindly or blatantly running it into the pit.

PRINCE

The Color Purple

t was a cold January day in Uptown Minneapolis in 1979 the first time I met Prince to talk on the record. He sat on the kitchen floor in Bobby Z's apartment, his hair in long, cornrow braids and his guard up. I sat opposite him against the stove and was lucky to get the few quotes that I did from the shy twenty-one-year-old with an immense, unimaginable lifetime ahead of him. The next official face-to-face I had with him was a couple weeks before Christmas in 1996. He lounged with his wife, Mayte, in a kitchen booth at Paisley Park, where today his ashes eerily sit above the kitchen doors inside a small replica of the 65,000-square-foot complex. Mayte had made a delicious vegetarian bean soup, a family recipe of her mother's from Puerto Rico, and shared it. A guitar noise erupted from a studio someplace.

Although it was seventeen years between official interviews, I had had many personal and professional encounters with Prince in the intervening years. During the interview at Paisley, the talkative Prince was the happiest, most relaxed I had seen him in all those years. Some of my other encounters included the following:

Prince birthday parties at the Prom Center, including the one where you could see Sheila E. snatching away Bobby Z's job as she climbed behind the drums for an impromptu jam. Prince quietly walking the red carpet at the Mann's Chinese Theatre in Hollywood for his first movie premiere, clutching a single rose, while MTV veejay Mark Goodman, broadcasting live, roused the hundreds of fans behind the police barricades and watching at home. At one point, he even used my line, penned three years earlier for *City Pages*, extolling the virtues of "His Royal Badness." Prince playing pop-up shows at First Avenue for those lucky enough to be on the grapevine. Prince rolling his warm-but-dismissing brown eyes at a casting call for extras for crowd scenes in *Purple Rain* when I gave him a battery-powered purple rose that would light up, which I'd bought as a joke at a James

Brown show a week earlier. Prince dressed all funky and shirtless at a New Year's Eve show with Miles Davis at Paisley Park. Prince holding his first international press conference at Paisley for the release on his NPG label of his three-record set, *Emancipation*, after changing his name to a runic figure that merged male and female symbols with an ancient Celtic cross.

There's no sense rehashing in depth his impact and his innovations, or his place on rock music's Mount Olympus, here other than to emphasize that the Pop Life he led left a lasting cultural imprint that few will ever match, from any walk of life. He fused and excelled in many music genres, challenged the music business model in the age of the internet, spurred fashion trends, took live performance higher and higher, and by example insisted on a social contract of equality where gender, sexual orientation, race, and age would be integral to the social fabric, not apart from it. I also think he may have invented, or at least anticipated, texting long before cell phones were a thing, with his interchanged numbers for words in his song titles and lyrics.

In 1992, Bill Pohlad from River Road Entertainment approached me to help script a low-budget documentary called *Prince: Unauthorized* for video store chains, featuring mostly interviews about his early life and where he was at that time. Interview subjects included his first manager, Owen Husney, who claimed he was a modern-day Mozart; Pepé Willie, with whom he played on the *94 East—Minneapolis Genius* sessions; Prince's cousin Chazz Smith; Chris Moon, who let Prince work and sleep in his studio; Steven Greenberg of Lipps, Inc., who beat him to a worldwide number one with "Funkytown"; rock critic and former *City Pages* editor Steve Perry; and First Avenue's Steve McClellan. Revolution guitarist Dez Dickerson and the Time's Morris Day appear in performance. None of us believed the doc would ever have a shelf life; we expected a cease-and-desist letter from Paisley Park at any time, but it never came. Maybe he liked it. Or, more likely, he never saw it. Now you can see it on YouTube.

The fifty-minute piece contains some now-prescient insights from Perry, Chazz, and me. I noted that many worry Prince will become the Howard Hughes of rock, holed up at the park by himself. Chazz said Prince was too isolated "out there" at Paisley, that he needs to come home. Steve echoed similar themes, citing how the truly stellar musical giants of the twentieth century shared collaborative relationships with other people who could afford to be honest with each other.

"The tragedy of Prince, who grew up isolated," Perry said, "is that he invented himself in this mold." Duke Ellington had Billy Strayhorn, James Brown had various sidemen over the years contributing to his sound and sensibility. Who did Prince have who would challenge him artistically? And most importantly, who could help safeguard his well-being, especially once he became addicted to opioids and needed help?

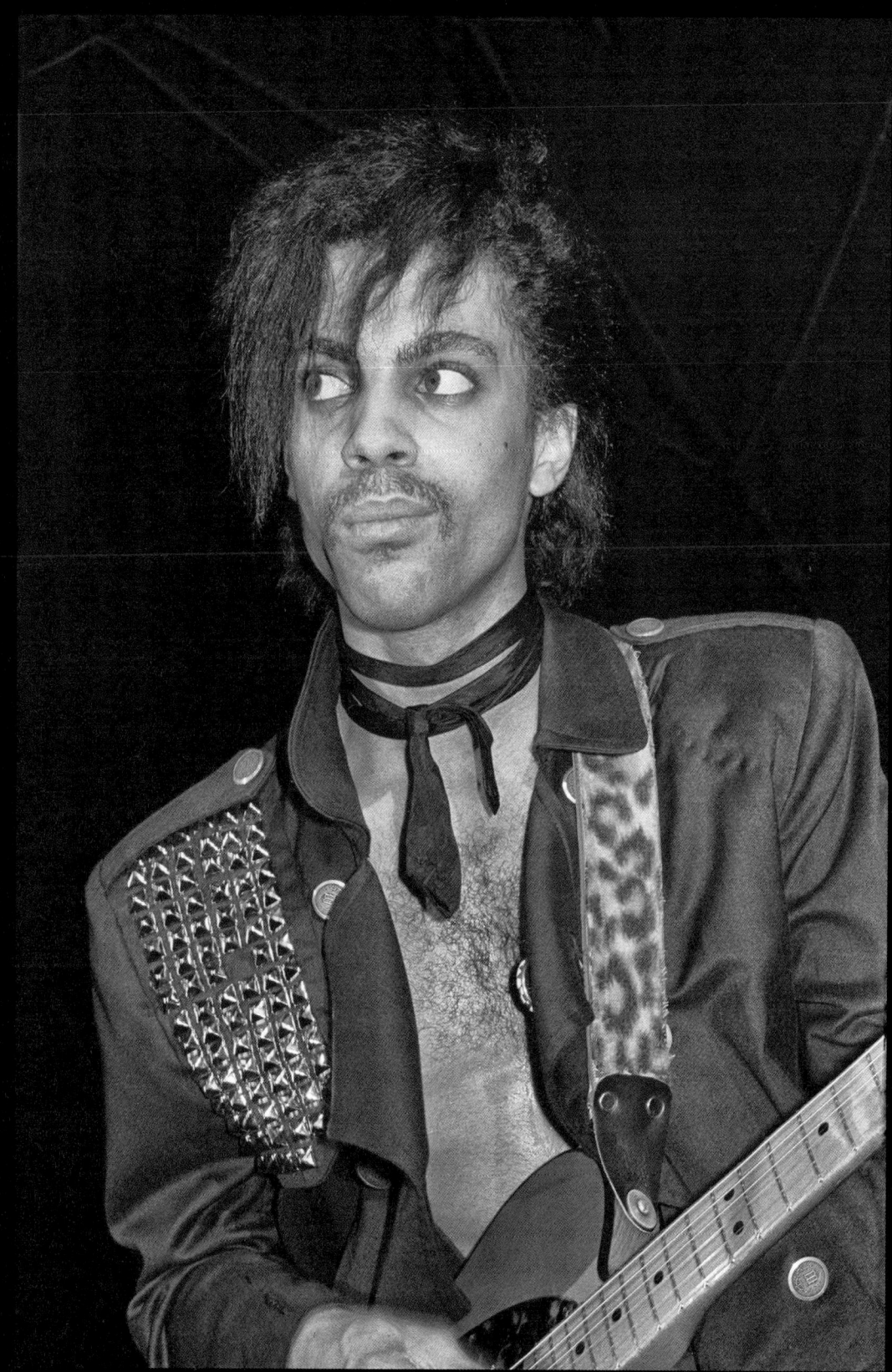

Prince in concert at First Avenue in 1982, during the era of his *Controversy* album

Looking back through my personal archives, I found that the 1979 *Reader* interview didn't reveal much, other than how much he liked "the quiet" in Minneapolis; what does any twenty-one-year-old know of the world or of himself? The piece in '96, however, a cover story for *Minnesota Monthly* magazine called "Portrait of the Artist as a Native Son," opened up sides of him I thought I'd never see: the philosophical, spiritual, and domesticated married man. By then, no note taking or tape recordings were allowed under any circumstances. But he said enough profound things that they were easy to remember and scrawl down on a notepad later, back in the car.

Comparing his married state, he talked about John and Yoko's life together, how if John had never found Yoko and settled down, he probably never would have written "Imagine"—"a song that will be around in two thousand years," whereas "I Am the Walrus" will not. Prince happily imagined a future where all kinds of kids would be running around Paisley Park, his kids. In the summer of 2018, I was reminded of that dream Prince and Mayte had before they lost their first and only child, right after childbirth.

I had been doing publicity for the New Power Generation for part of the year and a German film crew from ARTE Television was interviewing NPG players at the old Flyte Tyme Studios in Edina about Prince and his music. When the writer-director asked keyboard player Tommy Barbarella if he thought Prince was lonely, without hesitating Tommy B. said, "I think he was lonely all the time." It was heartbreaking to hear. Upon hearing it, it wasn't hard to wonder whether all his late-night Paisley Park pajama parties and surprise shows weren't somehow substitutes for a more conventional family vibe in the big soundstage area, where today there remains only expensive, shiny artifacts, fond performance videos, and ghosts piercing the veil.

During the *Minnesota Monthly* magazine interview, more than once he alluded to "The Sacrifice of Victor," a heavily autobiographical song. It was about growing up in north (and then south) Minneapolis and being bused to Kenwood for school and seeing how the have-lots and have-nots all lived within a few miles of each other. The lyrics also touched on the epilepsy he suffered from early in his life. According to Prince in several other interviews, his mother told him that he told her at one point in his childhood that he would no longer suffer from epilepsy. She wanted to know how he knew that, and he said an angel told him.

It's easy to dismiss the story as a fantasy of a young, creative, and imaginative boy. But he was, in fact, no longer epileptic as his grew into adolescence (although more than half can outgrow it, according to the Child Neurology Foundation). It's also easy to shrug off the rainbow that appeared over Paisley Park the day he died in 2016. However, when another one appeared a year later, on the exact same date, it has to give

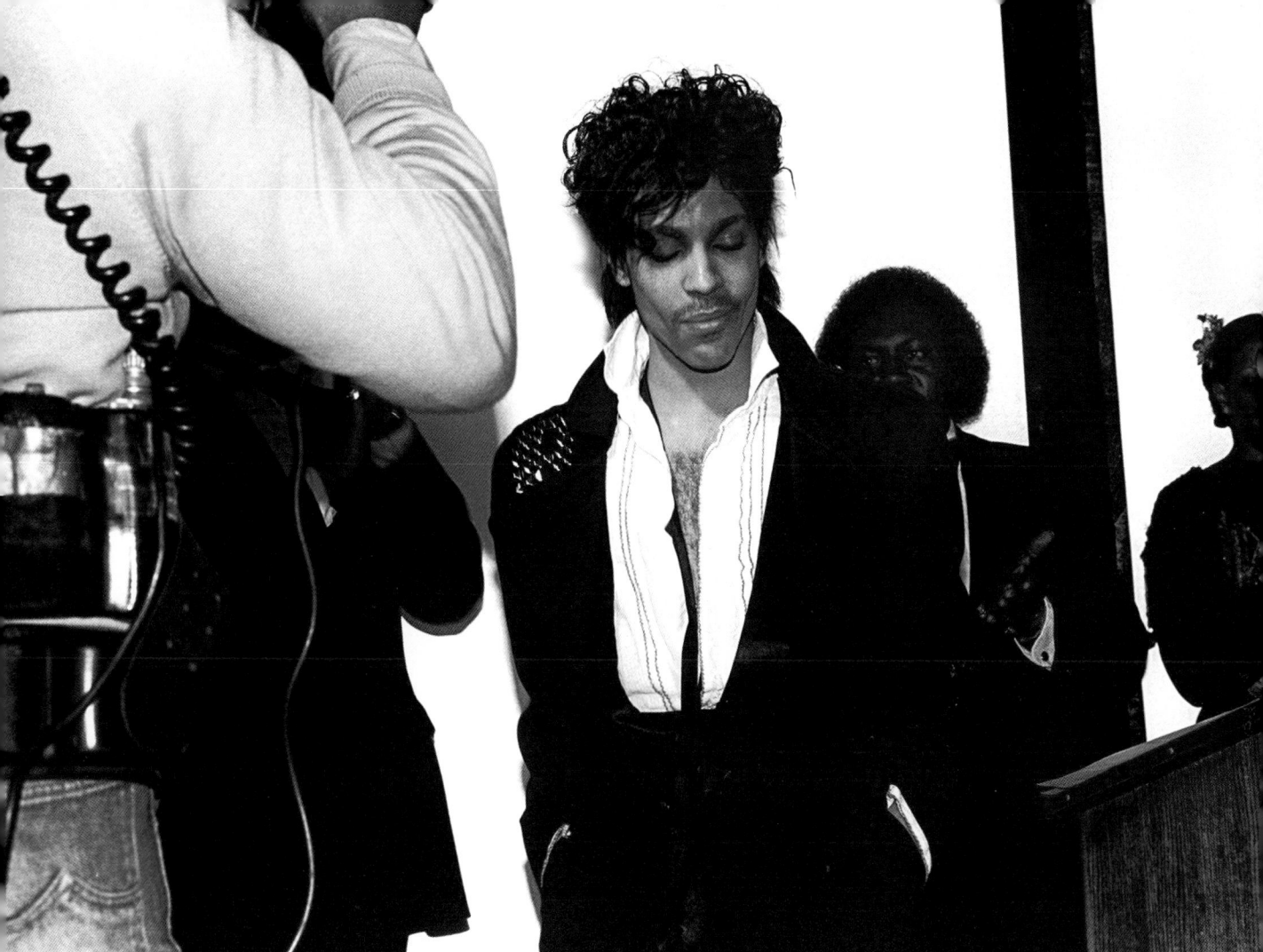

Prince avoids looking at the video camera during the 1980 Minnesota Music Awards ceremony at the Prom Center.

one pause. It certainly freaked out Morris Hayes, Prince's former music director, who had worked with "the boss" longer than anyone, at more than twelve years. Was it a paranormal event, a Prince prank from the other side, or just a meteorological coincidence? Morris mentioned in interviews that Prince often wanted to talk with him about "the eleventh dimension" and other far-out and far-in concepts. But the Arkansas native couldn't go that deep with him and told him as much.

Of course, the color purple also carried symbolic significance in Prince's life. A lot has been written through the ages about the color that lies near the invisible end of the electromagnetic energy spectrum and how it is associated with royalty and wealth, spirituality and exotic bearing, magic and mystery. All could equally apply to the diminutive giant, who perhaps also saw it as a powerful healing force.

At first hearing, I completely botched estimating the importance or longevity of the song "Purple Rain," which would become his signature

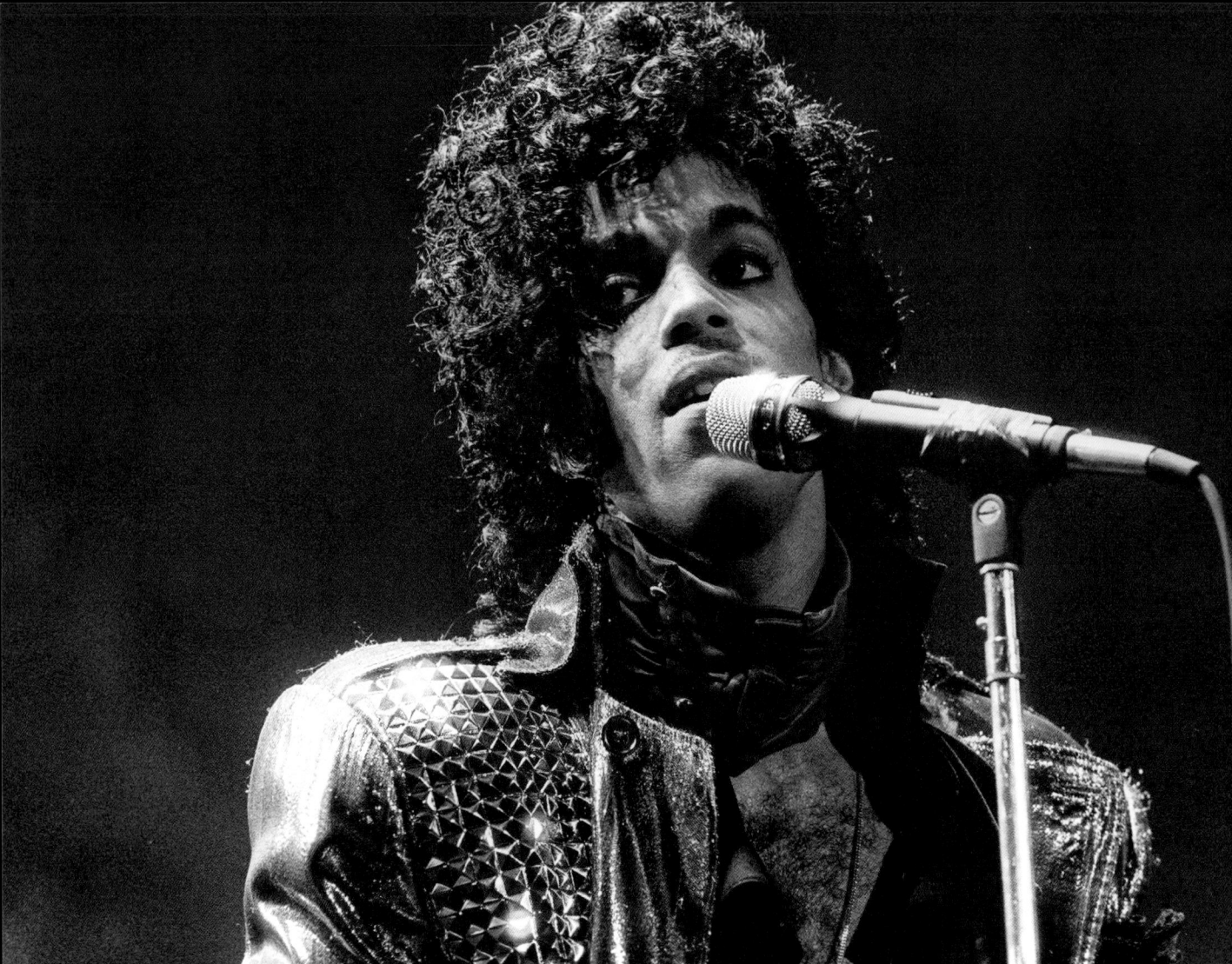

Prince at the St. Paul Civic Center during the *Purple Rain* period, December 1984

tune. When he introduced it—in an extended eleven-minute version—during the Minnesota Dance Theatre benefit at First Avenue, along with several other new songs that would become part of the movie's soundtrack, this music writer viewed it as the lesser number of the new ones in the set. But from that point forward, Prince's purple passion play was on.

In the later part of his life—and he admitted as much in the '96 interview—Prince made a conscious choice to reject the lifestyle and ideas that had propelled him to the material mountaintop. "The rock star thing is dead," he said. He also addressed the "karmic debts" from his younger days. Growing older, he became a devoted and devout Jehovah's Witness. He—and bassist Larry Graham from Sly Stone's band, who reportedly helped convert Prince to the religion—knocked on doors in Chanhassen to talk about the Bible with unsuspecting neighbors. Imagine opening your door to that superstar solicitor!

I was a little surprised (and silently thrilled) as we closed out our conversation and he asked where I had been since I quit writing full time and what I was doing. Very few musicians or others I'd interviewed over the years ever expressed much interest in what you, the writer, were up to (and why should they; writers were just willing and handy funnels to the public). His interest seemed to verify, if nothing else, what the Revolution's Lisa Coleman used to tell me: Prince considered me his top media supporter early in his career, even though I wasn't keen on all his projects.

Besides doing publicity and occasional freelance writing gigs, I had at that point been developing another TV pilot, called *Cosmic Highway*, for a series about the so-called paranormal—well before shows about ghosts and UFOs flooded cable networks. I had been exploring books about mysticism, the occult, and near-death experiences and had done an intense five-year stint as the communications contact for Dr. Steven Greer's controversial and visionary Center for the Study of Extraterrestrial Intelligence (CSETI). Prince listened intently as I tossed out other subjects that the show would pursue besides UFOs, like Elizabeth Kübler-Ross's life-after-death work. He offered sincerely, "You've got a hard job." We traded pat goodbyes and heartfelt gratitude, and then he turned on his high heels and headed off to a studio where the band was waiting to rehearse.

Ultimately, there is a deeper, perhaps more mystical, side of Prince that we may never know. The Purple Patriarch, who set in motion a kingdom of bands, songs, and staggering live performances, likewise created an empire of admiring fans, Prince scholars, and artists across the arts and entertainment spectrum. Still, he never forgot where he came from or why he was here.

"I think God puts you in the place you're supposed to be," he said, sitting in that Paisley Park kitchen booth so many years ago. "Flying back from a concert tour from around the world, and you look down over the land and all the beautiful lakes, and it just feels like home, that this is where I belong."

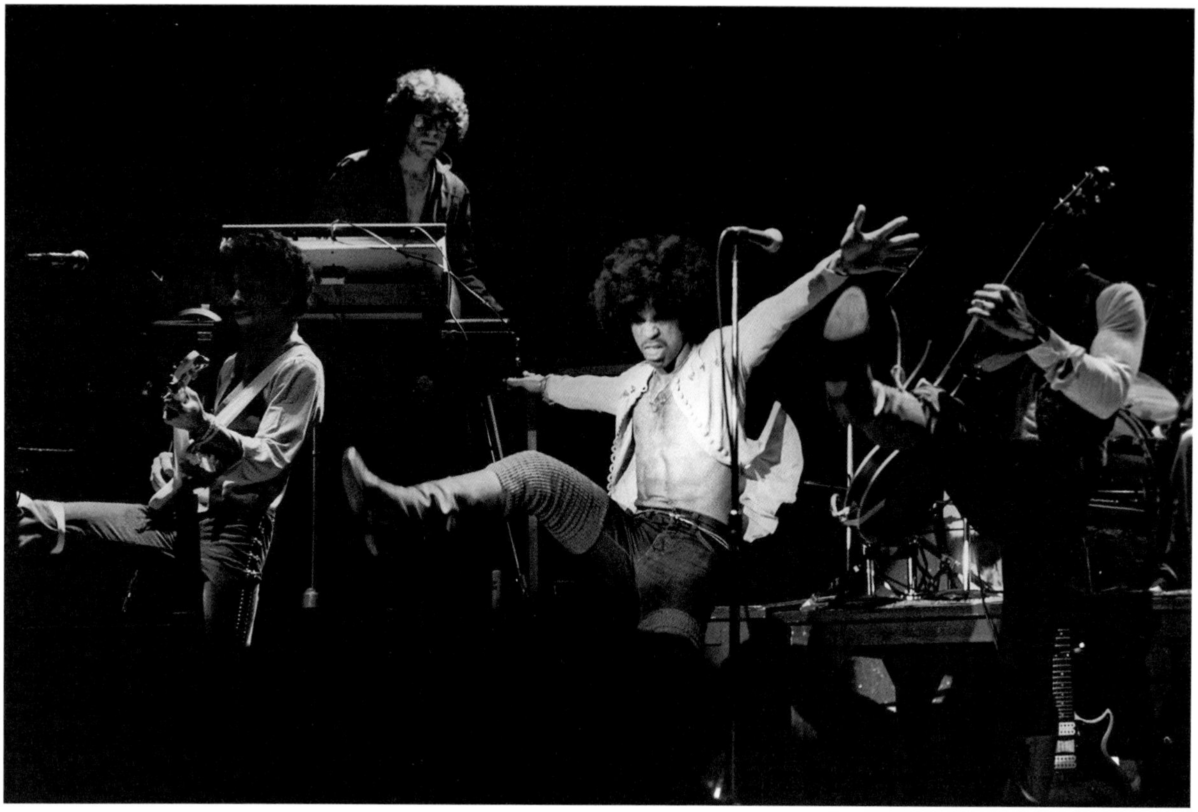

Prince's first gigs with his new band took place at the Capri Theater in north Minneapolis on January 5 and 6, 1979, featuring Matt "Dr." Fink on keyboards (top), André Cymone on bass (left), and Dez Dickerson on guitar (right).

(right) Executives from Warner Bros. records, which had released Prince's debut album, *For You*, in 1978, flew out to Minneapolis to catch the budding star's live show at the Capri. They left with a less-than-stellar assessment of the performance.

(far right) Prince digs down for a soulful moment at his Capri coming-out show.

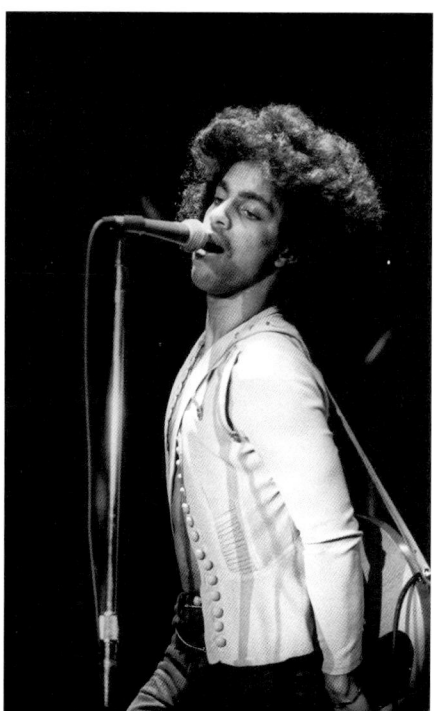
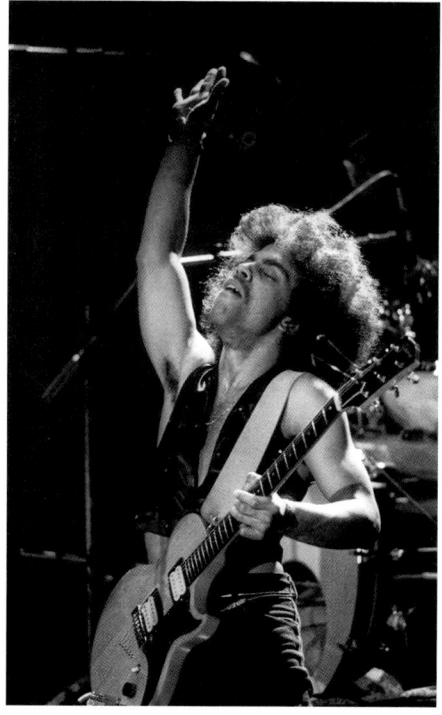

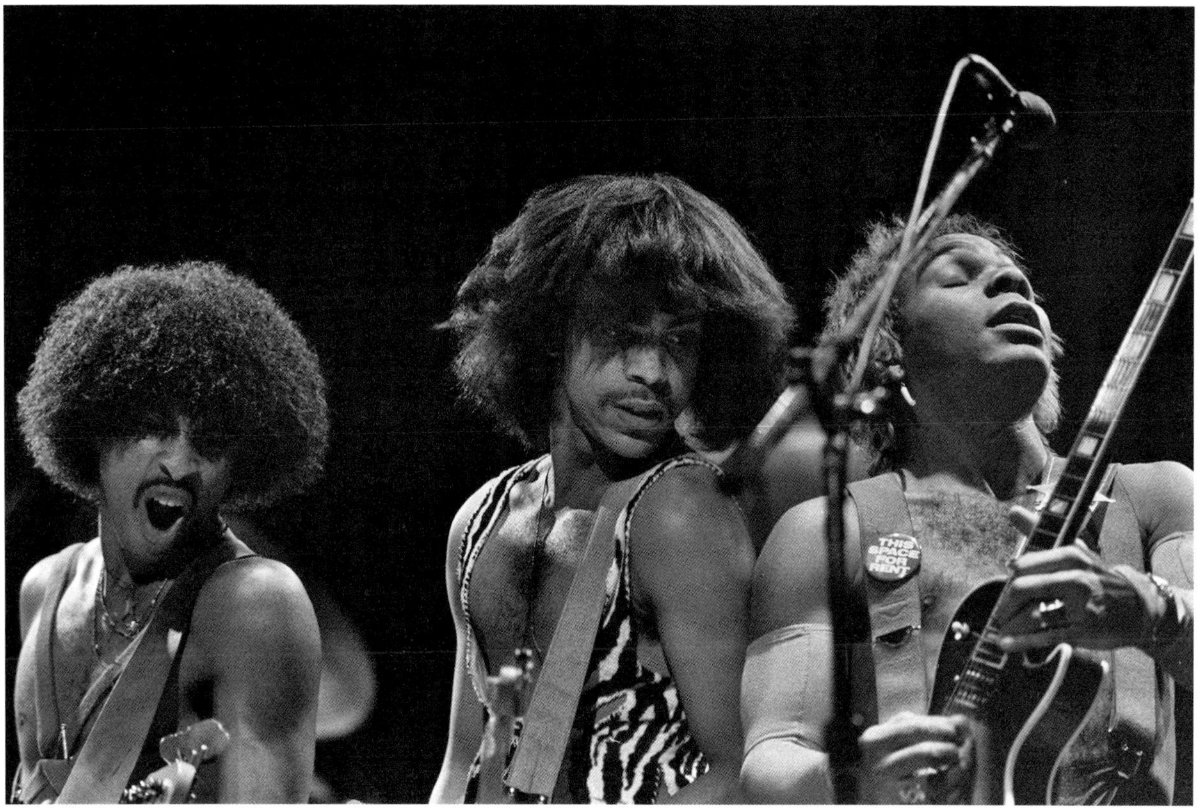

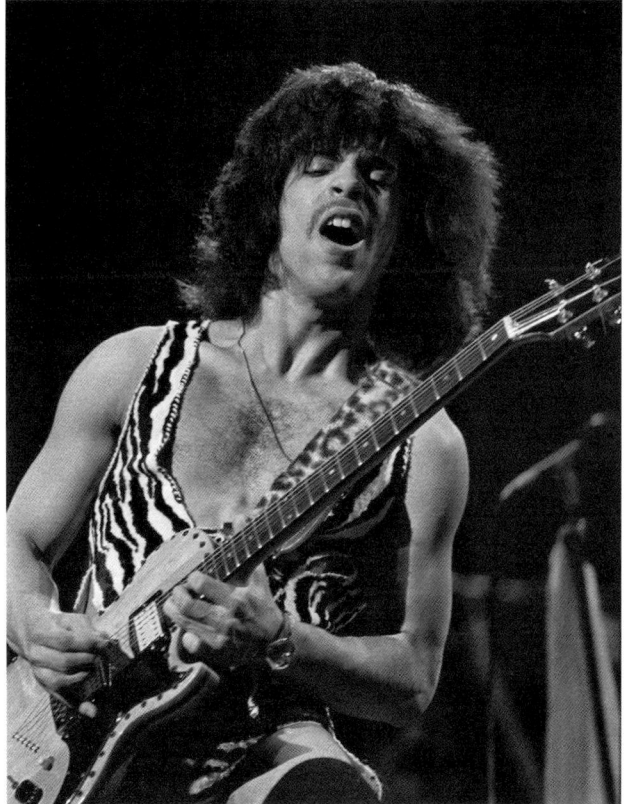

(above) More than a year after his Capri shows, Prince—here flanked by his brothers-in-arms, André Cymone and Dez Dickerson—was back onstage for another hometown performance, this time at the Orpheum Theatre on February 9, 1980. The theater was only about half full, and shortly thereafter Prince and company hit the road as the opening act for Rick James.

(left) Taking a solo in zebra-striped top, leg warmers, and bikini briefs during the Orpheum concert, Prince was continually refining his style and fashion sense throughout his career.

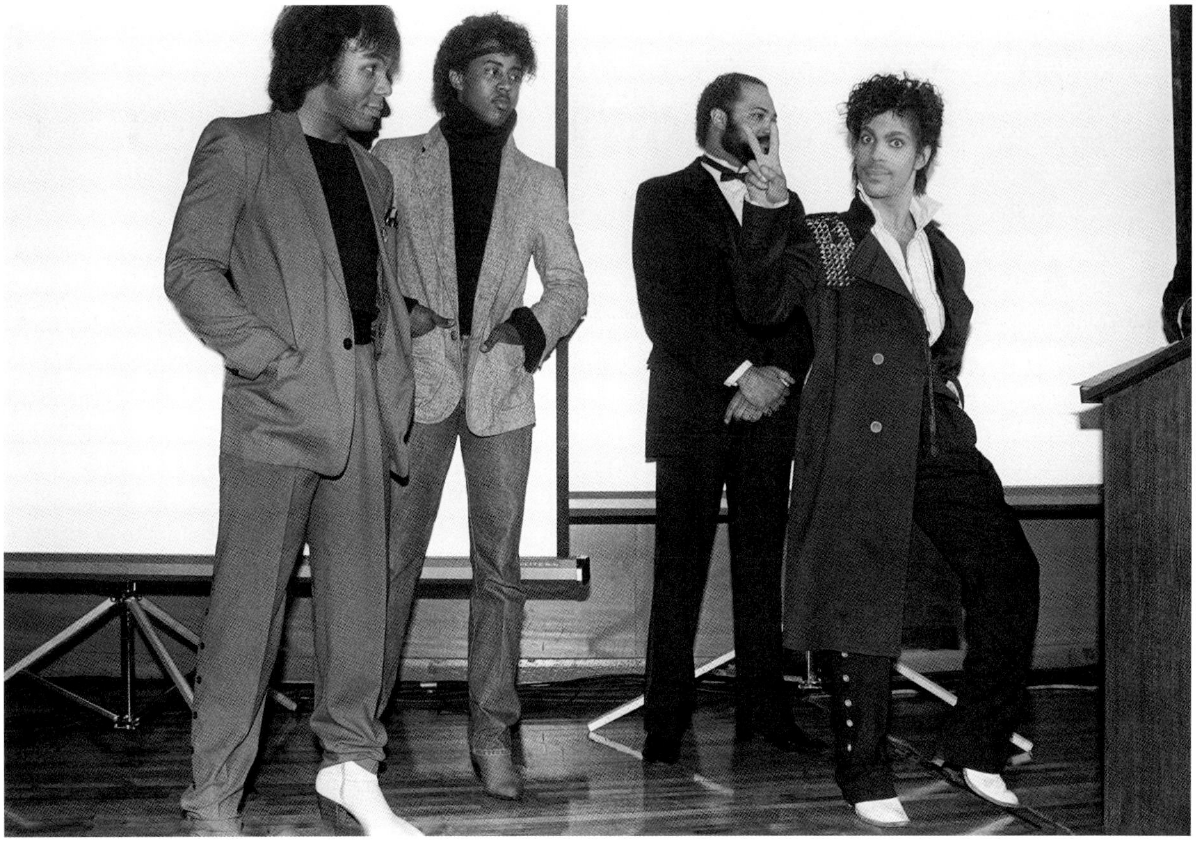

(above) Prince flashes the peace sign at the Minnesota Music Awards alongside bandmates Dez Dickerson (far left) and Brown Mark, who replaced André Cymone in the band in 1981.

(right) In another shot from the Orpheum concert in February 1980, "His Royal Badness" stripped down about as far as you can legally.

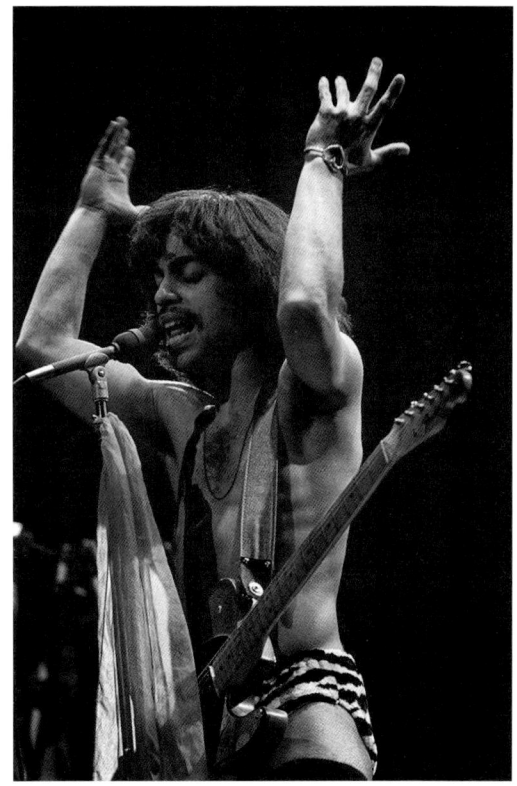

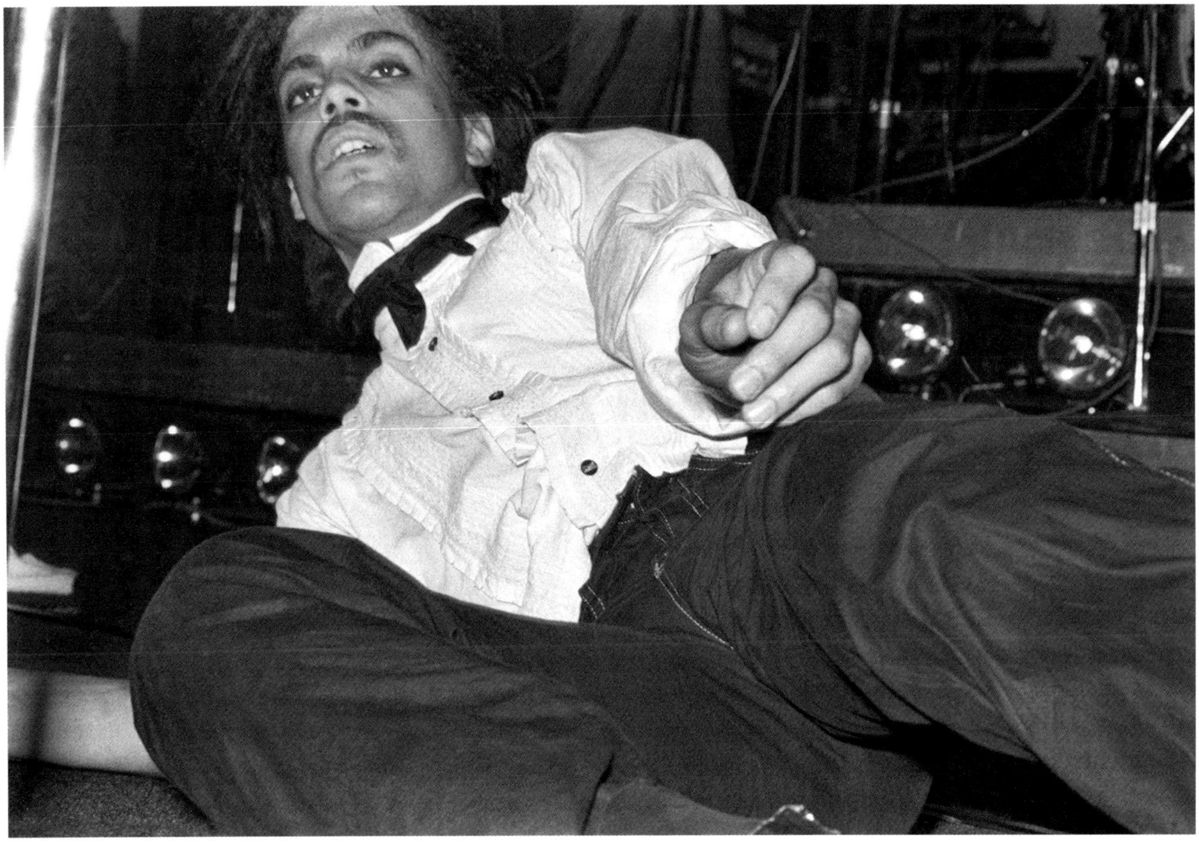

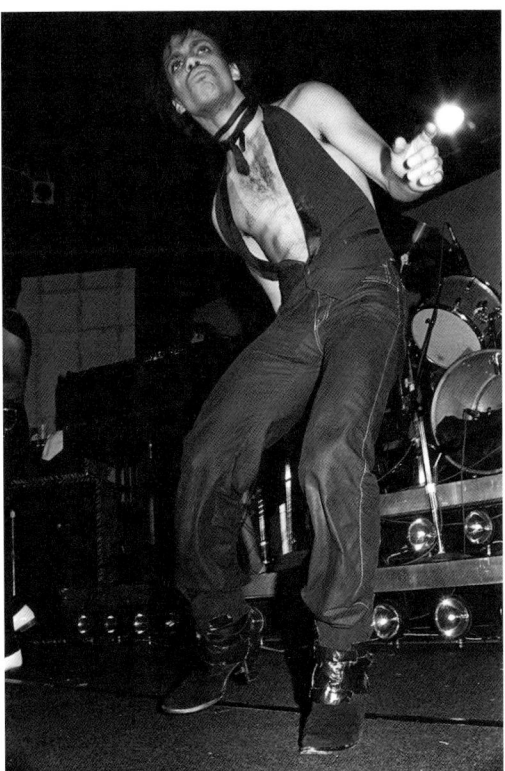

(above) Prince always put on an exciting and highly physical live show, especially at his early Minneapolis home away from home, First Avenue.

(left) Prince busts a move during his first concert at First Avenue (known as Sam's at the time) in March 1981 during the *Dirty Mind* album tour.

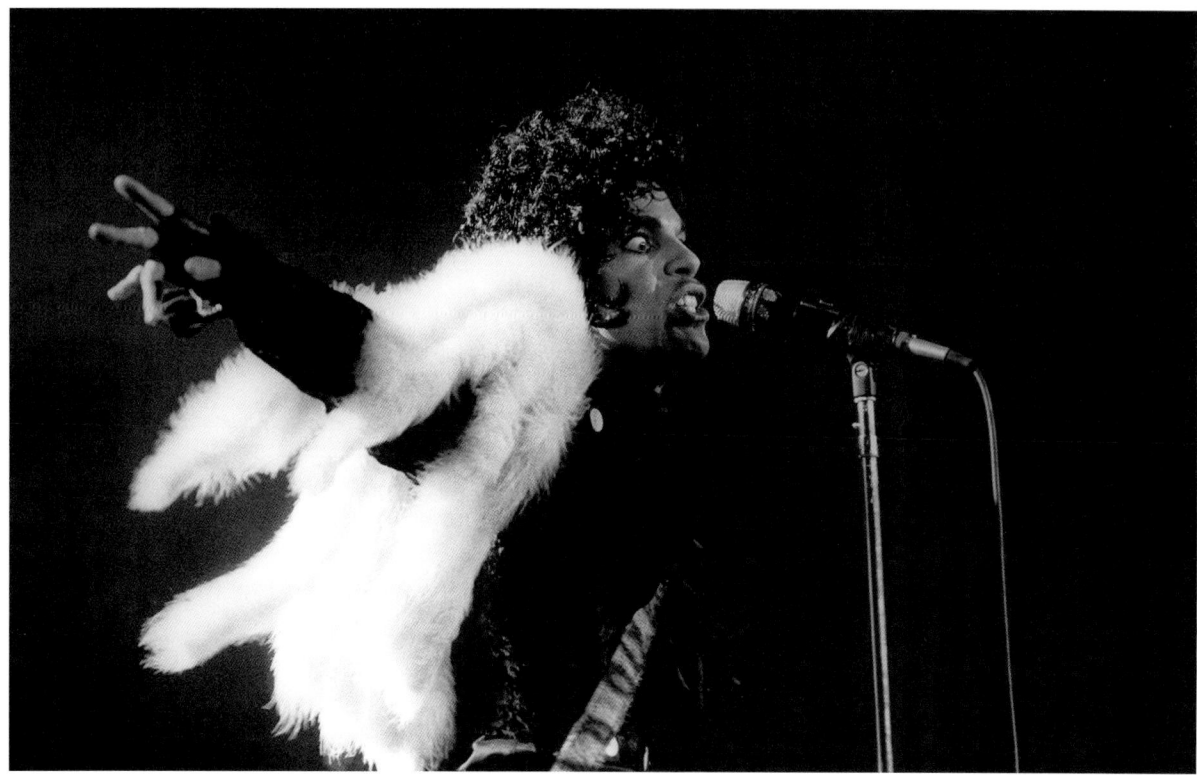

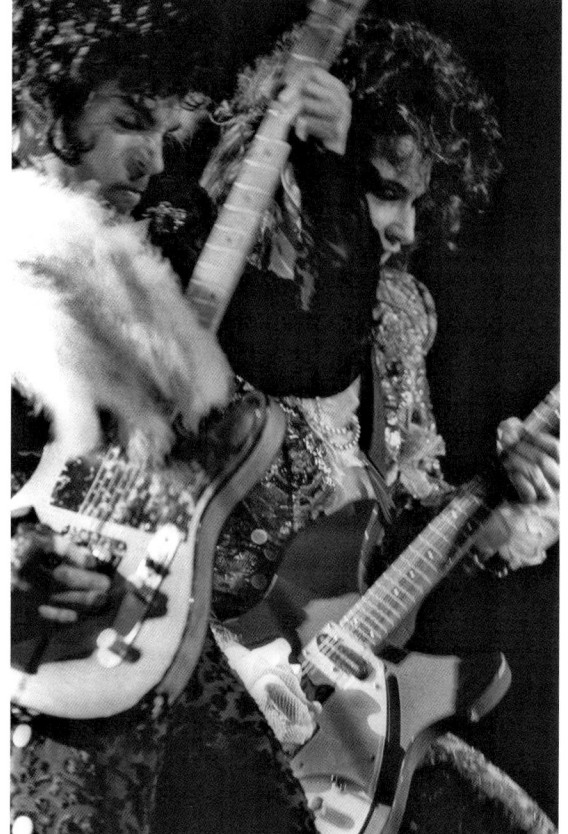

(above) During the extensive US tour that followed the cloudburst release of the *Purple Rain* album and film, Prince and the Revolution played a five-concert stand at the St. Paul Civic Center from December 23 to 28, 1984.

(right) Prince trades licks with Revolution guitarist Wendy Melvoin at the St. Paul Civic Center, December 1984.

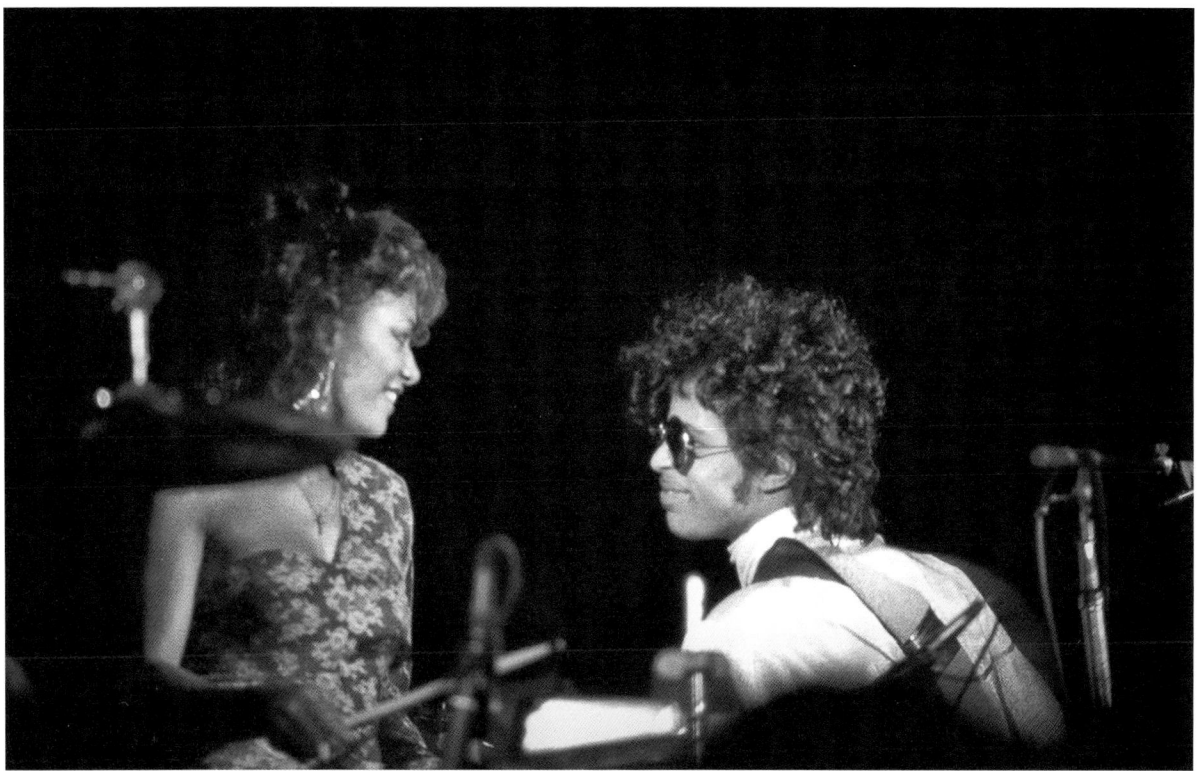

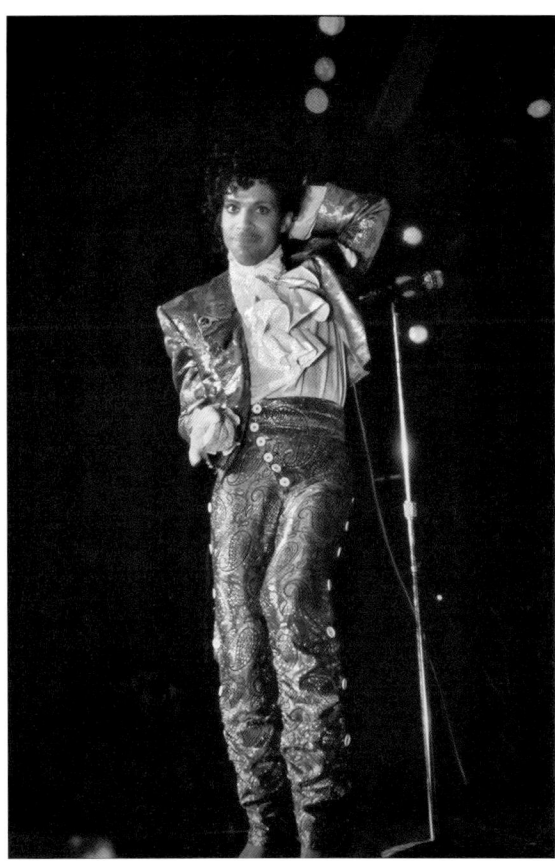

(above) Prince and Shelia E. share a moment onstage at First Avenue, October 25, 1984. It was a surprise appearance by His Royal Badness during Sheila E.'s first headlining set at the club.

(left) Prince plays to the camera at the Carlton Celebrity Room during the sixth annual Minnesota Music Awards in May 1986. The Helg was covering the event on assignment for *Rolling Stone* magazine.

(right) Dez Dickerson was Prince's lead guitarist during the early years, but Dickerson left the group before the formation of the Revolution and the beginning of the "purple reign."

(below) André Cymone shared a home and a musical journey with the teenaged Prince after the young star's home life shattered.

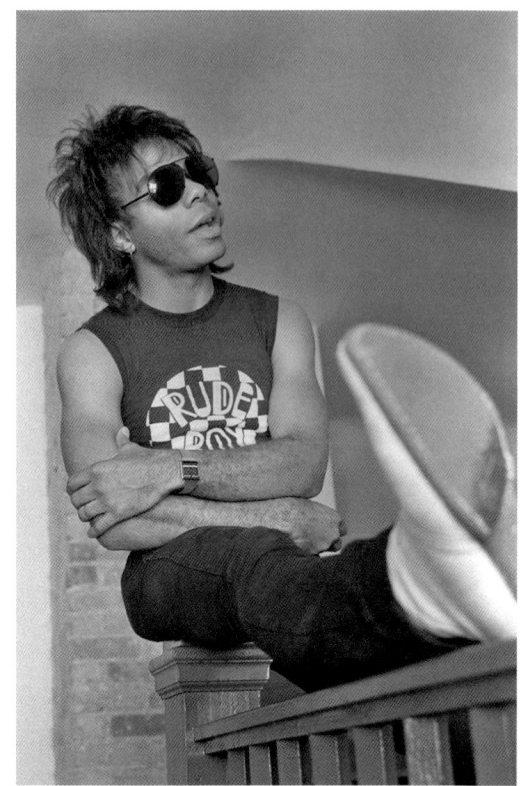

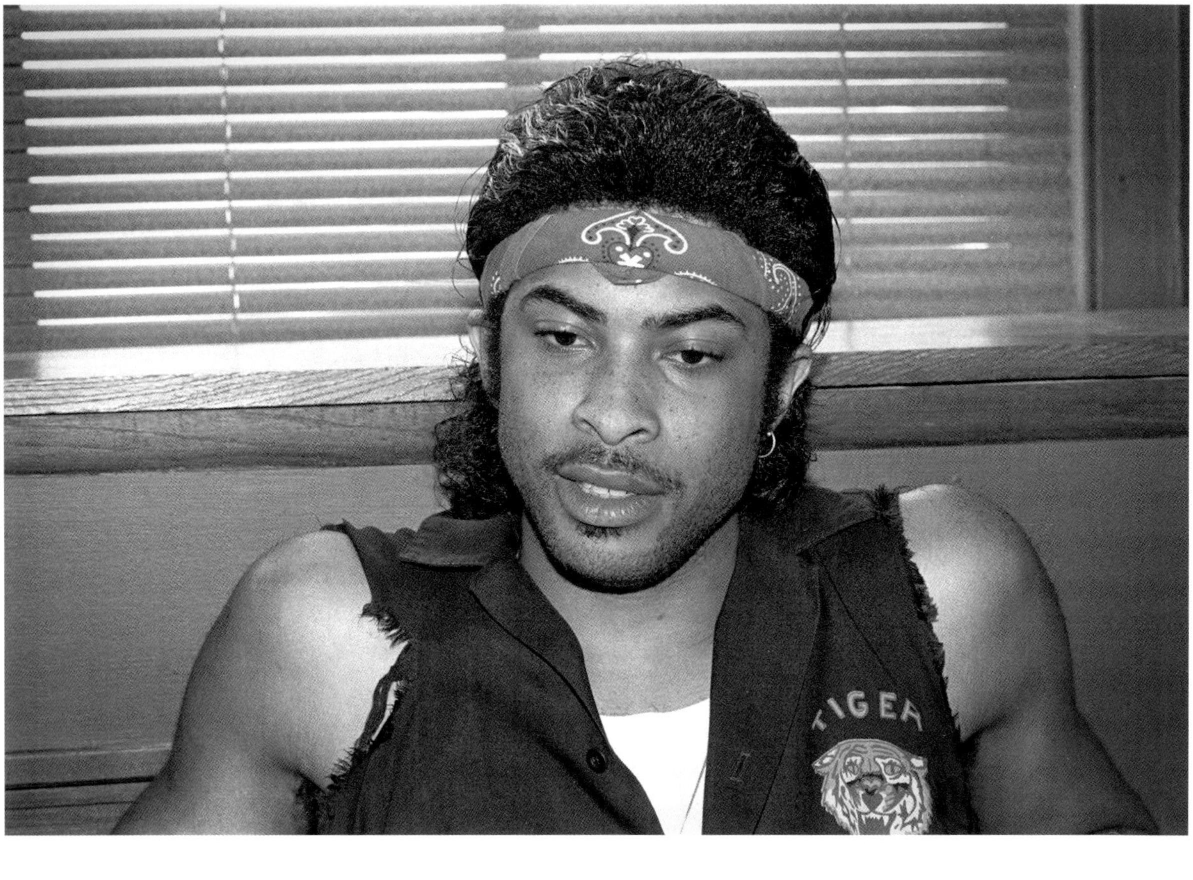

EPILOGUE

A Requiem for the Alternative Press, and Some Final Words for David Carr

||n March of 1997, almost a decade after Frank "Big Ears" Schwartz and I retired our regular bylines, the *Reader* was sold to *City Pages*, which had in turn been purchased by Village Voice Media Inc., which owned other weeklies around the country, including the influential *Village Voice*. For decades, the *Voice* set the bar for the alternative press. The acquisition was another sorry sign of the consolidation—and the slow death march—of weeklies that had their roots in the underground newspapers of the sixties. It was a free-form journalistic tradition, heavily informed by music and antiestablishment politics, that inspired both the Helg and me to join its ranks.

By '97, the internet also was already tearing up once-reliable business models as if they were losing pull tabs in the back bar. (Cue Kraftwerk's foreboding and beautiful "Computer World.") Without warning, the *Reader* was shut down the same week that its competitor bought it. An entire staff was out on the street, many of them ink-stained friends and acquaintances of many years. Without so much as a courtesy call, some of Helgeson's photo work from that era, negatives and the like, was thrown out. In 2018, the *Village Voice* was shuttered completely, after having been gutted many years earlier and turned into a digital-only media enterprise. You could almost hear Curtiss A's familiar Beatles requiem in the distance.

As we move on, the Spud Boyz couldn't bid farewell as you leave these pages without a few dedicated words (and one final image) about David Carr, whose presence vibrates in a handful of scenester tales herein. The Helg accidentally shot a photo of Carr while on assignment for a story about a halfway house in Minneapolis. As he rounded a corner inside the place, he encountered our old colleague.

"What are you doing here?!" they said, almost in unison.

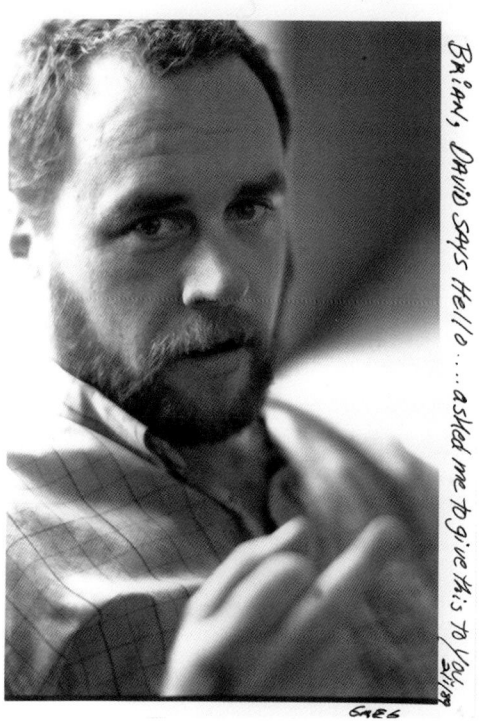

Brian, David says Hello ...asked me to give this to you 2/21/09

GREG

Still on the long road to what would culminate in an esteemed gig with the *New York Times*, David Carr offered a message to a fellow staffer at the *Reader* while at a halfway house following one of his many stints in rehab for drug addiction.

It was pretty clear what Dave was doing there: cleaning up and waiting to be freed from his Promethean rock of addiction. Eventually, he climbed to his better place out East in what is one of the best comeback stories I've ever seen.

Once the surprise wore off, the former *Reader* newsman and editor asked Greg if he would be seeing another *Reader* colleague, Brian Lambert. He covered film, occasional news, and whatever struck his fancy, like Cray supercomputers.

Helgeson confirmed he would be seeing Lambo.

"Give him this, would you?" Carr asked, raising his salute and signaling Greg to take a photo. Done!

The cliché "there are no second acts in American lives" was written by another local writer from St. Paul, F. Scott Fitzgerald, who had his own demons to free. Scotty, meet Dave, the guy who not only eked out a second act from his hard living into a brilliant writing career but was well into forging an entirely new play while working at the *New York Times*, which, frankly, is just not the same these days without his voice. To deploy another cliché, he was a beast.

So, D. C., a few final words before we all press on. You both darkened and enlightened our paths. We're grateful for both sides because we learned from each, even if one was at your horrible expense. Remember that time you used up my lunch hour to drive you to the north side? I forgive you for making me your mule when you were treading water in the abyss.

By the way, if you were still here, we *probably* would have hit you up to write the book's foreword. We don't care what the *Times*'s policy is; you would have made a perfect first choice, if only because you can verify that our analogue adventures happened pretty much the way they're laid out here in these images and words.

INDEX

Italicized page numbers indicate a photograph or its caption.

THANK YOU!

To my wife, Connie, for tolerating the long, late hours and believing in what I was doing; to my mom, Henrietta, for her musical interests that set the foundation for me; to the local music reps back when, for all their help; to the amazing world of artists and musicians in this book that I was fortunate enough to participate in; and to Bob Mehr, for deeply appreciating my photos so much and for writing the foreword.

Spud Boy 1 (Helgeson)

To my family and three-legged dog, for allowing me to disappear on weeknights and weekends to write for eight-plus months; to Scott Edelstein, for knowing the numbers; to former employers, good and bad, who gave us a shot; to Kevin Kirkendahl, Lance Grigsby, and Dean Brewington, for sharing their fond Morris Wilson memories and Sonny Rollins's sweet note; to Gary Marx, who I bugged while traveling in England, and Charlie Bingham, for being Charlie and for providing vital Lamont Cranston deets; to all the local and national record label people, gatekeepers, PR folks, club owners, and other music bizzers, for all the free stuff, gossip, and hard news and so much artist access; and to the many rainmakers in these pages who led us down so many roads.

Spud Boy 2 (Keller)

ABOUT THE AUTHORS

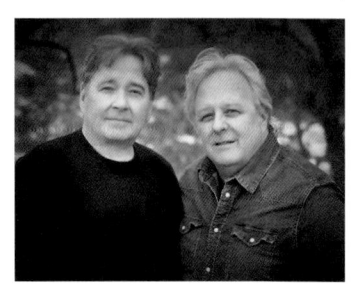

Martin Keller is a professional journalist, author, screenwriter, pop-culture critic, editor, and columnist. For the past twenty-five years, he has served as a public relations specialist. Keller covered the arts, business, and cultural affairs for several Twin Cities publications, including *Minnesota Monthly*, *Mpls.St.Paul Magazine*, the *Star Tribune*, the *Pioneer Press*, *City Pages*, and *Twin Cities Reader*. His work has also appeared in such national publications as *Rolling Stone*, *Billboard*, *Utne Reader*, the *Washington Post*, and the *Boston Globe*. He is the author of *Music Legends: A Rewind on the Minnesota Music Scene* and *Storms: Tales of Extreme Weather Events in Minnesota*.

Expertly working with Canon and Leica cameras for more than forty years, Greg Helgeson has fervently documented some of the most renowned artists and public figures in a variety of disciplines, from international superstars to local legends. His work has appeared in a range of periodicals, including *Rolling Stone*, the *New York Times*, the *Washington Post*, the *Los Angeles Times*, the *Village Voice*, *Du Monde* (Paris), *Mojo* (England), the *Star Tribune*, *City Pages*, and *Mpls.St.Paul Magazine*, as well as in numerous books and on album covers.